THE ROAD TO GLORIETA

A CONFEDERATE ARMY MARCHES THROUGH NEW MEXICO

DONALD W. HEALEY

HERITAGE BOOKS
2009

HERITAGE BOOKS
AN IMPRINT OF HERITAGE BOOKS, INC.

Books, CDs, and more—Worldwide

For our listing of thousands of titles see our website
at
www.HeritageBooks.com

Published 2009 by
HERITAGE BOOKS, INC.
Publishing Division
100 Railroad Ave. #104
Westminster, Maryland 21157

Copyright © 2003 Donald W. Healey

All rights reserved. No part of this book may be reproduced or transmitted in any form or by any means, electronic or mechanical, including photocopying, recording or by any information storage and retrieval system without written permission from the author, except for the inclusion of brief quotations in a review.

International Standard Book Numbers
Paperbound: 978-0-7884-2378-9
Clothbound: 978-0-7884-8210-6

*To the memory of my grandmother,
Antoinette Louise Kight,
who was justifiably proud of her
Texan heritage.*

CONTENTS

Illustrations   vii
Maps   ix
Acknowledgements   xi

Introduction - 1
1 Isaac Adair - 5
2 Plans and Ambition - 19
3 On to Fort Bliss - 37
4 A Gathering Storm - 61
5 Bloody Valverde - 81
6 Masterly Inactivity - 117
7 Pike's Peakers - 167
8 Apache Canyon - 191
9 Road to Glorieta - 209
10 Defeat - 249
11 Albuquerque and Peralta - 279
12 The long walk Home - 319
13 Shattered Dreams - 353

Notes - 379
Bibliography - 467
Index - 481

ILLUSTRATIONS

Captain Isaac Adair, Company H, 7th, Texas Volunteers - 10
Hon. John Titus Smith, Chief Justice of Houston County - 14
Brigadier General Henry Hopkins Sibley - 23
Captain David Alexander Nunn, Company I, 4th, Texas Mounted Volunteers - 27
Muster Roll of Company H, 7th, Texas Mounted Volunteers, Oct. 24, 1861 - 29
Lieutenant Colonel John R. Baylor, 2nd, Texas Mounted Rifles - 33
Requisition for Ordnance and Ordnance Stores - 43
"One of Sibley's Texas Rangers" - 50
"Fort Bliss - 1862" - 51
Colonel Edward Richard Sprigg Canby - 63
Colonel Christopher "Kit" Carson, 1st, New Mexico Volunteers - 65
Captain Trevanion Teel, 2nd, Texas Mounted Rifles - 66
Mountain Artillery - 70
Remains of Fort Craig - 72
"On the Line of Battle" - 86
Captain Theodore Dodd, Company A, 2nd, Colorado Infantry - 92
Private Alonzo Ickis, 2nd Colorado Infantry - 94
Colonel Thomas Green, 5th, Texas Mounted Volunteers - 101
"Battle of Valverde" - 103
Captain James "Santiago" Hubbell, 5th, New Mexico Volunteers - 106
Captain Alexander McRae, 3rd U.S. Cavalry - 108
Captain Rafael Chacon, 1st, New Mexico Volunteers - 119
Private Wady T. Williams, Company C, 5th, Texas Mounted Volunteers - 145
Governor William Gilpin of Colorado - 169
Company G, 1st Regiment, Colorado Volunteers - 173
Colonel John P. Slough, 1st Regiment, Colorado Infantry - 174
One of Governor William Gilpin's vouchers - 179

Colonel (General) Gabriel René Paul, 4th, New Mexico
   Volunteers - 192
Major John M. Chivington, 1st, Colorado Infantry - 199
"Captain Cook's Charge" or "Battle of Apache Canyon" - 203
Unidentified Texas soldier - 205
Lieutenant Colonel William Read Scurry, 4th, Texas
   Mounted Volunteers - 214
Pigeon's Ranch, Glorieta, New Mexico - 230
Lieutenant Colonel Samuel Tappan, 1st, Colorado Infantry - 234
Glorieta, New Mexico - 238
Colonel Manuel Chaves y Garcia de Noriega, 2nd, New
   Mexico Volunteers - 251
"Santa Fe, Looking North" - 269
Plaza, Santa Fe, New Mexico - 280
Plaza and Church, Albuquerque, New Mexico - 288
Henry H. Connelly, Territorial Governor of New Mexico - 303

MAPS

The Southwest in 1862 - 36
Route of Sibley Brigade - 47
Operations around Fort Craig - 76
Valverde - 98
Glorieta Pass - 232
Gen. Canby's Campaign in New Mexico - 322

ACKNOWLEDGEMENTS

I owe a debt of thanks to many people and organizations for their generous and unflagging assistance during the preparation of this book. First and foremost I want to thank Miss Eliza Bishop of the Houston County Historical Society. Without the initial leads she provided, and the contacts she helped me make, The Road to Glorieta would not have been possible. I also want to thank: James B. Evans, for preserving an important piece of Isaac Adair's history; Jerry Thompson for unwittingly setting me on a path; Donald Frazier for stoking my enthusiasm; Elisabeth Arrington Montgomery, Dr. Don Alberts, James H. Berry, Jr., Dr. F.R. Collard, Marion C. Grinstead, Mr. Emmett W. Muenker, Norma Mumey, Mr. Lawrence T. Jones III, Ed Whitted, Chuck Stern, Paul Harden, Ridley Politiski, Lannie Walker, Sr., Peggy Fox of The Harold B. Simpson Confederate Research Center at Hill College Hillsboro, Texas, Ms. Mavis Marek of the Crockett Public Library, Cassandra McCraw of the Special Collections section of the University of Arkansas Libraries, The staff of the Austin Public Library, The staff of the Denver Public Library, The Staff of the Colorado Historical Society, The staff of New Mexico State Records Center and Archives, The staff of Library of Congress Prints and Photographs Division, Arthur Olivas, Photographic Archivist at the Museum of New Mexico, Tod Butler and other staff of the National Archives and Records Administration, The staff of the Texas State Library, The United

Daughters of the Confederacy, The University of New Mexico Center for SW Research, The Center for American History University of Texas at Austin, Carol Finney of the Texas General Land Office; and Mrs. Huberta Nunn Wright, whom I nagged unmercifully.

Last, but of course not least, I want to thank my wife Denise and my son Austin for their loving support.

INTRODUCTION

"History has never been an absolute, even 100 hours after an event - let alone over 100 years."
- Burt Schmitz

By April 7th, 1862 the Civil War was raging in America. With their powerful legions locked in deadly combat, the eyes of both the Union and the Confederacy focused on the wooded tablelands of a charnel house called Shiloh. Seventeen hundred miles away in the Territory of New Mexico, Isaac Adair, a Rebel captain from Texas, lay dying. At that time, few people, east of the Mississippi, knew or cared what was happening in the Far West.

The grand stage of the Civil War was the East, but the Southwest also saw its share of conflict. Western battles were smaller in scale, but they were contested by soldiers who were every bit as committed and who fought just as courageously as their eastern counterparts. During the summer and fall of 1861, an army of 3,000 stalwart Texans assembled in San Antonio, under the command of an untried general named Henry Hopkins Sibley. With banners flying and the cheers of friends and family ringing in their ears, they advanced towards Arizona and New Mexico. These were not the ragged barefoot Rebels of later years. They were a zealous and determined army of committed volunteers marching off to war at a time when anything seemed possible. Their stated goal was the capture of the New Mexico Territory, but their general may have envisioned the banner of their new nation flying above the waters of the Pacific.

The chain of events that carried Captain Adair to his destiny and led to the clash of two small but rugged frontier armies, remains one of the most stirring and least known episodes of our nation's struggle. Near the end of the campaign a young Texan named Frank Starr wrote to his father, "We all think that our operations out here will all be lost in history." While not lost, the struggle in New Mexico has received little attention. If asked to name a battle from the American Civil War, most people can respond with names like: Gettysburg, Chickamagua, or Bull Run. If asked to name a battle west of the Mississippi, a few might scratch their heads and come up with Pleasant Hill or Pea Ridge. If asked to name a battle in New Mexico or Arizona, most people are surprised to learn that any took place.

When Sibley's 3,000 Confederates marched into New Mexico in early 1862, they were confronted by scattered Federal forces that together numbered nearly 5,000. How is it that 8,000 men, involved in a life or death struggle, left so little to mark their passing? The problem has not been a lack of interest, but rather a lack of easily accessible information. A casual reader finds little of their story in print because it is sequestered in personal collections and historical archives spread across the country. Much of the story's heart still lies buried in diaries, forgotten turn of the century magazine articles, and families' self-published copies of great granddad's memoirs.

Interest in the Civil War in the Southwest is on the upswing and in recent years a number of excellent books on the topic have appeared. Donald S. Frazier's "Blood and Treasure: Confederate Empire in the Southwest" focuses on the role of the New Mexico invasion in the fight for southern independence and adds a sense of historical and continental context. "Bloody Valverde" by John Taylor is a definitive hour-by-hour study of the conflict at Valverde ford, the largest battle ever fought in the Southwest. Other detailed monographs "The Battle of Glorieta" by Don

Alberts and "The Battle of Glorieta Pass" by Thomas Edrington and John Taylor apply a microscope to the fighting at Glorieta Pass and reassess the claim that this battle saved the West for the Union. While dramatic, the time spent in combat at Valverde and Glorieta was only four days. The Texan foray into the Southwest lasted nearly nine months! What happened during the rest of the invasion?

Using a solid combination of primary and secondary sources, the goal of this book is to bring this tale to life. Relying heavily on diaries, memoirs, and other first person accounts, it pushes personalities and emotions to the forefront. Often told in the participants' own words the story is a day-to-day account of the adventures of ordinary men living through extraordinary times.

Voices of soldiers long gone, again come to life. Felix R. Collard, a private in Company G, 7th Texas Mounted Volunteers, marched across country so barren that; "absolutely nothing existed except loose sand and buffalo bones, [...] not a drop of water on it, not a blade of grass nor any living thing." Sergeant Alfred B. Peticolas wrote in his diary; "I never thought I would ever be so pressed by hunger as to ask for bread when I had no means of paying for it, but I have done it, and without shame too." The journal of seventeen-year-old Ebenezer Hanna, ends with the entry; "Twas during the day of the 27th that we had the trial of burying the first one of the members of Company C. The enemy did not make their appearance during the day." Hours later, the young Texan was shot through the loins, bled internally, and died quietly. The reminiscences, hopes and fears, of these and many other gallant soldiers give form to the sound of distant trumpets, and forgotten tales of comrades in arms.

When General Sibley issued a call for troops, Isaac Adair a thirty-five-year-old planter from Crockett responded. Adair's sketchy story winds back and forth through the pages of this book and then ends abruptly before the saga is complete. He was chosen as a touchstone, not because he was famous or larger than life, rather because he is one of the nearly forgotten. Although an educated man, Adair kept no journal and if he wrote letters home, none have survived. Today, like the other men of his company, he is a shadow. The accounts of literally thousands, who contested the Civil War in the rugged Southwest, are lost forever. A few like Adair's can still be pieced together, and deserve to be remembered. With a family history of life on the frontier and a personal stake in the issue of slavery, Adair epitomizes the hardened Texas pioneer. The stories of Sibley's Confederates, the men they followed, the men they led, and the men they fought, are the sum and substance of the War of the Rebellion in the American West.

Chapter 1

ISAAC ADAIR

"He was Captain Adair of the famous Irish Adairs"
- Tommie Kight

Isaac Adair and his family were ardent supporters of the Southern Cause. In a letter to a soldier at the front in Virginia, his sister-in-law wrote; "[Isaac's wife Augusta] wants y-o-u to bring the Lincolnite family down here for her & some of her friends to whip. Mrs. Wall is to whip the 'Old Man', Sis. the 'Old Woman', Bet - Bob & if there are any more Miss May Albright & Miss Priscilla Adair will finish them." [1]

Working as Clerk of Houston County, Isaac Adair dealt on a daily basis with the probate of people's estates. On October 3rd, 1861, with the prospect of combat ahead of him, and "considering the uncertainty of this frail and transitory life," he sat down and wrote his own last will and testament. After settling his debts, Adair left the bulk of his estate to his wife. The only exceptions were 6 "negroe" children: "Patsy about 11 years old a girl; Jennie a girl about 9 years old; Sarah Jane a girl about 7 years old; Tobe a boy about 9 years old; Henry about 8 years old and Jack about 7 years old." These slaves Adair left to his own three children, a girl and a boy to each to be decided by lot. Adair instructed his wife to "use and take care of" the slaves until his children should marry or reach a marriageable age. Further, he stated that if "any of said negroes shall die run away or be disabled so as to be of little value," his wife was to use the proceeds of his estate to purchase suitable replacements so that his children would be sure to have "the above named negroes apiece- or their equivolent [sic] to commence the world with." [2]

Isaac Adair was born in 1825, the son of Zadock Adair and Sarah Kelley. His exact place of birth is unknown, but it was somewhere in Alabama, probably in either Perry or Sumpter counties. [3] At the time of his birth, the United States was barely 50-years-old, but Adair's ancestors had already been in America for nearly twice that long. Isaac's great-great-grandfather, Thomas Adair, left County Antrim in Ireland in 1730, and, accompanied by his three sons James, Joseph, and William, set out for the Colonies. [4]

By the time of the Revolutionary War the Adairs were a prominent family in the Carolinas. With their Irish descent, they held little love for the mother country and quickly sided with the American Colonies in their struggle. "There were no fewer than ten Adairs in the American Army from South Carolina." [5] Isaac's great-grandfather Joseph Adair, Sr., at the age of seventy years, served in the Revolution as the Commissary for Company D, Col. Levi Casey's Regiment.

Almost no information has survived about Isaac's father Zadock, and much of what remains derives from conflicting secondary sources. It seems that he was born in Laurens County, South Carolina in about 1780. Around 1804 he married Sarah Kelley, the daughter of Peter Kelley and Jane Ewing, both also from South Carolina. Zadock and Sarah raised at least 5 children and possibly more. Isaac was their youngest son. [6]

The pioneer spirit that brought his great-grandfather to America burned brightly in Zadock Adair. The War of 1812 put a stop to western migration, but by its end, around 1815, pioneers were again itching to be on the move. Eastern Georgia and the Carolinas were by that time worn and gullied from repeated plantings of tobacco. The Old Southwest, the southern backcountry stretching west to the Mississippi, beckoned to adventurous settlers and into these new lands poured a stream of humanity. In 1820 the population of Alabama was 127,000. By 1860 it was 964,000. Near the head of this tide moved Zadock Adair and his family. Like many small farmers, he was on the cutting edge of the frontier, probably goaded along by ambition and the unshakeable belief that greater success and prosperity were just over the next rise.

Zadock Adair's signature appears on a petition to the Congress of the United States, filed sometime in either 1817 or 1818. His endorsement suggests that the elder Adair was both civic-minded and suspicious of authority. The undated petition protested a proposed annexation of part of the Alabama Territory by the state of Mississippi. The petitioners wrote that they viewed "this proposed transfer of freeman, like the vassals of European potentates, from one sovereignty to another, as repugnant to justice & completely hostile to the principles of republican America." The petition was signed by "inhabitants of the Alabama Territory residing near the waters of the Mobile." [7]

On March 2, 1836 the Texas Republic declared its independence from Mexico. The Adairs were living in a land of plenty, but now a land of even greater opportunity opened before them. In 1836 Texas supported a population of 50,000 in an area the size of all of New England, New York, Pennsylvania, Ohio, and Illinois combined. In an effort to solidify its position, the newly independent republic was actively seeking colonists. To all those who would make the journey, Texas held out the promise of land, free for the taking. Sometime around 1837, Zadock Adair once again set his sights on the frontier. Uprooting his wife and two youngest children, Zadock headed west.

Of the Adairs' journey to Texas we know nothing, but on June 4, 1845 in the town of Crockett, the Republic of Texas issued Isaac an unconditional certificate for 320 acres of land, called a "3rd class headright." To be eligible for a Third Class land grant a settler needed to have arrived in Texas after October 1, 1837 and before January 1, 1842. Isaac listed his year of arrival as 1840. Three hundred and twenty acres went to single men and six hundred and forty to married. Strangely, no records remain to indicate that Zadock ever applied for a grant himself. [8]

Crockett was the county seat of Houston County, but only three-hours ride from the buffalo range; it was emphatically a frontier village. Danger from Indians and the usual inconvenience of a frontier country had long retarded the settlement of the county and growth of the village. Crockett owed its prominence to its being the only point, within reasonable distance of the San Antonio Road and the center of the county, where running water could be found. Although a log courthouse and jail had been erected in the town center, Crockett was still a wild place. Only one year before the Adairs' arrival in Texas, the danger from Indians was so great that families fortified the courthouse lot with pickets and took shelter inside until the immediate alarm passed. "The eastern and western mails arrived on an average twice a month. The northern mail for Fort Houston was sent whenever there was a chance, then generally in the crown of a hat." "Sassafras tea, rye coffee, milk and whiskey were the only beverages that could be depended on, as coffee frequently could not be had at any price. In the way of diet, steel mill bread and jerked beef were the great staples." [9]

Shortly after Adair was issued his land grant the Republic of Texas gave up its sovereignty to join the United States. This annexation brought to a boil long-simmering tensions with Mexico. Even though

Texas won its independence 10 years earlier, the Mexican government still regarded its annexation by the U.S. as an act of War. Armed conflict between the United States and Mexico broke out on April 25, 1846, with a Mexican attack on United States troops stationed along the southern border of Texas.

The fighting went on for almost a year before Isaac felt compelled to volunteer. During that time the constraints of work, family, and his newly acquired land kept him at home. News of the U.S. victory at Buena Vista on February 23rd may have fanned the flames of his patriotism. Conceivably his imagination was captured by Colonel Jefferson Davis's dramatic charge, that saved the day for the Americans. In Crockett on April 13, 1847, Isaac enrolled as an orderly sergeant for six months service with Captain John Long's cavalry company. The unit's muster roll lists his age as twenty-five, but it was really twenty-two. In a company where most of the officers and many of the enlisted men were his seniors, the young sergeant probably fudged his age a little to enhance his authority. After enrolling at Crockett, Long's Company proceeded to San Antonio, where they were mustered into national service as part of Colonel John C. "Jack" Hays's 1st Regiment Texas Mounted Volunteers. Isaac brought with him a seven-year-old brown horse valued at $200 and $15 worth of "horse equipments" [10]

The battle at Buena Vista was the last serious fighting to occur in northern Mexico. By the time young Adair shouldered his "Mississippi" rifle, the decisive campaign of the war was already underway and the battleground shifted to central Mexico. On April 18, 1847, U.S. Troops under General Winfield Scott fought the Battle of Cerro Gordo as they advanced towards Mexico City. There in a narrow pass troops commanded by the Mexican General, Santa Anna attempted to turn them back. U.S.

engineers, including such soon-to-be-familiar names as: Robert E. Lee, George B. McClellan, Joseph E. Johnston, and P.G.T. Beauregard, found a trail that allowed the Americans to surround and defeat Santa Anna's forces. By June the U.S. invasion force was at the gates of Mexico City. There was still some fierce fighting to come, but it was apparent that the war was over.

Captain Isaac Adair, Company H, 7th Regiment, Texas Mounted Volunteers. Probably taken in either Crockett or San Antonio in the fall of 1861, this is the only known photo of Captain Adair.
Author's collection.

Long's company was to have served six months, but with the conflict winding down, its services were unneeded. On June 2nd, at Alamo City, only fifty days after he signed up, Isaac Adair and the rest of the volunteers were told to go home.

Dated November 7, 1850, the Federal Census for Houston County, Texas states that Isaac, age 25, was living in a household with his father, Zadock, his mother, Sarah; and his twenty-one-year-old sister, Matilda. Zadock, who was by that time seventy, was still listed as the head of the household. He told the enumerator that he was a farmer. Sarah, who was fifty-six, was listed as a housewife. Isaac did not specify his profession, but because of his father's age, it can be assumed that, he was doing the real work of running their farm. No value was placed on the family's real estate, however the slave schedule for the same year shows that Zadock owned 5 slaves. Obviously the Adairs were prospering. [11]

About this same time, the John T. Smith family migrated to Houston County from Georgia. Smith was a native of New York, but he lived in Georgia for many years, operating a steamboat service on the Appalachacola River and serving in the state's legislature. Like Zadock Adair, he was a man who felt the call of the frontier. In 1849, he loaded his wife, Elizabeth Greene Gaines, their seven children, and many slaves into covered wagons and headed for Texas. Arriving in Houston County, the Smith family acquired a large plantation on the Trinity River, near the town of Alabama, and began to raise cotton. [12]

Both Isaac Adair and the older Smith were civic-minded and took an interest in local politics. In late 1850 they joined with other citizens, and petitioned the state's legislature to levy a special tax. The purpose was to raise funds for the erection of a new brick courthouse, the old log one being inadequate for the growing community. Acquaintance between the two men grew into friendship, and Isaac began to court Smith's oldest daughter, Augusta

Louise. [13] Augusta was amenable to the romance, and, after a proper interval, the couple was married. [14]

The next ten years of Isaac's life revolved around family, friends, and career; frequent business trips and frequent trips to visit neighbors; the rhythms of the weather and of seasonal plantings and harvests; and the comings and goings of steamboats on the Trinity river. Adair joined his business operations with those of his father-in-law and together the two men pursued a variety of agrarian enterprises. Isaac applied for and received a "pre-emption" land grant from the state of Texas, which increased his holdings by another three hundred and twenty acres. Much of the combined plantation was devoted to cotton. Some years the weather was good, the plantation received adequate rain, and bales of mature cotton were shipped by steamboat, down the Trinity River to Galveston. Other years the rains failed or the cotton was destroyed by frost. [15] When cotton production was off, the Adairs and the Smiths would fall back on other endeavors. Besides ever present garden crops, like "corn, squash, cucumbers, & beans," Isaac raised cattle and hogs. The family butchered and used the hogs locally, but the cattle were driven overland to the market in New Orleans. On one occasion, Isaac's mother-in-law reported that he set out with a "drove," "amidst rain, thunder, and lightening." [16]

Slavery was an integral part of the two families' economic and domestic lives. Slaves were used in the fields to plant and to harvest, they performed chores around the homes, they looked after the sick, and they were sent on various errands. Adair and his father-in-law both owned slaves, and, like their land, they managed their slaves in partnership. Slave labor was shared where it was most needed. Occasionally, slaves were also loaned to, or borrowed from, their neighbor, General John Beavers. In her diary, Isaac's mother-in-law devotes the same attention to slave illnesses, births, and deaths that she gives to these events among her own family. She also mentions the visit of a slave trader, and notes that because of a "Fuss between Johnson & negroes", that Mr. Johnson, their overseer, was discharged. [17]

The Adairs and the Smiths led busy gregarious lives. Roads in those days were bad and travelers frequently spent the night. It was the norm for neighbors passing by, to stay over and spend one or more evenings socializing. Besides friends and business associates, there were booksellers, horse hunters, and all manner of other peddlers. The two farms saw a steady stream of guests. Isaac Adair himself often traveled, making overnight business trips to Crockett, and less frequently to Galveston or New Orleans. The family also entertained, sometimes throwing parties. On one occasion they held a "raising" for their new "gin house." They attended traveling shows and camp meetings and, weather permitting, they spent days fishing with friends on the banks of the Trinity. [18]

Adair and his father-in-law continued their involvement with local politics and sometime before 1855, Smith, who was already an experienced politician, won the position of Chief Justice of Houston County. Isaac, meanwhile, became a County Commissioner. During the summer of 1858, both men again stood for public office. When it came time for the August 3rd vote, the balloting in Crockett was marred by street violence. Tempers flared and pistols were drawn; one man was killed and another wounded. The fracas, while emphasizing the rugged frontier nature of the community, made little difference to the election's outcome. Adair and his father-in-law both won their respective races. Isaac succeeded James Madison Hall to become the third District Clerk of Houston County, and John T. Smith won re-election as the county's Chief Justice. [19] Adair served as District Clerk until he resigned the post in 1861. John T. Smith continued to serve as Chief Justice, until elected to the state legislature in 1860.

Around 1854 Isaac's wife, Augusta, gave birth to their first child, John. Two years later, their second son, Ben, was born. It was also during 1856 that Zadock Adair died at the respectable age of seventy-six. The tempo of life and mortality continued in 1859 with the birth of Isaac's daughter, Emma Ada, and the death of his mother, Sarah. [20]

Hon. John Titus Smith, Chief Justice of Houston County.
Courtesy Houston County Historical Commission and the District Court of Houston County

Illness and disease were facts of life in rural Houston County of the mid 1800's and hardest hit were often the young and the elderly. Sarah Kelly-Adair outlived her husband, Zadock, by a couple of years, but it is known that during part of the time "the old lady" was "very sick." The diary of Isaac's mother-in-law is full of references to family illnesses, many of them serious. On one occasion, Augusta sent for her mother, sure that her son John was dying. John recovered, but tragedy struck the family full force in March 1860. Yellow fever swept through the county. The Adairs were unscathed, but the Smiths were ravaged. In a span of a few weeks, Augusta's mother, her sister Ada Smith, and her grandmother Louise Gaines Riviere all died. John Smith, who was on a business trip to Galveston, returned home to find his immediate family devastated. Elizabeth Smith's diary ends abruptly on Sunday, March 11, 1860. The last entry reads; "Clear Pleasant weather." [21]

Life in Texas was hard, but it was also good. In a span of twenty years, Isaac Adair carved a home for himself on the edge of the frontier, and went from young pioneer to pillar of a growing community. The 1860 census for Houston County lists Isaac as a thirty-three-year-old male born in Alabama with real estate valued at $5,000 and personal property of $3,000. He was head of a household consisting of: A.L. (Augusta Louise), a twenty-four-year-old housewife born in Georgia; three children, all born in Texas: John, age six; Ben, age four; and Ada, age 1. His occupation was listed as district clerk. Also listed in the household were Frank Edmundson, an eighteen-year-old clerk born in Kentucky; C.A. Wilkenson, a twenty-eight-year-old school mistress born in New York; C.R. Wilkinson, a twenty-five-year-old school mistress born in New York; and William Burnett, a fifteen-year-old male pupil born in Louisiana. The 1860 slave schedule for Houston

County for the same year recorded that Isaac Adair owned fifteen slaves. [22]

At the time of the 1860 Census, the population of Houston County was 8,058, including 2,819 slaves. Abraham Lincoln had just been elected president of the United States, and the nation was breaking up. In a span of less than thirty years Texas went from possession of Mexico to independent republic to the largest state in the Union. On February 1, 1861, smoldering tensions burst into flame. Texas, following the lead of South Carolina, Mississippi, Florida, Alabama, Georgia, and Louisiana, became the seventh southern state to secede. Three days later, delegates from these states met in Montgomery, Alabama and drafted a constitution for the Confederate States of America. On February 18, Jefferson Davis of Mississippi was selected as their provisional president. On Saturday, February 23, voters in Houston County ratified the act of secession. James Madison Hall, who proceeded Isaac Adair as District Clerk, recorded the voting in his diary; "Today I went with John Harwell to the polls, and while there had to act as one of the clerks to the election. The vote at precinct No.7 stood for Secession 31. against Secession 5. I voted for it." [23] Statewide the tally was 46,129 for, versus 14,697 against. [24]

A few days later, Hall reported that he and three other men "hoisted the Confederate flag on the top of a 30 foot pole and placed it on the top of [his] warehouse." After the flag was erected, he noted proudly; it "now floats to the breeze, the emblem of the free." [25] By April 12th, Confederate shells were falling on Fort Sumter. Presidents Lincoln and Davis both issued calls for troops. Few people thought that there would be a serious war, but martial excitement spread across the South. In Houston County companies of Texas Militia were formed to help defend the state and the new nation. Out of the less than 6,000 whites in the County nearly 1,000 eventually responded to the call to arms. [26]

According to Texas muster abstracts, a "call for 5,000 volunteers for field duty" was issued and Captain Edward Currie began to organize the first company of militia raised in Houston County. On April 26, 1861, Isaac Adair stepped forward with 117 of his friends and neighbors and enrolled as a private in the "Crockett Southerners." Other companies quickly followed suit, and by mid-May, James Hall recounted that men from all over Houston County were spending their evenings practicing "the manual of arms." [27] Captain Currie raised $1,650 to buy guns, but reported; "Most of the men will have six shooters or some other pistol and home-made knapsacks." This first group of enlistees never saw any action and in August they disbanded. [28]

Like the "Crockett Southerners", most of the militia companies, which formed in the spring and summer of 1861, were very fluid and short-lived. The war was still far from Texas and the men and boys who enthusiastically rushed to the southern banner frequently found themselves with little to do. Eager to learn the basics of soldiering, many recruits were soon disappointed. The State and the new Confederate government had not yet decided who was responsible for supplying and equipping the new soldiers. As a result volunteer companies were often left to fend for themselves. Many recruits found that when it came to even the basics of adequate food and shelter they were on their own. [29]

In May 1861 Isaac Adair sold 177 acres, of land for $450. The timing and size of this sale suggests that as a community leader and a man of means, Adair was raising cash to help arm and outfit his company. That spring was unusually wet, and the weather and inactivity took its toll on militias throughout Texas. Some companies disbanded and went home, or as in the case of the "Crockett Southerners" simply withered away as men left to join the "real" army. By July 1861, Isaac found himself a new company. This time he enrolled as private in Reserve Company Beat No. 1, Houston County, 11th Brigade Texas Militia under Captain John Blair. [30]

Chapter 2

PLANS AND AMBITION

"Boys, if you only knew it, I am the worst enemy you have."
- Captain Henry H. Sibley

While Isaac Adair discharged his duty on the home front, events unfolded elsewhere that would soon capture his imagination and launch the pivotal adventure of his life. The author of these events was Henry Hopkins Sibley, an ingenious dreamer and former officer of the 2nd United States Dragoons.

Sibley was a career soldier with a varied and extensive service record and strong ties to the West. He was born on the frontier at Natchitoches Parish, Louisiana, on May 25, 1816. His father died, when he was only seven, so he was raised by his grandfather, Dr. John Sibley . The elder Sibley was a noted frontier explorer, editor, and Indian agent. He was also and an influential figure in the conscious national movement westward. [1]

In 1833 at the age of seventeen young Henry was admitted to the United States Military Academy at West Point. He proved a poor student. Because of a deficiency in "Natural and Experimental Philosophy he was set back one year and required to repeat his Second Class Year, or his third year at the academy." [2] In 1838, Sibley graduated a lackluster 31st in a class of forty-five. Following graduation, he was ordered to Florida, where he fought in the second Seminole War and was promoted from brevet to regular 2nd lieutenant. Later, he served at a number of posts in New York, Louisiana, Texas, and the Indian Territory slowly rising to the rank of Captain. The high point of his military service came during the War with Mexico, when he was breveted to major for gallantry and heroism at Medellin near Vera Cruz. [3]

Well liked by many, Sibley was at times both contentious and arrogant. These qualities did little to advance him in his chosen profession. In 1847, while serving with the occupation forces near Mexico City, he squabbled with his immediate superior, Major Edward V. Sumner. As the rancor grew heated, Sumner warned Sibley to watch how he spoke to a higher ranked officer. Sibley responded by shouting, "I will speak to you in that way or in any other way I please." The next day Sumner preferred charges, accusing the captain of "conduct highly disrespectful towards his commanding officer." [4] Sibley was most likely saved from a court-martial because of an acquaintance with General Winfield Scott. The charges were dropped, but in return Scott forced Sibley to swallow his pride and apologize to Sumner.

Eleven years later, while stationed in Utah, Sibley got into a shouting match with his colonel, Philip St. George Cooke. This time he stood trial for his impulsiveness. Cooke charged Sibley with "neglect of duty" and "conduct to the prejudice of good order and military discipline." The trial ran for several days, with both the prosecution and the defense calling a number of witnesses. After "mature deliberation," the court decided that, although some specifications of the charges were true, there was no criminality involved. [5]

Henry Hopkins Sibley was a mediocre career soldier, whose star never shined very brightly. Just the same, he was endowed with an excess of pent-up ambition and ingenuity. While serving in Kansas, he designed and patented, "Sibley's Improved Conical Tent." Patterned after the teepee of the plains Indians, the "Improved Conical Tent" was far superior to any the army then used. It was was eighteen feet in diameter, and was supported internally by a nine-foot pole, mounted on a three-foot tripod. There was fly at the top, that could be trimmed to improve circulation. Unlike other existing tents, a fire could be safely built inside. [6] An army board of inspection, evaluating the tent, found it well ventilated, spacious, resistant to winds and comfortable. The officers who examined it recommended "without reservations" that the military adopt it. Sibley believed his fortune was made but wide scale acceptance of the tent remained elusive. [7]

By the time of secession, Sibley had been stationed in the West for ten dreary years. He served on the Texas border and saw duty in "Bleeding Kansas," where he fought free soil and slavery guerrillas. He also accompanied the Mormon Expedition of 1857, and helped to subdue the Navajos in 1860. The outbreak of the Civil War found him still serving as a captain (brevet major), in the New Mexico Territory. In late April 1861, after carefully weighing his options, and over the spirited objections of his New York-born wife Charlotte, Sibley resigned his commission to cast his lot with the Confederacy. His letter of resignation was short and to the point: "I have the honor to enclose herewith the resignation of my commission in the Army of the United States and request authority to leave this Dept. immediately." [8] Sibley underlined the word immediately, but decided to remain at his post in Taos until relieved. By the end of May, he could wait no longer. Receiving no official response to his resignation, he took matters into his own hands. The captain issued orders giving himself seven days leave of absence, said goodbye to his troops, and caught a stagecoach for Las Vegas. The same day Sibley left his post the United States sent orders offering him the rank of full major. After fourteen years at the same rank, the attempt to bolster his loyalty came too late. [9]

By May 31 Sibley was on the road to Texas, his brain reeling with a grandiose plan of conquest. After his long tenure in the Southwest, the captain was convinced that the Union's hold on the region was tenuous. With a bold initiative he believed the territories could be led into the Confederacy. Western lands lay ripe for the picking, and Sibley was cocksure that he was just the man to do the harvesting. He was so wrapped up in his scheme that, as he passed through Fort Fillmore, north of current day El Paso, he leaned from his wagon and yelled at a group of U.S. soldiers, "Boys, if you only knew it, I am the worst enemy you have." [10]

After he reached Texas, Sibley hurried on to Virginia. Arriving in Richmond in early June, he quickly arranged a meeting with Jefferson Davis and laid out his plan of conquest. The details of the meeting are speculative and second-hand, but it is purported that Sibley told the Confederate President that the Union troops in Arizona were in disarray, and proposed leading an invasion of the Territory. Resistance, he advised Davis, would be minimal. He would recruit troops in Texas and equip them with supplies from abandoned or captured Federal garrisons. His army would live off the land, and Southern sympathizers would flock to his banner. Davis was impressed with Sibley's knowledge of the situation in Arizona and New Mexico; "and as to the condition of the United States forces in those Territories, the quantity of government stores, supplies, transportation, etc." [11] The low risk and possible high benefit of the plan interested the President, and he was quick to see the value of a military victory in the Far West. Part of France's and England's reluctance to recognize his new nation came from the South's lack of offensive success. The scheme risked the new Confederate nation little, but if it succeeded the potential rewards were huge. Davis commissioned Sibley a Brigadier General and authorized him to raise a command in Texas with which to carry out his invasion. Sibley was entrusted "with the important duty of driving the Federal troops from [the Department of New Mexico] and at the same time securing all arms, supplies, and materials of war." [12]

Brigadier General Henry Hopkins Sibley.
Courtesy Library of Congress, LC-B8172-1976DLC

An officer serving with Sibley later wrote that the newly appointed brigadier may have taken leave of Davis without telling the President the full scope of his scheme. Sibley envisioned himself a Napoleon of the West. As soon as he occupied New Mexico, he planned to recruit an army of advance. This army would come from Southern men who he believed were spread across the Western States and Territories, "anxiously awaiting an opportunity to join the Confederate army." [13] Once formed, his army would push on to Colorado. It would capture the gold and silver fields of the Rockies, and the territory's riches would flow into Confederate coffers. Finally, his men would continue the march west, and "On to San Francisco" would be the watchword. [14] What Sibley hoped for was nothing less than the establishment of a Western Confederacy.

With glory and laurels on his mind, the Brigadier General hurried back to Texas to raise his army. By August, he had established a headquarters in San Antonio and begun the organization of his troops. Authorized to enroll two regiments of cavalry and a battery of howitzers, Sibley expected to get his invasion underway within a matter of weeks. He was sorely disappointed. Governor Clark of Texas had promised him that, sufficient companies of Texas Militia were already formed and ready go. The reality was that the militia system was in disarray. Like Isaac Adair's companies in Crockett, many that existed on paper had left for the East, disbanded, or were seriously under strength. Early in his military career, General Sibley was a recruiter. He now found himself forced to fall back on those skills. He placed notices in newspapers calling for volunteers for the purpose of invading New Mexico. War fever was already running high in Texas, and with the help of the patriotic press, he began to have modest success. [15]

The horrors of war were still sometime away, and many youthful Texans held romantic notions about the proposed campaign. Young men, their heads filled with thoughts of: "gallant soldiers", a "noble steed", and going "off to the wars," began to rally to Sibley's banner. [16] Despite recruiting competition from the Eastern Front, General Sibley received letters from dozens of future company commanders offering their services. He responded, authorizing these men to raise their own companies and offered captains bars to any who succeeded.

By early September, David Alexander Nunn, Crockett's first mayor, was signing up a company of volunteers. He was followed shortly by Isaac Adair and Reddin Smith Pridgen. [17] Crockett was the only large town in Houston County and it is likely that all three men placed recruiting notices in the local newspaper, the "Crockett Courier." No copies of the Courier remain from this period, but any notices undoubtedly resembled the following placed by another captain in the Austin State Gazette of September 7, 1861.

> **Attention Volunteers!**
> I am authorized by Gen. Sibley, Gov. Clark, and the Adjutant General, to raise a company of Cavalry, to be mustered into the Confederate service, and attached to Gen. Sibley's Brigade. It will consist of one Captain; one first Lieutenant; two second Lieutenants; four Sergeants; four Corporals; one Farrier, one Black smith; two Buglers, and sixty-four privates minimum, one hundred and fourteen maximum.
>
> Volunteers are required to furnish themselves with a good horse, saddle, bridle and blanket; a good double barrel shot gun or rifle certain, a bowie knife and six shooter, if the latter can possibly be obtained. all necessary camp equippage will be furnished at San Antonio.
>
> The company will be organized at Austin or on the road to San Antonio, as a majority may determine.
>
> I shall be pleased to receive applications for enrollment up to the 25th inst., at my office on Congress Avenue in Austin, at which time and place the company will rendezvous and immediately move forward to San Antonio, where it will be mustered into Col. Reily's 1st Regiment, Col. Green's 2nd, or _____ 3rd, as a majority may elect.
>
>   W. L. ROBARDS
> Austin, Sep. 5 1861 [18]

Sibley's plan caused a stir among the strictly rural and sparsely settled populace of Houston County. Men and boys from the plantations, farms, and piney-woods of Houston and Madison Counties responded and on September 9th, 1861, Captain Nunn reported his "Crockett Boys" for duty in the town of Rusk. The officer to whom he reported sent the following message to the state's Adjutant General:

Rusk, Texas, Sept. 9,1861
William Byrd, Adj. Genl. , State of Texas

Sir:

I have the honor to report the foregoing muster of the company of "Crockett Boys" D.A. Nunn Captain to whom I have gave orders to march on the 17th inst. for San Antonio,
and report there to Brig Genl Sibley.

   Very respectfully
   Your obt servt
   Jas. S. Hogg

aide de camp
5th Military Dist of Texas [19]

The Crockett Boys joined the Sibley Brigade as Company I of the 4th Texas Mounted Volunteers. There is no record why it took Isaac Adair and "Red" Pridgen longer to get their companies organized, but it was nearly a month after the Crockett Boys departed before Adair and Pridgen mustered their troops.

Captain David Alexander Nunn, Company I, 4th Regiment, Texas Mounted Volunteers.
Courtesy Mrs. Huberta Nunn Wright, Princeton, NJ

Most regions supplying men to Sibley's Brigade were heavily engaged in cotton production. Oddly, comparatively few of those, who joined the campaign held slaves. [20] Adair's ownership of negroes and large tracts of land marked him as part of a privileged Southern elite. The Adairs were slaveholders, descended from generations of slaveholders. While motivation varied from recruit to recruit, Captain Adair probably saw the issues at hand very clearly. Jefferson Davis stated that secession was justified as an act of self-defense against black Republicans, whose plans to exclude slavery from the territories would make "property in slaves so insecure as to be comparatively worthless [...] thereby annihilating in effect property worth thousands of millions of dollars." [21] To Adair and his family, negroes, like land or cattle, were valuable property, and a belligerent and pompous North was trying to take their property away. [22]

As far as we know, Isaac Adair never wrote down his reasons for going to war. If he had however they would likely have echoed the words of another Confederate Captain who vowed; "to fight forever, rather than submit to freeing negroes among us ... [We are fighting for] rights and property bequeathed to us by our ancestors." [23]

On October 5, 1861, "Red" Pridgen stood in front of T.W. Dailey's Store in the town of Elkhart and swore in his recruits. One of the "men" who joined Pridgen's "Elkhart Cavalry" was sixteen-year-old Frank [B.F.] Edens. [24] The Crockett Courier took note of young Frank's boldness saying that Edens enlisted to defend Southern rights because he "was thrilled with the spirit that thrilled and animated the heart of every true Southern man." [25] Slavery was at the core of the war, but many of the recruits, like young Frank Edens, saw their own liberty and freedom at stake. Time and time again those flocking to the Confederate banner described their motivation in terms of the pursuit of independence. Invoking the memory of 1776, one young infantryman wrote: "How trifling were the wrongs complained of by our Revolutionary forefathers, in comparison with ours! If the mere imposition of a tax could raise such a tumult what should be the result of the terrible system of oppression instituted by the Yankees?" [26]

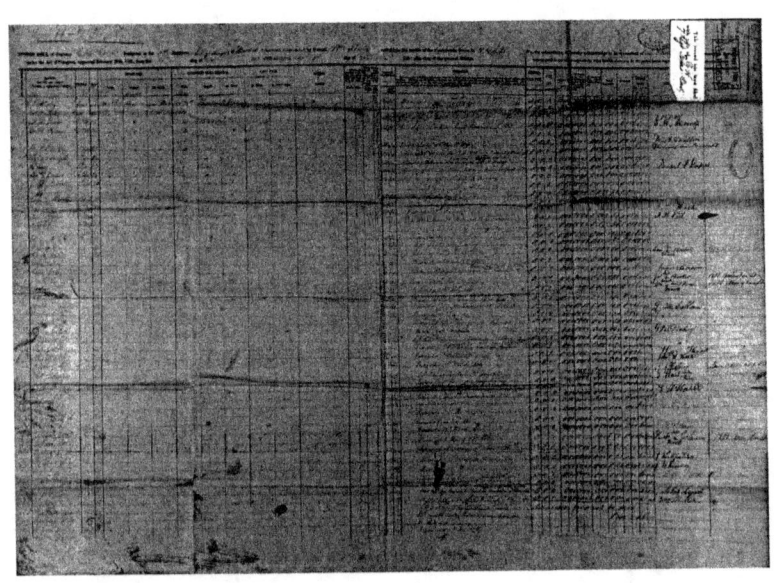

Muster Roll of Company H, 7th Regiment, Texas Mounted Volunteers, Oct. 24, 1861.
Courtesy National Archives

Like Red Pridgen, Isaac Adair chose October 5 to assemble his company. With most of his affairs in order, he stood proudly in front of Crockett's courthouse and enrolled his own ninety-three recruits. Most of the "boys" who signed up to go adventuring with Adair came from Houston County. Twenty-four of his would-be soldiers rode in from nearby Leon County and the balance trickled in from other outlying areas. The majority of his recruits were Anglos, but at least three Mexicans also enlisted. The youngest men who joined the company were ten, eighteen-year-old privates. The oldest recruit was Private S.E. Kennedy, age fifty-nine. As a whole the company was slightly older than the rest of the brigade they were joining. Adair's men were also a close mix of relatives, neighbors, and friends. This pattern repeated itself over and over, among the companies of the Sibley

Brigade. There were several sets of brothers among the recruits, and possibly a father and son or two. Bennett Bunn Arrington the company's 2nd Lieutenant would soon marry Georgia Smith, who was Adair's sister-in-law. Among the privates was John W. Murchison, twenty-three, also a relative through marriage. [27]

No writings have surfaced from any of Adair's men, so we know little of their individual motives. For the most part, the rank and file of Sibley's Brigade enlisted unsure of how and even where they would be utilized. A few recruits, knowing the campaign's objective to be the Western Territories, were aroused by the Texan's long held-belief, that the annexation of New Mexico was part of the state's destiny. Others saw the campaign as an opportunity for personal gain or plunder. Some simply wanted to defend the Confederacy and fight Yankees wherever they might find them. A few even believed that they were going to battle in Missouri or Virginia! During the heady days of 1861 many young Texans were simply raring for a fight. By the year's close Sibley's recruits were only a part of almost 25,000 who had enrolled in the Confederate army. [28]

During the last days of October, Captain Adair's' Company tarried in Crockett making final preparations. Adair, like various other newly appointed and overeager officers, liquidated part of his holdings to support his company and further his ambitions. On the 12th, he made a precipitous sale of land for $600. Apparently he was raising cash for the upcoming campaign. Later in the month, with arrangements finally complete, the company marched out of Crockett and headed for San Antonio. Georgia Smith, Isaac's sister-in-law, reported that when her friends took leave, Miss Hattie King presented one of the men, Charles Stokes, with a battle flag. Flag presentations were one of the highlights of early military life for most Texas volunteers, so it is possible that friends and family turned out to see the soldiers off. Typically, local townspeople would assemble for patriotic speeches and maybe a barbecue or parade. After the festivities, someone would present the departing soldiers with either the Confederate flag or a special unit flag. These ceremonies were often solemn affairs, looked upon by many as the last act of the farewell drama. [29]

By October 28, 1861 Adair's men had ridden the 350 miles to San Antonio. There the unit was mustered into Confederate service for "term of the war," as company H, 7th Regiment Texas Mounted Volunteers. At the time of this second muster, Captain Adair was riding a horse that the Confederate authorities valued at $135 and carrying personal equipment they valued at $40. [30]

Adair and his men were late. For almost two months the rolling country near San Antonio had echoed with shouts, commands, and bugle calls as officers drilled their "greenhorn" recruits and attempted to teach them "how it goes in war." The training in "the most improved methods" called for drilling as infantry in the morning and as cavalry in the afternoon. There were "roll calls by morning and by night, as also tattoo and reveille, all performed according to the forms prescribed on page 2299 of the revised edition of the military statutes." [31]

While Adair's Company formed in Crockett, the assembled brigade had completed its training. On October 21, it held a grand march and review through the narrow streets of San Antonio cheered on by the town's patriotic citizens. After viewing the parade, a reporter for the Houston Tri-Weekly Telegraph wrote: "A finer brigade of men and horses I do not believe can be found in the Confederate Army." "Most of the men ... have entered the service for the war, not for pay, but for love of country." [32]

Brigade camps, outside San Antonio, were named: "Sibley", "Manassas", and "Pickett," and were spread along the west bank of Salado Creek on the Austin Road. While Adair and his men were pitching their tents, other units were already striking theirs. General Sibley had long since decided the time for action was at hand. Preparations had taken much longer than he planned. Recruiting had gone slowly and weapons proved difficult to procure. Equipment was in such short supply that the General even had trouble finding himself a saddle. For almost sixty days each of the brigade's nearly 4,000 animals had consumed six to twelve pounds of feed a day. Meanwhile, Sibley's soldiers ate thousands of dollars worth of food and wore out their clothing. Just sitting and waiting was literally devouring the brigade's supplies. Also weighing heavily on the General's mind was the situation of Colonel John Robert Baylor. [33]

Baylor was an audacious Confederate officer, who struck the first blows of rebellion in the Southwest. In early 1861, communities in the Mesilla Valley and the Pinos Altos mining district, some 700 miles west of San Antonio, endorsed resolutions declaring their support for the Confederacy and asking its protection. Acting on these requests, the Confederate military commander of Texas dispatched Colonel Baylor to the area with about 630 men from the 2nd Regiment of Texas Mounted Rifles.

Combative by nature, Baylor immediately put his troops into action. In July of 1861, with only about half his command present, he moved against the Federal garrison at fort Fillmore just outside the town of Mesilla. As Baylor, dressed in "a blue jacket, red sash, and big silver buckle embossed with the Lone Star," led his troops through town, the secessionist population turned out to cheer them on. [34] In response, Major Isaac Lynde, the Union commander of the nearby fort, turned out his entire garrison of nearly 700 men and advanced toward Mesilla. Lynde positioned his artillery, lined up his troops, and sent forward a white flag, demanding Baylor's immediate and unconditional surrender.

Lieutenant Colonel John R. Baylor,
2nd Regiment, Texas Mounted Rifles.
Courtesy Colorado Historical Society, negative F-24389

Contemptuously, Baylor sent back that, he "would fight first and surrender afterward." "If you wish the town and my forces," he told Lynde, "Come and take them." [35] Stunned by Baylor's unexpected response the major advanced on the town and began a half-hearted assault. The Confederates took up defensive positions on rooftops, behind corrals, and in other sheltered locations and a desultory skirmish ensued. After three Union soldiers were killed and six wounded, Major Lynde broke off the attack, regrouped his forces and marched impotently back to the fort. [36]

Lynde's courage failed him. Although his troops outnumbered Baylor's more than two to one, the major decided his only course of action was a desperate cross-country retreat to Fort Stanton. Stanton was the closest Federal outpost, but it still lay nearly 140 miles across the desert to the northeast. Just before dawn on July 26, the Union garrison destroyed supplies they could not carry, set fire to Fort Fillmore, and shepherding their families, embarked on the ill-conceived march. With the hot desert sun baking down and Baylor in pursuit, Lynde's strategic retreat quickly became a rout. By noon his infantry had marched twenty miles and were without water. Captain Alfred Gibbs of the 3rd U.S. Cavalry, assigned to guard the column's rear, reported that, "by the side of the road over 150 men were lying, unable to rise or to carry their muskets, and useless and disorganized in every way." [37] Moving swiftly, Baylor's relatively fresh mounted troops overtook the Federal force at San Augustine Springs. Major Lynde ordered the "Call to Arms" sounded and found that he "could not bring more than one hundred men of the infantry battalion on parade." [38] With his command in disarray, he completely lost the will to fight. To the chagrin and anger of many of his men, Lynde surrendered his entire command, "eight companies of infantry and four of cavalry, with four pieces of artillery, the whole numbering nearly 700 men," without firing a single shot. [39] One of Baylor's soldiers noted that "good, bad, and indifferent," the entire

Confederate force "consisted all told of about 280 long-eared, ragged Texans." [40]

Lynde's surrender was a debacle for Union forces in the Southwest. Colonel Baylor was left in possession of the southern portion of the region and in control of large quantities of Federal ammunition, quartermaster stores, and treasury notes. After his success, Baylor established the Confederate Territory of Arizona, declared Mesilla its capital, and appointed himself governor. [41]

General Sibley was well aware of the colonel's accomplishments and planned to use them as a springboard for his own invasion. By late October 1861, however, Baylor's tenuous grip on his new territory was slipping. His small command was simply not large enough to hold the vast area he conquered. Much of the native Mexican population was decidedly pro-Northern in their sentiments and actively non-cooperative. Colonel Baylor wrote, the Mexicans "avail themselves of the first opportunity to rob us or join the enemy. Nothing but a strong force will keep them quiet." [42] Constant Indian depredations were also a problem. The pro-Confederate populace was becoming dissatisfied with his governing, and he received rumor after rumor about large well-equipped Federal forces moving against him. Baylor did not know what was true and what was not, and his requests to his superiors for reinforcement became more and more strident. [43] General Sibley understood that if Baylor's gains were not to be lost, speed and decisive action were needed. Sibley also knew that he had already delayed much too long. On October 23, deciding to advance with those portions of his brigade which were ready, he finally gave his men the orders to march.

Chapter 3

ON TO FORT BLISS

"You'll soon be way up yonder where the wolves howls and the chickens never crows."
- Sam Maxwell

Before Isaac Adair's Company even reached the brigade rendezvous, the men of the 4th Regiment departed. On October 22, 1861, the clear morning air along Salado Creek was broken by the shrill of a bugle. First, came the call to "boots and saddles" and then "assembly." The men of the 4th Regiment promptly mounted and formed into a solid square. Colonel James Reily the regiment's commander addressed the troops. Reily told the waiting soldiers; "Much was to be done; much would be done, and that he felt confident of the result." [1] After closing, the Colonel removed his hat and read an inspirational prayer written by Alexander Gregg the Episcopal bishop of Texas. Private Theophilus Noel, who was listening, wrote that it was "one of the most reverent and eloquent prayers that it has ever been my lot to hear. Everyone was moved to tears and solemn thoughts." [2] After a few moments of quiet reflection, the mood was shattered by the shouted command, "By the fours from the right, march!" As the troops left Camp Sibley and headed for San Antonio, spirits were high. At first everyone rode in silence, but soon having no brass band the boys were calling for "vocal strains of harmonious tunes." The called-for music came forth and the men sang as they rode. The sentimental ballad "The Texas Ranger never sounded half so beautiful or appropriate as it did at that time." [3] With only unknown adventures before them, each man from the General downward was confident of victory and success. In those heady hours, it seemed as if fame and glory lay just down the road.

As the column passed through San Antonio with flags waving and drums beating, the citizens turned out to cheer the men on their way. General Sibley ordered the 4th to assemble in companies in the plaza in front of the Alamo. There, before that revered symbol of Texan strength and defiance, they received a battle flag from the ladies of Nacogdoches and listened to more speeches from their commanders. Private Noel of the 4th later commented that General Sibley's turn came and "in a few unguarded remarks, convinced all that he was no orator." Adding distraction to tediousness, Sibley's horse pranced about the whole time he spoke. Noel went on to say that although the General's speech was nothing special, at least it was short and it "displayed a great deal of originality and much determination." When the General closed, he bowed to his assembled soldiers, and after three rousing cheers the 4th was on the march. 4

Ten miles to the west the regiment paused along Leon Creek to make final preparations for the long trek ahead. The Brigade's path to New Mexico lay along the stage road between San Antonio and Fort Bliss, a journey of almost 700 miles through desolate inhospitable wastes. Sources of water were scarce, and many that existed were inadequate for the needs of a regiment. Because water was such a concern, General Sibley decided to divide his command. The brigade would take up the line of march a few companies at a time, eventually regrouping at Fort Bliss. On November 9, the vanguard of his troops, two companies of the 4th Regiment and a battery of artillery under the command of Major Henry Raguet, turned their horses west. The great adventure had begun. The next day, four more companies departed under the command of Lieutenant Colonel William

Read Scurry. One day after that, Colonel James Reily was in the saddle and the 4th Regiment's last four companies were on the road. 5

During that same week, the soldiers of 5th Regiment also began their move. Pulling up their stakes at Camp Manassas, they followed the 4th's lead westward. Benton Bell Seat, a lieutenant with Company F, recalled that while drawn up in a line waiting to leave an old man on a small mule approached his men. The codger faced the company and said,

> "Boys, I want to say good bye to you all for they is a good many of you I may never see any more, and I want to tell you ... You are goin' on a long dangerous journey an' you'll soon be way up yonder where the wolves howls and the chickens never crows, and ye won't have mammy's apronstrings to tie to up thar, so ef thar's ary one of you boys that ain't made up his mind, that he be willin' to hug a blackjack ef he knowed that lightenin' was goin' to strike it, you better fall out of ranks and go back home 'long o' me." 6

The old man's name was Sam Maxwell, and many of the men were his neighbors. According to Lieutenant Seat, one of the soldiers took Maxwell's advice and decided then and there not to go. The rest of the men ignored the codger's plea, and the regiment rode away.

The troops of the 5th passed through San Antonio with little fanfare. The only exception was "the grand display made by the two companies who were armed with lances." 7 Each man in these two units was equipped with a six-shooter and a 9-foot spear. General Sibley had ordered the lances, and each was topped by a three inch by twelve inch blade and a large red pennant. Sibley was a romantic at heart, and the lancers were his pride and joy. As the companies paraded through the narrow streets of San Antonio with the pennants flying, they were "truly grand." [8]

The 5th Texas rode together until they arrived at San Felipe Springs. Two weeks out of San Antonio and some fifteen miles from the Rio Grande, San Felipe Springs was considered by many of to be the end of civilization. There, the 5th divided into three squadrons. The first was under the command of Major Samuel Lockridge, the second under Lieutenant Colonel Henry McNeill, and the third under the regimental commander Colonel Thomas Green. Each of the brigade's squadrons was accompanied by supply wagons, wagons containing personal possessions, and herds of beef cattle. "There were three six-mule wagons furnished to each company, and the general regimental and medical headquarters were abundantly supplied with teams." [9] The soldiers and their equipment were an impressive sight as they formed huge columns that stretched for miles along the road.

Isaac Adair and the other soldiers of the 7th Regiment must have felt a mixture of pride and urgency as they watched the rest of the brigade march away. They too wanted to be underway for the Arizona Territory, but much remained to be done. Some of the 7th's companies were yet to be organized. Others, like Company H, were still drawing equipment.

One soldier "of the Fifth Regiment wrote that he was given a full military uniform, which included a haversack, pants, drawers, pantaloon boots, and a broadcloth coat with brass buttons." [10] Quartermaster stores like these were certainly exhausted long before Adair and his Houston and Leon County recruits showed up. Almost from the start, General Sibley had difficulty locating adequate supplies for his brigade. Company H, as late comers, probably received the dregs of what was gathered. Most of Sibley's soldiers lacked uniforms and simply wore the civilian clothes they brought from home. Some enterprising recruits talked their mothers, wives, or sweethearts into making them "soldiers shirts" so that they would present a more martial appearance. [11] Captain Adair probably fell into this category. The brass-buttoned battle shirt he is pictured wearing in his one surviving photograph could have come from government stores, but it is more likely that it was made by his caring wife, Augusta.

Of more concern to General Sibley, than the nondescript nature of his soldiers' dress, was the fact that most of the recruits lacked proper winter clothing. From his years of service in New Mexico and Utah, Sibley was familiar with the harsh conditions his men would face. When it turned out that existing Confederate storehouses could not meet his needs or did not have the authority to issue requested equipment, Sibley turned to the state's residents for assistance. The general and his regimental officers made public pleas, asking the patriotic citizens of Texas to contribute clothing and blankets for the campaign. The appeals paid off, and through the efforts of individuals and the San Antonio Ladies Southern Aid Society, much was collected. The brigade received donations of "blankets, comforters, quilts, flannel shirts, socks, drawers, and other items, as well as some cash." [12] Still it was not enough. Many of the soldiers were forced to rely on the charity of friends and family at home, and requested that they be sent boots and other clothing. Despite the best efforts of Sibley and his Quartermasters, most of the men were ill-equipped as they embarked on their expedition.

Weapons were another serious problem. When Sibley originally outlined his plan to President Davis, the two men agreed that the brigade would draw ordnance from Federal supplies seized in Texas. By the time organizing began, much of this seized material was already on its way to defend the coast and the Rio Grande valley. Recruiting advertisements asked enlistees to furnish themselves with "a good double barrel shot gun or rifle certain, a bowie knife and six shooter, if the latter can possibly be obtained." [13] Even so, some of the companies reported for duty, virtually unarmed. For some the prospect of free firearms was part of their motivation to sign up in the first place. One young soldier wrote to friends back home; "I am afraid so many companies have gone ahead of us that it will be doubtful about us getting Six Shooters, but if I don't get one I know the way home and will go straight back." [14]

To fully arm his troops, General Sibley eventually turned to the open market. Using his access to Confederate government credit, he purchased whatever weapons happened to be available. Additionally, patriotic citizens donated guns of all kinds. As a result the brigade was outfitted with every type of firearm imaginable. According to private Noel of the 4th, when his fellows left San Antonio they were "armed with squirrel guns, bear guns, sportsman's guns, shotguns, both single and double barrels, in fact guns of all sorts." [15]

By the time Captain Adair and Company H got their turn to draw weapons, things were well picked over. Undaunted, Adair still managed to put together a requisition for "Ordnance and Ordnance Stores" that the arsenal was able to fill. His shopping list included eleven Sharps rifles, five Mississippi Rifles, eight double-barrel shotguns, and several revolvers. In all Captain Adair asked for forty-eight long arms and five pistols. Presuming that everyone in his company was armed, many of the men must have supplied their own weapons. On November 20, 1861, all the requested items were delivered to Adair and his men waiting at Camp Pickett. [16] Sometime afterwards, soldiers at Fort Hudson watched two companies of the

7th regiment pass by. Commenting on how they were armed, one wag wrote in the post weekly; "We suggest as our Regiment is called Texas Mounted Rifles, that they be called 'TEXAS MOUNTED SHOT GUNS;' fo this is the weapon they are armed with." [17]

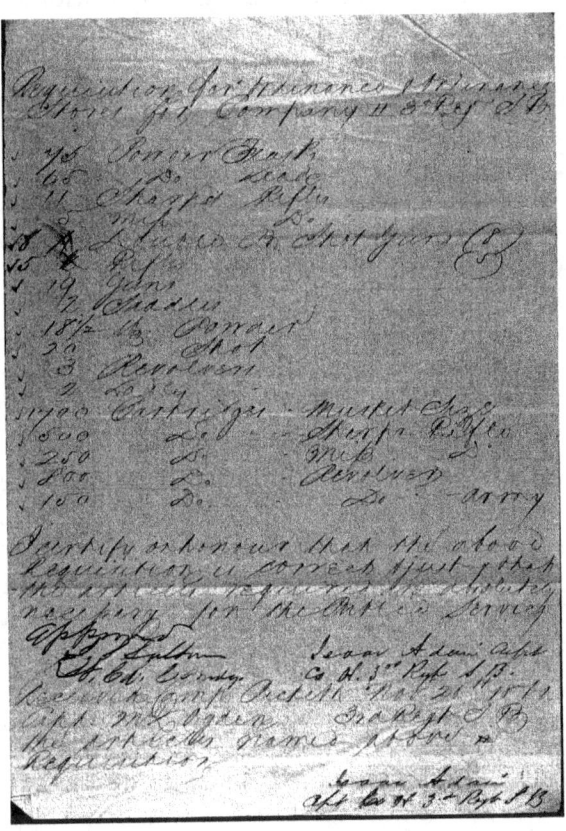

"Requisition for Ordnance and Ordnance Stores
for Company H 3rd Regt. SB,"
Courtesy, National Archives

Confederate officers were responsible for their own side arms, so about this time Captain Adair spent $8.85 to purchase himself a sword from the Texas

Arsenal. [18] It may be that the officers of the brigade were required to carry swords, or Captain Adair may simply have thought he would cut a more dashing figure with it strapped to his side. If the latter was the case, he certainly was not the only man in the brigade to hold romantic and chivalrous notions of the enterprise at hand. From General Sibley to the lowliest private, the Texans were dreamers. Despite a lack of weapons, clothing, and just about everything else needed for a successful campaign the soldiers saw nothing but victory ahead. Underscoring the lack of reality that attended the preparations, one quartermaster sergeant wrote, "It was the most complete and perfectly equipped brigade sent out by the Confederacy during the war." [19]

While Company H waited for their arms and equipment to be delivered General Sibley decided that it was high time he personally set out for Fort Bliss. A recent message from Colonel Baylor in the Mesilla Valley told him that Baylor's position was becoming untenable. With New Mexico's Union commander about to invade the lower valley with a superior force, Baylor was preparing to fall back to Fort Bliss or beyond. "Hurry up," he told Sibley, "if you want to fight." [20] With two of his regiments already on the road and the third soon to follow, it was time to leave. On November 18th, the General and his staff quit their rooms at the Plaza Hotel in San Antonio set out after his columns. Isaac Adair's sister-in-law, in a letter to a friend, proudly reported, "They selected nine of Mr. Adair's men for Gen. Sibly's [sic] body guard." [21]

The General's departure left the 7th to complete its organization and equipping under the eyes of its regimental commander, Colonel William Steele. Steele, a Northerner by birth, married a Miss Annie Du Val and joining her family, became a Texan by "friendly persuasion" or "matrimonial coincidence." [22] Besides the few companies that were still unorganized and the ones like Isaac Adair's that were drawing equipment, Colonel Steele was given command of all the men from other regiments who were left behind as too sick or temporarily unfit to travel. Eager to have at least some of his troops on the road, Steele ordered Lieutenant Colonel John Sutton to take the five most nearly ready companies and head for New Mexico. On November 28, Sutton assembled Company H and four other companies A, B, F, and I left Camp Pickett and headed west. Unlike the earlier brigade departures, the battalion under Sutton left San Antonio quietly and with little fuss. [23]

General Sibley did not assign batteries to the 7th Regiment, so no artillery accompanied Sutton's battalion. Like the columns that went before them, however, they were encumbered by beef herds and large numbers of slow-moving baggage wagons. They were also escorting a sutler's train, loaded with goods the merchants hoped to sell to the rest of the brigade. How far the cattle could be driven and the distance between water holes set the limits of daily travel. [24]

The road to Fort Bliss that lay before the battalion, was little more than a pair of wagon ruts stretching for hundreds and hundreds of miles. Writing about the company's journey, Isaac's sister-in-law speculated whether her beau, Second Lieutenant, Arrington had "seen any snakes since he started?" Rattlesnakes epitomized the hostile nature of the land through which the men were marching, and they were "said to be around in abundance." [25] On reaching the Frio River some seventy-five miles west of San Antonio, guards received orders to load their guns. The river marked the beginning of hostile Indian territory that reached nearly to the edge of Fort Bliss. From this point on there were few white settlements, and danger and hardship would be daily companions. As one trooper remembered, "A considerable crowd of camp followers had been with us but as they did not care to take the chances of encountering the Indians they left us at that point." [26]

The distance the columns traveled each day varied greatly depending on the terrain. On some days the men would ride as much as twenty-eight miles, on other days the best they could manage might be seven. As the soldiers plodded along, a great deal of the journey was monotonous. Frequently they "rode eight hours without leaving the saddle," and time and time again they described their surroundings as "desolate country." [27] A few found a stark beauty in the emptiness, but to most it was simply bitter with "Thorns and Spanish daggers very plenty, indeed." [28] When they were not marching, the Texans' time was filled with the mundane. They would cook, wash clothes, shoe their horses and listen to the occasional preaching. At Mud Creek and on the Rio Grande the "boys" went fishing and supplemented their dinners with a "great many fish." As the trek continued, the weather became progressively colder. Equipped with only a saddle blanket for warmth, some of the men spent nights awake, "trying [not] to freeze," huddled over fires of green mesquite. [29]

Some 150 miles west of San Antonio the columns reached the Devil's River, near Fort Hudson. After passing "through a country where mesquite could not grow, cactus were drying up, and grass and such good things were not to be thought of," the tired soldiers found the stream beautiful and declared it some of "the best water on the route." [30] The river was located in a country of "rock bluff" that was "very hilly, rocky, and rough," and which soon tempered their pleasure. [31] Before the troops left the area, they found themselves forced to ford the stream thirteen times, five times in a single day. Despite their proximity to water, they rode through almost insufferable clouds of dust. [32]

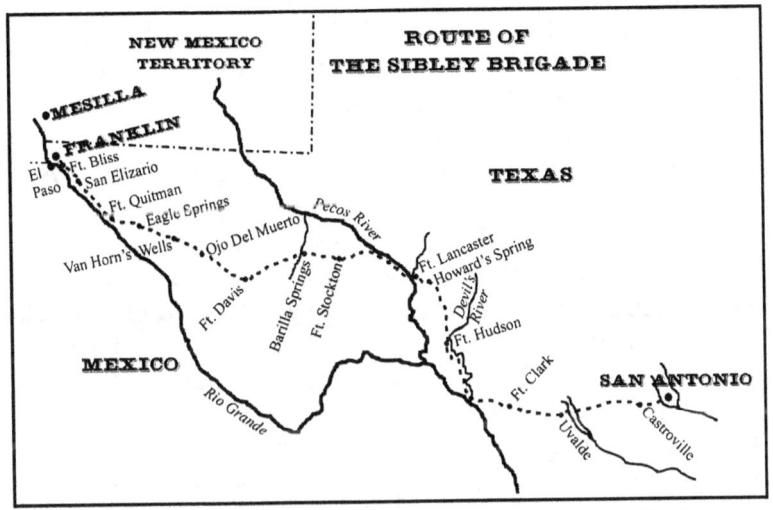

As each squadron left the Devil's River, the men prepared two-days rations of bread and beef. Private William Howell, of the 5th Regiment, told how his party broke camp at noon and headed in a northwesterly direction. Their march lasted until late that night and still the squadron failed to reach the next water. The weather was bitterly cold and the men were forced to make a dry camp. At daybreak they set out again "at a very brisk rate in order to get to water as early as possible." 33 By afternoon the thirsty troops reached their goal, Howard Spring in the channel of a dry creek bed. "Here immense stones had been blasted or dug out, making a kind of stair-way down to the water, which could be reached by only one man at a time." 34 Other men stood on the stairway and the water was passed up in buckets, hand to hand. It was a great deal of trouble getting the precious liquid to the surface and in the end only the soldiers and their mounts got to drink. The draft animals and beef herds did without. Howard Spring was only one of several difficult watering places along the trail. Many miles further on, "Dead Man's Hole was under an overhanging cliff of a boulder, which would cover a square in a city." "A man could walk erect, then stoop, then crawl to the water." [35] Here again the soldiers were forced to draw out the water in buckets. At Eagle Springs the water was so scarce they "were compelled to fill the buckets with [their] tin cups." [36]

After Howard Spring came more marching, more dust, and more dry camps. Wood was often scarce. As supplies of food ran low, the soldiers' meals came to consist solely of "beef and wormy crackers." [37] Expressing the feelings of all, a trooper in the 4th regiment commented; "When I go to another war, I'm goin' to it a way I can get to it quicker than this 'ere one." [38] Because of inadequate provisioning, much of the army marched on reduced rations. The diary of Lieutenant Julius Giesecke, Company G of the 4th Regiment, contains fifty-five entries for the journey from San Antonio to Fort Bliss. Of these, no fewer than sixteen mention the lack of food and water. At one point the soldiers were issued some corn for their horses but were so hungry that they kept it for themselves. The enterprising Giesecke used his coffee mill to grind it into flour, and his men made themselves cornbread. [39] Typically, the troops experienced several days of shortage and hardship, and then reached a spot were provisions could be obtained. When this occurred, the men often gorged themselves. A private describing one such meal wrote, "Three days full rations of flour, bacon, beef and onions were drawn and taken out to the river, a short distance off, where in a few moments the work of cooking went bravely on, and no recall was sounded until the last vestige was consumed." [40]

As the columns crawled past the various frontier forts and outposts that dotted the road, there were opportunities for the men to post letters to the friends and loved ones back home. The mail was uncertain, and it was a lucky soldier whose messages were always delivered. It was an even luckier soldier who regularly received mail in reply. Isaac Adair's sister-in-law wrote that her friends still had farther to go but already; "It takes their letters a long time to reach us; a month or frequently six weeks & more often than not they are lost." [41]

So far from home, Christmas brought little cheer to the men of the Sibley brigade. It was just another day taking them farther on their journey. They missed the "Egg Nog" of Christmas Eves past and could not help but contemplate the difference between that Christmas and pleasant ones spent at home. About to pass the night standing guard duty, Private Howell lamented; "Christmas gone and I not enjoyed anything but work." [42]

Christmas was also the day on which Colonel James Reily commander of the 4th Regiment bade farewell to his troops. Reily, who was already at Fort Bliss, was about to strike out for Mexico. General Sibley was interested in establishing diplomatic relations with the governors of Chihuahua and Sonora and he selected Reily for the mission. The Colonel was well suited for the assignment. Previously he was the Texas Republic's Charge d'Affaires to the United States and in 1856, President Buchanan had appointed him United States Minister to Russia. Reily was a zealous advocate of succession and the first of Sibley's regimental commanders to receive his commission. With his diplomatic background, Sibley hoped the Colonel could establish "satisfactory relations with the adjacent Mexican States of Chihuahua and Sonora." [43] Carrying his General's dispatches and armed with letters of accreditation, Sibley's second in command hastened on his way. In the course of events Reily's mission achieved little, but it effectively removed him as a player in the campaign.

"One of Sibley's Texas Rangers" "These Rangers who went into the rebellion were described as being, many of them, a desperate set of fellows, having no higher motive than plunder and adventure. They were half savage, and each was mounted on a mustang horse. Each man carried a rifle, a tomahawk, a bowie-knife, a pair of Colt's revolvers, and a lasso for catching and throwing the horses of a flying foe. The above picture is from a sketch by one of Colonel Canby's subalterns." From: Lossing, Benson John. Pictorial history of the Civil War in the United States of America.

The next day on December 26th, Captain Adair and his escorts, privates William Booker and J.H. Gibson, led Company H into Fort Stockton. "The weather [was] very disagreeable, dust flying so thick that it [was] impossible to see a horse fifty yards away." 44 Major John S. Shropshire wrote to his wife Carrie, "I candidly confess I never would have come this way had I imagined the country was so mean [...] If I had the Yankees at my disposal, I would give them this country and force them to live in it." 45 In the twenty-nine days since Adair and his men left San Antonio, they had traveled almost 380 miles. El Paso was still 300 miles away.

Around January 18th after another grueling twenty-three days, the battalion of the 7th arrived at Fort Bliss. Following their long and tiring journey, the volunteers found little to recommend their destination. Private Felix Collard of Company G wrote that where the city of El Paso now stands, "There was not a house on the east side of the river except the fort. Juarez, on the west side was a mere hamlet of a few adobe houses - not more than five hundred inhabitants. There were no fences of any kind." 46

"Fort Bliss - 1862," From: Twitchell, Ralph Emerson. "Old Santa Fe, a magazine of history, archaeology, genealogy, and biography." Vol: III, 1916 "The Confederate Invasion of New Mexico 1861-62."

Unencumbered by cattle and wagons, a rapidly moving General Sibley had arrived in the area more than a month earlier. Hurrying across the deserts of

West Texas, Sibley had quickly outdistanced his advancing columns. The General's small party passed three squadrons of the 5th Regiment at San Felipe Springs and the remainder of the regiment at the Devil's River. After camping with his troops, he pressed on to Fort Lancaster, passing through that outpost on November 28th. This was the same day that Isaac Adair with Sutton's battalion left San Antonio.

Third Lieutenant Isaac W. Clark, in command of the small Lancaster post, was anxious to make a favorable impression on the visiting general. To that end, he ordered his company to "appear in Uniform and mounted, with their Arms, at 7 o'clk A M, for the purpose of escorting Gen'l Sibley and paying the necessary honors." Excited by the opportunity, the small command carried out the orders with gusto. They were especially energetic when, to see how well the men were drilled, Sibley personally took charge of the company. As the garrison marched proudly by in a column of two's, the General ordered, "file left." The soldiers were so focused on their performance that the order went unheard. Away they moved at a brisk trot. As they ascended a nearby rise and disappeared from view, Sibley was heard to mutter, "gone to hell." [47] When the company finally returned, their guest had departed.

Sibley's party reached Fort Bliss on December 13, 1861. He established his brigade headquarters at the fort and the next day assumed command "of all the forces of the Confederate States on the Rio Grande at and above Fort Quitman and all in the Territory of New Mexico and Arizona." He went on to declare that, hereafter all these forces would be known collectively as the "Army of New Mexico." [48] Even though his command was only brigade sized, an ambitious Sibley styled himself the leader of an army.

By decree, all troops that were at the time serving under Lieutenant Colonel Baylor were added to the new army. As reward for his heroic efforts in the Mesilla Valley, Baylor was effectively stripped of his military command. In a clarification several days later, Sibley wrote, that he did not intend to "abrogate or supersede the powers of Baylor, as civil and military governor of Arizona." He also stated the Colonel would continue "the full exercise of the functions of that office." [49] Unfortunately, it was an office for which the Indian fighter showed little talent.

Eclipsing Baylor, Sibley bolstered his own position to the detriment of Confederate aspirations in the Southwest. In later years one of Sibley's trusted officers wrote about the campaign; "Had Colonel John R. Baylor continued to command, the result might have been different." [50] At the time, Baylor's men held none of these misgivings. General Sibley excelled at winning people's confidence, and he quickly exercised his authority over the Colonel's former troops to gain their support. This was accomplished by the simple expedient of giving promotions to a number of Baylor's key officers.

Six days later on December 20th, the General issued a far-reaching proclamation to the people of New Mexico. The proclamation began:

> "An army under my command enters New Mexico, to take possession of it in the name and for the benefit of the Confederate States. By geographical position, by similarity of institutions, by commercial interests, and by future destinies New Mexico pertains to the Confederacy." [51]

Sibley told the "peaceful people of New Mexico" that the Texans came as friends not conquerors, and pledged to "liberate them from the yoke of a military despotism." He promised that persons, family, and property would be respected, and that all forage and supplies needed by his army would "be purchased in open market and paid for at fair prices." If the people continued quietly about their "peaceful avocations," they would have nothing to fear. General Sibley also told the New Mexicans that he knew that many of them were intimidated and forced in to Federal service. He encouraged these conscripts to lay down their arms and disperse to their homes, but he also warned them, "persist in the service and you are lost." 52

By January 9, 1862 all elements of the 4th and 5th regiments safely completed their march from San Antonio and were united near Fort Bliss. With Lieutenant Colonel Sutton's battalion of the 7th then only ten days away, General Sibley was again ready to advance. Gathering his troops, he congratulated them on "a successful and rapid march of seven hundred miles in mid-winter, and through a country entirely devoid of resources." Seeking to stiffen their resolve, he concluded by reminding them of an earlier boast that; "We could go any where, and do any thing." 53 The brief remarks complete, Sibley ordered the Army of New Mexico to take up the march for Fort Thorn. The Confederates would rendezvous at the old fort, about forty miles north of Mesilla, as their last stop before taking the offensive.

It was about this same time that General Sibley's weakness as a commander began to appear. Henry Hopkins Sibley was a visionary. He may have been one of the few people of his time who truly understood the strategic value of the American Southwest. He could picture a Confederacy that stretched from ocean to ocean, and he understood the grand benefits that entailed. Fortunately for the Union, the ability to dream does not go hand in hand with the ability to strategize and lead. Although Sibley managed to pull his campaign together, he did not have the expertise and forethought needed to see it to a successful conclusion. The problems of commanding large numbers of men, hundreds of miles from their base of supply, needed someone of greater talent. After the war Major Trevanion T. Teel, Sibley's close friend and trusted chief of artillery, summed up the situation saying, "General Sibley was not a good administrative officer. He did not husband his resources and was too prone to let the morrow take care of itself." [54]

Sibley was also plagued by personal problems. He spent much of his military career at isolated frontier outposts on the outskirts of civilization. Temperance influences at these remote posts were weak, and it was common for whiskey to be relied upon for medicine, relaxation and amusement. Like many old frontier officers, he drank heavily. Early in the New Mexico expedition, Sibley was also in bad health, suffering from what one staff doctor described as "colic." Evidence suggests that this was renal colic, a painful and debilitating kidney ailment. It is uncertain whether drink exacerbated the General's illness or whether he drank to ease the pain of the disease. What is certain is that by the time his men took the field, his overindulgence and his lack of physical strength were hindering his ability to command. [55]

A central feature of General Sibley's strategy for the New Mexico campaign was that it would be self-sustaining. This was also the plan's weakest link. The valley of the Rio Grande in 1862 was barely able to support its indigenous population. Into this area Sibley marched an additional 3,000 mounted soldiers, who were supposed to live off the land. As an experienced cavalry officer, intimately familiar with the area, Sibley should have known that the course was a risky one. Despite his experience to the contrary, he was sure that adequate supplies could be obtained in the West. The General was so sanguine that when his regiments left San Antonio, they carried only enough provisions to sustain them en route. By the time they concentrated around Fort Bliss supplies were already a problem. In the words of Private Noel of the 4th, "the cold season was coming on; clothing was being needed; all of which the country afforded none." [56] The brigade's quartermasters did not bring sufficient stores with them, and there were none to be obtained in the territory. The plight of Sibley's troops was obvious even to the enemy. On January 17th, 1862, the Union commander of the Department forwarded an intelligence report to Washington, stating; Sibley's troops are "badly provisioned and armed" and that their only hope is "to march into New Mexico in quick time, or engage in a war with Mexico to procure provisions." [57]

At the heart of the Army of New Mexico's predicament was its commander's overconfidence. Defending the General in later years, Private Noel wrote, "Gen. Sibley had all confidence in his ability to move with his Brigade upon the Territory, and without resistance take possession of all its garrisons, forts and depots of supplies, and thus subsist his army on the enemy's country." [58] General Sibley tried to lay a solid foundation for his invasion. His failing as a commander was that he did not prepare alternatives should his schemes go awry.

While organizing in San Antonio, the General made plans for supplying his army once it reached the Arizona Territory. Working with Colonel Baylor he made contact with leading secessionists from the Mesilla Valley. Men of considerable means agreed to procure supplies for the Sibley Brigade from Old Mexico and sent the General repeated assurances of their ability to do so. One wrote, that he made arrangements through a responsible party to "buy up a quantity of corn, beans, &c.," for the army's use. He also stated; he would "engage all the arms and munitions possible to be had." [59] The picture painted by another was even more positive, writing in part; "I will order the purchase of more flour, beans, salt, beef, soap, corn, &c. I have there already some 10,000 pounds of corn and 300,000 pounds of flour, all for your brigade." He closed his letter to Sibley saying; "Be easy about your supplies; we shall get all we want from Sonora - what this valley cannot furnish - until such time as you may be in full possession of New Mexico and can avail of its resources [...]." [60] With guarantees like these in hand, Sibley put more effort into procuring wagons to carry the brigade's provisions than in securing the supplies themselves.

When General Sibley reached Fort Bliss, he learned to his shock that the promised supplies had not been collected. The problem was hard currency. The agents needed it to make purchases, and Sibley had not provided them any. Sufficient supplies of foodstuffs and other items were available, especially in Sonora, but the Mexicans refused to sell anything for Confederate scrip. Merchants and people on the north side of the Rio Grande were also reluctant to accept paper money. Sibley did not have even a single dollar in specie and the credit of the Confederate government was virtually non-existent in the Far West. To make matters worse, Colonel Baylor's 2nd Texas Mounted Rifles had garrisoned in the area for nearly two months. While awaiting the brigade's arrival, they consumed practically all food and forage immediately at hand.

Despite the hardship and suffering caused by the lack of adequate food and supplies, the spirits of Sibley's men and their confidence in their commander remained high. A correspondent for the New Orleans Daily Picayune wrote of the volunteers' feelings for their General, "They all love him, and have every confidence in his bravery, prudence and capability. Wherever he wills they should go, even into 'The mouth of Hell or jaws of Death.'" [61]

Supply shortages were not the brigade's only problem. On the march, and while gathering around Fort Thorn, the Confederate columns were attractive targets for hostile Apaches. The army's horses and cattle were windfalls for the Apaches, and their warriors made the most of the opportunity. Unimpressed by the brigade's size or its armaments, the natives conducted numerous minor raids against the army's herds and small detachments. Most of the Texans were not experienced Indian fighters, and the Apaches were frequently successful. "The mountains here are full of Indians," wrote one soldier, "and we dread them worse than we do the Lincolnites, by odds." Private Felix Collard of the 7th remembered how on dark nights "they would slip up to and surround the camp, each one with a bow in his hand." "One Indian, oiled all over, would lie down and wallow in the dirt and grass." "Then quiet as a cat, he would step over the sleeping men, and be among the horses." During one such raid a sergeant shot an Indian who crawled off into the darkness badly wounded. Fearful to follow the Texans let him alone until daylight. In the morning they followed his drag and came upon the brave three-quarters of a mile away. When discovered, the Apache raised himself to a sitting position and let fly and arrow. "We had to back off and shoot him with a rifle," reported Collard. "They neither give nor ask quarter." [62]

Although the soldiers killed some Indians, scarcely a day went by that the Confederates did not have horses stolen or run off. In a raid at Willow Bar, near Fort Fillmore, Indians stole "75 or 80 mules and about the same number of horses." [63] On another occasion, the Apaches burned several of the brigade's wagons. There is some evidence to suggest that Captain Adair's men were involved in at least one encounter with the hostiles. While Company H was en route to Fort Bliss, a twenty-two-year-old Private, M.A.

Dickey, was wounded and left behind at Fort Lancaster. Although other explanations are possible for Dickey's wound, it may be that Adair's company had a brush with the Apaches. [64]

In all, the Texans "had about 200 horses stolen" from them while in the area. [65] This loss was a serious difficulty for an army, whose animals were already in poor condition. Lack of feed corn and adequate forage weakened the brigade's stock, and draft animals were in disastrously short supply. Weak and useless animals and the depredations of the Apaches meant that dozens of the supply wagons, that General Sibley had so carefully assembled, were immobilized. "This, in turn, caused a shortage of transportation for carrying vital food and ammunition forward with the army." [66]

Waiting took a toll on the Brigade. As the men loitered around El Paso and Fort Thorn, there was occasional violence that led to casualties. In one instance, Seth Platner a soldier from Company F of the 5th Regiment was killed in Juarez on the Mexican side of the river. Platner got drunk, picked a fight with the locals, and "was brought back filled with Mexican bullets." In another incident, Commissary Sergeant M.C. Higgins got into a quarrel with Dan Ragsdale, the Captain of Company D, over a game of billiards. Pistols were drawn, and Higgins "was shot in the knee, from which he afterwards died." [67]

Illness among the troops was also a problem. Smallpox broke out amid Colonel Baylor's 2nd Regiment of Texas Mounted Rifles, forcing a hurried vaccination of those not infected. Colonel Reily whose troops were encamped only one day away from Baylor's, wrote; "on account of rumors of small pox," "Three hundred men have been vaccinated and we will have every soldier, teamster, servant, etc., attended to." [68] Strangely, the soldiers of one company contracted measles while on the march. This "company lost 15 men, all of whom died of that loathsome and painful disease; many whose highest ambition would have been to have fallen on the field of honor." [69] As the brigade waited near Fort Thorn for all its elements to rendezvous, pneumonia also became prevalent. Cold weather, inadequate clothing, and lack of blankets all worked to thin the army's ranks. By the time the brigade was ready to leave, so many men were laid low, that General Sibley was forced to establish a general hospital at Doña Ana.

Chapter 4

A GATHERING STORM

"Grand beyond description was the sight of our camps."
— Private Theophilus Noel

When he first dreamed up his invasion, Sibley planned for his army to take the offensive in New Mexico by early September. Thanks to innumerable delays it was now the first week of February, and the Army of New Mexico was still waiting at Fort Thorn. "Poorly armed, thinly clad, and almost destitute of blankets", his two-and-a-half regiments were now facing a winter campaign. [1] Despite these obstacles, the morale of the Confederates rode high. On February first, a combative and optimistic Colonel Baylor issued a statement typifying their mood. It read in part; "So far Mr. Lincoln is not making much headway in suppressing the rebellion. He has got himself thrashed at every fight from Manassas to Mesilla, and today we dare them to attack us at any point." [2]

Three days later Lieutenant Colonel John S. Sutton finally arrived at Fort Thorn with the five advance companies of the 7th Regiment. Isaac Adair's men in Company H, along with the other soldiers in companies: A, B, F, and I, had "made an almost unprecedented march from San Antonio." [3] With the arrival of half of his third regiment, General Sibley "determined to move forward with the force at hand." [4] Colonel Tom Green's 5th Regiment was ordered to mount up and take the advance. Several days later, the 5th broke camp and headed toward Fort Craig and the enemy.

Lying about seventy miles to the north, Fort Craig was the first Union stronghold blocking the Texans' way. Sprawled over nearly twenty acres located on the west bank of the Rio Grande, Craig was a formidable Indian fighting post. At its heart was an odd shaped compound that enclosed twenty-two adobe and basaltic-rock buildings. An adobe wall ten feet high and four feet thick at the bottom surrounded the compound. This sturdy structure had firing holes for the garrison and strong ramparts on the southeast and northwest corners. Mounted in each of these corner bastions was a four-gun battery able to command the two adjacent walls. Into this fort, designed to house 200 men, and recently expanded to hold 300, the Union had packed an army ten times that size. [5]

When Henry Sibley and other secessionist officers, deserted their posts and headed South, Union forces in the Department of New Mexico were left in the hands of Lieutenant Colonel Edward Richard Sprigg Canby. The forty-four-year-old Canby was a tall, sober, Kentuckian. Vigorous and energetic, he was a consummate organizer and exactly what the department needed. The resignations of so many officers demoralized the soldiers who remained at their posts, and the army Canby inherited was in a shambles. Troops had gone unpaid for many months; and even if he distributed all the funds at his disposal, many soldiers would still have been uncompensated for months of service. The department was short of officers, horses, draft animals, and forage, and the members of its garrisons were divided by doubts about each other's loyalty. It was this disarray that made General Sibley confident that he could march into New Mexico and overwhelm its defenses. What he failed to consider was that while he organized his command, Edward Canby would be working assertively to reorganize and strengthen his.

Colonel (Major General) Edward Richard Sprigg Canby. Courtesy Library of Congress, LC-B8172-6574DLC

Sibley and Canby were well acquainted. The two men attended West Point at the same time. They both served on the Mormon Expedition of 1857 and later campaiged against the Navajo together. Their ante-bellum comradeship was close enough that it would later give rise to false rumors that Canby stood as best man at Henry's wedding and that he was married to a cousin of Sibley's wife. Despite their acquaintance or perhaps because of it, General Sibley grossly underestimated his adversary. [6]

By the time Sibley's troops advanced on Fort Craig, the Union was ready. Waiting in and around the fort, Colonel Canby had assembled an army of 3,810 men. Of these, about 1,200 were regulars, 1,500 or so were New Mexico Volunteers, and the balance "about 1,000 hastily-collected and unorganized militia." [7] Canby also had at his disposal a hard-marching company of Colorado Volunteers. Commanded by Captain Theodore H. Dodd, the company of seventy-one miners and frontiersmen had rushed from Fort Garland in the Colorado Territory to join in Fort Craig's defense. Private Alonzo Ferdinand Ickis described the last part of their journey saying we arrived after "a tedious force march of 200 miles over sandy roads living on half rations of sandy flour poor beef & transparent bacon." [8] Impressed with their determination and stamina, the other Federals dubbed Dodd's men the "Foot Volunteers." [9] Rounding out the Union command was an independent Spy Company organized by a boisterous and colorful saloon owner and former dragoon named James "Paddy" Graydon. Captain Alexander McRae's provisional six-gun battery and Lieutenant Robert H. Hall's two-gun provisional battery of twenty-four-pounders provided Canby's artillery support. [10]

Washington planners may have placed little importance on remote New Mexico, but hardly a man of consequence in the territory failed to answer Canby's call. To protect against the impending invasion notables gathered at Fort Craig including Colonel Christopher "Kit" Carson, the renowned veteran scout, Major J. Francisco Chaves, the stepson of Henry Connelly, New Mexico's Governor, and popular local politician, Nicolás Pino. Governor

Connelly himself arrived at the fort a few days before the Texans and was delighted with what he found. Despite the language barrier, frictions, and misunderstandings, a general air of enthusiasm prevailed. "The militia were in high spirits and Colonel Canby had the entire confidence of his army." [11] On February 6th, Connelly wrote, "I have no fears as to the result here. We will conquer the Texan forces, if not in the first battle, it will be done in the second or subsequent battles." [12] The Texans had other ideas.

Colonel Christopher "Kit" Carson, 1st Regiment, New Mexico Volunteers. Courtesy Colorado Historical Society, negative F-3554A

Colonel Green's command accompanied by Major Trevanion Teel's battery of four six-pounder field howitzers was advancing steadily toward the Union bastion. The rest of the Texan force followed at daily intervals. General Sibley intended for his whole army to concentrate just below Fort Craig. On

February 9, 1862, after only four days of rest at Fort Thorn, Isaac Adair's men again took up the line of march. The 4th Texas, led by Lieutenant Colonel Scurry followed Lieutenant Colonel Sutton's battalion of the 7th the next morning. After innumerable delays, The Army of New Mexico was again on the move. [13]

Captain Trevanion Teel, 2nd Regiment, Texas Mounted Rifles. Courtesy Archives Division - Texas State Library

For several days the detachments traveled "slowly and cautiously." [14] Some thirty-five miles to the west, the soldiers could see the snow capped peaks of the Black Range. Mush ice was floating down the Rio Grande and the water was "almost too cold to drink." [15] Because of the decrepit condition of its draft animals, the brigade was forced to leave fully half its supply wagons at Fort Thorn. The ones the Confederates did take were filled first with ammunition, then with food. As a result the men were forced to travel on half-rations. Also left behind were "luxuries" like company tents and extra shoes. The winter weather was freezing and the Texans suffered accordingly. [16] Marching along the Rio Grande, the chill seemed worse because of the snowy mountains that glistened "perfectly white" in the distance. "The breeze that comes off them is verry [sic] cold," complained Private William Smith of the 5th Regiment, "This day has been as cold as any I ever felt in any land or country." [17]

By the 12th, Green's men were within twenty miles of Fort Craig and their scouting parties were starting to see "Yanks." [18] The Texans expected to be attacked at any time. That night Colonel Green laid out his camp in a two-rank battle formation and placed his artillery in a commanding position on a nearby hill. "If the Yankees come," wrote a private "we can feed them on grape shot & bombshells." [19] The men were told to graze their horses carefully and to keep their weapons loaded and ready. No attack came during night, but Major Charles Pyron leading three companies from Baylor's command and one company from the 4th Regiment joined Green's men in camp. The next morning, "All hands" left camp for a position about twelve miles closer to Fort Craig. The troops were encamped in their new position for "about one hour when a picket hurries in and reports the enemy advancing." [20] As the Union troops approached, Colonel Green deployed his men. Holding his artillery and most of his troops in reserve, he ordered four companies to move forward to meet the challenge. Prudently, Green also sent messengers back down the Rio Grande to hurry forward the rest of the army. [21]

As Green's four companies moved forward, the advancing Federals "took a position in a ravine patiently waiting an attack." Like Green, the Union commander, Captain Benjamin Wingate of the 5th U.S. Infantry, also sent an express requesting additional support. In response, Colonel Canby hurried down from the fort, bringing both reinforcements and artillery. Reaching Wingate, these troops also took up a concealed position behind the banks of the ravine. A private in the Union ranks wrote that, they were "lying behind the bank every moment expecting an attack our force is 1000 white and 2000 Greasers the enemy between 3000 and 3500." [22]

Faced for the first time with their enemy in force, both commands were exceedingly guarded. Green's advance companies proceeded about four miles, formed a line of battle and waited in that position. Officers and men alike, the Texans "all seemed cool and anxious for a fight. Some were cursing the Yankees, some were careless and unconcerned, while others were almost praying for an attack." [23] Everyone's blood was up, but neither side was willing to initiate an encounter. Because of the extreme wariness, the expected confrontation never materialized. Private Howell, waiting in the Texan line reported, "We remain in position until dark and as the enemy don't come, we return to camp." [24] The Union perspective was that, the "Texans smell a mice and retreat out of our sight." [25] Canby's men lingered in their positions until about 9 P.M. and then returned to their fort. That night the Texans remained at camp in line of battle as a heavy snow began to fall.

At about 9 A.M. on the morning of February 14th, the 4th Regiment and the battalion of the 7th arrived at Green's camp. Isaac Adair and the other soldiers suffered through the most arduous trek yet faced. Leaving their camps around midnight, in answer to Colonel Green's summons, they made a thirty-five-mile forced march in a swirling snowstorm. "The men had to face a north wind with sleet and snow falling so hard 'as to almost pelt the skin off their faces'." [26] Having outdistanced the brigade's slow moving supply train the men "were compelled to camp without bedding and provisions." [27]

For the first time, the strength of the Army of New Mexico was concentrated in one place. Sibley's forces camped below Fort Craig now consisted of the 4th Regiment, under the command of Lieutenant Colonel Scurry; the 5th Regiment led by Colonel Tom Green; and companies A, B, F, H, I of the 7th, commanded by Lieutenant Colonel Sutton. Also present were Major Pyron's three companies of the 2nd Texas Mounted Rifles and three independent companies of volunteers. This last group included Captain George M. Frazer's "Arizona Rangers", Captain Bethel Coopwood's "San Elizario Spy Company", and Captain John Phillips' "Brigands." [28]

The Brigands were an informal collection of drifters, gamblers, and desperadoes who proffered their services to General Sibley at Fort Thorn. Referred to by the rest of the army as the "Santa Fe Gamblers," this unseemly pack of ne'er-do-wells was less interested in the Confederate cause than they were in opportunities for plunder and adventure. They later caused problems by stealing from the Mexican population along the way, but they also proved aggressive fighters and valuable scouts. [29]

Major Trevanion Teel's Light Company B, 1st Texas Artillery, supported the Army of New Mexico. The Artillery Chief's company consisted of four field guns he brought with him from Baylor's command and the brigade's two four-gun batteries of Mountain howitzers. [30] Designed for use in rugged terrain, the mountain howitzers were so small and light-weight that many volunteers were amused by their appearance. Private Theophilus Noel described them as "guns in the shape of cannons," [31] while another soldier recalled that they were "about the size of a pocket derringer." [32] The howitzers were limited to a maximum effective range of 1,000 yards, but provided significant firepower for close range antipersonnel work. [33]

Mountain Artillery, U.S. Ordnance Manual 1861

Completing the Army of New Mexico was a long supply train and thousands of draft and beef animals. In all General Sibley had between 2,500 and 2,600 men gathered before the enemy. Three men from Isaac Adair's Company, who were medically unfit, were left behind in San Antonio. Another five of his men, two of whom later died, were left sick along the way. A twenty-three-year-old private, C.C. Castron, deserted while en route and a new man joined the company. On the eve on the invasion Company H had 83 men in camp, awaiting their orders. [34] One soldier later wrote that an admiring viewer had never beheld such a sight. The scene reminded him of the stories he read in his youth of armies in the "tented field" and of "Napoleon's army by night." The camp was "Grand beyond description." [35]

On February 16, 1862, having decided that a direct frontal assault on Fort Craig was too risky Sibley resolved to challenge his enemy to battle on an open plain south of the stronghold. The fort's defenses were substantial, and the general was concerned about the Union artillery's superior firepower. The broad relatively flat terrain at the fort's southern face was good ground. It offered the Confederates strong, semi-concealed, defensive positions and high ground on which to place their batteries. Believing that Canby could be enticed to fight in the open, Sibley ordered his army toward the fort. [36]

For several days, the General was either sick or drunk, or both. Ultimately, he became so violently ill that his surgeon, Dr. Covey, found him "entirely too unwell for service." [37] Colonel Tom Green was the Texans' next ranking officer. With battle impending, Sibley retired from the field and the colonel assumed command. Henry Sibley spent the next five days in his tent or ambulance, ill and drinking heavily the whole time. Rumors, frequently distorted, spread quickly through the Army of New Mexico. In time, many of those he led "came to question not only the general's tactics but also his ability to command." [38]

About a mile and three-quarters from the fort, Green deployed the brigade into a line of battle and slowly advanced. A tense wait began for the Federal reaction. Between Isaac Adair's company of the 7th Regiment and David Nunn's company of the 4th, men mustered in Houston County, Texas accounted for as many as 170 of the Confederate soldiers present on the 16th. Company I, Nunn's command, was positioned near the center of the Texan line. The battalion of the 7th, including Captain Adair and Company H, waited in reserve some distance back, with the brigade artillery. [39]

The wait was not long. "The place seemed to be deserted at first, but soon the old Stars and Stripes are run up and men begin to swarm in all directions." [40] Canby's soldiers were now clearly visible to the Confederates as they poured out of the fort and took up defensive positions just outside its walls. After their endless march from San Antonio the Texans were finally face to face with the enemy. Many of them were confident that "Canby's Greasers" would not put up much of a fight. [41] After the Union flag was run up, Major Samuel Lockridge of the 5th Regiment joked to his fellows that; "he would make his wife a shimmy out of the flag and that if he could get a wife as easy as he would get the flag, he will never sleep by himself anymore!" [42]

Remains of Fort Craig as it appeared on Sept. 1, 1957, Note Mesa Del Contadero, right background. Courtesy Colorado Historical Society, negative F-38087

The Texans advanced until they reached a position about 800 yards south of the Federal lines. Here they stopped just below the lip of a gulch, the bulk of their force hidden from the Union troops. Close enough to hear the shouts of Canby's officers, they waited with battle flags flying. The Confederates remained in position for several hours, but Canby refused to take the bait. The Union commander placed little confidence in his New Mexico Volunteers and none in his militia. Long before Green's demonstration, Canby had determined that if possible he would only offer battle "where the New Mexican troops wouldn't be obliged to maneuver in the presence of or under the fire of the enemy." [43] His bias was so strong that he suspected some Confederate officers were trying to draw him into open battle, because they had lived or served in the territory and, "thoroughly understood and appreciated the [low] character of its people." [44]

Canby wanted none of it. Instead, he tried to lure the Texans into a frontal assault on his fortified position. He ordered volunteer cavalry under captains Rafael Chacón, Paddy Graydon and Charles Deus, to "go out to the front and gallop [their] horses along a stretch between the two armies." [45] Canby hoped the provocative action would draw the Texans out, especially those concealed in the gulch. The Texans, seeing what appeared to be a charge, "yell and wave their hats at Yankeedom and beckon them on" in hopes of attracting the New Mexicans in range of their artillery. [46] To the Confederates' disappointment the cavalry stopped short. Captain Graydon made a target of himself "turning and wheeling like a circus man" before Green's troops, but the best reaction the volunteers could raise was some desultory, though accurate small-arms fire. [47] In two such sorties, the New Mexicans "shot perhaps three cartridges per man", but could not provoke fire from the entire Confederate line. [48] Canby's cavalry suffered two casualties. Private Benjamin Baum, from Deus' company, was killed, and another soldier was wounded. On the Texan side the men "heard several bullets whistle by" but no one was injured. [49] Private Alonzo F. Ickis, serving with Dodd's Colorado Company, wrote in his diary; the "Enemies Sharp Shooters threw a few shots among Canby's escort, but not a muscle moved on the Col. He sat erect on [his horse] Old Chas with that ever present cigar which he never smokes between his lips." [50] With daylight fading, it became apparent to the Rebels that Canby could not be induced to fight. As Colonel Green was equally unwilling to commit to an assault, another almost-battle spluttered to a close. Their baptism of fire over, the Texans withdrew to their camps.

That night the weather changed from unpleasant to severe. Swirling snow flurries were replaced by fiercely blowing winds, and out of the southwest came clouds of stinging sand and dust. Regular operations became impossible. For the next two days, both armies hunkered down and protected themselves as best they could. During the wait, "Daddy" Green called a council of war. Sibley's troops faced a dilemma. Canby refused to fight. The brigade's artillery was too light for an effective bombardment, and Fort Craig was too strong to be stormed. With barely ten days of food remaining in the Texans' commissary, a siege was out of the question. Because Fort Bliss and the Mesilla Valley were stripped of provisions the brigade could not fall back or resupply. Something needed to be done, and done quickly. [51]

While most of the Texans rested in camps south of the fort, the brigade's commanders formulated a plan. After careful reconnoitering and deliberation, they decided that there was still a chance to draw Canby into battle. The Texans felt that their "only hope for success was to force the enemy to an open-field fight." [52] Sibley and his officers decided to backtrack a couple of miles and cross the Rio Grande. They would then push north "turn the fort," and recross at Valverde ford. This bold and unorthodox move would place the brigade across Canby's line of supply and force him to either fight or be cut off. The strategy was fraught with hazards. The Texans would need to cross the frigid Rio Grande twice under the guns of their enemy. They would also have to force a passage through deep sand, and make a dry camp less than four miles from the Union bastion. Worst of all, if their objective failed, the enemy force would sit squarely across their own line of supply and retreat.

The risk was high, but if the plan worked, the Brigade could force Canby to battle on ground of its own choosing.

For two days the Texans remained in camp preparing rations and looking to their weapons, then on the morning of the 19th the wind abated. Breaking camp early, they moved down river a short distance and began to ford. The movement confused the defenders at Fort Craig and only the icy waters of the Rio Grande opposed the Confederates' crossing. By evening, the entire Army of New Mexico including the wagon train and beef herd were safely on the far bank. [53] Most of the Texans were still ignorant of the reason for their move and according to hearsay from Private Noel "Ten thousand times ten thousand conjectures were afloat amongst the men, and questions innumerable asked in relation to what was to be done, and where we were going." [54] That night, the Texans left their horses saddled and slept with their weapons at hand.

The land on the eastern shore was a rough country or malpais, consisting of ancient lava flows and deep sandy plains. The morning of February 20, 1862, found Sibley's men again in the saddle. The Brigade was divided into two parts with the wagon train placed in the middle for protection. In this formation the Texans marched, paralleling the Rio Grande until they caught sight of the Federal Fort on the bluffs across the river. [55]

As the brigade marched, Fort Craig on the opposite bank loomed closer and closer. About noon, wishing to avoid Canby's artillery, Sibley ordered his men to turn right and move northeast. Up to this time the way was hard-packed and "the journey had been performed with but little trouble." [56] Now, the Confederates began to blaze their own trail. Playing "tug of war" with their heavy supply train, they crawled up a steep rocky ravine toward higher ground.

After considerable effort, they found themselves on "a level sandy plain in which the wagons would settle nearly to their hubs." With "some pulling, some pushing, and no few cursing", the Texans covered only 7 miles before calling a halt. [57] It was only four in the afternoon, but the soldiers were exhausted and their teams were fast giving out due to lack of food and water.

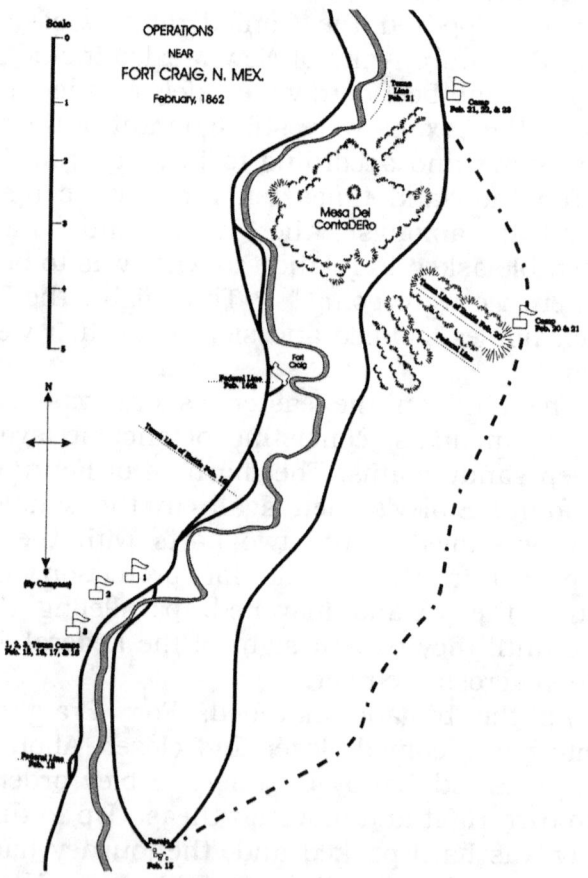

Operations around Fort Craig

While the Confederates rested and struggled with their wagons, Colonel Canby finally concluded that they were sidestepping his fort and moved to contest their passage. A short while before sundown, he crossed the river with a section of artillery and most of his infantry and cavalry. From the heights above, the Texans watched the Federals ford the river and climb the sandy ravines leading to their position. "Gen. Sibley being sick, Col. Green took command and formed his men along a ridge in the shape of a crescent." [58] The artillerymen of the 4th and 5th Regiments readied their little mountain howitzers, and in the middle of the Texan line, Captain Trevanion Teel's men unlimbered their four six-pounder field pieces. As Union troops began to force in their pickets, Sibley's men unfurled their regimental battle flags. Positioned on a little eminence, the brigade's tiny brass band struck up "Dixie." [59] As the Federals approached, Isaac Adair's immediate commander Lieutenant Colonel Sutton rode among the men of the 7th urging them to "think of their rights, and remember the honor of Texas." [60]

The ground in front of Colonel Canby's troops "was exceedingly difficult for the operations of cavalry or artillery," but he decided to continue his attack. [61] Cautiously, he deployed his men and threw forward skirmishers. As soon as the Federals were within range, Colonel Green ordered Teel's six-pounders to open fire. For the first the time the Rebels "heard the roar of cannon blazing at the enemy." [62] At about 1,000 yards, the Federals formed a line of battle and fired two harmless volleys and a few shots from their artillery. In reply the Texans added the weight of Reily's and Wood's mountain howitzers to their cannonade. Soon the mesa was echoing and booming with the sound of the Confederate guns. Private Frank Starr, attached to Reily's battery, wrote to his father, "Every time the balls fell among the enemy shouts rose from one end of our line to the other." [63]. Although the shells inflicted little damage, they succeeded in unnerving a portion of Canby's green volunteer troops. Some of the volunteers were mustered as recently as January, and the explosions, smoke, and raining debris were more than they had bargained for. [64]

Colonel Green noticed their restlessness and ordered his guns "to play upon their volunteers." [65] The New Mexicans cowered as Teel's rounds showered them with rock fragments. Ultimately, as the fire became hotter, they broke and fled. Colonel Canby was disgusted. He wrote that the volunteers were "thrown into such utter confusion by a few harmless cannon-shots that it was impossible to restore them to any kind of order." [66] With night fast approaching and a significant portion of his force already in retreat, the Union commander decided to retire to the safety of his fort. The Texans did not get the decisive battle they wanted, but nevertheless they carried the day. Seventeen-year-old Ebeneezer Hanna wrote in his diary; "the yankees came out to meet us. We fired them a salute with our artillery and they taken some exceptions to our introductory [...] took to their heels and went back to their dens." [67]

After the Federals departed, Colonel Green decided to move farther away from the fort. With their "wagons going four abreast in order to strengthen [their] line of march," the Texans pressed on across the pedregal and its drifting ridges of sand. [68] Only scant miles from the river, their animals were suffering terribly from thirst. As Second Lieutenant Philip Fulcrod remembered,"We had now been from water two whole days and one night, and our mules were so completely exhausted that near night they broke down and could go no further, and we had to camp in a desert of sand." [69] Wagons that failed to keep up with the column were scattered for miles along the trail. It took weary soldiers and teamsters most of the night to bring them to camp and in the end; some were abandoned and later burnt by Union patrols. [70]

Feeling nearly as thirsty as their mules, the Texans settled down for an unpleasant night amid the mesquite groves of the open mesa. Water was extremely scarce so cooking was out of the question. Conserving the little water that remained the Confederates huddled around small fires and prepared meager meals of cold bread and dried beef. [71] "They talked and cast bullets from lead bars melted over the glowing coals. Some replaced missing or defective shoes on their mounts." [72] A few brave men, under cover of darkness, risked a perilous trip down the mesa to fill canteens. They crawled through the Texan lines, "made their way to the river, crawled through the enemy lines and obtained water for themselves and their sick companions." [73] Elsewhere men slept on their arms. Near Isaac Adair rifles flashed as pickets from the 7th Regiment fired at enemy scouts.

Later after the camps quieted down and a majority of men drifted off to sleep, the most outlandish action of the entire campaign began to unfold. Captain James "Paddy" Graydon, the colorful commander of Canby's Independent Spy Company, formulated a plan to stampede Sibley's horses. No sooner was the bizarre scheme conceived, than Graydon proposed it to Canby, "who, nothing loath, consented." That the Federals would harass the Texans was expected, but it was the nature of Paddy's proposed "raid" that set it apart. Graydon intended to equip a broken down mule with a packsaddle upon which was mounted a display of fireworks. He reasoned that, if he could slip in among the Confederate mounts and set the thing going it would be "astounding and startling to all horsekind." [74]

Under cover of darkness, Captain Graydon slipped across the river with his infernal machine. Passing over the few miles to the Rebel camp, he stole past the Texan sentries and found himself in the midst of their grazing cattle. "Now was the time for action, the accomplishment of the grand 'coup' the unrestrainable Irishman had evolved." With his solitary mule in position, Paddy struck a match and lit the fuse that was to set the whole mass of explosives spitting, fizzing, and buzzing." Unfortunately for the success of this enterprise, [Graydon's] education in pyrotechny had been neglected, and rockets, Roman candles, blue devils and grasshoppers burst all together, blowing the ever patient and self-sacrificing mule into that everlasting eternity, where it is doubtful if two ribs were ever collected." [75] Unharmed, but crestfallen and vanquished, Graydon crawled through the darkness outside the Texans' now alert camp. Once in the open he footed it for the Federal lines, all the while "philosophizing upon the uncertainty of all human calculations." [76]

Despite its seeming failure, Graydon's plan may actually have met with limited success. The Texans' animals "were suffering terribly for water" and sometime around midnight 150 poorly secured draft mules stampeded. [77] The mules ran until they reached the Rio Grande, where they stopped to appease their thirst. The drinking animals were quickly rounded up by Union pickets, who herded them to Fort Craig. Maybe the noise and commotion of Graydon's explosions spooked these "deserters" or maybe their thirst simply became too much. Whatever the cause, the result was that more than two dozen of the 4th Regiment's wagons were immobilized. The brigade also lost its unfortunate wagonmaster, who stumbled into Federal hands while searching for his wayward charges. [78]

Chapter 5

BLOODY VALVERDE

"Forward boys forward, glory lies in front."
- Lieutenant Colonel John Schuyler Sutton

As the 21st "dawned verry cold & cloudy", General Sibley pondered how to deal with the loss of the 4th Regiment's mules. [1] Deciding that the best course was to abandon his crippled wagons, he ordered Lieutenant Colonel Scurry to lighten some of the wagons and burn the rest. Nearly thirty wagons "containing the entire kits, blankets, books and papers" of the 4th Regiment were consigned to the flames. [2] Among the companies that lost their belongings was David Nunn's from Crockett. Captain Nunn reported that the "Crockett Boys" "lost all their blankets, overcoats and etc. which loss [later] caused much suffering." [3]

General Sibley was still "quite sick" and "rode nearly all the time in his ambulance", but he reluctantly took to the saddle at early dawn to personally direct his operations. [4] "Green's regiment, with a battalion of the Seventh, under Lieutenant-Colonel Sutton, and Captain Teel's battery, were ordered to make a strong, threatening demonstration on the fort, while Scurry, with the Fourth, well flanked by Pyron's command on the left, should feel his way cautiously to the river." [5] Because of the fiasco with the 4th Regiment's wagons the intended movements were delayed and slightly altered. Green's regiment remained on the south side of the mesa to threaten the fort, but everyone else headed for the river. "What was left of the trains was kept in motion over the sand hills, which the enemy had deemed impossible." [6] Captain Adair's company and the other 400 men of the battalion of the 7th moved out with the train. The wagons now lightened of all unnecessary equipment, crept slowly across the sandy highlands behind the mesa. "Streched out for several miles," they pushed northward, following in Scurry's wake. [7]

At first light General Sibley had dispatched Major Charles Pyron and his 180 man detachment from Baylor's command to reconnoiter the road to the ford. Riding far in advance of Scurry's column, the major and his men reached the northwest edge of the mesa. Spread before them in the cold morning light was the still darkened valley and the quiet river bottom. Supposing the ford to be free of enemy troops, Pyron sent back a message that "the road was clear and the water in sight." [8] The small command then leisurely proceeded to the river to water their thirsty horses.

The valley containing the ford, or more properly fords, is bordered on the southeast by a monolithic rise called Mesa Del Contadero. The valley's eastern edge was more or less formed by the dry arroyo of an old river channel. Over time the Rio Grande had changed its course many times and not far back from its banks lay a series of small hills and sand ridges. In February of 1862, these hills and ridges ran northward for nearly a mile until they met another lower mesa. Some of the valley was open, but other parts were thickly wooded with "bosques" or groves of cottonwoods. The river itself swept through the basin in wide curve that bowed to the northwest. As it slowed and broadened it became shallow and easy to cross. [9]

Sometime between 7:00 and 7:30 in the morning, Pyron's men finished watering their horses and filling their canteens. As they turned to leave a stand of cottonwoods and return to the main column, they spotted a body of Union cavalry only a couple of hundred yards downstream. [10]

Sibley's Texans planned for the day's operations, but back at Fort Craig, Colonel Canby had laid plans of his own. With pickets and scouts strung out along the river and atop the mesa, he was promptly informed when the Confederates began their predawn march. Based on this intelligence, Canby decided to contest Scurry's advance. To deny the Texans their objective he immediately ordered six cannon and close to 850 men to rush to the Valverde ford. As a safeguard against Green's continued presence south of the mesa the Union commander built his defensive position on the eastern bank of the Rio Grande to nearly 1,400. Satisfied with his preparations, Canby waited at the fort with the remainder of his forces to see how and where the action would develop. [11]

In due time a section of Union cavalry, commanded by Major Thomas Duncan reached the ford. Hurrying ahead of his slower foot soldiers, Duncan was under orders "to cross the river and hold the bosque on the opposite side, so as to prevent the enemy from reaching the water." [12] When he arrived at the ford, he found two mounted companies of New Mexico Volunteers, Rafael Chacón's and Paddy Graydon's, already there. No sooner did the Federals reach the river than "a large force of the enemy's cavalry could be seen in the woods a few hundred yards" away on the far bank. Duncan immediately ordered Lieutenant Ira Claflin's Company G, First U.S. Cavalry to proceed up the river and observe the Texans' movements. Meanwhile he ordered the New Mexico Volunteers and the rest of his command to cross over as promptly as possible. [13]

The Confederates were of course Pyron's battalion, and it was probably Chacón's and Graydon's dismounted companys they spotted as they turned from the river. When Pyron saw the Union skirmishers, he sensed an opportunity. At least for the moment, he believed his enemy was outnumbered. As the New Mexico Volunteers cautiously withdrew, Pyron wheeled his command and set out in pursuit. Chasing the retreating Federals through the heavy bosque the Texans came to the bank of an old river channel and suddenly found themselves "in front of a large force of all arms." [14] Arranged before him, with their backs to the river, Pyron had run into the balance of Duncan's command. The Rebel major immediately dismounted his men and established a defensive position behind the embankments of the old channel. Erroneously believing that he was greatly outnumbered, Major Duncan also assumed a defensive posture.

The better-armed Federals opened a brisk fire on the Texans, and as Confederate Sergeant Major William Laughter put it, it was soon apparent that we "bit off more then we could chew." [15] As a light snow began to fall Pyron dispatched a message to Lieutenant Colonel Scurry. The message warned "that large masses of the enemy were in his front and threatening an attack." [16] During the next hour, "by the courage and determination of [his] men, [Pyron] was enabled to maintain the position in the unequal struggle." [17]

The major's dispatch caused a flurry of excitement when it reached the Confederate column. Fearing that Pyron and his men would be overpowered, Colonel Scurry ordered his men to push forward as fast as their horses could carry them. Hurrying for all they were worth, Scurry and Major Henry Raguet's 310 man battalion of the 4th Regiment quickly reached Pyron and deployed to his right. Hot on their heels, the first of Reily's 12-pounder mountain howitzers arrived on the scene and took up a position on the far left. For a short while the two forces in the valley were near evenly matched, with approximately 500 men each. Scurry, believing that he held an advantage, began to press the Unionists in an attempt to control the lower ford. At about the same time, Lieutenant Colonel Benjamin S. Roberts arrived with the Union infantry and artillery and waded into the fight. Without waiting to cross the river, Roberts positioned his cannon and began shelling the Confederates in the bosque. [18]

Maybe half an hour behind Raguet's companies followed the rest of the 4th Regiment. In superb spirits, the 4th Texas rode over the high table land at a brisk trot, singing songs as they came. As they descended a long slant to the valley bottom, they began to hear the booming discharge of Robert's Federal cannon. By the time they dismounted in the cottonwoods the fighting was general. They could hear the rapid discharge of small arms, and every half minute the heavier crash of artillery as the enemy threw shells and balls at the Texan positions. It was only 9:00 A.M. and despite the snowy ground both sides knew they were in for a hot day. [19]

Isaac Adair and his Houston and Leon County Company were still atop the mesa guarding the Confederate train, but their friends and neighbors were already hard at it in the valley below. Captain David Nunn's "Crockett Boys," were met with "volley after volley of musketry" as they advanced into line. As the men attempted to take cover in the safety of the sand banks, the enemy's balls greeted them "with a viper's hiss." Second Lieutenant J.P. Stephenson was the first to fall, a bullet in his ankle. Lead whizzed by in rapid succession and "the enemy cannon balls came just over [their] heads, tearing the trees, and cutting the limbs that fell thick amongst [them]." Captain Nunn later divulged to his diary; "Now, for the first time, did I fully realize the terror of the battlefield!" [20]

"On the Line of Battle," From: Ladd, Horatio O. The Story of New Mexico. D. Lothrop Company, 1891

Over the next two hours the struggle at the ford seesawed back and forth as the two forces each sought an advantage. Fighting with great determination the Texans made several desperate efforts to obtain the crossing. Colonel Scurry dispatched a strong dismounted force and one of Reily's cannon down through the timber toward the Mesa del Contadero with the intention of assailing Major Duncan's right flank. Before the Texans were in position Roberts, who was still on the opposite bank with McRae's and Hall's artillery, saw the move and sent a warning. Duncan immediately dispatched reinforcements to the woods. Following several minutes of spirited skirmishing Scurry's men were driven back. After being pushed from the woods by the dismounted cavalry, the Texans regrouped and swarmed back. Three times, each with accumulated strength they rushed the bosque, but three times they were again "driven out by the slaughter of McRae's and Hall's guns." [21]

During the skirmishing Lieutenant Colonel Roberts grew increasingly frustrated by Major Duncan's relative inaction. Some months before, Roberts had examined the area of the ford and he was convinced of the importance of seizing and holding the thick grove of cottonwoods. As he watched the 4th Texas swarm down from the mesa, he repeatedly sent orders to Duncan to take this key part of the field and "hold it at all hazards." Roberts' anxiety to gain the position was extreme, and three times he sent his adjutant, Lieutenant Meinhold, across the icy river to urge Major Duncan to act aggressively. The Lieutenant Colonel believed that if Duncan could secure the woods for just 20 minutes, his artillery could cross the river. Once across and placed in a commanding position, he was sure McRae's guns and Hall's howitzers could force the Confederates back to the mesa. To Roberts' chagrin, Major Duncan seemed either unable or unwilling to take and hold the timber. [22]

Denied the water and unable to advance against the combined strength of Robert's better armed troops and the artillery across the river the Texans were nevertheless well situated. Sheltered behind the first sandbank of the old river channel, they dominated the bosque and were relatively unhampered as they consolidated their positions.

Just before noon Captain Travanion Teel came thundering down off the mesa with two of his 6-pounder howitzers. The canyon down which he careened was steep and rocky and to the amusement of some of the Rebels below, the cannoneers had to cling to the seats of the wildly bucking caissons to keep from being thrown off. [23] When the battery reached the ford, "shout after shout went up as it charged up in front."[24]

In a flash Captain Teel unlimbered his two guns and engaged McRae's artillery across the river. Just as quickly the Federals changed their battery's front and responded with its whole force. The area around the Rebel howitzers became hot indeed as a spirited artillery duel commenced. Showers of round shot and rifle bullets whistled past the battery and over the heads of soldiers huddled to its rear. Shells burst all around, trees were shattered and limbs were cut. Behind the men of the 4th Texas, horses were screaming and dying. The Texan guns only "boomed once or twice, perhaps four or five times," when one of the Confederate gunners was carried off severely wounded. [25] At nearly the same instant, another was shot dead.

"When Teel's men fell, the others in panic deserted." [26] The cannonade from McRae's and Hall's 8 guns was furious. "So heavy was their fire that [Teel] soon found himself with but five men to work the two guns." A shell exploded under the Captain's pieces setting "the grass on fire; still this gallant officer held his position and continued his firing upon the enemy." [27] Standing bravely at his post, amid a hail of bullets, Teel seized a rammer and assisted in the loading of his undermanned guns. With only five cannoneers left, the beleaguered Teel was forced to alternate between his pieces and it was impossible to keep up a steady and effective fire. Seeing his plight, Lieutenant Colonel Scurry called on Lieutenant John Reily and his men from one of the ineffective mountain howitzers to man the guns. As soon as Reily's artillerymen were advised of the situation, they rushed to Teel's support. Then, amidst the storm, they stood their ground with "heroic daring." [28] The artillery duel continued a while longer, until the Union gunners tired of the game and changed their front. [29]

By noon, the action at the ford was furious and the commanders of both armies started sending in all their available reinforcements. On the strength of messages from Lieutenant Colonel Roberts, Canby decided to commit most of his remaining forces to the growing battle. Leaving a mixed command of about 890 volunteers and militia to guard against any remaining threat to Fort Craig, he ordered another 1,200 men to cross below the fort and hurry to Robert's aid. [30] For his part, General Sibley discontinued his feint against the fort. Colonel Green with all his disposable force was ordered to rush to the support of Scurry and Pyron.

With its wagons stretched for miles across the rough sandy plateau, the Confederate train needed protection. Aware of the New Mexico Volunteers and militia operating south of the mesa, Green ordered the battalion of the 7th under Colonel Sutton, and companies C and H of his own regiment to remain with the wagons. Leaving four of the brigade's mountain howitzers with Sutton, Green took the remaining two guns and hurried for the ford. With pennants flying, Major Lockridge led the way with the two companies of lancers. The remaining six companies of the 5th regiment followed closely. In all Colonel Green was bringing about 670 men and another two cannon into the fight. [31]

As the reinforcements from both sides poured into the battle, the Federals took the upper hand. On the Confederate left the Texans' one piece of artillery was silenced by the heavier metal of the enemy and the men of the 4th Texas and Pyron's battalion were being driven back. Major Lockridge arrived on the scene with three companies, but could do little. The Union numbers were so great and their fire so heavy that Lockridge and Pyron pulled back to the safety of a sandbank about 100 yards further to their rear.[32]

On the right, the rest of Lieutenant Colonel Scurry's command was hunkered down behind another sandbank of the old river channel and was fairing little better. Union troops discovered a lightly guarded ford where the water "proved to be not over three and a half or four feet deep." 33 Wading into the freezing water Theodore Dodd's Colorado Volunteers and Union regular infantry under Captain Henry Seldon had crossed with minimal loss. On the far bank they were joined by Captain Rafael Chacón's company. Selden's orders were to advance against the Texans and "engage them with the bayonet." 34 About 600 yards from Scurry's lines, the storming force made their preparations. Amid intermittent snow flurries the cavalry drew their sabers, and the foot soldiers fixed bayonets. With all in readiness, the order was given, and the combined force of nearly 630 stepped forward into the woods. 35

Facing a real danger that he would be flanked Lieutenant Colonel Scurry extended his line. As the Union troops began their advance, Scurry ordered his men to grab their horses and ride 250 yards to the right. Moving to their new position, the men of the 4th Texas "dismounted in a perfect hail of bullets." 36 Captain Nunn recalled; as "we ran up to the trees to hitch our horses, the bullets whizzed by us, as thick as bees in a swarm." 37 Now came some of the heaviest fighting of the day. As the Federals approached, firing rapidly, the Confederates could do little but lay behind their sandbank and keep their heads down. Only a few of the Texans were armed with modern rifled muskets and the remainder simply could not respond to the longer-range Union weapons.

The bullets took a heavy toll on the 4th's horses, tied just behind the lines, and men began falling in the ranks. In David Nunn's company, nineteen year-old Zebedde Gossett was shot through the back as he raised to load. With heart rending groans, Gossett fell to the ground. Although dying, "Zeb" asked someone to load his gun and fired at the enemy one last time. 38 All along the line men were being hit. On Captain Nunn's left, three men from Company C were wounded. With a cry of "O God, I'm shot." William H. Onderdonk was shot through the mouth. [39] Corporal Al Field was struck in the arm as he took cover behind a large tree, and Private S. Schmidt took a Minie ball through both thighs.

Lieutenant Phil Fulcrod, manning a section of Teel's artillery, later recounted; "Our center having only shotguns [and unrifled muskets] were silent with the exception of my two six-pounders which we kept working, the enemies long-range guns doing us considerable damage." [40] Finally, Selden's advance brought his soldiers within the Rebel's range. Shooting as quickly as they could load, the 4th Texas poured their fire into the enemy with deadly intent. The Unionists found little cover on the field and the Confederate fire soon became extremely galling. Captain Nunn wrote, "The enemy concealed themselves behind the trees. We picked them off so well, that they could not stand it." [41] Faced with stiff opposition, the Federal advance slowed, but continued to force the Texan extreme right.

About this time Captain Willis Lang of the 5th Texas approached Scurry and asked for permission to charge with his and Captain Jerome McCown's lancers. The Lieutenant Colonel refused. Soon the persistent Lang was back with the same petition. This time Scurry gave in. The Captain's objective was to be a body of troops on the Federal extreme left, wearing the gray uniform of the New Mexico Volunteers. [42] Lieutenant Phil Clough, of the 5th Texas, remembered that as the companies were readied, "the gleaming lance blades and fluttering pennons [sic] could be seen through the smoke of battle forming a line." Captain Lang made a short speech to the assembled lancers, "brought them to attention and gave the fearful order 'charge'!" [43] In a column of fours, the lancers burst through a gap in the sandbank and headed for the Federal lines. Through some confusion, possibly a last minute countermand by Colonel Green, only Lang's company made the attack.

Captain (Lieutenant Colonel) Theodore Dodd, Company A, 2nd Regiment, Colorado Infantry. Courtesy Colorado Historical Society, negative F-2028

"Like an avalanche the intrepid Lang with his squadron of lancers charged the serried lines of the foe." 44 A private among the waiting Federals wrote, "Not a sound in our ranks, could hear my own heart beat. Oh what suspense." 45 Unfortunately for the Captain and his men, the Union troops in the gray were not the raw native militia they expected. Instead, they were the hardy miners and frontiersmen of Captain Theodore Dodd's Colorado Volunteers. The battle lines were only one hundred yards apart, but owing to the volunteers' position, "the direction of the charge was so oblique that the lancers had to traverse about two hundred an fifty yards" before reaching their goal. 46 While skirmishers coolly picked off men and horses, Captain Plympton, who commanded the point towards which the lancers were thundering, rallied the left platoon of his company and the right platoon of Dodd's company. The disciplined regulars and Coloradans reacted instantly and "threw themselves in position 'to resist cavalry' the front lines on their knees with braced muskets presented a wall of bayonets, while the second lines delivered fire into the breast of the heroic lancers." 47

At about 40 yards the Coloradans fired their first volley. Private Alonzo Ickis reported: "when they got to us we were loaded again and we gave them the 'buck and ball'." 48 Lang's desperate charge broke against the fierce wall of steel and lead. The Texans flowed around Dodd's and Plympton's men, only to be met by reinforcing columns, who poured a deadly musket fire into the hapless lancers. "Lang and his men rode through and over them, wheeled and rode through them again, all the while emptying their pistols in the enemies faces." 49 Despite their boldness, the lancers were no match for the determined Federals, and "they were soon butchered ... by the bayonet." The slaughter was terrible. "Private G. Simpson ran his bayonet through one [of the Texans] and then shot the top of his head off." 50 Lang was shot from the saddle, and Lieutenant Demetrius M. Bass was wounded in 7 places. Many of the lancers were killed inside the Federal lines and "many were

Private Alonzo Ickis, 2nd Colorado Infantry, Courtesy Dr. Nolie Mumey and Fred A. Rosenstock

dismounted and had to fight their way back." In moments, the pride of 5th Texas was decimated. Twenty of Lang's men lay dead or dying, and virtually all the horses were maimed or killed. "If Captain Lang's men had not had their six-shooters, and had depended on their lances, they would all have been killed instead of half." [51] "Desperate courage was ineffectual against great odds and superior arms, and the company there sustained the greatest loss of life of any company of the brigade." [52]

While Lang's attack cast a gloom over the entire Texan line, it also caused the Federal advance against Scurry's right flank to lose momentum. Enticed forward, the Union troops were met with an effective small-arms fire from the Confederate line. Teel's howitzers also reopened with killing effect. The firefight raged for another half-hour at which point the Union infantry fell back and the assault spluttered to a halt. [53]

As the Union soldiers retreated out of range, one of Captain Nunn's men noticed, that a Yankee he shot and wounded was still shooting back. The Rebel known as "Uncle Jannis" approached Nunn and said; "Captain, yonder is a d__d son of a __ that I have shot who is lying behind a tree shooting at us. May I go out and kill him?" [54] Captain Nunn gave his permission, and Uncle Jannis went out to murder the Yank. When he reached the wounded fellow, the soldier begged so piteously that Jannis could not kill him. Instead he disarmed the man and left him where he was. Jannis then gathered up four rifled muskets and some ammunition and brought them back to his fellows.

The Texans blunted Seldon's attack, but everywhere they were forced from the woods and away from the river. Although they were in a strong defensive position, behind the sandbanks of the old river bed, the Confederates were clearly in trouble. In some places Scurry's "men were scattered in a single rank, the men being four or five feet apart." [55] Additionally, ammunition was running low. Private William Lott Davidson of Company A of the 5th Texas wrote; "Here I sent my last bullet, and my rifle was of no more use that day, so I fell back on my shot-gun and laid in the ravine with my company." 56 Satisfied with the morning's results and feeling that the fords were now secure, Benjamin Roberts ordered all of his Union artillery to cross the river. After splashing across the middle ford, the guns were soon back in action at even closer range. 57

General Sibley had not been a factor in the battle and by this time he was too ill and drunk to remain in the saddle. Exhausted, he ordered his aides and other staff officers to report to Colonel Green and once again retired to his ambulance. Although the general kept some of his headquarters staff busy rushing between his ambulance and his officers on the field, command effectively passed to Colonel Green. Concerned with the deteriorating situation at the front "Daddy" Green decided to send in his last reserves. Dispatching a messenger to Lieutenant Colonel Sutton he ordered him to reinforce as quickly as possible. 58

Before the Texans' wagon train had barely gotten out of camp in the morning, Isaac Adair and its other guards could already hear the sullen roar of cannon. For hours they slowly pushed the wagons through the deep sand and listened to the distant sounds of battle. During this whole time, the men worried that they would have no share in the conflict. When Green's messenger arrived with the order to move to the battlefield, they were chomping at the bit. Lieutenant Colonel Sutton decided to risk leaving the train with a significantly reduced guard. Detaching companies A and H of the 7th and company C of the 5th, He ordered the balance of his men to the scene of the action. 59 Captain Adair's men, and the other soldiers detailed to the wagons, watched their comrades gallop away and brooded about being left behind. They worried that others would think it was their fault that they were not in the fight. Consoling themselves that their job was important, the men told each other that they were needed "to keep Kit Carson's regiment off [the] train." [60] In a letter to his father, Private Howell, with company C wrote, "We were in great danger with that train [there were] so few of us [that] had not the enemy needed all his force at the battlefield we would have been attacked." Despite their feelings, their orders were clear. The three companies of the rear guard had "to stay with those old wagons until they were out of danger." [61]

While Lieutenant Colonel Sutton and his five companies "went at a gallop" toward the battlefield, Colonel Canby moved in the same direction. All morning long, the Union commander had remained at Fort Craig. With receipt of information that the Rebels' had only about 500 men still south of the mesa, Canby decided that his own place was now at the ford. Leaving a few regulars and a mixed command of militia and volunteers to garrison the fort, he made for the upper crossing. [62]

On the battlefield, things had settled into a temporary lull. After hard fighting all morning, both armies were worn out. Stubborn Texan resistance had thwarted Colonel Roberts attempt to roll up the Texas line. With the Confederates positioned behind the strong defensive barrier of sand hills, Roberts consolidated his own position and waited for Canby's arrival. As 5th Sergeant Alfred B. Peticolas described it; "Both parties ceased their firing for a while and paid exclusive attention to maneuvering." [63] Both armies also took the opportunity to care for their dead and wounded, removing them from the field and tending to them as best they could. With the fighting abated, the men of both sides used the lull to eat a little and refill empty cartridge boxes and ammunition chests. Because of their failure to gain a foothold at the river, the Texans suffered for want of water. One group of Texan artillery men went so far as to dig a makeshift well with their spades. The water table in the old river bottom was very near the surface and with only a little digging they were able to expose the water below. Off and on during the lull, it continued to snow lightly. The soldiers wrapped blankets around themselves and worried lest their firing caps should become wet. [64]

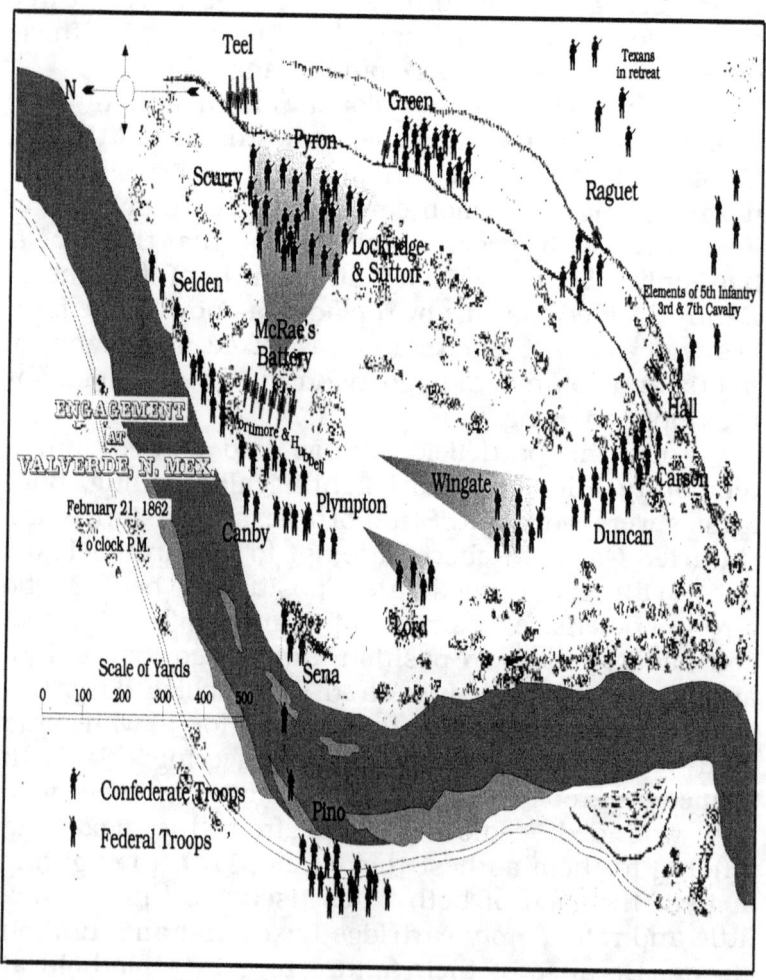

Around 2:45 P.M. Colonel Canby arrived from Fort Craig, accompanied by the Federal ammunition

train and McRae's two six-pounders. Close behind followed Colonel Miguel Pino's 590 men of the 2nd Regiment of New Mexico Volunteers. Met by thunderous cheers from his men, Canby quickly forded the two howitzers. Pino's regiment, "then just coming up, was ordered to cross the river as the reserve for [the Union] left and an additional support for the battery." Satisfied that he understood the tactical situation, Canby immediately redeployed his command. McRae's six cannon were run out to within point-blank range of the Texans. Heavily supported by a mix of regulars and volunteers, the battery was to anchor Canby's line. Formed to the left of the guns were Selden's regular infantry. Canby intended Carson's volunteers to hold the center and Hall's twenty-four-pounder howitzer battery, supported by Duncan's dismounted cavalry, his right. Canby felt that he was securely in control of the field and he was confident that the Texan line could be forced. He planned to push forward his right and center, pivoting on McRae's battery and then advance his right until it could enfilade the Texan position. [65]

As soon as McRae's guns were in position, he began to play canister and shell upon the Rebels. As the "leaden shower" pinned their men, Major Lockridge and Colonel Scurry walked coolly through the ranks telling the Texans to keep their heads down and not to expose themselves. [66] Now, the battle grew very hot indeed. Canby ordered Carson's 1st New Mexico Volunteers and Graydon's spy company to move up and reinforce Duncan. Braced by Hall's twenty-four pounder this force of nearly 1,200 men began the Union pivot. "Slowly but surely, the heavy columns of infantry and artillery on the [right began] driving back [the Texan] lines." [67] The Confederates could not hold against the close heavy cannonading and galling fire of the Federals longer range small arms. The "Crockett Boys" watched nervously as dismounted Union cavalry began flanking their position. Close behind, Hall's battery inched forward, pouring a deadly fire amongst the Texans. Canby's plan was working. Captain Nunn wrote, "Our left was so weakened, that the enemy was marching with confidence of flanking and routing us." [68] In minutes Federal fire would rake the Texan lines from the side. Suddenly, above the din of battle, "came the stentorian voice of old Captain 'Red Bridgeon' (sic), 'Capt. Nunn, Tell Gen. Green the enemy are enfilading us on the left." [69]

With shells and canister flying everywhere and few options left, the Confederate field commander made a fateful decision. One of his soldiers later wrote, "Col. Green knows nothing about military science, but he knows how to fight and win battles." [70] Looking across the field at McRae's cannons, Colonel Green said; "We must charge that battery, boys." [71] Instinctively, he knew that if his men did not seize the initiative the day was lost. Accordingly, he ordered Major Henry Raguet and his men to prepare for a charge as cavalry. He then sent them back to menace the Union troops who were now flanking the left of the Texas line in force. Gathering Lieutenant Thomas P. Ochiltree and the other staff officers, Colonel Green ordered them to move through the brigade, telling the men to prepare for a second charge on the Texan right. Green was running out of options and his only hope was to carry the fight to the Federals. He intended to have Raguet's cavalry charge on the left. He would wait just long enough for the Federals to react, then he would attack at the opposite end of the field with the balance of his force. A charge against a well supported battery of cannons was a desperate proposition but remaining in position was equally risky. If the charge succeeded Green believed he might desynchronize the Union advance, split Canby's forces and achieve a local numerical advantage. [72]

Colonel (General) Thomas Green, 5th Regiment, Texas Mounted Volunteers, Courtesy Library of Congress, LC-B8184-5304

When all was in readiness, Major Raguet aligned his men into a single rank and hurled them at Hall's battery. Although he held a clear numerical advantage over the charging Texans, Duncan stopped his advance and immediately sent "urgent and repeated messages" for help to his commander. [73] Reacting instantly, Canby detached first Ingraham's company of the 7th Infantry and then Wingate's battalion of the 5th to aid in repelling the attack. Carson's regiment, that had just crossed the river, also heard the firing and rushed to Duncan's defense.

Raguet's command thundered into a maelstrom of Union artillery and small arms fire. Charging across the field at an angle, his men were exposed to a deadly discharge of rifles and musketry from both the side and the front. At a distance of about 100 yards, Hall's howitzer dropped a shell into the Texans' midst. Major Raguet looked back and saw a great confusion of wounded and fallen horses. With Duncan's and Carson's men pouring volley after volley into his command, the major knew the Union line would hold. Reluctantly, Raguet ordered his men to fall back. Disorganized and panicked, the Rebels wheeled their mounts and retreated. [74] Rafael Chacón, who was stationed with Carson's volunteers during the assault, remembered; "We received the order to advance and attack their flank, sabers in hand. We made the attack. full of courage and almost in a frenzy. First checking and then driving the enemy back through blood and fire." [75] Raguet's cavalry fell back precipitously and although he tried to rally them, it was to no avail. Watching the Rebels flee, and sensing victory, the Federals set out in pursuit.

"Daddy" Green was probably unaware of what was unfolding on his left but his timing was good. As the fury of Raguet's charge reached its peak, Green looked to his men and said; "Boys, I want Colonel Canby's guns! When I yell, raise the Rebel yell and follow me!" [76] Then, with the words "Up boys, and at them!," the assault began. [77] The "old Texas war-shout" rang in the air and the first wave of two hundred men jumped over the sandbank. Close behind at intervals of thirty to forty yards came the second and third waves. In all some seven hundred men began a wild dash toward "the belching cannon and the solid lines of infantry supporting them." [78] Twenty-three year old Private Davidson, who had the end of the little finger of his left hand shot off at Valverde, remembered that there was, "One yell as they started and then ominous silence, broken only by our gallant officers as they cheer their men onward." [79]

"Battle of Valverde, Our Men Commanded by Col. Tom Green, 7000 Yankees to 1500 Texans," Feb. 21, 1862, D.F. Brown. Courtesy Archives Division - Texas State Library

The stretch to the Union guns was over 600 yards. According to Captain Teel, whose battery provided covering fire, it took Green's volunteers nearly eight minutes to cover the distance. [80] From the moment they rose the Texans were exposed to a "driving storm of grape, canister and musket balls." [81] Lieutenant Colonel Scurry, Lieutenant Colonel Sutton,

Major Lockridge, and the other field officers advanced with their troops, shouting words of encouragement as they ran. "On, on my gallant 4th, and plant your flag on their battery!" yelled Scurry. "Follow me my noble boys," bellowed Lockridge. Sutton screamed "Forward boys forward, glory lies in front." The voice of Captain James Walker, the forty-eight-year-old commander of Pyron's company D, rang loud and clear over the field. "On boys on! I'm an old man and a little one, but I'm ahead of some of you young fellows!" The clear ringing tones of twenty-three-year-old, George Little, the flag bearer for Company A of the 4th Texas, could also be heard urging the men forward. "Follow, and stick by your flag boys!" [82] Captains, Charles M. Lesuer, William P. Hardeman, and James M. Crosson followed close behind, shouting as they waved their swords, "Come on, my boys, don't stop here." [83] As cannister plowed up the dust before them and whistled past as they ran, the charging Texans fixed their eyes on the Union cannon and double-timed it for all they were worth. [84]

The chief defenders of McRae's battery were two companies of inexperienced New Mexico Volunteers, commanded by Captains William Mortimore and James "Santiago" Hubbell. Nearby in reserve on the guns' left, Canby had positioned Captain Peter Plympton of the 7th U.S. Infantry. Plympton's command consisted of four companies of regulars and Dodd's Colorado Volunteers. Captain Benjamin Wingate and a battalion of the 5th U.S. Infantry had been positioned nearby on the right, but when Canby was told of Raguet's charge he had dispatched them to support Major Duncan. Behind the battery and slightly to the rear Captain Richard Lord of the 1st U.S. Cavalry and his company waited as a another reserve. Canby himself was just behind the battery. [85]

From his vantage point astride his horse, "Old Chas," the Union commander was one of the first to see the charging rebels. Scanning the field Canby realized his battery was in danger. The redeployment to repulse Raguet's cavalry had left McRae's right flank "in the air." Green's ploy was working. Even if the right was recalled immediately, the Texans would win the footrace to the guns. Reacting swiftly, Canby wheeled his horse and galloped to Plympton who "was entirely unsuspicious of the danger that threatened the battery." [86] As quickly as possible, arrangements were made to close and defend the cannons.

Meanwhile the Confederates covered two-thirds of the distance to the battery. McRae's gunners fired steadily, but with little effect. It took the artillerymen time to find the Texan's range and initially much of their shot passed over the heads of the running Rebels. The fire from Mortimore's and Hubbell's New Mexicans was also ineffective. Like the Texans, the native troops were armed with older weapons whose accurate range was 200 yards or less. Despite the fact that Green's men were relatively unscathed, many of the Federals thought they were wrecking havoc on the attackers. This was largely because Colonel Green "instructed the men to fall at the flash of the enemy's cannons and after the shot passed over to rise and go on." [87] Each time McRae's gunners fired, the Union soldiers saw large numbers of their enemy fall to the ground apparently slaughtered by the cannon.

As the Texans neared their goal their path grew bloody. McRae's men depressed their guns and fired canister and shot as quickly as they could load and ram. On the left, Union small arms fire started to find its marks. Among the charging Confederates men began to fall. "A Minie ball shot through [16 year old] Abe Hanna's hat, grazed his head, and knocked him flat." [88] Only dazed, the young soldier was soon back on his feet. Dr. A.J. Dawson, serving as a private in David Nunn's company, "was knocked down by a ball that grazed his neck," but he also rallied and

Captain James "Santiago" Hubbell, 5th Regiment, New Mexico Volunteers. Courtesy New Mexico State Records Center and Archives, Neg. 12306

continued the charge. [89] Others were less fortunate. With men dropping all around, the Texans continued to close. Lieutenant Colonel "Sutton was thrown to the ground, his leg shattered by a grape shot. Nevertheless, he raised himself up on his elbow, pointed toward the battery, and urged his men on as they passed." [90] "On they came," remembered one of McRae's gunners, "without order, each man for himself and the 'devil for the vanquished,' in true ranger style, down almost to the muzzles of our guns." [91]

About forty yards from the Union line, the Texans opened with their shotguns. The shock proved overwhelming to some inexperienced New Mexico Volunteers. Faced with a seemingly unstoppable onrushing wave to their front and a hail of canister and shell which Teel was dropping over their heads, the volunteers broke. When struck by the shower of lead from Texan shotguns, the Union "lines seemed to melt away." [92] McRae, his right arm shattered, ran a few yards back and implored the infantrymen to "for God's sake assist him in maintaining his position and save the guns." [93] It was too late. Mortimore's panicked volunteers fled into Plympton's advancing battalion. In passing through, they "communicated their panic, and carried with them part of his men." [94] Private Davidson of the 5th Texas afterwards remembered, the "regiment of infantry while compelled to retreat with the crowd do so sullenly, and wheel and fire back at us, but they kill more of their own men than they do ours." [95] Colonel Canby, "ordered-nay, implored" the Union troops to charge the enemy, but to no avail. Governor Connelly who was on the field wrote painfully, "Of the forces in position for protection of the battery not one company advanced to its relief or even fired upon the enemy as he approached." [96]

On the Union right, a group of Confederate sharpshooters gained the cover of a grove of cottonwoods. Moving cautiously from tree to tree, they began to pick off the cannoneers. As their comrades fell and much of their support deserted, McRae's gunners stuck gamely to their posts. At point-blank range they continued to operate their pieces until the Texans, "desperate enough to bathe their bayonets in the flame of guns," surged among them. [97] The main Confederate storming party, not bothering to reload their shotguns, "drew their pistols and pressed on over the cannon." [98] In the act of ramming a final charge, Lieutenant Lyman Mishler, McRae's subaltern, was shot through the chest.

Captain Alexander McRae, 3rd Regiment U.S. Cavalry. Courtesy McRae descendants and Mrs. Marion C. Grinstead, Alamogordo, NM

Major Lockridge was among the first Confederates to reach the Union guns. "With his left hand on one of their cannon and with his right waving his sword above his head" [99] he yelled, "This is mine"! [100] Captain McRae was reported to have yelled back,

"Shoot the son-of-a-bitch!" [101] At McRae's words, "a sergeant of artillery seized a musket from a wounded infantryman and shot [Lockridge] dead." [102] The Major's dying words were "Go on my boys, don't stop here." [103] The Rebels surged among the now silent cannon, but still McRae and his men refused to yield. The cannoneers pulled their pistols and short swords and began a furious hand-to-hand defense of their overrun position. Many of the battery's supporting troops fled, but those that remained fought with courage and abandon. In the midst of the melee a Texan leapt atop a caisson and shot one of McRae's gunners. He was in the act of leveling his pistol at another when in an instant the brave artilleryman "thrust his fuse into the caisson box, which blew up with a dreadful explosion." [104] "The smoke was so thick that you could scarcely tell one man from another," remembered one Confederate, "our faces so black with powder and dirt that we looked more like negroes than white men." [105]

Desperate resolve alone could not prevail and as more and more Texans reached the guns the defenders were overwhelmed. Captain McRae, a southerner whom Colonel Canby described as "deaf to the seductions of family and friends," fell among his guns shot through the head. [106] According to Confederate Sergeant Peticolas, "The artillerymen brave to the last were shot down at their posts" and "two other companies were entirely cut to pieces." [107]

Just to the rear, Colonel Canby tried to avert disaster. Lord's cavalry squadron, was coming up from the right and Canby ordered them to charge. With a shout the Captain wheeled his men to the left and started for the battery. [108] Advancing they were exposed to fire from their own troops as well as that of the Texans. For reasons that Canby never found entirely satisfactory, Lord dismounted his command and told them to fight on foot. [109]

On the far left, Captain Selden was alerted to the emergency. At once, he recalled Captain Benjamin Wingate from the right, with four companies of infantry, to recapture the guns. By this time, the Union soldiers around McRae's guns had lost nearly one-half of their effective force. Wingate's battalion ran across the field and "coming up at the double-quick, poured upon the Confederates a rapid and destructive fire, under which they recoiled in disorder." 110 So great was the Texans' confusion at this sudden and unexpected counterattack that for some moments Canby "entertained the confident hope that the battery, and with it the fortunes of the day would yet be saved." 111 The Union Commander's optimism was short-lived. Even as the Rebel lines shuddered under Wingate's assault, more men from the second and third waves of the storming party joined the conflict. "Here the firing was so rapid that it sounded like one solid crash of musketry."112

With his position becoming more precarious by the moment, Colonel Canby held his ground. When "Old Chas" was shot from under him he picked up a musket and continued to urge his men on. His bravery was not lost on his enemies. Twenty-five years later William Davidson wrote; "We have no mean and cowardly foe to fight. The grand and noble Canby stands amid his men and cheers them by words and deeds, and he stands there until his men all flee." 113 As the Colonel looked around he realized that Wingate and Lord were not stemming the tide and that the battle for the battery was lost. Union reserves across the river were not crossing in force, and Duncan was too far away to reinforce in time. Convinced "that to prolong the contest would only add to the number of casualties...without changing the result," Canby reluctantly ordered his bugler to sound "retreat." 114

McRae's men continued firing their cannons until overrun so two of the pieces were still loaded when the Texan's took them. Captains Hardeman and Walker ordered the guns turned by hand and promptly began using them against their previous owners. Lieutenant Colonel Scurry saw that Charles Raguet from Reily's battery was present and placed him in charge of another piece. Manning the gun with such men as were nearest, Raguet also opened on the retreating Federals. "The rammer being gone, a flag-staff was used in its stead." [115] Within minutes they were joined in the cannonade by Captain Teel who had limbered his guns and charged across the casualty strewn battlefield.

Colonel Canby's after-action report describes an ordered withdrawal across the river. While it is certain that some of Canby's command retired in a careful steady manner, it is equally certain that other portions simply fled. Confederate accounts describe a rout. Colonel Green stated, that his victory was "complete" and that both the Federal cavalry and infantry fled "in the utmost disorder, many of them dropping their guns to lighten their heels." [116] Another Texan wrote that as they chased the flying Union force "all go into the river together, their cavalry actually riding over their infantry." [117] As the Federals struggled through the icy armpit-deep water of the Rio Grande, the Texans crowded the bank and shot at them as they fled. Alfred Peticolas wrote, "The mortality amongst them in the river was terrible. The shot guns then came into play and did great execution." [118] Private Daniel Robinson of the 7th U.S. Infantry remembered, "I struck across the river and when about halfway over the Texans opened up on us and made the water rattle like a shower of hail." [119] Alonzo Ickis from Dodd's Company echoed Robinson, writing in his diary; "We crossed the Rio Grande under a perfect shower of shot from the enemies double barreled shot guns and navies." [120] In later years some

Confederates reminiscenced that the river ran red with Yankee blood.

On the Union right, far from the overrun battery, orders to retreat were met with consternation and disbelief. Duncan's and Carson's men had repulsed Raguet's cavalry charge so violently that they had pushed deep into Texan territory. Major Raguet's men eventually rallied behind a set of sand hills, but they were on the defensive and in danger of being flanked. Union Captain Rafael Chacón wrote, we "did not understand the order at first for we considered that our charge upon the enemy's main cavalry had won the battle." [121] The Federals were reluctant to abandon their gains, but Duncan and Carson followed orders. Leaving the field to the Texans, they moved their men to the lower ford and recrossed the river in good order. With the pressure off his front and word of Green's success ringing in his ears, Major Raguet abandoned his defensive position and galloped down to support Scurry. Moments later, he arrived at the river with two mounted companies that he collected along the way. [122]

When Colonel Canby reached the west bank, the scene was one of chaos and disorder. "The troops that had escaped from the battle were found to be much scattered." [123] Everyone was wet and cold and many of the soldiers who had defended the battery, were wounded. Some of the whipped volunteers and regulars, together with about 100 less-than-motivated men from Miguel Pino's regiment, simply deserted from the field. In other companies the wildest confusion reigned, and no efforts of their officers or Canby's staff could restore any kind of order. According to the Union commander, the pandemonium was greatest among the volunteers, but "the regular troops were easily collected and sent forward in the direction of the fort." [124]

By this time the Confederate wagon train was quite close to the battlefield and, except for the Union recall, would have been in extreme danger. With the battle apparently won and Canby's soldiers in full retreat, it was decided to pull the train's escort. According to Lieutenant J.P. "Phil" Clough, "Some of our best fighting men were detailed to guard our train and bring it into the valley which they did successfully and great praise is due them for performing their duty so well." [125] These fresh troops were "brought forward to pursue and follow the discomfited column of the enemy." [126] Although too late to participate in the brilliant charge that gave the Texans victory, it looked like Isaac Adair and his men would finally get into the fray. Isaac's company, along with Company A of the 7th and Company C of the 5th, left the wagons with the teamsters and headed for the river at "full speed." [127] Arriving on the heels of Major Raguet, the three companies reported themselves to Lieutenant Colonel Scurry. Flush with success and presented with five mounted companies, "Scurry asked permission of Colonel Green to cross and pursue the enemy." [128] Green gave his consent, and with the sun rapidly setting, the horsemen plunged into the water and made for the opposite bank. No sooner did the head of their column reach the far shore however than they were ordered to call off the pursuit. [129]

With his army in full retreat and the safety of his fort still some distance away, Colonel Canby had presented a flag of truce. Colonel Green wrote in his after action report that "the enemy's white flag, asking permission to gather up their dead and wounded, came almost before the sound of the last cannon had ceased to reverberate in the hills." [130] The arrival of the flag was precipitous, but Colonel Green chivalrously agreed to the request. The Battle of Valverde was at an end. As night fell the weary Federals filed into their bastion. A dispirited Colonel Canby believing himself outnumbered, and still fearing imminent pursuit, ordered his beef herds driven in and all public property collected.

While Colonel Green understood the object of the Federal truce, the majority of his troops did not. For the next two hours, most of Sibley's soldiers jubilantly believed that Canby's flag was "a proposition to surrender." [131] When the truth was learned, some of the men felt that Green had allowed himself to be hoodwinked. Private Howell expressed the confusion of many an average soldier when he wrote in his diary, "Our victory would have been complete, as we could easily have followed the enemy into the fort and been in no danger of the guns at the fort. I must leave this subject for older and wiser heads to discuss." [132] More outspoken was Captain William Lee Alexander of Company H of the 4th regiment who wrote; "In my humble opinion, the Battle of Valverde ought to have settled the question of the conquest of N.M. by 7 o'clock of the same night we could have taken Ft. Craig with [out] losing one man more than we lost at Valverde. The enemy was totally routed and scattered and all we had to do was to push on and the fort was ours." [133] Even General Sibley wrote, "This signal victory should have resulted in the capture of the fort, as fresh troops had been brought forward to pursue and follow the discomfited column of the enemy." [134] For the rest of their lives, many of the Texans contended that Canby used the truce to protect his retreat where force of arms would have failed him.

If Isaac Adair and his men were chagrined that their duty with the supply train kept them out of the fighting, they should have been grateful. Between the wounded and the dead, the Confederate victory cost the Texans 229 casualties. This 10 percent casualty rate on the field was one of the highest in North America at that time. Among the twenty-five companies of the 4th, 5th, and 7th Regiments, only

Captain Adair's Company H and Captain Jordan's Company A escaped unscathed. Although Texan's losses were severe, Union losses were even worse. Colonel Canby initially estimated his casualties at 284, but as more and more men turned up wounded, dead, or missing, the number grew to a mind numbing 475. Of the approximately 2,800 troops he took onto the battlefield, fully seventeen percent were eventually listed as casualties. The companies supporting McRae's battery were decimated. Company F of the 7th U.S. Infantry suffered a staggering seventy-one percent loss. Dodd's Coloradans, who were one of the first companies in action and one of the last to leave the field, suffered fifty-six percent casualties. Santiago Hubbell's New Mexico Volunteers also took a beating, sustaining losses of fifty-one percent. [135] After the retreat, Union Private, Alonzo Ickis confided to his diary; "The wounded were in every room in the Ft. and scenes as I there beheld I hope are seldom seen. Men mutilated in every conceivable manner." [136] While the engagement at Valverde is but a footnote compared to the Promethean struggles that were fought in the East; on a wintry February 21, 1862 in New Mexico it was unprecedented.

Chapter 6

MASTERLY INACTIVITY

"The truth is the marches show as much or more heroism than the battles."
- Private William Lott Davidson

After the battle, the victorious Texans "shook hands with acquaintances and congratulated each other on being alive. They laughed and danced and shook hands with more real joy than friends must after years of absence in ordinary circumstances." [1] Masters of the field, the Sibley Brigade "camped on the river in strange confusion at night, wagons and men all together and regiments mixed." [2] The nine hours of fighting left both men and horses completely worn out. The exhausted soldiers, "thankful to the great King of Kings, who is the God of Battles" for their victory, simply made camp wherever they found themselves. [3]

That night, most of the Confederates took supper "on provisions abandoned by the Abs in their flight. Every Yank had one or more canteens and a haversack (bread basket), and everyone disrobed himself on leaving the field." [4] Each of the haversacks was stuffed with a three-day supply of rations including light bread, coffee, sugar and bacon. To the poorly supplied Texans, the scattered provisions were a bonanza. As Private Theophilus Noel put it, "Our half-starved boys 'gormandised sumptuously' on Yankee light bread and other most delicious eatables."[5]

While part of the men ate and rested, others wandered the darkened field looking for missing friends or relations. Some searchers held lanterns; others simply followed the moans of the stricken. As the night progressed, fires were built in various parts of the battleground, and under the flag of truce, soldiers both North and South began the arduous task of collecting and caring for their wounded. The night was cold, and there was little the Confederates could do for their injured. Those lucky enough to be found by their comrades were laid around the fires "with blankets over them, as comfortable as circumstances would permit." To Sergeant Peticolas, "It was a sad sight to see these young men, so lately in the strength and vigor of manhood, now lying pale and weak around these fires suffering." [6] The Texans did their best for the injured, but they were hampered by a severe shortage of supplies. During one of the many Indian raids, which occurred while the brigade passed through Horn Valley, "Apache Injuns burnt nearly all their medicine and destroyed surgical instruments." [7]

By daybreak most of the wounded were located, and both sides started the gloomy duty of collecting their dead. As the morning light illuminated the field, for the first time the men could truly see the results of the previous days work. With the flame of battle no longer hot upon them, the men were shocked by the picture that greeted them. The area where McRae's battery was taken "was covered with blood, horses, torn and dismembered limbs, and heads separated from their bodies - a spectacle that was horrible." [8] Gazing upon this and other scenes of devastation, Private William Howell wrote to his father, "The battlefield was a sad sight after the fighting had ceased - to see so many poor fellows lieing [sic] cold in death and others biting the earth, horses dead and wounded and the whole seemed to be the abode of death itself..." [9] In the face of such destruction, many of the Confederates found themselves subdued and despondent. Alfred Peticolas confided to his diary, "I feel extremely sad today." [10] Abe Hanna wrote; "I think the most melancholy scene I ever witnessed was on the valley of the Rio Grande where the Texas Boys thrashed out the Yankees." [11]

Captain Rafael Chacon, 1st Regiment, New Mexico Volunteers.
Courtesy Museum of New Mexico, Neg. 148455

The task of collecting the Union dead and wounded fell to captains Chacón and Graydon, and their respective companies. Colonel Canby sent out carts to bring in those left on the field, and he assigned the volunteers as escorts. Like their Confederate counterparts the Federal mortuary detail was affected by the chaos that lay before them. Nevertheless, amid the death and suffering, Captain Chacón found something that raised his spirits and gave him satisfaction. "When we arrived at the battlefield," he wrote, "the Texans were already gathering their own men, and it was a great pleasure for us to see the chivalry and courtesy with which we treated each other, forgetting the anger and the antagonisms in the solemn presence of the dead." [12]

Once the carts were loaded with their sad cargo, the Northerners returned to Fort Craig. "The dead were collected in a large room at the fort while the coffins were prepared, and each one was identified before being buried." [13] Each Union soldier was interred in his own coffin and was accorded military honors. More than one Federal later commented with pride about the care given those who died. All day long the Confederates could hear volleys from the fort, telling them that another of the enemy was laid to rest. [14] For their part, the Texans afforded their fallen what honor they could. In the words of one aging veteran, "We dug a ditch four feet deep, and wrapped forty of our boys in their blankets and laid them in the ditch as their last resting place." [15] Despite the spartan conditions, the Southern dead were buried with all the pomp and ceremony their comrades could muster.

Sometime during the day, Lieutenant Colonel Sutton of the 7th Texas died. Isaac Adair's friend and regimental commander refused to have his leg amputated saying, "he did not intend to hobble round the balance of his days on one leg, and that when his leg went that he would go with it." [16] In a letter home, Assistant Surgeon Jacob "Hal" Hunter described Sutton's internment.

> "It was the most impressive funeral I ever witnessed, A detachment of his command with arms reversed followed his remains in silence to the grave. All was silence profound - not a word was spoken, not a gun fired - no sound was heard but the chilling rattle of the sod as it was thrown on the body of our lost colonel. 'Farewell, Gallant Eagle, thou art buried in light!...Godspeed thee to heaven, lost star of our night'" [17]

Other activities, besides caring for their dead and wounded, also busied the Texans on the 22nd. One of the most important was scavenging the battlefield. In addition to dropping haversacks loaded with food, Canby's fleeing troops discarded all manner of equipment. Regardless of the Union commander's assertion that; "Nothing was abandoned on the field except some tents and fixtures of the field hospital", [18] the Confederates collected "large quantities of provisions, small arms and accoutrements." [19] McRae's six pieces of artillery were the Texans' main prize from the battle, but Sibley's men also picked up nearly 130 stand of small arms, several six-shooters, and a considerable quantity of ammunition. Of particular and immediate importance to the Rebels were the large number of cast-off overcoats and blankets they found. Most of the brigade's tents and extra clothing were abandoned and had been burnt the morning of the battle. Without the captured goods they would have suffered severely from the harsh New Mexico winter. A number of wandering horses were also rounded up and quickly distributed. [20]

The Texans were soon disgusted to learn that they were not the only ones scavenging. In what the Southerners regarded as a clear violation of the truce, Union medical and mortuary details, roaming the battlefield gathered and removed equipment. General Sibley in his report of the battle wrote, "This flag had for its object the burying of the dead and removal of their wounded; and I regret to state here, for the sake of old associations, that, under this flag and another sent the next day, the enemy availed himself of our generosity and confidence in his honor." [21] The Federals not only loaded their dead-wagons with small arms they picked up, they "sent a force up and actually succeeded in recovering from the river one 24-pounder." [22] The heavy cannon was one of Lieutenant Hall's two pieces from the Union right. In the midst of the retreat, it broke an axle recrossing the Rio Grande and was abandoned into Texan hands. Sibley also wrote; "Even a guidon and a flag, taken in the same way, under the cover of night, and a white flag were boastingly pointed to, in an interview between one of my aides and the Federal commander at the fort, as trophies of the fight." [23] These alleged acts were a shock to the Southerners' Victorian sense of chivalry and honor. Colonel Tom Green expressed the feeling saying; "I do not believe that the commanding officer of the enemy is aware of these facts, as he would not have spoken of stolen flags as trophies." [24]

The interview Sibley referred to was between Colonel Canby and Colonel Scurry, and took place on the 22nd. By the morning after the battle, General Sibley recovered his health sufficiently to resume command of the brigade. On the chance that Canby felt himself fully defeated Sibley dispatched Scurry to Fort Craig to discuss terms of surrender. The Colonel, with an escort of ten men, headed to the fort under a flag of truce. The little party rode to within forty or fifty yards of the walls. There, they stopped and asked permission to speak with Colonel Canby. This was granted, and Colonel Scurry and Captain Denman W. Shannon were taken inside. [25] After an initial exchange of pleasantries Colonel Scurry told Canby that, "in the name of the Confederate States, Sibley demanded the surrender of the fort." The Union colonel "turned pale, his beard shook in anger, and he responded, 'You tell Sibley that he can come to take it, that I have a sufficient force to defend it. If this is your only mission you can return because this ends our meeting.'" [26]

Canby's brusque refusal left General Sibley with a substantial dilemma. Although his troops were clearly victorious on the battlefield, the Southern commander had gained no significant advantage over his Union counterpart. Colonel Canby still held Fort Craig, and its thick adobe walls were just as formidable as when the Texans decided to bypass them less than a week before. Even with the addition of McRae's captured battery, Sibley still lacked enough artillery to pound Craig into submission. A siege was out of the question. Day by day the Confederate larder was growing smaller and smaller. With the failure to capture additional supplies in quantity, it had reached a critical level. Unless something was done immediately, the Texans would run out of food in five days! [27]

In a "council of war" Sibley and his officers discussed the only options still open to them. They could move rapidly up the river and hope that "supplies of breadstuffs and meat could be procured" en route or they could pack up and head back to Confederate Arizona. [28] Neither path was very attractive, but the only real choice was to go forward. During its stay in the Mesilla Valley, the brigade stripped the area bare of supplies. A retreat back spelled starvation. On the other hand, the alternative was a desperate gamble. Marching forward meant moving into "the very heart of the enemy's country." [29] Although the remainder of the New Mexico territory was lightly held, Sibley would be placing his army between Canby's force and a garrison of undetermined strength believed to be holding Fort Union to the north. Worst of all, Fort Craig and its garrison still sat squarely across the brigade's only line of resupply or retreat. Even if the move succeeded, the territory the Rebels were about to occupy "was no storehouse." [30] There was no guarantee adequate provisions could be collected. After careful deliberation, the council of war resolved to advance.

During the twilight and evening hours of the 22nd and the morning hours of the 23rd, the burying of the dead and the caring for the wounded continued. Despite the decision to move, the brigade remained on the battlefield. "The whole talk in camp ... was about the fight, of course, and every man was recounting his individual exploits with great zest." [31] Counted among the few Confederate non-combatants, Isaac Adair's men must surely have felt left out. Listening to the banter of their fellows, the men of Company H probably consoled themselves with the knowledge that the campaign was far from over and other chances for glory still lay ahead. With each retelling, accounts of individual exploits were embellished and the number of Yankees killed became more astonishing. The exaggeration got so outrageous, that it prompted Alfred Peticolas to write in his diary, "a fool blows his own horn, a smart man get his blown for him, and a man of genius would rather die than blow his own horn or get any other man to do it for him." [32]

The business of exchanging prisoners and attending to fallen comrades notwithstanding, the Texans were slow to get moving. Among other things, the loss and injury of key officers hampered their advance. Lieutenant Colonel John Sutton, Major Samuel Lockridge, and Captain Marinus Van Der Heuvel were all dead. Colonel Tom Green, Major Henry Raguet, and Captain Trevanion Teel were slightly wounded. Captain Willis Lang, Lieutenant Demetrius

Bass, Lieutenant David R. McCormick, and 2nd Lieutenant David Hubbard were grievously wounded and would succumb. [33] The casualties among the Rebel leaders prompted Private Davidson of the 5th Texas to write, "Our loss in officers has been particularly heavy because they have exposed themselves the entire day, while they have tried in every way to shield the men. The boys all say now that they have no desire to become officers." [34] The battle left the brigade disorganized. As Lieutenant Phil Fulcrod put it, "The command was badly torn up, the batteries shot to pieces and things in general in a dilapidated condition." [35]

Transport was also a shambles. In addition to the 150 mules lost on the night of the 20th, hundreds of horses and mules were killed during the fight. Tied some distance behind the Rebel lines these animals were frequently the only opportune targets for Federal gunners and sharpshooters. As a result, large numbers of soldiers from each regiment were now without mounts. Because of those abandoned south of the mesa, wagons were also a problem. With nearly twenty percent of their train destroyed and insufficient draft animals for what was left, the Texans were again forced to discard equipment. Ultimately, the Confederates "burnt a number of saddles and old clothes" and abandoned still more wagons. [36] Around noon on the 23rd, the Army of New Mexico turned its back on communication with Texas and Confederate Arizona and resumed its march north.

Shaken by the events of the past few days, Canby recovered his equilibrium more quickly than did Sibley and his officers. The Union commander was defeated on the battlefield, but he was still an efficient officer and a consummate organizer. On the night of the clash, while the Southerners milled around on the battlefield complimenting each other on their victory, Canby plotted his next move. He believed Sibley's reliable force much larger than his own. Rather than "bring on a second battle with the Confederate Army," or endeavor to throw his troops above the enemy and try to impede their progress, Canby decided his best plan of action was to stay put. He had previously requested reinforcements and while he awaited their arrival he planned to strengthen Fort Craig and defend it "to the last extremity." [37]

His first act was to "disembarrass" himself of a portion of the militia by simply allowing the men to go home. Fort Craig was not designed to sustain the number of soldiers crowded within its walls and the Union commander deemed the New Mexicans troops near worthless. Just the same, he "arranged with the officers of that force to impede the operations of the enemy" by "removing from his route the cattle, grain, and other supplies [...] that would aid him in sustaining his force." [38] Canby knew well the barren nature of the Territory, and understood that starvation was a weapon that could be used just as effectively as cannons and muskets.

On the night of the 21st instructions were sent to the commander north of Fort Craig to remove or destroy any public property that might fall into the hands of the enemy." [39] The next night Colonel Nicholás Pino, Major Charles Wesche, and a 280-man detachment of the 2nd Regiment New Mexico Militia slipped north with resolve. Riding with the militia was Major James Donaldson, Canby's quartermaster. Donaldson had volunteered for the purpose and was "charged with the duty of superintending the removal of the public property, procuring supplies, and collecting troops for future operations." [40] Canby was optimistic as he watched them depart. If he could deny the Texans provisions, he was sure their invasion would fail.

With their late start on the 23rd, the Texans only managed to travel about six miles and cross the river. Near the village of Valverde, they stopped to ransack a store, where they discovered: bales of Federal uniforms, hundreds of pounds of wheat, salt, and sugar, some oxen and a flock of sheep. The building was part of a ranch belonging to militia Colonel Robert H. Stapleton, and the Confederates were able to confiscate some $3,000 worth of badly needed supplies.

After the short move, the Texan camp was still so near the battlefield that Colonel Canby was unsure of their objective. Having refused the Texan demand to surrender, he fully expected Sibley to attack in an attempt to enforce it. The Confederates' slow progress made their intentions unclear and for a couple of days Canby remained in the dark as to their purpose. The Texans on the other hand, saw the militia go up from Craig during the night. To counter this move, Sibley dispatched five mounted companies of the 5th Texas and two pieces of artillery under the command of Lieutenant Colonel Henry C. McNeill. This battalion was to act as a fast-moving advance and secure whatever supplies could be found at the town of Socorro. [41]

The 24th dawned warm with a feel of spring. Isaac Adair's company and most of the Rebel army remained in the same camp. During the day, Sibley's quartermasters busied themselves, dividing and distributing the goods confiscated from Stapleton's store. "The wearing apparel was divided out to the different regiments and companies" and the sheep became mutton for breakfast and dinner. [42] Other soldiers attended to men who had recently died from their wounds. Another burial was held and the Texans saluted their fallen comrades by firing over the bodies. While waiting in camp the Confederates also took the opportunity to release their prisoners on parole. Throughout the Civil War, both sides used parole as a way to avoid the responsibility and burden of guarding, feeding, clothing, and providing medical care for captured enemy soldiers. Basically, prisoners were sternly lectured and then required to give their oath of honor that they would no longer take up arms or perform duty that soldiers normally perform. Once their oath was given, the prisoners were reminded of the dire consequences of breaking it and were released. Surprisingly, most soldiers' Victorian sense of honor was so strong that the system worked. [43]

As the day wound to a close most of the Army of New Mexico lit cook fires and readied their beds. At the same time, twenty-five miles to the north, its vanguard under Lieutenant Colonel McNeill reached Socorro. Only hours before the town was reported unguarded, but now it was swarming with New Mexico Militia. Shortly after passing through Socorro Colonel Nicholás Pino's 280-man contingent from Fort Craig had received a dispatch telling them to drop back and defend the town. Faced with unexpected opposition McNeill deployed his force on a commanding elevation southwest of Socorro. At about 8 p.m., when all was in readiness, he ordered one of his howitzers to fire a warning shot over the town. [44]

Colonel Canby considered his native militia unreliable and as a consequence had sent them away from Fort Craig. At Socorro they demonstrated the exact lack of resolve that had fueled his fears. Many of the New Mexican soldiers did not wanted to be there in the first place and from the moment McNeill's one cannon ball flew overhead Pino's "men began to desert and hide themselves away." [45] Only days before the demoralized citizen soldiers witnessed the rout of Canby's army. Now, they were facing the same unstoppable force of Texans. Texans who clearly had artillery while they had none.

Believing that volunteers stationed at Camp Connelly near Polvadera might ride to their assistance, Colonel Pino and Major Charles Wesche tried to hold the Texans in position and stall for time. Over the next couple of hours they negotiated with McNeill and pretended that they still commanded a significant force. In truth, only thirty-seven men remained at their posts. Wesche visited the houses of some influential Mexicans and tried his best "to make them take up arms in defense of their Government, their homes and firesides. Vain endeavor!" If anything, the people of Socorro were less motivated than the troops who deserted. One prominent citizen, Don Pedro Baca "went even so far as to say that the United States Government was a curse to this Territory, and if the Texans would take and keep possession of New Mexico the change could only be for the better." [46]

Near 2 A.M. at McNeill's repeated request Pino and Wesche rode over to the Confederate camp to see the force arrayed against them. Pino took one look at the long line of rebels and quickly surrendered. For the rest of the morning the New Mexican officers suffered the indignity of watching their troops reappear. At about 10 A.M. at least 150 of the militiamen took the oath of neutrality, promising to lay down their arms and return to their homes. Major Wesche wrote; "If it had been disgusting to us to see our militiamen abscond in the hours of trial, it was provoking to see them come out of their hiding places when the danger was over." [47]

After their bloodless victory McNeill's troops secured Socorro and fitted up a hospital for the arrival of the brigade's sick and wounded. "A few supplies were found where the Yankees had hidden them, together with a considerable quantity of medicines and hospital necessaries, all of which came in good time." [48] In addition to badly needed medicine the Texans seized 300 stand of arms, some 150 mules, nearly the same number of horses, 8,000 barrels of flour, and a number of Government wagons. [49] The capture of the flour was particularly fortuitous as Sibley's army was again going hungry.

Throughout the remainder of the 25th and most of the 26th, the main body of the brigade slowly made its way to Socorro. The condition of the wounded hindered the army's progress and made the twenty-four miles extremely difficult. The brigade's surgeons believed that bumping and jolting along in the wagons would kill many of the sick and injured. As a result, crude litters were constructed, and their friends tediously carried the more severely incapacitated. Despite the care, some of the wounded never completed the trek. Lieutenant David McCormick of Company F and several others died during the night of the 25th, and were buried the next morning. Other men who managed to walk the first day found they could no longer continue. On the 26th many more were packed in litters than on the day before. [50]

For Isaac Adair and the other uninjured, the worn out condition of the army made the marches weary affairs. The men were on half rations of flour, coffee, and beef; and nothing else was available. The Texans' beeves and the mules meanwhile were so starved and exhausted they could barely walk. According to William Davidson, "Our mules are about worked down and can hardly pull the empty wagons, the consequence is the boys have to put their shoulders to the wheels and roll the wagons along." [51] Isaac and his men were fortunate that they still had their horses. Many of their comrades did not. Because of the number of animals killed in the battle, a large portion of the brigade was now dismounted. As they plodded along Ebeneezer Hanna sarcastically scribbled in his diary; "I am now afoot and I now feel the pleasure of soldiering in New Mexico more plainly than I have ever done before." [52]

The weather was harsh, and wood for fires extremely scarce. Grass along the trail proved worse than straw for the horses and more of the animals gave out each day. On the 26th, the journal of Private Howell of the 5th Regiment records succinctly, "Have no bread tonight." [53] Despite the hardship, many of the Rebels were still sanguine about their prospects. William Davidson wrote, the "men are in good spirits and around the fire crack their jokes and sing as merrily as we did when in Texas." [54] Other soldiers found their situation more distressing. Private Hanna described his lot as "being now a thousand miles from home afoot & without a dog. Surrounded on all sides by enemy and no prospect before us only to fight our way through & having no idea where or when our destination should end." [55]

Around three in the afternoon of the 26th the army arrived gratefully at Socorro. A general hospital was established and nearly 150 men were admitted. Besides those wounded in the battle, many were sick with pneumonia. Since leaving Fort Thorn more than a month before the brigade's sick had been without a roof over their heads. Now the unwell were quickly sheltered in the town's adobe houses. The men were cared for by the army's head "Medical Purveyor," Dr. Edward N. Covey, who was chief surgeon. He was "assisted by Dr. Samuel B. Maney, a private in Company A of the [4th] Regiment who, for his ability as a practitioner, his devoted kindness to the sick, wounded and weary, as well as for his unbounded popularity, was shortly afterwards promoted Assistant Surgeon." [56]

On the 27th the army lay in bivouac just north of Socorro. Although there was no marching and nothing was heard of the enemy at Craig, there was still plenty of activity in camp. Four of the brigade's officers who had talked of quitting after Fort Craig was taken, resigned in the morning. Among the four was

David Nunn from Crockett. For some time the ex-mayor and his men had not been getting along. During the battle, Nunn courageously led the "Crockett Boys" "in the last brilliant and successful charge, which decided the fortunes of the day." 57 Nonetheless, shortly afterwards the Company petitioned him to step down. While Nunn saddled up and headed for home, his men elected Lieutenant James Mitchell Odell to replace him. Most of the men were happy to see David Nunn go, but not everyone was comfortable with the changes in their company. Private B.G. Hartgraves and his brother John D. Hartgraves decided that they would be happier with Isaac Adair and transferred accordingly. The Hartgraves were prominent farmers of South Houston County, whose homes were in Gayle Creek bottom about seven or eight miles southeast of Crockett. 58

The resignation of Captain Nunn and the other three officers was important to the companies they left, but the big news of the day was that the 4th Regiment was to be permanently dismounted. Between the horses lost in battle, those that were stampeded on the night of the 20th, and those that died for want of forage, half of each of the brigade's regiments were now afoot. General Sibley and his officers knew that for the army to continue to function efficiently the remaining cavalry needed to be concentrated. After seriously debating alternatives they decided to ask the men of the 4th to voluntarily turn over their remaining horses. The Quartermaster could then redistribute the 4th's mounts as replacements to the other regiments. Since the horses were the soldiers' private property, each man would be promised reimbursement equal to the appraised value of his horse and equipment. 59

The self-sacrifice asked of the men of the 4th Regiment was enormous. Already, it was winter. The soldiers were subsisting on half rations and they were all at least one thousand miles from home. Now they were being petitioned to deliberately give up their mounts. Faced with the prospect of watching their animals starve, however, the idea of turning over their horses was "not as repugnant to them as one would naturally suppose it would be to the cowboy of Texas." [60] Personal verbal pledges from General Sibley and more importantly Colonel Scurry swung the day. The brigade's quartermaster was nearly broke, but Scurry gave the men his word of honor that they would eventually be paid for their animals and equipment. Each horse and kit was duly appraised and given to the Quartermaster. When the task was complete 5th Sergeant Peticolas jotted in his diary; "Our horses are all turned over, and afoot and without bread, the regiment is more depressed that it has been in months." [61]

The Confederate officers were extremely proud of the Regiment's action. General Sibley wrote that the men were "worthy of high praise, and the more commendable because they are Texans. Without a dissenting voice, a cavalry regiment, which had proudly flaunted its banner before the enemy [...], took the line of march [...] a strong and reliable regiment of infantry." [62] Praise notwithstanding, the men of the 4th never saw a penny of repayment for their sacrifice. Many of the troopers were well mounted and the cost of the horses turned over was no small matter. Alfred Peticolas said his horse and saddle were appraised at $110, but it was not uncommon to see valuations of $175, $180, or more. In an army where a 2nd lieutenant earned only $90 a month, this was real money. [63] For more than two years after the campaign, Colonel Reily, Captain Hardeman, and Captain Alexander made repeated attempts to have their men compensated. Despite assurances that the claims would be honored, the Departmental Headquarters never took any action. Eventually, the Confederacy died owing the debt. Years later, Theophilus Noel wrote in disgust, "This goes too plainly to show the manner in which things are conducted by those whose business it is to look after the comfort, well being and good condition of the army in the field." [64]

The condition of his army in the field was foremost on Sibley's mind on the morning of 28th. His commissary was still dangerously low and only by capturing more Federal rations could his men hope to sustain themselves. With that goal in mind Sibley ordered the brigade to march toward Albuquerque and its stockpile of Union supplies. Knowing that the infantry and wagons would move slowly, the General dispatched Major Charles Pyron and his battalion of the 2nd Texas Mounted Rifles to hurry ahead and secure what provisions they could. "Mid shouts and cheers, the cavalry commands moved off at a brisk pace, followed by the artillery, close behind which came the 'foot pads' [infantry], as they designed to call themselves." [65]

With no bread for breakfast, the entire brigade was soon plodding forward. Since their stomachs were nearly empty and it was the 4th Regiment's first day traveling afoot, "there was considerable growling among the boys." [66] By the time the men covered twelve miles, everyone was tired and hungry and many a foot was blistered. Reaching camp Alfred Peticolas wrote; "I have a blister on my heel about as large as a quarter of a dollar tonight, from which the skin is peeled, but I washed my feet thoroughly in cold water, and they feel tolerably comfortable now." [67] For other men suffering from more serious maladies, the rigors of the day proved too much. Bill Davidson buried four of his friends in camp commenting wryly, "pneumonia, measles, small-pox, itch and body lice are getting their work on us." [68] That night the men ate poor beef and beans with a little bacon. Before retiring, they were issued some corn meal for the next day.

The first day of March blew in cloudy and depressing. The wind was bitingly cold and snow swirled whitely about as the weary soldiers struggled over a sandy monotonous road. Upon the battlefield, faced with the fierce din of conflict and danger, Sibley's men were sustained by the courage of their convictions and the importance of winning the day. Now, as they trudged "along day after day with nothing to eat save beans, with no teams fit to transport [their] baggage, and no forage", spirits plummeted. [69] Abe Hanna's diary reads; "We have eaten our last piece of bread this morning and no more in the Brigade and but few beeves and a little bacon and things in such a state of confusion our prospect is but a gloomy one." [70] In an even darker mood, Bill Davidson wrote; "From this time on [...] our trail is one of gloom and death, for at every camp we bury some of our comrades who have succumbed to this terrible winter campaign and exposure." [71]

Plugging along through the sand, 5th Sergeant Peticolas, grumbled. He felt a gnawing hunger and he was angered to see the brigade's officers, "every one of them with great sacks of flour and sides of bacon, living high while the men are really suffering for something to eat." [72] The "foot pads" of the newly constituted infantry were stuck with their privation, but for enterprising men in the cavalry, it was a different story. When Private William Howell felt the pangs of hunger, he decided to do something about it. Howell, who was still mounted, rode off in the company of his friend John C. Naile of the Grimes County Rangers, to do some personal foraging. The two troopers crossed the Rio Grande and spent the day in the little east bank village of La Joya. Howell wrote in his journal that they were able to get "plenty [of] corn and tops for my horse and two or three 'tortillas' dinners for my self." [73] Later, when the two men returned to camp, they were able to carry back feed corn. As foraging became more and more important to the army's survival the unhorsed men of the 4th Regiment consistently found themselves at a disadvantage. Fully mounted units, like Isaac Adair's Company H, were able to range far and wide in search of provisions. The best the infantry could hope for was that their comrades would leave something behind.

After a long fifteen-mile tramp "through desolate sandy and desert," the soldiers finally "went into camp late in the evening." [74] The brigade's wagons were stalled in the deep sand, and it was after 9 o'clock before the last of the command straggled in. Wood was now more scarce than at anytime before, and the men's "only chance for a fire was to gather old dry cow chips." [75] The camp was in the level valley of the Rio Grande. With nothing to break its force, a bitterly cold wind blew clouds of sand in the men's' faces. Cooking was a "desperate undertaking," and many of the exhausted Texans simply gave up and went to sleep hungry. [76]

The next day was a Sunday and the worn-out troops spent much of it just lying in camp. It was extremely cold, and in the morning the soldiers watched ruefully as large blocks of ice floated by on the river. The country along the Rio Grande was entirely destitute of timber, so around two in the afternoon the Confederates made a five or six mile march to Sabinal, a little Mexican town where they could buy wood for fuel. [77] Despite the harsh weather and the lack of trees, this part of New Mexico was more desirable than any the Texans had yet seen. As the men marched passed irrigated ranches, Sergeant Peticolas noted; "The valley is very wide and fertile and thickly settled. Some of the churches are very neatly built, and the houses, inside, are very well furnished." Wistfully, he also scribbled, "Some of them are papered and some of them neatly whitewashed, and they are perfectly air-tight." [78] Near Sabinal, Judge Spruce M. Baird joined the Texans. Baird, an ardent Southern sympathizer, had ridden hard from his home nearly 40 miles north to bring the Rebels word of their vanguard.

Earlier in the day, Major Pyron and his command had marched into Albuquerque and easily captured the city. Fortunately for the Union, the advance party still failed its principal mission. By the time the Rebels reached the outskirts of the city Albuquerque's Federal supply depot was in flames. From a distance Major Pyron and the others could see "three large columns of smoke ascending, as it were, to the very heavens. This told the tale." [79] The badly needed equipment and provisions were lost. Although not a shot was fired this was one of the most serious defeats handed the Sibley Brigade during its' campaign. The General's plan counted on the capture of Federal rations to sustain his army. Without them the invasion was in serious trouble. The architect of this disaster was Captain Herbert M. Enos, the U.S. Army's Assistant Quartermaster in Albuquerque.

Spreading the alarm from Fort Craig, Major Donaldson passed through the city several days before Pyron's arrival. He informed Captain Enos of the their army's defeat at Valverde and charged him to keep Albuquerque's supply depot out of Confederate hands. His duty fulfilled the Major and his party quickly moved on to Santa Fe. Enos watched them ride out and felt the enormity of his responsibility. After Donaldson's warnings the Captain no longer considered the militia and volunteer companies reliable. Without them, his "only dependence" was a tiny garrison of twelve regular soldiers. [80] Undaunted, the Assistant Quartermaster assumed command of these twelve and set out to do what he could.

On the afternoon of the 1st, Captain Enos received reliable information that Pyron's vanguard had entered the town of Belen only thirty-five miles south. "Upon this intelligence [he] ordered that every preparation be made for destroying the public stores, both quartermaster's and subsistence, which could not be carried off." [81] At about 6 p.m. an express rider came pounding in and reported that fifty of the Texans had reached the town of Los Lunas and captured a citizen train carrying supplies for Fort Craig. Enos had already loaded all the depot's ammunition and ordnance stores into wagons. Now, he started them on the road to Santa Fe. With the ordnance on its way, he ordered his remaining eight or nine teams harnessed so they would be ready to move at a moment's warning.

The rest of the night passed without incident, but the Assistant Quartermaster was running out of time. He heard no word about relief troops from Santa Fe and so correctly assumed that he was on his own. Faced with an enemy force reported to be 400 strong, he knew that his own command was too small for even a delaying action. At 6:30 A.M. on the morning of the 2nd, believing that the Texans would soon be upon him, Captain Enos gave the order to burn all Union property in Albuquerque.

Like the tiny Union garrison, much of the city's native population was up the whole night waiting to see what would happen. Their interest, however, was not the approaching Confederates, but rather the valuable supply depot itself. The people saw an opportunity for plunder and were waiting excitedly to see what they could lay their hands on. With his small force and the short time at his disposal, Enos decided to burn the provisions buildings and all. Watching the waiting New Mexicans, he was convinced that if he tried to remove any property before burning it, the natives would overpower his troops and save the stores for the enemy. Flames had barely begun to lick the depot's twelve buildings when "a great rush of Mexican men, women and children" ran inside to carry off what they could. [82] From the subsistence department they grabbed candles, molasses, vinegar, and soap. From among the quartermaster's stores, they saved some office furniture, carpenter's tools, and a few saddles. The crowd was so large that Enos and his small band were powerless to stop the thievery. In the end, the flames were quicker than the looters and a good portion of the supplies went up in smoke. When the destruction was nearly complete the steadfast Captain took his remaining wagons and departed for Santa Fe.

Many of Sibley's soldiers later felt that if they could have captured the supplies that Enos burned, "the Army of New Mexico would never have experienced any inconvenience for want of either clothing or commissaries." Had the property fallen into Southern hands, it is quite possible that "Fort Craig with its entire garrison would have been compelled to surrender." [83] As it was, when Pyron's men reached the site, all that was left of the Union depot was "a pool of grease three or four feet deep just in front of their commissary building." [84] The grease was the runoff from hundreds of pounds of Federal bacon that disappeared in the flames. As the hungry Texans milled about gazing on the destruction, 2nd Lieutenant Phil Fulcrod reflected, "it looked like a sin to destroy the necessities of life in such a manner." [85] Colonel Canby's astute evaluation and quick action after his defeat at Valverde were paying off.

Denied the Union supplies depot the Confederate vanguard nevertheless took formal possession of Albuquerque. Major Pyron gathered his men in the main plaza and after a few words, "The Stars and Bars was raised on the flag staff." The regimental "band played 'Dixie' and 'The Girl I Left

Behind Me' and the men raised three cheers for the Confederacy." [86] The formalities were soon dispensed, and the Texans moved on to the work of securing quarters and salvaging what they could.

Farther north in Santa Fe Major Donaldson "deemed it necessary to pursue the same course" as Captain Enos. [87] The city was commanded on all sides by hills and the Major did not believe it could be defended. On Donaldson's orders, 120 wagons were loaded with the most valuable stores remaining in the department. When the train was ready the U.S. Army evacuated Santa Fe. With an escort consisting of two companies of infantry, one of cavalry, two howitzers and an assortment of volunteers the precious supplies moved slowly but surely northward. Within a matter of days a quarter of a million dollars worth of food and equipment was "under the guns of Fort Union" and forever beyond Confederate grasp. [88] The Texans knew that Canby's men had out maneuvered them. Twenty years later Phil Fulcrod wrote, "The greatest mistake that was made was in not sending a force on to Albuquerque as soon as Valverde was won, and not have delayed a day. If a force had been dispatched on that night, the result might have been different." [89]

The invasion would now have ground to a halt except for an unlikely stroke of luck. Major Pyron and his men were in Albuquerque less than an hour when a man, by the name of Richmond Gillespie, came riding up. Gillespie was a Southern sympathizer from Cubero, a small town sixty miles to the west. He had just ridden alone through dangerous hostile Indian country to bring word that he and three companions had captured the town's garrison and its well-stocked post. Meeting with Pyron, he urged "the importance of a small force being sent there without delay." [90] The Major acted quickly, ordering Captain Alfred S. Thurmond of the 7th Regiment to take his company and ride to the sympathizers' aid. When Thurmond arrived at Cubero at two in the afternoon on March 5th, he was greeted by Gillespie's cohorts Dr. F.E. Kavenaugh, Mr. R.T. Thompson, and Mr. George Gardenhier. The Captain soon learned that the little party had pulled off a surprising feat of bravado.

The four partisans were long-time residents of Cubero and their secessionist sympathies were well known. The Federal Government of the area took a dim view of their sentiment and had harassed them for espousing it. Consequently, when Sibley's army arrived the four chose to throw in their lot with the Texans. As Captain Thurmond put it, "there was but one game to play, and they did play it with profit to the Confederate States and great credit to themselves." [91] Encouraged by Sibley's success at Valverde, Gillespie and the others decided to take action of their own. On the morning of March 3rd, Dr. Kavenaugh, the group's leader, approached the Federal outpost in Cubero and demanded to speak with Captain Francisco Aragon, the garrison commander. In the name of "The Kavenaugh Regiment" and the Confederate States of America, he gave Aragon ten minutes to surrender the post peaceably or face the consequences. Aragon did not know what to do. Plainly his small command of forty-two New Mexican soldiers and three regulars was no match for a "regiment" of marauding Texans. At the end of the ten minutes the stunned Union officer had still not responded. Kavenaugh took the silence as a yes. Confidently he sent one of the others to formally demand surrender and receive the garrison's arms. Confronted with an obviously self-assured enemy of unknown size, Aragon threw in the towel. Later, when the Union Captain learned the true nature of his opponent, it was too late. He had already formally surrendered the post and his honor prevented him from further action. In his report of the affair, Captain Thurmond wrote that although Kavenaugh's action had the effect of a bluff, that was not its intent. Thurmond believed that if Aragon had refused to surrender the "Kavenaugh Regiment" might actually have stormed the garrison! "In conversing with both friends and enemies [Thurmond] found the above to be substantially true; yea, more than true, for such an act of bravery, under the circumstances, could not be expected from [only four] men." [92]

The action of Dr. Kavenaugh and his companions could not have come at a better time for the fortunes of the Sibley Brigade. The isolated post at Cubero was a temporary Union supply depot. It was established before the war for a proposed campaign against the Navajos, but its supplies were never used. "Apparently Major Donaldson, in carrying out Canby's orders to remove or destroy all property, had forgotten about Cubero." [93] The hungry men of Thurmond's company took full advantage of the windfall and "soon the boys were enjoying good eating as well as good drinking." [94] In a further show of support, Dr. Kavenaugh opened his own store to the Texans. In short notice the company was not only well fed, but also well clad.

The supplies secured at Cubero went well beyond the immediate needs of Captain Thurmond and his men. Thanks to the "Kavenaugh Regiment," the Texans had captured "a large and valuable lot of quartermaster's, commissary, and ordnance stores. The surgery [was] also well supplied with valuable medicines, &c. There was not less than 60 arms and 3,000 rounds of ammunition turned over." [95] The little outpost was so well stocked that Captain Thurmond was able to send 25 wagonloads of commissaries and ammunition back to Major Pyron. [96]

The partial success of its vanguard gave Sibley's army a reprieve. With supplies captured at Cubero, and what Major Pyron's men were able to salvage or liberate in Albuquerque, the Texans now "had a sufficiency for some three months." [97] On March 2, Captain Julius Giesecke recorded in his diary, "In the evening we received the news that New Mexico had declared itself defeated, and that we would be well treated in the principal towns." [98] Despite the encouraging prospects, only Major Pyron's troops found immediate relief. Captain Giesecke, along with Isaac Adair and most of the other Confederates were still some distance below Albuquerque. Several more days passed before they reached the provisions. In the meantime, they continued to suffer. Abe Hanna wrote in his diary, "We are now entirely out of everything in the way of provisions and yet thirty miles to Albuquerke [sic], our promised paradise." [99]

By this time the Rebels had good reason to regard Albuquerque as the Promised Land. Most of them had been on reduced rations since Valverde and were slowly starving. To make matters worse, many were also ill-clothed. Extra clothing was one of the first things the brigade discarded, and like food, the territory offered little chance for replacement. Private Davidson recalled the army's impoverished condition saying, the average soldier had "but one old ragged suit of clothes, soaked with mud and lined with lice."[100]

The weather on March 3 chilled the men to the bone as they tramped through a thickly settled, but poorer region. To the weary Texans the country looked "destitute of everything," "having the appearance of a desolate old waste farm." [101] One soldier was prompted to remark that New Mexico was "never intended for white folks" and that "the first man that ever came to the country ought to have been killed by the Indians." [102] After marching ten or twelve miles the men encamped near the little Mexican village of Sabinal. That night, wood was again a problem. So little fuel was collected that Colonel Scurry bought the roof poles off a fodder shed from the town's inhabitants.

With only two poles issued per company, the shivering Texans had to choose between having coffee that night or warming their breakfast of beans in the morning.[103]

The roof poles were not the only items that Sabinal surrendered to the Confederate cause. When the brigade left, William Howell noted laconically that it was "after confiscating some goods." [104] Although the Texans occasionally purchased supplies from the locals, more frequently they merely took what they wanted. Foraging was now a matter of survival. Private Davidson wrote; "The enemy have moved everything to eat out of the country and have persuaded the Mexicans to hide their corn and wheat and drive their cattle and sheep beyond our reach." [105]

Most residents of the Rio Grande Valley tried to conceal their property, but for many small towns the Rebels' passage still proved a disaster. As the Texans moved, they stripped the little Mexican "villages of all the food, animals, and transportation they could find." [106] At the village of Belén, fifty-five miles north of Socorro, the Texans seized, "thirteen horses, twenty-two mules, eighteen cows and five calves, thirty-six sheep, two bulls, two oxen, two hogs, two heifers, two burros, and forty-two chickens." Besides livestock, Confederate foragers also stole "three hundred thirty-eight sacks of corn and one hundred sixty sacks of flour." [107] The brigade's horses and draft animals were turned loose to graze in the fields around Belén and promptly devoured 95 acres of early beans and fodder. Adding insult to injury, the Texans were not above pilfering. When the army left, the "villagers also found themselves to be missing revolvers, carriages, saddles and bridles, brass kettles, blankets, two bundles of carpets, and a cart loaded with firewood." [108] During the course of the invasion, violations, like those at Belén, were repeated again and again.

Private Wady T. Williams, Company C, 5th Regiment, Texas Mounted Volunteers. Courtesy Lawrence T. Jones, III collection, Austin, TX

Making matters worse, Confederate confiscations came on the heels of similar Union appropriations. To ensure adequate supplies for the Territorial Militia, "citizens were ordered to place their riding animals, arms, and ammunition at the disposal of militia officers who also were authorized to purchase or take by force provisions to subsist their men." [109] Before the Texans ever arrived in Belén, its unfortunate citizens complained that militia officers went into poor people's homes and took their "last mouthful of flour," while the homes of the wealthy were left untouched. The regular Union army also commandeered supplies, or forced the populace to sell against their will. Issued at Fort Craig, a typical confiscation order of the period reads; "If the people of Paraja have corn for sale, they must supply your camp, and if they refuse to do so or ask more than three dollars a fanega, you are directed to take the corn, giving receipts for the amounts." [110] One year later, Union and Texan depredations and a devastating summer flood caused serious starvation up and down the valley.

    In the short run, the Army of New Mexico's high-handedness and ruffian behavior did little to win support for the Southern cause. Instead, it reinforced many natives' dread of the Texans and even angered some that counted themselves neutral or Confederate sympathizers. Just the same, the Hispanic population of the Rio Grande Valley had little use for the Union or its far-off Federal Government. In individual encounters with the New Mexicans the Confederates found many a friendly face.

    Around noon on March 4th, an exhausted Alfred Peticolas dropped out of ranks. An ice-cold crossing of the Rio Grande and several miles of marching had left the 5th Sergeant tired and hungry. With a smattering of Spanish at his command, he decided to try and raise something to eat from the numerous Mexican houses scattered along the way. Stopping at the first place where he saw any inhabitants Peticolas asked if they would give him a little bread. Everyone said they had none, but as they sat there in the hot sun one of the women began talking. "Tears came to her eyes as she spoke." [111] A few moments later she gave a key to one of the men in the group and he beckoned the Texan to follow him. Nearby on the road, Peticolas' friend, Frank D. Kneiber was listening. Since he spoke the better Spanish of the two, he decided to tag along. As the two men trudged behind the villager a third hungry companion, twenty-year-old B.A. Jones joined them. Their guide soon led the men to his house where a young boy cooked all three Texans a meal of boiled beef, eggs, and a sort of mush with sugar and grease. While the Southerners ate, the man recounted how the Federals had tried to force him into military service. He said that he was knocked down and showed the three "a bayonet wound where they stabbed him trying to force him along anyhow." [112] He also said that many a sick man was forced into service and marched away without being allowed to rest or stop. The three Texans did not have any money, but their host "seemed to give with a free will." Feeling a need to repay the kindness, the sergeant and his friends gave the man all their tobacco. The villager "said he wanted no pay" and could hardly be persuaded to accept their offering. [113] Peticolas later wrote, "I never thought I would ever be so pressed by hunger as to ask for bread when I had no means of paying for it, but I have done it, and without shame too." [114]

That same day the brigade tramped about ten miles and stopped in a stand of cottonwoods near the village of Peralta. The men made camp and spirits brightened a little. Wood was more plentiful and in anticipation of resupply the soldiers were allowed to draw a small amount of flour. [115] The flour was quickly baked into bread which, "tasted very sweet [...] after living on poor beef and beans for so many days." [116] That night all the talk was of Albuquerque. Judge

Baird had ridden with the men during the day and had expounded a good deal about the encouraging prospects for provisions ahead. As the soldiers lay around camp, Baird's words were repeated from fire to fire. "He says that the inhabitants of the towns above are all for us and are willing to sell to us anything they have on the credit of our government." "In Alberkeurque [sic] it would take a very strong force to get us out." "In Santa Fe, 40,000 men would hardly do it." [117]

By morning much of the optimism faded, replaced by the realities of sore aching feet and the prospect of another long march. The brigade's destination for the day was Judge Baird's ranch, just seven miles from Albuquerque. [118] The troops set out at a leisurely pace intending to cover the twelve miles to the ranch with as much ease as possible. After a short distance however, the road turned sandy and only strenuous labor kept their wagons moving. Because of the "low condition" of the teams, the officers decided to abandon the direct route along the sandy river bottom and seek better ground. [119] Turning to the right, the train headed up a large canyon toward the foot of the mountains. Some of the men could not stomach the idea of a more round about route and struck out on their own along the river. Isaac Adair and his company stuck with the wagons as did the two other Houston County companies and the bulk of the command. Although the new road was easier to travel the distance proved far longer than anticipated. Wagon teams began to give out and progress slowed to a crawl. Soon night overtook the exhausted column. "The wind blew at a hard rate off the snow mountains" and the going became extremely unpleasant. [120] It was 9 o'clock at night before the wearied soldiers spied the Confederate flag flying above Judge Baird's house and finally stumbled into camp. Abe Hanna wrote in his diary; "I was more exhausted from this days travel than any I had before experienced." [121]

The soldiers who continued up the river bottom fared much better. Alfred Peticolas took the shorter route and was already at the ranch collecting cow chips for fuel when the regiments arrived. "Every man was mad enough to bite a tenpenny nail in two. Every one swore they had walked twenty-three miles; that the officers were fools for marching them so far around instead of taking them the short road, etc.,etc." Peticolas could not remember when he had seen the regiments so universally angry. [122]

Since leaving Socorro, the Confederates had seen almost nothing of their enemy. Foragers occasionally spotted small Yankee patrols in the distance, but little else. Just before reaching Baird's ranch the men learned that two companies of Union cavalry were operating in the area. The Federals never materialized, but the supposed threat was enough to keep the men on their toes all through the next day.

While the soldiers idled in camp, rumors made the rounds. One much repeated tale said, "that Canby has left Craig and is making for Ft. Union to make another stand; that he has only 800 men with him; that all the Mexicans have left him, glad of an excuse to leave." Another said "6000 Mexicans under a certain nameless Mexican Col. have attacked and taken Ft. Union [...] and that now the Confederate [flag] is flying over the place." Getting into the spirit of things, Judge Baird said, "that to his certain knowledge there were 8000 men at Craig and 1300 were regulars and Pikes Peak men. Of these, the morning after the fight, only 900 were there to answer to their names at roll call." [123] The telling of these tales helped the men pass the time, but like most rumors they were all either false or exaggerated.

That night as a further gesture of his support the Judge hosted the brigade's officers to dinner. Most of the army was still on short rations and some of the uninvited were indignant that their officers got to feast and make merry. Listening to the party, Private Howell grumbled, "Officers get some butter this evening, but privates continue to live hard as usual." [124]

Fortunately for morale, on March 7th, captured supplies from Albuquerque reached the troops. For the first time in a long while the men received full rations. They were also given "corn and tops" for their horses. [125] Alfred Peticolas noted, "We are drawing flour enough to feed us men and are living better than we have for some time before." [126] To augment what they captured at Cubero and Albuquerque, the Texans confiscated a number of small "Yankee" stores located in and about the city. [127] These businesses were owned by sutlers who supplied the Federal army and by prominent Union sympathizers. Most of the seizures were forcible, but on at least one occasion supplies were turned over willingly. The brothers, Rafael and Manuel Armijo, two of the wealthiest and most respectable native merchants in New Mexico, stepped boldly forward and offered their support to the Texans. After meeting with General Sibley, the two men placed an extraordinary $200,000 worth of merchandise at the brigade's disposal. [128]

The influx of rations and the chance to relax made a big change in the average soldier's disposition. William Howell, who just the night before was grumbling about rations, took the opportunity to wander into nearby Albuquerque and do a little sightseeing. In the plaza, he was cheered by the Confederate flag waving atop a "splendid pole", once occupied by "the old Stars and Stripes." Spread around the square, he noted, "several things that look a little similar to a civilized country." [129] After so long in the wilds, just the sight of dry goods stores, churches and frame houses was enough to lighten the young private's mood.

On the night of the 7th the war and the enemy seemed far away. Lounging in camps, the Rebels paid little heed to either their organization or their weapons. As Abe Hanna put it, "The boys now begin to get tolerable easy and careless." [130] The carelessness soon caused a short-lived excitement. After dark several pickets hurried in and reported that an unknown body of men was approaching from the mountains. Many of the men had wandered away from their companies and guns and accoutrements were scattered about. The disorganized Texans thought the Yankees were upon them, and "there was considerable commotion in camps for several minutes." [131] The alarm proved false, but the reminder of their situation was clear.

Next morning the army was again on the move. The 4th Regiment, along with parts of both the 5th and 7th, packed up and headed east. Meanwhile, General Sibley and his remaining units entered Albuquerque in triumph. Major Pyron welcomed his commander at the town plaza and the vanguard fired a 13-gun salute in the Sibley's honor. With a cold March breeze blowing through town and the "Stars and Bars" fluttering overhead, the Texans then held another formal occupation ceremony. [132]

After the speech-making and posturing were completed, Sibley established a temporary headquarters in the city and pondered his next move. Despite the desertion of large numbers of New Mexicans from the Federal ranks, the attitude of the native population toward the Texans remained uncertain. The largess shown by the Armijo brothers was unusual and was in sharp contrast to the indifference or outright hostility of most of the territory's well to do. From the beginning, Sibley counted on winning the support of a large portion of the territory's Spanish-speaking population. Knowing that his campaign might flounder without it, the

General again issued a proclamation intended to weaken the Union army and gain the backing of the local citizens.

> "TO THE PEOPLE OF NEW MEXICO:
> The signal victory which crowned our arms at Valverde on the 21st of February proves the truth of the assertions contained in my first Proclamation in regard to our powers and ability to accomplish the purposes therein declared. Those of you who volunteered in the Federal service were doubtless deceived by designing officials and interested citizens. The militia were driven to the field by force of arms. Under these circumstances I deem it proper and but just to declare a complete and absolute amnesty to all citizens who have, or may within ten days lay aside their arms and return to their homes and avocations.
> The conduct of this army since its entrance into the Territory of New Mexico attests the honesty and integrity of our purpose, and the protection it has and can afford to the citizens of the country.
> Return then with confidence to your homes and to your avocations, and fear not the result." [133]

Sibley believed that the positive conciliatory tone of his proclamation would encourage prominent natives to step forward and throw their support behind the Confederacy. For all his effort, he was just shouting in the wind. Neither the proclamation nor other efforts to solicit more support produced any tangible results. Acknowledging his failure, Sibley disgustedly wrote; "The ricos, or wealthy citizens of New Mexico, [...] have no distinct sentiment or opinion on the vital question at issue. Power and interest alone control the expression of their sympathies." They have "been completely drained by the Federal Powers, and, adhering to them, [have] become absolute followers of their army for dear life and their invested dollars." [134]

Because of captured and confiscated supplies the Texans now had adequate food and clothing. They continued, however, to be plagued by shortages of firewood and forage for their animals. To solve these problems, General Sibley decided to split his brigade. Holding back a portion of the 5th Regiment to garrison Albuquerque, he sent the bulk of his command eastward into the Sandia Mountains. Grass and wood were plentiful there, and Sibley planned for his troops to rest and recuperate in the mountains' sheltered canyons and villages. The move would also put his army astride the main road from Fort Craig to Fort Union. The General reasoned that his men could slowly work their way north, at the same time keeping a lookout for Federal activity. While the men and animals regained their strength, their presence would interfere with communication between the two Union outposts. When the time was right, the brigade would reunite above Santa Fe and overpower Fort Union. The plan seemed reasonable. The road, running through Tijeras Canyon via the villages of San Antonio and Galisteo was mountainous, but direct. Water sources were dependable, grass was ample, and pinon and juniper wood was readily available. The only factor that proved unreliable was the weather. [135]

While Sibley was welcomed into Albuquerque, Isaac Adair and his men were riding east with a near hurricane howling at their backs. March 8th was a terrible day for man and beast alike. As the nine companies of the 4th Texas and the five-company battalion of the 7th headed for the Sandia Mountains, sand and gravel blew in a way that few of the men had ever experienced. According to Alfred Peticolas, "Clouds of sand came driving against our backs, and the whole atmosphere was dark with heavy clouds of sand." [136] "It was so windy and dusty that you would not distinguish a person fifty steps away." [137] Pebbles dashed stingingly against the men and their eyes were almost put out by the sand. As the dust bit his face, Abe Hanna was reminded of descriptions "of the sand storms of the great desert of Sahara." [138] Thankful that the gale was at their backs, the Texans pulled their hats down and hurried on. With the wind pushing them the columns traveled rapidly and towards evening they reached the shelter of the mountains. Passing down a long descent, the regiments "reached a deep canyon where the wind did not blow with so much violence." [139] About a mile in they made camp along a little stream. Wood was still scarce, but the men were able to gather enough green cedar to make tolerable fires. After a time, the wind abated a bit, and the temperature began to drop.

On March 9th, the hapless Southerners shivered around their guttering fires and tried to keep warm. The weather between the high mountains was windy and cold and frequent showers of snow fell throughout the day. Wrapped in their overcoats the suffering soldiers huddled about camp and waited for the storm to pass. [140] One soldier later wrote, "During the period of our encampment at this place, we were destitute of tents and almost entirely without clothing or blankets." [141] In the evening the detached companies of the 5th Regiment stumbled into camp. Trailing behind their comrades, they had traveled through swirling snow almost the entire day. In the cold and dark, William Howell wrote in his diary, "Nearly freeze tonight." [142]

The storm passed, but the next day was again spent lying in camps. Happily, the weather was pleasant enough that the men could finally find some comfort. Alfred Peticolas spent the hours reading a novel entitled, "The King and the Cobbler." [143] Others discussed the news from the Eastern front or sat with sick friends. The sick were already abundant. Marching day after day on short rations had whittled away the Texans' physical reserves. After the extreme exposure of the past couple of days, pneumonia was again making the rounds. [144]

Crouched around fires of cactus and green cedar, some of the men speculated that their leadership had lost its direction. They debated the wisdom that sent them to the mountains in the first place and wondered when, if ever, their ordeal would end. Abe Hanna dejectedly scribbled, "Still in camps and do not know when we will leave here as headquarters is generally but a figurehead and has never been any other way lately." [145] Ever since his failure to appear on the field at Valverde, General Sibley had steadily lost the confidence of his men.

Despite these concerns not everyone in the camps was gloomy. Many soldiers took heart in the news that Captain John G. Phillips' "Brigands" had entered Santa Fe. Shortly after occupying Albuquerque, Major Pyron dispatched eleven of the volunteers toward the territorial capital. On March 10th, this advance scouting party of irregulars entered the city unopposed. Finding that the Federal garrison had fled, the volunteers terrorized some of the citizens and indulged in petty thievery and pilfering. When their husbands left, a number of Union wives were forced to remain in Santa Fe and some of the Brigands began to seize their belongings. Luckily, Captain Hiram Ford's wife was among the ladies and was acquainted with Lieutenant Battles, the irregulars' officer. At her request, Battles ordered his men to stop their looting and respect the women's property. [146]

After waiting for General Sibley's victorious welcome into Albuquerque to conclude, Major Pyron also hopped back into the saddle. Only three days behind the scouting party, his seventy-five-man advance rode into Santa Fe on March 13. The city looked deserted. The territorial government had fled to the safety of Las Vegas, and most of the locals were hiding from the "terrible Tejanos." Just as in Albuquerque, Pyron quickly discovered that he had arrived too late to capture any significant Federal stores. Union soldiers burned what they could not evacuate, and once again the sight of blackened warehouses greeted the Major's men. In a final act of defiance, the retreating garrison even cut down the plaza's flagpole. The cursed Texans might have the town, but at least they could not raise their damnable banner.

Pyron took formal possession of Santa Fe, and despite the Union vandalism, the Stars and Bars were soon waving over the 250-year-old Palace of the Governors. The next day, the Major seized the presses of the pro-Union Santa Fe Gazette and reissued copies of Sibley's recent proclamation. The notices were no more effective in Santa Fe than they were in Albuquerque. Pyron's men went into quarters in town and the Confederate advance spluttered to a halt. [147]

East of Albuquerque, the columns of the 4th and the 7th advanced deeper into the mountains and camped near the village of Tijeras. The area was covered with a good growth of pine and cedar and nearby was a clear brook. Provisions were plentiful. In the words of Captain Julius Giesecke, the men "had nothing to do but eat and drink." [148] The time might have been idyllic except for the continued foul weather. On the same day that Major Pyron entered Santa Fe, the men in the Sandia Mountains woke to find their beds covered with an inch of snow. Alfred Peticolas thought, "It was amusing to see the men as they woke and looked around with bewildered expressions, raking the snow out of hats and shoes, but it was not very pleasant." [149] Not very pleasant indeed! "The whole face of the earth was covered with snow," wrote Private William Henry Smith. "It is severe upon our soldiers without any tents or anything to shelter from the snow." Smith "and some friends found a cave in the rocks & built a fire" and struggled to keep warm. [150]

From the moment the trek east began a trickle of weak and ailing men left the columns. Helped along by their fellows these sick soldiers slowly made the long walk back to Albuquerque and the Confederate hospital. By the 13th, "deep snow in the mountains [was driving] in [a] great many poor fellows with pneumonia." [151] The trickle became a torrent. In good health himself, Private William Howell of the 5th Regiment accompanied his friend John Naile back to Albuquerque. Waiting at the hospital and watching over the dying Naile, Howell watched the sick arrive. His diary for March 13, 1862 reads, "Great many more come in from the mountains and report the snow all over everything, blankets and all. That foolish move out in those mountains will cause the death of many a poor fellow." [152] Huddled in the cold near Tijeras, Private Bill Davidson painted an even darker picture, "Sleeting and snowing all the time. At this camp we remain a week and bury fifty men, and if this weather and exposure continues much longer we'll have to bury the whole brigade." [153]

Davidson's statement that fifty men were buried is an exaggeration. Just the same, it is a tragic fact of the New Mexico campaign that many more soldiers were laid low by the gruesome inroads of disease than fell fighting in battle. In Isaac Adair's company alone, thirty-seven Texans took ill. Of these sick, eleven were captured while hospitalized, four were medically discharged, and ten eventually died from pneumonia, dysentery, or other assorted ailments. This works out to an appalling thirty percent casualty rate from disease. By contrast, Company H's ultimate losses at the hands of the enemy would come to only five! [154]

"As there seemed to be no stopping to the snowing," the Rebels decided to break camp and find shelter in nearby Mexican villages. [155] "On account of not having teams sufficient to bring them," the regiments were long before "compelled to throw away [their] tents." [156] With the snow already four inches deep and still falling, the protection of Mexican huts seemed far better than another night in the woods.

For the next week the soldiers quartered in the homes of the villagers. Most of the houses were small and poor, and the Texans filled them to overflowing. While twenty or more men squeezed inside each of the "miserable little hacienda[s]," the former owners found themselves relegated to a single room or corner. [157] Because of the jam of sleeping and lounging soldiers, cooking inside was out of the question. Mess fires were built outside and the men continued to prepare their meals standing in the snow. In spite of being rudely displaced by the Confederates, some of the Mexican families acted as gracious hosts to their uninvited guests. The owners of the home in which Alfred Peticolas was quartered spread out a bed for him by the fire and "kindly furnished" the men with pillows. [158] Julius Giesecke reported; "our mess sergeant befriended a family with whom he found quarters and once again we spent a pleasant evening in a family circle." [159]

The respite from the elements was greatly appreciated by the Texans. After so long outside, most of the men found the simple quarters "real comfortable." [160] For a lucky few it was a chance to enjoy the luxury of sleeping on a real bed for the first time in eight months. Alfred Peticolas thought the room in which he was staying was "altogether the most comfortable quarters I have yet found to stand guard in." [161] Nonetheless, the constant coughing of his fellows distressed the Sergeant. Outside the huts, the snow was now six inches deep. To everyone's relief, on the 14th the weather turned fine and the sun began to shine. The regiments were without orders and accordingly the men passed the time playing cards, reading, or just lying about.

While idle in the villages, the men received melancholy news from below. In the brigade's hospital at Socorro seventeen of their wounded comrades had died. Among them was Captain Willis Lang, who so bravely led the lancer charge against the Federal lines. The Captain was severely wounded and was unlikely to make a full recovery. In a fit of depression over his condition he asked his slave to hand him a pistol and "shot himself through the brain." "Lang was a modest nice man, well educated," and it made those who knew him "almost sick to hear the sad news of his death." [162]

March 16th was a Sunday, but the lives of the Confederates were now so changed that it went almost unnoticed. For many, the Chaplain's regular service was their only reminder that the Lord's Day had come once more. One soldier lamented, "Alas! Sometimes I almost forget the day entirely, so much does it resemble other days in camp life." [163]

At about 8 o'clock in the morning word reached the Texans in San Antonio that a train of Federal wagons was trying to slip north along a road no more than a mile from the village. The escort of the train was reported to be only twenty. Sunday or not, Major Raguet immediately called for volunteers to intercept the wagons. Twenty-five or thirty men responded, including 5th Sergeant Peticolas and Private Abe Hanna. The men collected their guns and ammunition and in short order set off across the piney hills at the double quick. The chase soon reached the road, where the Texans discovered that the wagons had already passed. Unwilling to let their prize escape, the men lengthened their stride and hurried in pursuit. With their officers loping ahead on horseback the party kept up a punishing pace for nearly five miles. The Rebels were just beginning to think that the train had eluded them when they turned a point of wood and caught sight of the wagons. As Abe Hanna put it, they "was considerably disappointed." [164] After their arduous effort the Texans discovered that they had overtaken "some Mexican sheep herders with two wagons and a cart or two." [165] Adding to the chagrin, it turned out that the party "was traveling with a passport from Gen'l Sibley." [166] After milling in the road, coughing for five minutes, the dejected would be heroes headed back to camp. Abe Hanna noted that the chase only took about an hour, but "it was not such fast time going back." [167] The men now noticed that the day was chill and that a cold wind was blowing constantly from the North. No longer buoyed by the excitement of the hunt it took the volunteers three hours to make the long walk back to the village.

The next morning the snow returned and the weather was colder than ever. Following the death of Lieutenant Colonel Sutton at Valverde, Powhatan Jordan, the captain of Company A was promoted to Major and placed in command of the battalion of the 7th. Jordan, who originally hailed from Virginia, was a physician by profession. He earned a bachelor's degree from a Virginia military academy and later a doctor of medicine from The Columbian College of the District of Columbia. When General Sibley ordered the 7th into the mountains, Jordan left Company A in Albuquerque and proceeded east with his remaining four companies. The battalion was camping somewhere below the main body, possibly in Tijeras, but on the 17th, the Major ordered his men to saddle up and join the 4th Regiment at San Antonio. Isaac Adair and his men, along with companies B, F, and I rode through the snow and made camp just above the village. [168]

Fueled by the 7th's arrival, there was much speculation among the troops that a move was imminent. Everyone was sure they would soon be on the march, but the "place of destination uncertain." [169] The 18th was the coldest day that the men experienced all winter and talk notwithstanding, nothing of note occurred. Julius Giesecke's diary for the 18th and 19th reads simply, "Remained here." [170]

It was time for the Texans to get their stalled campaign moving again. General Sibley knew that if he was ever to consolidate his gains and secure the Territory, it was imperative that his army overrun Fort Union. Provided that the garrison did not destroy them first, the fort's seizure would mean a second chance to capture some of the invaluable supplies lost at Albuquerque and Santa Fe. The fall of the fort would also mean that Canby was helplessly cut off from aid. With the exception of the isolated Fort Craig, the whole of New Mexico would be under Confederate control. Sibley planned for his army to move against Fort Union in three columns. Major Pyron would move eastward from Santa Fe along the Santa Fe trail and Colonel Green would move from Albuquerque along a more southern route leading to Anton Chico. Meanwhile Colonel Scurry, commanding his 4th Regiment and the battalion of the 7th, would proceed northward through the Sandia Mountains to Galisteo. From there he could support either Pyron or Green and a reunited army would proceed to Fort Union in force. [171]

To put the strategy in motion, General Sibley ordered the four best-mounted companies of the 5th to leave Albuquerque. Under the care of Major John Samuel Shropshire, they were to make for Santa Fe and reinforce Pyron. Shropshire was formerly the Captain of Company A, but he was promoted to replace the dead Lockridge. Since transportation was something of a problem for the 5th, its remaining companies were recalled from the mountains to garrison Albuquerque. The six companies were joined on the walk back by all the sick and infirm from the other two regiments. [172]

Isaac Adair and the other soldiers remaining with Colonel Scurry drew ten-days rations and on March 21st once more took up a line of march. An entire month had slipped past since the victory at Valverde and the rank and file Texans had watched as the initiative and momentum of their campaign drained slowly away. Despite the hardships suffered and the uncertainty of where they were headed the men were pleased to be back on the offensive. The first day out of San Antonio Scurry's column only covered seven miles, but at least the Army of New Mexico was again an army of advance. Marching along, the boys reminisced about the battle gloriously won exactly one month to the day before. They also indulged in speculation about their "probable condition as individuals at the end of the war should it last three years." [173] Bringing up the rear, Company H and the other three companies of the 7th resumed their old role as guardians of the supply train.

From the 21st through the 25th the column and the train leapfrogged northward. Even though the weather turned moderate, the mountainous road made the going slow. The men on foot would quickly outdistance the ponderous wagons, then they would need to make camp and wait for the train to catch up. The country through which the Texans marched was desolate and lonely. Alfred Peticolas remarked, "No living thing can we see as we travel on, save animals and men accompanying us, and not even a bird flies across the road or chirrups in the bushes as we pass." [174] Many of the men were struck by the region's austere natural beauty. For the first couple of days, the scenery remained picturesque and interesting. Snow-capped mountains, dotted with immense stands of pinion trees rolled away on every side. Gradually, as the men moved farther north, their surroundings became less timbered and scrubby pine again became predominate.

Other than the scenery, the area held little of regard for the men. One exception was Real de Dolores. This village was the center of a gold and silver mining district. The foot of the mountains near the community was covered all around with diggings and in the town itself was machinery for working the mines and a mill for processing ore. Some of Scurry's bored soldiers were fascinated. While camped at Real de Dolores, Abe Hanna wrote; "here we found the first interesting curiosity we had found in the Territory." [175] Alfred Peticolas collected several specimens of quartz, toured the mill, and made notes about its yield. Even Captain Giesecke's terse journal mentions the mining town. [176]

After Real de Dolores the Texans' road sloped down out of the piney country. By the 25th they left the Sandia Mountains behind and once again reached the broad flat valley of the Rio Grande. In the valley the troops "traveled a good distance over a first-rate road" and made camp at the community of Galisteo. [177] Galisteo was situated on a small creek of the same name. Located some twenty-five miles from Santa Fe, it lay on one of the main roads from Fort Craig to Fort Union. It was near dusk when the Confederates reached the village. The strenuous march through the mountains left the men considerably fatigued and as Sergeant Peticolas put it, "We were not sorry to know that we had at last reached a point where we could rest a little." [178]

When the 4th Regiment reached Galisteo they were nearly a half-day's march ahead of their supply wagons. On the 26th they lay over in camp and waited for further orders. Private John M. Rogers who "died with swelling of the throat" was buried. [179] Around midday Major Jordan and the four companies of the 7th rolled in with the slow-moving train. Corporal Sharp Whitley of Company F reported that the rations for the column were already running short. As soon as the 7th made camp, foragers went into the little Mexican town in search of provisions. They succeeded in requisitioning a small quantity of corn and a flock of sheep. "They were naturally very small sheep and were so very poor that many of them could scarcely walk but [the Texans] slaughtered them and cooked them and ate them with relish." [180]

While the soldiers were enjoying their early supper of mutton, they "happened to look across the prairie and saw the dust rising and it was only a few minutes until it showed to be a man." Moments later the rider was pounding into camp. "He had a paper in his hand and loped up to Colonel Scurry's tent and handed the paper to the colonel." [181] The men standing about did not immediately learn the content of the note, but they could read their Colonel's reaction. Seeing Scurry's face, one soldier turned to his fellows and commented, "Hell is brewing and not a mile off." [182] The paper was an express from Major Pyron.

> "Col. William R. Scurry, Commanding Camp Galisteo.
> Col. - The enemy has moved down from Fort Union and is in full force in my front, and we have had heavy skirmishing during the day. I have a strong position. Will hold them at bay, and wait your arrival.
> Most respectfully
> Chas L. Pyron
> Commanding camp of observation." [183]

"Pyron with two hundred and fifty men, had been attacked by the Yankees with twelve hundred and fifty men in Apache Canyon!" [184] After fighting a losing battle for nearly three hours Pyron and his outnumbered command "had fallen back to wood and water, which he would hold till" reinforced. [185] The message sent shockwaves through the camp at Galisteo. The order was immediately given to prepare to move out. Sixteen miles separated Scurry and his command from their beleaguered comrades. Every minute counted. The men of the 4th and 7th "at once broke camp and by sundown were on the march." [186] Isaac Adair and the other men of Major Jordan's battalion had not finished their meal and they set out at the quick step, eating supper as they went. [187]

Chapter 7

PIKE'S PEAKERS

"They were regular demons, that iron and lead had no effect upon."

- George M. Brown

Confederate intelligence indicated that Fort Union was lightly held and that Canby's army was still bottled up at Fort Craig. So who were the troops who had attacked Major Pyron? The answer was both a surprise and a shock to the Texans. Some of the Federals were Regulars from Fort Union, but the bulk of the force consisted of infantry and cavalry from the 1st Regiment Colorado Volunteers! While General Sibley's Army had languished in Albuquerque, Santa Fe, and the Sandia Mountains, volunteers from in and around Denver City had force marched to the Union's defense. Instead of a small demoralized garrison from Fort Union the Rebels were facing a large, highly motivated, army of hardy miners and frontiersmen.

If any one man could claim credit for throwing these troops against the Texans it was the first governor of the Colorado Territory, Major William Gilpin. Gilpin was appointed by Abraham Lincoln, who gave him orders to keep Colorado loyal to the Union. Arriving in Denver in May of 1861, just as the Civil War was commencing, Gilpin possessed the right qualities for the job. He "was a man of foresight and energy, and of marked intelligence, courage and patriotism." Born in eastern Pennsylvania October, 1813, he was a graduate of University of Pennsylvania and later from the U.S. Military academy at West Point. Like his classmate Henry Sibley, Gilpin saw hard service in the War with Mexico and fought Indians in Florida and the Far West. He made at least forty exploring tours of the Rocky Mountains at various points and through the country to the Pacific Coast. At one point he represented the earliest settlers in Oregon's Willamette Valley, urging congress to provide them a territorial government. He is even credited by some as a founder of the city of Portland Oregon on the Columbia River. Gilpin was a true frontiersman. While a lawyer and an able territorial administrator, he was equally happy "sleeping off a drunken fandango on the dirt floor of a peon's shack, or talking to his little ponies on lonesome mountain trails." In the summer of 1861, he was just what the Union needed. [1]

When Gilpin arrived at his post he found that the "overwhelming popular majority" of Coloradans favored the Union. Still, he felt the situation was precarious. A recent election had demonstrated the depth of Union loyalty, but it had also revealed "a strong malignant element essential to be controlled." The new governor wrote worriedly to Colonel Canby in New Mexico that almost one-third of the population in Denver and the mining camps were secessionists. Gilpin believed the Southern sympathizers to be "ably and secretly organized" and felt that "extreme and extraordinary measures" were required to control their onslaught. Evidence from the early days of the governor's administration shows that the Rebel sympathizers were active and influential. Much of the Colorado public feared that the Territory would "drift away into the folds of the Confederacy." Isolated Confederate flags were flown over a few stores and saloons and one Denver newspaper was outspoken for secession. [2]

Governor William Gilpin of Colorado. Courtesy Colorado Historical Society, negative F-643

In late April a Confederate flag was run up over the Wallingford & Murphy general merchandise store on Denver's principle business street. The incident sparked a near riot as a crowd of excited and angry men gathered and "declared that the flag of disunion should not float in the town." Others felt it should remain and violence seemed near at hand. The Union men in the crowd were in the majority and directly had their way. One of their number, Samuel M. Logan, scrambled to the top of the building and tore down the offending banner. The flag had not "fluttered long enough to smooth out its creases and wrinkles" but it flew long enough to emphasize the deep rift developing in the territory. 3

In May, 1861 there was no formal military presence in the Pike's Peak area. Denver had previously boasted two companies of city militia, but they were no longer active. If he was to save Colorado for the Union, its new governor believed a military establishment was essential. In April, Gilpin asked the War Department for authority to raise a territorial militia. His request was denied. Not someone who accepted "no" as an answer, Gilpin forged ahead and took action anyway. If he could not legally raise troops at least he could plan. Under the legal authority he did hold, Gilpin created a military staff. He named "Richard Whitsett, adjutant general; Samuel Moer, quartermaster; John Fillmore, paymaster; and Morton Fisher, purchasing agent." Together with these four Gilpin set out to prepare for Colorado's defense. 4

Shortly after the appointments the governor ordered Fisher and others to go through the region buying up guns and ammunition of any sort. These agents moved quickly among the people, promising to pay high prices for weapons irrespective of condition or caliber. As most men owned either a rifle or shotgun, a large quantity of ordinance was soon collected. The arms, however, were poorly adapted for organized soldiers since almost no two guns were alike. It is unclear whether Gilpin was buying the weapons to build an arsenal or simply to prevent them from falling into Southern hands. What is clear is that he soon had stiff competition. On seeing the governor's actions, some Confederate sympathizers "threw off restraint, and entered the field for the purchase of rifles and shotguns wherever they could obtain them, together with ammunition to make them effective." Led by Captain Joel McKee, a transplanted Texan and ex-Indian fighter, these secessionists openly solicited arms. They even went so far as to post notices in Denver and the nearby mining camps "in which they named places where good prices would be paid for guns, powder, and so forth, mentioning an especial desire for a supply of percussion caps." The competition continued until Gilpin got fed up and arrested McKee and about 40 others for treason. [5]

Soon afterwards the imminent Southern threat in the territory subsided. Many sympathizers felt that they could be of more use to the Confederacy by taking up arms in the East. Subsequently men began to leave Colorado quietly in ones and twos. Governor Gilpin described the departure of the "malignant secession element" saying, "The core of its strength has at present withdrawn to gather strength from Texas, Utah, Arkansas, and from the country of the Confederated Cherokee, Creek, and other Indians." The exodus of outspoken Southerners gave Gilpin some breathing room, but the governor expected the respite to be temporary. He still believed Colorado was in peril and expected that sooner or later the Rebels would return in "overwhelming strength" and together with Indian allies attempt to conquer the region. To meet this perceived threat, Gilpin focused all of his energy on plans to muster a "sufficient force to meet the enemy in the field." [7]

In July 1861 the secessionist threat in the Colorado Territory was home grown. Henry Sibley was far to the east in Richmond. He had laid his invasion plan before Jefferson Davis, but was still awaiting official approval. Sibley's Texans were more than a thousand miles away, most of them tending their farms or stores. Nearer to Denver, a harried Colonel Canby was trying to reorganize his command. The U.S. Army in the New Mexico Territory was badly depleted by the resignation of Southern sympathizers and Canby did not have enough troops to garrison his posts. With Indian hostilities on the rise he turned to

Governor Gilpin for aid. Fort Garland was at the edge of Colonel Canby's command. Because it lay inside the Colorado Territory, he reasoned that it would be expedient for Gilpin to provide soldiers to defend it. Up to this point, Gilpin's lack of authority to raise troops had severely limited his schemes to provide for Colorado's defense. All that changed on July 6 when a letter from Colonel Canby arrived requesting the governor to enroll two companies of infantry. Canby asked that the volunteers be sent to Fort Garland, "to be mustered into the service of the United States at as early a period as possible." The authority was shaky, but Canby's letter expressly asked Gilpin to raise troops. The governor was looking for a loophole and he had found it. 8

    Almost immediately Gilpin embarked on the great military undertaking of his administration, the enlisting and getting into shape of an entire regiment of loyal Coloradans. By mid July the work was underway and he was appointing officers and recruiters. On the 27th, Samuel M. Logan, the man who tore down the Confederate flag above the Wallingford & Murphy store, was commissioned an "unattached" 1st lieutenant. Recruiting offices were opened in Denver, Boulder City, Colorado City, Gregory Idaho, the Clear Creek mining towns and several other places. 9

    The rough and tumble mining towns proved an especially fertile source of recruits. The volunteers came "in from all quarters, from the mines, the shops, and stores, all ready to fight for their country." The lure of gold had filled the Rocky Mountains with hopeful miners, but for most it was a luckless pursuit. If they could make enough from their claims to keep themselves fed many were satisfied. The work was hard and thankless. Those with a strong hope in the future and a stronger sense of luck worked steadily always hopeful that wealth was just a shovel away.

Others worked spasmodically. While the larder was full they would loaf and daydream about what they would do when they struck it rich. As supplies ran low they would return to digging, looking for the next bit of "color" to stave off hunger. For many this hand to mouth existence quickly lost its luster.

Company G, 1st Regiment, Colorado Volunteers, drilling at Empire, Colorado during the summer of 1861, Colorado Historical Society, negative F-2034

Gilpin's recruiting proceeded at a fast pace. Denver was all confusion and bustle. Bands paraded the streets and as one resident related, "The sound of fife and drum is heard from morn til night." Soon two companies were fully formed and a number of others were well on their way toward completion. While the work proceeded most of the new volunteers were quartered in and around Denver. On the Platte river, two miles from the center of town, work was under way on a new military post to house the regiment.[14]

Colonel John P. Slough, 1st Regiment, Colorado Infantry. Courtesy Colorado Historical Society, negative F-4055

Near the end of August, Gilpin named the principle officers who would lead his little army. As Colonel he appointed John P. Slough, the recruiting captain of Company A. Slough, who was originally from Ohio, was a prominent lawyer in Denver and a fast-rising territorial politician. He was also an outspoken pro-Union crusader. Not only did Slough recruit a company for Gilpin, but his family donated substantial sums of money to the effort. A very capable man, Slough would later prove a less than ideal military leader. [15]

Another recruiting captain of Company B., Samuel F. Tappan, was promoted to Lieutenant Colonel. Tappan, who recruited Company B in and around Central City and Black Hawk, was a military veteran and Colorado pioneer. The most colorful of Gilpin's regimental officers was John M. Chivington. Chivington was a "Bull Roaring" Methodist preacher who held the post of presiding elder of the Rocky Mountain District. Born in Warren County Ohio in 1821, he had migrated to Illinois where he joined the Illinois Conference of the Methodist Episcopal Church. He later joined the Missouri Conference and became a missionary to the Wyandotte Indians. In 1860 Chivington had moved to Colorado and assumed the head of its large Methodist congregation. When Gilpin approached him, it was to tender the position of regimental chaplain. Chivington would have none of it. He was a large man used to thundering from the pulpit and every bit as rough and tumble as the miners to whom he preached. He told Gilpin, "If there's fighting to be done, I want to fight. ... There is no force more evil on earth than the Confederacy and its people." Gilpin took the hint and subsequently appointed Chivington a major. [16]

In 1861, most everyone in the Colorado Territory was from somewhere else. Accordingly, the men who stepped forward to join Gilpin's 1st Colorado Volunteers came from far and wide. A physician's report for Company A listed the following nativity for its members: "New York, 17; Pennsylvania, 4; Ohio, 9; Ireland,7; Canada, 6; Vermont, 5; Scotland, 4; Illinois, 3; Germany, England, Virginia, Indiana, New Jersey, each 2; Rhode Island, Maine, Maryland, Massachusetts, Michigan, Missouri, Iowa, and Wales, each 1." The bulk of the recruits were "hardy miners inured to toil and privation." A Denver newspaper reported proudly that the "physique" of the men was first rate, and that they "look hale and hearty, and are in excellent spirits." By October 1, the ranks of most of the companies were completely filled. [17]

Despite his success, Governor Gilpin was left with some nagging concerns. First and foremost was Colonel Canby in New Mexico. On August 14, Canby sent another message to Gilpin recommending that the Governor organize one or two companies of men and send them to Fort Wise. Clearly, Canby knew about the mustering in and around Denver and was asking, where were his volunteers? Gilpin stalled. Canby's original request may have given the Governor authority to raise troops, but actually sending the volunteers to Fort Wise did not fit into his plans. The word among the men volunteering was that Gilpin's regiment "will not leave Colo., and perhaps not Denver." [18]

The Governor was in a quandary. He had not raised a fine body of men for Colorado's defense just to send them traipsing off. Still, he needed to make some effort to support Canby and follow orders. Despite already having nearly 2,700 men under arms, Gilpin decided that the best response was to raise more companies specifically for the task. He was already thinking about a second regiment and two new "Independent" companies would make a good beginning. [20]

On August 29, the Governor appointed James H. Ford a captain and authorized him to raise a company. The next day, Gilpin appointed a West Point graduate and former regular army officer, C.D. Hendron as captain of another company with Theodore H. Dodd as his second lieutenant. These newly appointed officers quickly began enlisting volunteers in and around Canyon City. Despite Colonel Canby's urgency the effort took the rest of the fall. Along the way Dodd replaced Hendron as captain of the second company and it was not until December that the ranks of both companies were filled.

Popularly, the two companies mustered at Canyon City became known as "Captain 'Jim' Ford's Independent Company" and "Captain Dodd's Independent Company." [21]

Shortly after the recruiting effort began, Governor Gilpin wrote to Colonel Canby in New Mexico. He told the Colonel that two companies of volunteer infantry were being readied and soon would report to Fort Garland for muster into the United States service. Gilpin also warned that if any further troops were required then Canby would need to send an authorized mustering officer to Denver and supply all arms and ammunition for their complete equipment. [22]

Colonel Canby was recently advised by telegraphic dispatch that two additional regiments of volunteers were authorized for the New Mexico Territory. He confided in Gilpin, "In my judgment they cannot be raised here, and it may be necessary to ask your excellency to organize four or six companies in the Colorado Territory." If that necessity arose, Colonel Canby promised to send the requested mustering officer and necessary arms to the place of rendezvous. Ironically, while Canby had the authority to raise troops and to a lesser degree the ability to equip them Governor Gilpin was the one with the manpower. [23]

The organization of the of the independent companies notwithstanding, Gilpin delayed sending Canby any troops. In early October the Governor wrote to Captain Elmer Otis, commanding Fort Wise, and advised him; "there is no volunteer force available to relieve your command or enable it to retire from Fort Wise." Otis informed his colonel and Canby immediately sent a dispatch to Gilpin expressing his "very great disappointment" at the governor's attitude. Canby was counting on the garrison from Fort Wise as part "of the force intended for active operation at the

South." Now, it was nearly too late to make other plans. Chidingly, Canby told Gilpin that he was sorry the determination was not made in a more seasonable fashion. At least that way, he could have arranged to replace the troops at Fort Wise from some other quarter. Gilpin responded on October 26. Ingeniously he told Canby that the population of the region near Fort Wise was not numerous enough to provide even one company. To send them from the mining region, he complained, was impossible because of "want of arms, ammunition, food, clothing, transportation, or money to procure any of these essentials." Gilpin protested that with such obstacles in his path, he was doing the best he could. He assured Canby, "I am incessantly occupied to comply with your requisitions at the earliest moment." [24]

What Governor Gilpin failed to mention to Canby was that he was trying to provide for the needs of fourteen companies, not two! By mid October Gilpin had recruited ten companies for his regiment, the two independent companies under Ford and Dodd, and two companies designated ,"home guards." All these soldiers rightfully expected to be paid, fed, housed, clothed, and armed at government expense. The expenditure required to organize and maintain the force for even a short time was going to be huge. Unfortunately for Gilpin he had no resources with which to meet the need. The Territory was practically without money for military purposes. Washington had not provided him with war funds and he was not authorized to borrow any. With no other means at his disposal Gilpin took a bold and foolhardy step. A man of action, in late July he approached a local Denver printer and ordered him to print up $355,000 in United States Treasury Notes. Short of cash, the enterprising Governor simply printed his own money![25]

The day the notes were delivered was the beginning of the end of William Gilpin's political career. $355,000 was an even more impressive sum of money in 1861 than it is today. It was more than the entire annual budget of the Colorado Territory. Gilpin was sure that his actions would be vindicated when he saved the territory from insurrection, so he was not concerned. If he managed to thwart a Confederate takeover, Washington could not help but support him. Certain of his government's backing, he informed President Lincoln and the Secretary of War of his action and began issuing the notes. [26]

Locally, Gilpin was viewed as an experienced Washington insider. Area merchants, who had complete faith in his understanding of government red tape, accepted the sight drafts without question. Pike's Peak mines were not producing well and most leading businesses were happy for the perceived influx of capital. For several months, the notes were accepted at face value and Gilpin put them to good use. The most prominent being the establishment of Camp Weld his new military camp on the Platte river. [27]

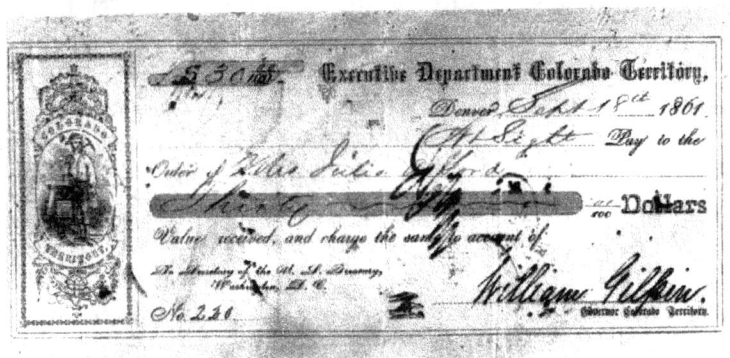

One of Governor William Gilpin's vouchers. Courtesy Colorado Historical Society, negative F-712A

Constructed for the extravagant sum of $40,000, the camp buildings were "built in the most substantial and comfortable manner." There was grumbling in Denver that the new camp was too lavish for a bunch of soldiers and local newspapers quickly dubbed the men of the 1st Colorado, Gilpin's "Pet Lambs." [28]

Gilpin's use of the bogus notes went far beyond the establishment of Camp Weld. He created a Quartermaster Corp and the script was spent far and wide on everything from food and uniforms to wagons, horses, and weapons. Large amounts were used to pay the wages of carpenters, teamsters, and others. The script was even used to pay the wages of the volunteers themselves. For a time the drafts were readily accepted and even circulated as currency. By September the wind had shifted. Worried holders of the notes started to voice concern about their money. In early November the roof fell. The first of the notes began to show up at the United States Treasury and a startled Treasury quickly repudiated the claims. On November 2, an assistant quartermaster of the United States Army, Captain Charles H. Alley, arrived in Denver and announced his grim opinion that the notes would never be honored. [29]

The value of the drafts immediately dropped 10 per cent and with it Gilpin's popularity. Businessmen who were his friends were now his enemies. "As an old army officer he was held to have known the government's rigid financial methods and it was principally because of his presumed knowledge of such matters that the people had unquestioningly accepted his irregular and illegal orders upon the national treasury." The value of the notes continued to fall, reaching a low of only forty cents on the dollar. Near panic prevailed in Denver's business community. Merchants of everything from lumber to dry goods and food found themselves holding tens of thousands of dollars of heavily discounted and possibly worthless script. Holders of the illicit drafts sent complaint after complaint to Washington. Some wrote to President Lincoln, others even made the long trek East to seek restitution. [30]

Making matters worse, William's "Pet Lambs" also turned their backs on him. When the 1st Colorado learned the truth about the Governor's drafts there was near mutiny in the ranks. For almost four months the soldiers had received no hard currency. Everything was paid for in vouchers. Some of the volunteers, who carefully saved their pay now believed their savings worthless. At Camp Weld there was talk of forming a lynch mob. Things would probably have gone badly except for the oratory skill of Major Chivington. Bringing to play all the talents he had honed during years in the pulpit, the Major appealed for calm. Speaking to the assembled troops, he reminded them why they were there. "It is not about pay," he thundered, "it is about good versus evil. It is about saving our Territory. It is about protecting our wives and children. It is about saving the United States of America from an evil aggressor." Chivington kept at it for 30 minutes. When he finally wound down there were still a few boos and some muttering among the troops, but the crisis was past. Over the next few days more than half the regiment walked away from camp and never returned. It is a tribute to Major Chivington's powers of persuasion that, even without pay, 1,200 men chose to remain in their barracks. [31]

Beleaguered on all sides, November and December of 1861, were the worst months in William Gilpin's life. The situation in Denver was angry and contentious. The "Rocky Mountain News," one of the area's two large Republican newspapers, turned on the Governor. Once a supporter, it became more and more critical of his actions and administration. Eventually the News became the rallying point for Gilpin's frustrated creditors and political enemies. Idle and unpaid, companies of volunteers, still housed in town, began to make a nuisance of themselves. They engaged in pilfering and brawls, upsetting the citizens and further souring opinion against the Governor. By early December the clamor in Washington grew so loud and the situation at home so precarious that something had to be done. Gilpin decided his only solution was to personally travel to the nation's capital, answer accusations, and try to procure payment. Appointing Lewis Weld, the Territorial Secretary, as interim governor, Gilpin headed East. It was late February before he returned.[32]

Weld evidently held very different ideas about how Colorado could best serve the Union and itself. Shortly after Gilpin's departure the two Independent Companies under captains Ford and Dodd were sent to assist Canby in New Mexico. No longer held in check these companies became the first Colorado organizations to leave the Territory for service in the war. Dodd's Company left Canyon City on December 7, 1861 and began the 110 mile trek to Fort Garland. Five days later, Ford's Company took up the line of march. By Christmas Eve both parties reached the fort and were mustered into United States service for periods of three years. Dodd's Company was immediately hurried on to Santa Fe and then on to Fort Craig. By a series of long hard marches Dodd's men covered the distance between themselves and Colonel Canby. The badly needed volunteers reached Fort Craig just in time to face down Willis Lang's lancers and then be decimated in the defense of McRae's battery. In early February Ford's Company, which had remained at Fort Garland, was also ordered to Santa Fe. Leaving the fort on February 4, the company made a strenuous twenty-eight day march to the territorial capital. Their route took them through the Sangre de Cristo mountains, where they struggled through deep snow, often pushing their wagons. The Coloradans reached Santa Fe on March 4, only to find that Canby was defeated at Valverde and that Major Donaldson was evacuating the city. The next morning the Major's 120 supply wagons rolled towards Fort Union. Ford's weary "foot volunteers" marched along as escort. [33]

While Dodd and Ford saw service with Canby, the rest of Gilpin's volunteers remained in Denver. During December Colonel Slough and Major Chivington drilled the 1st Colorado regularly and tried to hold the unit together. Moral among the troops was extremely low. Men who enlisted with a desire for action and a "thirst for fame" now believed that their sphere of action would always be confined to Denver and vicinity." This was a service they viewed as "inactive and inglorious alike." According to one soldier, "Idleness, the mother of mischief was busily sowing the seeds of ruin among them." Besides intolerable boredom the soldiers were faced with deteriorating living conditions. With the Governor's vouchers discredited almost no funds were available for the regiment's support. The quality of uniforms and clothing issued to the men deteriorated. Eventually nothing at all was issued. Rations consisted of plentiful amounts of dirty coffee, bread and beef, and little else. Desertions were commonplace, as men snuck off to join the war in the East or merely get away. Occasionally, an incorrigible drunk was drummed out of the regiment or an officer was cashiered, but in general no one seemed able or disposed to maintain much discipline among those remaining. One recruit described those days saying, "we drilled and raised merry kane." In early December, the "good people of Denver, alarmed at the growing insolence of the soldiers," "organized a police to preserve order in town." [34]

As Christmas drew near, conflicts between the soldiers and the citizenry increased sharply. Most of the volunteers were broke. What money they possessed when they enlisted was long since spent. Ovando Hollister of Company F wrote, "we had been dogs now four months without pay. No money in the company. We could not live over Christmas on bread and beef. It already stunk in our nostrils like quails in those of Israel." More to the point, Benjamin Ferris of Company F noted that there was "no prospect of a Christmas dinner unless we stole it and we did." The soldiers scoured the country stealing everything they could lay their hands on. Under cover of darkness, pigs, eggs, oysters, champagne, hams, cheese and vegetables all were "foraged." In one incident men from Company F, at great risk of detection, carried a 40 gallon barrel of vinegar to their quarters, mistaking it for whiskey. The thieves booty was not what they expected, but as vinegar was worth $1 a gallon, they still deemed their raid a success. Eventually, the idle soldiers became so bold that they started stealing in broad daylight. One volunteer, who was a good runner, grabbed a hat containing 25 eggs from a man who had just purchased them for $2.50. The thief then sprinted for the barracks chased by his hatless victim. At the door, the unfortunate pursuer was turned away as "no citizen was allowed to pass the guard." On Christmas day the city police attempted to arrest a drunken soldier. The rumpus attracted a crowd and a fist fight soon broke out between the soldiers and the citizenry. After "a little sparring was exchanged" the citizens and the police gave up. Unable to control or best them the locals left the soldiers to manage their own affair's. As Ovando Hollister remembered, for the rest of the week the city was "lawful loot." [35]

Colonel Slough and Major Chivington knew that if tensions continued to flair a genuine crisis was just around the corner. On January 1, 1862 a partial solution arrived in the form of another letter from Canby in New Mexico. The letter, which was addressed to William Gilpin, again requested, the Governor of Colorado send troops to Forts Wise and Garland. The two forts protected Canby's line of communication to the East and although he was desperate for their garrisons of regulars to join him, he could not leave the forts undefended. It was essential that New Mexico's life line to the East remain open. This meant that Wise and Garland needed to stay manned. By this time Sibley and his invasion force were concentrating around Fort Bliss and Canby's letter carried a tone of urgency. As acting governor it was Lewis Weld that opened the message. With Gilpin away in Washington, Weld, Slough, and Chivington decided to meet Canby's request and at the same time relieve the pressure in Denver. [36]

A key feature of the problems between soldiers and citizens in Denver was, that several companies of volunteers were still billeted in the city. The soldiers and the locals were constantly in each other's presence. If troops from Camp Weld were dispatched to Fort Wise it would free enough barracks space to allow the last remaining companies to be removed from Denver. The regimental officers reasoned that if the troops and the populace were physically separated conditions might improve. Fort Wise, later called Fort Lyon, was situated on the Arkansas River some 200 miles southeast of Denver. Canby's request was approved, and Lieutenant Colonel Tappan was quickly ordered to proceed with 3 companies of men and garrison the post. [37]

At the height of conflict between the soldiers and the citizenry, the Rocky Mountain News reported that the "soldiers only returned to Camp Weld for their meals, and spent the remainder of their time causing trouble in the city." Without the impending threat from Sibley's Texans there is no telling how far the clash might eventually have escalated. Fortunately Tappan's departure and the news that Texan invaders were in the Mesilla Valley had the desired effect. The 1st Colorado Regiment concentrated at Camp Weld and got down to the now pressing business of preparing to meet the Rebel threat. [38]

On February 10, with the Confederate Army of New Mexico only days away from Fort Craig, General David Hunter, at Fort Leavenworth, Kansas, sent the following wire to Lewis Weld, "Send all available forces you can possibly spare to re-enforce Colonel Canby, commanding Department of New Mexico, and to keep open his communication through Fort Wise. Act promptly and with all the discretion of your latest information as to what may be necessary and where the troops of Colorado can do most service." The wire was a godsend for Weld. Although improved, tensions around Denver were still high.[39]

Unlike Governor Gilpin, Lewis Weld did not need to be asked twice. Within days of receiving the wire from Hunter the acting governor ordered Colonel Slough to take the seven companies remaining in camp and march immediately for Santa Fe. He also contacted Lieutenant Colonel Tappan at Fort Wise and told him to consider himself under Colonel Canby's orders and to be prepared to join the regiment at a moments notice. Informing Canby that the troops were on the way, Weld wrote "You will find this regiment, I hope, a most efficient one and of great support to you. It has had, of course, no experience in the field, but I trust that their enthusiasm and patriotic bravery will make amends." [40]

When the telegrams were read to the assembled volunteers cheers rang loudly through their camp. On February 22, the day after Sibley's victorious Texans swept the field at Valverde, the 1st Regiment Colorado Volunteer Infantry tramped out of Denver. Between them and New Mexico lay hundreds of miles of sparsely populated country. [41]

On about March 1, express riders from the south reached both Fort Wise and the advancing regiment with the first reports of Canby's defeat. Initial details were sketchy and confused. Consequently it was reported that Captain Dodd's company of volunteers were all killed but two. The news galvanized the Coloradans. To the universal joy of his men Lieutenant Colonel Tappan immediately published marching orders. He ordered all baggage except a pair of blankets and a change of shorts for each man left behind. Traveling light, his three companies left Fort Wise and hurried to join the rest of the regiment. Likewise Colonel Slough's main column discarded everything except actual necessities and hastened to Canby's relief. The two groups advanced southward with as much speed as they could muster. Even though several inches of snow covered the ground, they still managed to average 40 miles per day. [42]

On March 7, amid loud cheering, the two columns united at Gray's Ranch near the headwaters of the Purgatoire River. That night their camp was alive with "the bustle and hum of a small town." To celebrate their reunion the men fell in and gave Colonel Slough "three cheers and a tiger." The Colonel's reaction disappointed his men. Excited and on the eve of an important undertaking the soldiers expected a rousing speech. Instead Slough tipped his hat and remained silent. In the six months since the regiment was organized the Colonel had never addressed his men. The volunteers thought their Colonel presented a noble appearance, but his silence undermined their confidence. Some felt that, "his aristocratic style favors more of eastern society than of the free-and-easy border to which he should have become acclimated." 43

Early the next morning, the regiment followed the Santa Fe Trail over the Raton Mountains. Their way led through a wild and picturesque gorge lying between Simpson's Rest and Fisher's Peak. Just as Isaac Adair and the other Texans had been taken by the strength and solitude of the Sandia Mountains, the Colorado Volunteers were struck by the grandeur of their surroundings. The view was magnificent. Whichever way the soldiers turned, mountains met their eyes. Away to the west the Spanish Peaks rose grand and towering, "their bald temples silvered with snowy lines, like the gray hairs of some old-time Anaks -- their crowns encircled with a wreath of storms." Off to the east the soldiers could see a spur of the Raton mountains, torn from the parent chain by a deep gorge. The spur, broken and worn by the elements and original upheavals consisted of the "boldest, bluffest and most fantastic crags imaginable." Away to the south the men imagined, rather than saw, New Mexico, "the promised land where battles were to be fought and glory achieved." 44

After the column crested the mountain and began its descent the grand scenery was lost from sight. The troops followed a rough winding road which crossed and recrossed a little brook leading them toward the Red River. About the time the mountains were turning into foothills and a plain of short yellow crisp grass was opening before them the volunteers were met by an ambulance coming from the south. The occupants of the wagon gave Colonel Slough some jumbled intelligence about Texans threatening Fort Union. Taking the information at face value Slough ordered his men to pick up their pace. With wings added to their speed the Coloradans raced forward. At about three in the afternoon the column reached the Red River. Here the weary soldiers, "camped for a short hour, made some coffee and ate some bread and raw bacon fat." By this time Colonel Slough had convinced himself that a crisis was at hand and that not a moment could be lost. Cutting short the rest stop, he determined to push on. To speed his men forward Slough ordered them to leave behind everything except their arms and two blankets each. The regiment's supply wagons were hastily unloaded and refilled with passengers. Leaving their equipment in charge of a corporal's guard, the volunteers resumed their march. Even with all the wagons filled to capacity 300 to 400 men were still left to tramp it on foot. [45]

What followed next was an amazing feat of endurance. With boisterous cheers, the troops moved out. For a while the miles they had already come were forgotten. As the men marched or road along they sang gay songs and told each other glib stories. By the wee hours of the morning these cheery sounds had died a natural death. "Nothing broke the stillness of the night but the steady tramp of men and the rattle of wagons." The volunteers covered more than 30 miles that night, stopping only briefly when their animals began to drop in their harnesses from overwork. Many of the Coloradans would later remember the march as among their finest hours. At the time they questioned its wisdom. The men were willing to put forth any exertion that might be demanded of them, but the intelligence that had sent them rushing forward was sketchy and incomplete. Many viewed the night's effort as nothing more than the caprice of their commander. Further souring the mood, Colonel Slough rode the whole way in the relative comfort of his coach. As his men huddled over fires of willow brush during their brief stop, they grumbled bitterly. One private afterwards recalled, the "curses were not loud but deep." [46]

The next morning dawned bitter and cold. The wind increased until it became a veritable hurricane driving snow and bits of ice. Scarcely rested and more like machines than men, the soldiers stumbled along. So severe was the weather that both Major Chivington's big gray horse and his saddle mule dropped dead from exhaustion. As more and more of the regiment's animals weakened the pace of the advance slowed. Fortunately by the night of March 10, the column reached the ranch of Lucien Maxwell on the Cimarron River. Here behind the stout adobe walls of the hacienda style compound, the Coloradans obtained shelter. Maxwell, who was a friend of "Kit" Carson and John C. Fremont, did what he could to make the soldiers comfortable. He distributed 100 pounds of coffee and 160 pounds of sugar to the men and accommodated several companies in his main house. Tired beyond all human endurance the remaining volunteers huddled in the courtyard and took what respite they could. Outside the compound the wind howled against its walls. [47]

On March 11, 1862, after another hard day, the 1st Regiment Colorado Volunteer Infantry finally arrived at Fort Union. Some distance from the post the troops dismounted from their wagons and formed into columns. With drums beating and colors flying, the exhausted volunteers then marched proudly into the fort and presented themselves to its commander, Colonel Gabriel R. Paul. In all the 950 men of the regiment had ridden and walked over 400 miles in thirteen days. They covered the last ninety-two miles in an incredible thirty-six hours! [48]

Chapter 8

APACHE CANYON

"The captains and lieutenants stood around like Stoughton bottles until it became every man for himself."
- John D. Miller

Colonel Canby, who was still holed up at Fort Craig, was aware of the Colorado Volunteers' arrival in his theater of operations and planned to coordinate their actions with his own. He sent orders to Colonel Gabriel René Paul commanding the garrison at Fort Union and authorized the Colonel to "harass the enemy by partisan operations; obstruct his movements, and remove or destroy any supplies that might fall into his hands." [1] When the time was right, Canby wrote, he would move from Fort Craig and effect a juncture of the two commands. Until that time, he admonished Paul not to move from Fort Union.

Colonel Slough commanding the Colorado Regiment immediately disagreed with Colonel Paul over the interpretation of the orders. Paul took them literally and argued that their combined force should continue to garrison Fort Union, holding it at all costs. Slough's assessment was more liberal. Canby said to harass the enemy and Slough could think of no better way to do it than to advance upon the Territory's capital. He reasoned that by moving down the Santa Fe Trail he could remain squarely in the Texans' path to Fort Union, but at the same time carry the fight to the enemy. Intelligence indicated the Texan occupation force in Santa Fe consisted of only one hundred men with two cannon. Slough thought that a modest advance might let him retake the capital. The

Coloradans came to New Mexico to fight and that is what he intended to do.

Colonel (General) Gabriel René Paul, 4th Regiment, New Mexico Volunteers. Courtesy Library of Congress, LC-B8184-4489

Colonel Slough's commission was senior to Colonel Paul's and he settled their argument by assuming command of their combined forces. Paul was mortified. He was an officer with years of experience. He had frequently been tried in battle. Nonetheless, he was forced to relinquish authority to an officer of only six months service and no experience. [2]

On the morning of March 22nd, despite Colonel Paul's vigorous protest, Colonel Slough sallied from

Fort Union, leaving behind a skeleton garrison of regulars and volunteers. Among the Coloradans, it was clear what was afoot. Charles Gardiner of Company A of the 1st Colorado wrote, "We left in direct opposition to the wishes of Gen. Canby, as it was his order for us to remain there until further orders from him. But Col. Slough, thinking Canby too tardy in his movements, or something else (I won't say what) put us on the march." [3] The force that tramped away under Slough's command tallied 1,342 men. [4]

As the Colorado Volunteers advanced towards Santa Fe elements of the Confederate Army of New Mexico moved along the same road. Major Pyron, after occupying Santa Fe for about two weeks, had moved toward the Sangre de Cristo Mountains and Glorieta pass. On March 25, he left the city and headed north leading a force of about 280. The command consisted of his own battalion, Major Shropshire's four recently arrived companies of the 5th Regiment, three locally recruited "spy companies," and a 2-gun section of Teel's artillery. The forage around the capital proved inadequate for a force this large so the two majors decided to proceed up the Santa Fe Trail in search of better grazing for their animals. By nightfall the column reached Apache Canyon, which seemed to fill the bill. Located at the mouth of Glorieta Pass, the canyon was a small valley of cultivated fields bisected by Apache Creek. Both water and grass were abundant and the Confederates made camp about a mile and a half from an old homestead called Johnson's Ranch. [5]

Like the Texans who had marched east from Albuquerque, Major Pyron's men soon discovered that winter still held sway in New Mexico's mountains. As Bill Davidson related, "The weather was so cold and our covering so light that we could not sleep much at night." Assigned to the camp guard, the young private vividly recalled, "pacing a weary beat for two long hours with bare feet on the cold frozen snow covered earth." [6]

"Coronado, the Spanish explorer, passed through Glorieta Pass in 1542, and gave it its name - [Bower], from the many beautiful trees of juniper, cedar, pine and cotton wood which fill the canyon." [7] In 1862 it was the only accessible pass through the mountains for many miles north and south. Unknown to Pyron's shivering Texans, only a short distance away a superior Federal force was pushing into the pass's eastern entrance.

On the night of March 25 a 418-man detachment under the command of Major John M. Chivington was nearing Pyron's position. Still convinced that Santa Fe was lightly held Slough had ordered Chivington to dash ahead, surprise the Texans, and retake the capital. [8] The Major's orders were, to proceed as far as he could that night before encamping. "He was to remain at his camp during all of the following day. When nightfall came he was to march rapidly to the capital and fall upon the small enemy garrison." [9] As Chivington hurried his men forward, "verry [sic] few knew what to expect, but all expected a fight soon." [10] What none of them suspected was that Majors Pyron and Shropshire with about 280 weary Confederates were waiting unawares at the western end of the pass.

The night was dark and still as the Federals wound through the mountainous partially settled country that separated the two forces. Sometime near midnight they reached a well-known stopping place for travelers called Kozlowski's Ranch and Major Chivington called a halt.[11]

The Union raiders were now only twenty-seven miles from the capital. While making camp and eating a cold supper from their knapsacks, they learned from the ranch's owner, Poland-born Martin Kozlowski, that enemy pickets were nearby. Major Chivington was not expecting to encounter any Texans until he reached Santa Fe. Surprised and wary, he quickly threw out his own guards. With pickets in place his camp was secure, but he needed to know the nature of the force before him. The Texan pickets were reported to be at another ranch five miles nearer to Santa Fe. At about 2 A.M. Chivington ordered 1st Lieutenant George Nelson of the Colorado Cavalry to go out and see if he could capture a Rebel or two. Nelson selected twenty of his men and road off into the dark. [12]

The place they were headed was Pigeon's Ranch. Located about one mile east of the high point of Glorieta Pass it was the largest hostelry on the Santa Fe Trail between Santa Fe and Las Vegas. The ranch belonged to a Franco-American named Alexander Vallé who acquired the nickname "Pigeon" because of his peculiar style of dancing at fandangos. [13]

At the nearby Confederate camp Major Pyron had placed Captain John Phillips' company of Santa Fe Gamblers on picket duty. Four of these men, led by 2nd Lieutenant John McIntyre were indeed at Pigeon's hostelry. McIntyre, who previously held a Union commission, was on Colonel Canby's staff at Valverde. Since the battle his loyalties had changed. [14] The four Brigands spent the night standing their watch and playing cards. A little before dawn they saddled up and headed back to join their fellows. Nelson and his men made good time to Pigeon's Ranch, but when they arrived the Texans had already flown the coop. Moving hurriedly by a circuitous route the Lieutenant contrived to get between the Rebels and their camp. Just at daybreak McIntyre and his men rode into Nelson's party. Because of obscurity of the hour and the direction from which they came, the Texans mistook the Union patrol as one of their own coming to relieve them. By the time they realized their mistake it was too late. Despite being well armed and splendidly mounted the Texans were so surprised and confused by Nelson's order to surrender that they made no resistance. The Coloradans quickly disarmed the bewildered Rebels and herded them back toward the main Federal force. [15] One of those taken prisoner was Henry Hall. Hall was a Confederate agitator in Colorado and was well known in Denver. Commenting on his capture, Ovando Hollister of Company F wrote, "Being a Northern man, I can conceive no excuse for his conduct. He never should be allowed to taint the fair soil he has disgraced by his silly and despicable treachery." As to McIntyre, who was also known to the Federals, Hollister expected that he would "probably expiate his treason on the scaffold." [16]

After interrogating the prisoners Major Chivington knew or at least guessed that a substantial enemy force lay close at hand. Discarding his original plan to lay over until dark, he decided to find the Texans and engage them in a daylight battle. By 11 a.m. on March 26, his troops were moving west. The detachment consisted of three companies of United States cavalry commanded by Captain G.W. Howland, Company F of the Colorado Cavalry commanded by Captain Samuel Cook, and 180 infantrymen from the First Colorado. The Federals marched in order of their rank with the infantry in the lead. While they slowly advanced, their scouts kept coming in, confirming the intelligence of the night before. Ovando Hollister wrote, "We thought likely we would meet a force of Texans during the day, but it's doubtful if many realized the issues involved in the meeting. If we had we would have stolen a longer and tenderer look at some of our comrades whose countenances were soon to be robed in death." [17]

Without incident the column passed Pigeon's ranch and gained the summit of Glorieta Pass. Proceeding down the trail the Union advance guard entered Apache Canyon and marched into a narrow defile studded with pinon pine, gamble oak, and juniper. Coming from the opposite direction was a party of mounted Texans. As a precaution Major Pyron had dispatched two lieutenants and thirty troopers to make a reconnaissance through the canyon. Rounding a sharp bend in the trail the Confederates rode smack into the middle of the Union advance. No less surprised and dumbfounded than their pickets, this group was also captured without a struggle. [18] Elated with their success the Coloradans in the advance rushed their prisoners back to the main body crying, "We've got them corralled this time. Give them h--l, boys. Hurrah for the Pike's Peakers." [19] Instantly, Chivington's men closed ranks. The cavalry took open order by fours, and the entire command rushed forward. "Knapsacks, canteens, overcoats and clothing of all kinds were flung along the road as the boys stripped for the encounter." [20] With hearts pounding the volunteers and regulars rounded a short bend and surged into the canyon proper. A short distance away lay Pyron's Texans.

    A little over two miles long, Apache Canyon is quite steep with high mountainous bluffs on each side. The Santa Fe Trail ran down its center often with little or no surplus room on either side. Near its east and west ends are two wider grassy flats with sufficient room for troops to maneuver. It was into the upper of these two fields that Chivington's men were pouring. Pyron's command was totally unprepared for the onslaught. As no encounter with the enemy was expected, Pyron and Shropshire had allowed their companies spread the length of the canyon in search of good camping spots. Additionally, the night before many of the lightly clothed Texans were unable to sleep because of the cold. When the early afternoon sun finally made it warm enough to rest comfortably the officers told the men to get some sleep. Trusting in their pickets the two majors were letting their boys doze in the warm afternoon sun. Chivington's appearance threw the Rebel camps into utter confusion. [21]

Pyron was accompanied by a 2-gun section of Teel's battery, but as no major encounter was expected, Lieutenants Joseph H. McGinnis and Jordan W. Bennett who regularly worked the guns had remained in Santa Fe. With Union troops forming up a scant 200 yards away the two six-pounder howitzers were in the charge of three noncommissioned officers, Peyton Hume, Adolphus Norman, and Timothy Nettles. Recently detailed to work the cannons these three soldiers had only days before been privates in Company A of the 5th Regiment. To their credit, within a matter of minutes the two howitzers were throwing shell and canister at the advancing Yankees. [22] The sound of Norman's cannon was the first warning for many of the Texans that they were under attack. Others "were rudely awakened from [their] slumbers by a volley of musketry fired into camp. In a moment every fellow was on his feet gun in hand to repel the assailants." [23]

Fearing that their artillery was about to be overrun Rebels individually and in groups put on their best speed to reach the guns. A mounted company who unfurled their battle flag and prepared to make a stand soon attended the battery. A small red banner emblazoned with the lone star of Texas, it was the first rebel flag that most of the Colorado Volunteers had ever seen. Benjamin Ferris thought, "It looked very sausy and wicked at the head of their column of men." [24] The appearance of these "lions in the path" and the thunder of their artillery, for a moment stunned the largely untried Union troops. [25] With "shells tearing and screaming overhead" all was confusion. "The regular officers in command of the cavalry plunged wildly here and there, and seemed to have no control of themselves or of their men. Everyone was talking-no one talking to any purpose." [26] John D. Miller of the Colorado Cavalry was thoroughly displeased with the way the battle opened, "No head," he wrote, "no one to go ahead and give orders. The captains and lieutenants stood around like Stoughton bottles until it became every man for himself." [27]

Major John M. Chivington, 1st Regiment, Colorado Infantry. Courtesy Colorado Historical Society, negative F-22

Spread out down the canyon, the Confederates could hear their cannon speaking "in clear ringing tones." Peyton, Norman, and Nettles worked the guns with vigor, but it soon became apparent that their cannonade was largely ineffective. The inexperienced gunners kept it up for five to ten minutes, loading and firing as quickly as they could. Although the range was close, most of their fire whistled over the Federals' heads and did no damage. Each time the shells flew over, Chivington, a "Bull Roaring" Methodist preacher, yelled to his men; "Look out boys there goes the gospel." [28] Meanwhile, he kept edging his flanks forward. Shortly men on the mountainsides were making it too hot for the gunners. "The Texans soon found their position in the road untenable." [29] Fearing for the battery, the three sergeants quickly limbered up and with flag flying beat a rapid retreat. [30]

Rushing to the sounds of battle Pyron and Shropshire were met by their artillery coming at full speed from the opposite direction. Many who were out of sight of the fighting feared their guns lost. These "heaved a sigh of relief" as the battery thundered into view. [31] By this time the Texans had fallen back about 800 yards. The lower or western part of Apache canyon was more readily defended so the two majors decided to make another stand. Pyron and Shropshire began "rapidly moving back and forth, calm, cool and deliberately restoring order and forming [their men] in a line to meet the foe." [32] The companies, in picking their camping spots were considerably scattered and although the two majors succeeded in establishing a line, it was some time before they gathered their force sufficiently for concerted action.

Pyron and Shropshire hurriedly formed their men at a point where the canyon made an abrupt bend to their left. A rocky bluff like the bastion of a fort commanded the bend and a company of men climbed to its top. Other troops were positioned to completely cover the steep canyon sides. The center of the Rebel line was protected by another natural defense, a deep ditch. The water worn gulch that snaked its way down the canyon floor was spanned at this point by a rough timber bridge. Once across the Texans destroyed the bridge leaving their pursuers to face a gully perhaps 5 feet deep and 10 feet wide. The Rebel battery unlimbered on a smaller mound at the bluff's base. The road was narrow and crooked and the ground altogether unfavorable to cavalry. With their howitzers positioned, where it was impossible for the enemy to approach in column except directly into the guns, the Confederates nervously awaited Chivington's arrival. [33]

It was a fleeting wait. The mountainous "six-feet-four-and-one-half two-hundred-and-sixty-pound" Methodist preacher was hot on the Texans' heels. [34] Approaching the second Rebel line Chivington again concentrated his men on the canyon's sides. This time he dismounted all his regular cavalry and ordered them to assist in clearing the hills. The Texans were strongly situated, but Chivington had them outnumbered. By extending his own line as far as possible and concentrating on the Rebels' flanks he knew Pyron's position could be forced.

While the infantry and dismounted troops tried to drive in the Texan flanks, Cook's Colorado Cavalry waited in reserve. Chivington instructed Cook that the moment the Texans gave way before the fire of the Union infantry, he was to charge. [35]

It was now 3:30 in the afternoon and for the next hour the two commands struggled for position. The Confederate artillery managed to hold the Federals at bay in the center. As one Texan remembered, "Norman, Hume, and Nettles were beginning to preach to them in true war-like style from our six-pounders." [36] With no cannon of his own Chivington ignored the center and pushed the flanks. Given the circumstances and the terrain the double envelopment strategy worked to the Union advantage. The battle seesawed as the skirmishers fought to control the canyon's sides. On the Confederates' extreme right companies from the 5th Texas began to push forward. At almost the same time Union troops broke through on the left. Pyron straightaway realized that he was flanked. He shouted for his men to shift their front to the left and ordered a hasty withdrawal.

Major Chivington saw the preparations for retreat and immediately shouted for Cook's cavalry. The Coloradans double quicked to their horses, mounted, and were at once ordered forward. The commands rang out, "draw pistols, trot, gallop, charge!" As the cavalry surged forward the report of a rifle was heard. One of the riders "threw up his hands, high above his head, and fell backwards from his horse" crying; "Oh boys, don't leave me!" [37] The shot almost seemed a signal because immediately puffs of smoke sprang from behind every rock. As the cavalry closed, shorter ranged Texan muskets came into play. Ovando Hollister remembered, "The old United States musket cartridges, containing an ounce ball and three buck'shot, began to zip by our heads so sharply, that many, unused to this kind of business, took them for shells." [38] At the head of the column, Captain Cook was struck in the thigh by the "buck and ball", but managed to stay in the saddle. About 200 yards further on; his horse stumbled and fell on him, badly spraining his ankle.

As Cook limped to the side, the charge "swept down the canyon like a hurricane." [39] With Lieutenant Nelson now in command, Company F let out a hair-raising yell and jumped the ditch. All of the 103 horses, except one, managed to leap the obstruction. [40] Pyron's men who thought themselves safe were stunned. One Texan later wrote to his wife; "they were regular demons, that iron and lead had no effect upon." "At full charge, with swords and revolvers drawn," the "Pike's Peakers" looked "like so many flying devils." [41] Discharging their revolvers, the Colorado Cavalry dashed around the bend in the canyon, broke through the Texan center and trampled down the Rebel reserve. Amid the dust and smoke the men of Cook's Company busily emptied their pistols at the fleeing foe. Despite the cavalry's success, Pyron's artillery was too fleet-footed for the Coloradans and escaped down the canyon. The Texans stationed in the road, however, were scattered and confused. When other Federals came down from the hills "like a parcel of wild Indians, cheering at the top of their lungs," some of the Confederates simply dropped their weapons and surrendered. Others "made for cover and stood like a tiger at bay." 42

"Captain Cook's Charge" or "Battle of Apache Canyon," by Willard H. Andrews, oil, 36 1/4 x 56, 1972-73. Courtesy Museum of New Mexico, Neg. 152188

Company A of the 5th Texas never received Pyron's order to withdraw. When the other companies moved off they stood their ground. Now, with Union troops moving upon them from above and below they found themselves encircled. Completely cut off from the rest of the command and surrounded, their plight caught the eye of Major Shropshire. Before his promotion Shropshire was the captain of Company A. These were his boys and he was devoted to them. Private Bill Davidson remembered his Captain, sitting at the campfire "his mild dark-blue eyes beaming in love" at his men. On March 26, 1862 it was not love, but "the fierce light of battle" that gleamed in Shropshire's eyes. Like an "avalanche," the Major spurred his horse forward and burst through the Union lines to his beleaguered men. "The storm cloud of war rested dark and deep upon his brow." Standing amid a shower of death-dealing missiles, Shropshire rallied the company, shouting, "Boys, follow me!" Someone said, "We are out of cartridges." The Major coolly replied, "Then take out your knives and follow me." [43]

Shropshire, at his own expense, had ordered made for each of his men a knife, "the blade about eighteen-inches long, a guard over the handle and made very heavy." According to Bill Davidson, "It was a terrible weapon as it was easy to cut a man in two with every blow." With the Major at their head, Company A hurled themselves at the encircling Union troops. The Texans fought ferociously and managed to break the Federal line. In so doing, the company lost twenty-seven men wounded, killed or captured. Those who made it through believed they owed their escape completely to Shropshire. Not only did the Major lead them, but also mounted on his horse and wearing a conspicuous white hat he personally drew much of the enemy's fire. Bill Davidson afterwards wrote, "Shropshire was a noble man, but on that day and at that particular time, he was grand, mighty and magnificent." [44]

"It was a terrible weapon as it was easy to cut a man in two with every blow." Unidentified Texas soldier. Courtesy Lawrence T. Jones, III collection, Austin, TX

In another pocket Captain Denman Shannon and his company were surrounded on three sides. Shannon also broke out of his trap, but likewise lost a good many of his men along the way. It was only "by dent of hard fighting and good running" that the remainder managed to escape. [45] Individually and in groups other Confederates were not so lucky. Two Colorado Volunteers, Boon and Dixon, captured fifteen Texans hiding in a house near the road. Even though the Texans outnumbered their captors they surrendered as soon as discovered. While the prisoners were being disarmed, "Somebody cried out,

'Shoot the s--s of b-----s.' 'No!'," yelled Boon, "'I'm d----d if you do! I'm d----d if you do! You didn't take 'em. I took these prisoners myself, prisoners of wah [sic]. Fall in thar, prisoners! Forward, double quick.'" With that, Boon and Dixon marched the Texans off to the rear. [46]

Private D.L. "Doc" Walker of the 5th Texas squeezed through the Union lines, but was again cut off. Trying to get away he ran into a cedar thicket on the side of the mountain. There, he saw a large rock and under it a big hole. Immediately the twenty-nine-year-old private dove inside. Walker might have escaped detection except that his friend, Sergeant Lovard Tooke, spotted him. "Love", who was also looking for a hiding place, scrambled in behind Walker. Unfortunately, the sergeant was too long and passing Union soldiers spied a foot or two of his legs hanging out. Unaware that Doc was in the hole they grabbed onto Sergeant Tooke and commenced to pull. Tooke grabbed onto his friend and for a moment a tug-o-war ensued. "After several long hard pulls Walker cried out, 'Hold like hell, Love; I've a good lock around this rock and they'll have to pull down the side of this mountain to get us." [47] The surprised Federals, realizing that they were dealing with two gophers instead of one, ordered the Texans to stop their nonsense and come out. Walker and Tooke both surrendered and were promptly marched away.

Other incidents were uglier. Captain Samuel Logan of the 1st Colorado found a Rebel lying behind a rock. Logan, who was already wounded in the face, leveled his revolver at the man. The Confederate called out that he was wounded and wished to surrender whereupon Logan lowered his gun and advanced to disarm him. As the Captain approached the man coolly drew up his pistol and fired. "The ball, which was meant for a center shot, passed through Logan's arm. 'O, you son of a b---h,' exclaimed Logan, 'I'll kill you now, G-d d--n you,' and suiting the action to the word, put a bullet through his head." [48]

As the Texans fell rapidly back the widespread fighting turned into long range skirmishing. With the sun setting and the canyon falling into darkness the firing gradually ceased at every point of the field. Major Chivington, victorious, ordered a recall and assembled his men in the road. The minister turned soldier had won his first battle. In so doing he handed Sibley's Army the first defeat of its campaign. Although the number of men on each side was relatively small and the engagement was only two or three hours long, the fighting was furious while it lasted. [49]

Casualties among the Colorado Volunteers and Union regulars were: five killed, fourteen wounded, and three missing. [50] With daylight quickly fading the Federals decided to retire from the field. They were wildly successful, but Major Chivington was not prepared to pursue Pyron in the dark. He was concerned about Texan re-enforcements and he was also wary of the Rebel artillery. The cannon were mostly ineffective during the fight, but Chivington had none of his own should the situation change. Since there was no water in the canyon the Major left Captain Charles J. Walker's regular cavalry as a rear guard, and collecting his dead and wounded, fell back to Pigeon's Ranch. Walker and his company remained in the road until about 9:30 o'clock that night and then retired to join Chivington. [51]

Pyron's unprepared Texans were badly mauled. His report of the engagement has been lost so the exact numbers of Confederate casualties are unknown. Major Chivington reported the Rebel losses as thirty-two killed, forty-three wounded, and seventy-one taken prisoners. These numbers are probably inflated. Texan Abe Hanna recorded the losses in his diary as four killed and six wounded and Alfred

Peticolas wrote in his journal that only two were killed and three wounded. [52] About those captured there is little doubt. The Texans made a good fight, but as Cook's cavalry rode them down, "they finally collapsed and gave it up and surrendered in a bunch." One of Cook's men wrote, "We were obliged to make prisoners of some forty or fifty - all there were in the road; for when they found us in their midst, as if descended from the clouds, they forgot that one of them was equal to five of us and insisted on surrendering." [53] Benjamin Ferris remembered that as the Texans were marched away, "The ground was strewed with all kinds of soldiers fixtures, including many guns of all patterns." [54] Having lost almost one third of his effective force, Pyron fell back to Johnson's Ranch at Canōncito and grimly awaited reinforcements.

Chapter 9

THE ROAD TO GLORIETA

"The character of the country was such as to make the engagement of the bushwhacking kind."
- Colonel John P. Slough

When Pyron and Chivington each fired off messages describing the action in Apache Canyon and requesting prompt reinforcement the skirmish primed the pump for the second major battle of the Texan invasion. Pyron's express went straight to Colonel Scurry encamped at Galisteo. Chivington's went to Colonel Slough waiting at Bernal Springs. Only hours after the echoes of the fight quit ringing through the canyon, both commands were on the march.

Informed of "the critical condition of Major Pyron and his gallant comrades," Scurry and his men took only ten minutes to form their column. [1] "In an hour," wrote Alfred Peticolas, "we were all under way." [2] The shortest distance between Galisteo and Apache Canyon was along a rough road, straight through the mountains. The trail was suitable for men and horses, but not for the Texans' ponderous supply wagons. With time of the essence Scurry decided to divest himself of his baggage train. The slow moving wagons were ordered to take a longer but less strenuous road and approach Pyron's position from a point six miles to the rear. The duty of guarding the train again fell to the 7th Regiment. This time, however, only Lieutenant John W. Taylor and one hundred men from Company I were assigned to the task. [3] For the rest of the 7th the onerous work of shepherding the wagons was over. With a fight expected before morning it looked like Isaac Adair and his boys from Crockett would finally see some action.

It was about 8 o'clock and already dark when the Texans set out at a brisk gait. For the first six miles they made good time, but as the night became oppressively cold their pace slackened. Isaac Adair and the rest of Major Jordan's command had spent a long day in the saddle and the 4th Regiment was footsore from days of marching. All the men were weary, but none of them murmured about their suffering or growled at the discomfort. Instead, "every man marched bravely along and did not complain at the length of the road, the coldness of the weather, or the necessity that compelled the march." 4

As the Confederates neared Apache Canyon their road led them through a high mountain pass. Here they slowed to a crawl. The men were tired, but their draft animals were exhausted and the grade proved too steep. The wearied horses simply could not drag their artillery and ammunition wagons to the top. Rather than turn around or leave the cannons behind, the Texans fastened long ropes to the heavy pieces and set about the task by hand. One or two hours later, Scurry's soldiers succeeded in getting both the artillery and the wagons up the grade. The Colonel later reported to General Sibley that just as they marched without complaint, "the men cheerfully pulled [the cannon] over the difficulties of the way." 5 Another soldier wrote, "Patriotic and heroic men, they would sacrifice every comfort to gratify the wants of their suffering comrades, and to attain success for the cause." 6 Describing the motivation that led Scurry's command on foot at night through snow, winds, and sleet, the soldier continued, "These men were not mercenary hirelings, but were men of fortune, and went into the war with justice and right as their shield. Rocked in their infancy in the cradle of liberty and smiled upon by freedom, these men were fighting for civil and political liberty as their reward." 7

Pyron's and Shropshire's Texans had hightailed it from the battlefield, but the two majors rallied their men at Johnson's Ranch. Everyone knew that Scurry was only twelve to fifteen miles away, but they did not expect to be reinforced until morning. What they did expect was another Federal assault. Throughout the long night they remained in line, under arms, waiting to be set upon by the enemy. In later years, one old soldier quipped; "I almost believe that evening made my hair turn gray, at least, it was very black up to that evening, its pretty gray now. Three hundred men fighting three thousand; it was terrible." [8] Pyron's command was so completely routed that even twenty years later many of the men still believed they had faced Canby's entire army!

About 3 o'clock in the morning, as the men lay wearily on their arms watching for the next attack, a faint sound began to grow in the distance. Young Bill Davidson wrote, "Placing our ears to the ground we could hear it more distinctly still, it was the tramp, tramp, tramp of soldiers on the march, not the regular step but the 'rout step,' not the clear ringing of men well shod striking the cold frozen earth, but some hard clear ringing, others soft, showing sandals or barefeet." [9] Instantly, the men were on their feet, cheering at the top of their lungs. The canyon rang with their shouts and in response they heard the cheers of the 4th and the 7th. Within minutes the head of Scurry's column arrived. What a round of hand shaking and back slapping ensued. Private Davidson thought the reinforcements were "the finest looking men I ever saw in my life." [10]

Colonel Scurry ordered his soldiers to gather what wood they could find and build fires. Since their supply train was still miles away, none of the men had blankets. A few attempted to sleep, but most just huddled around their fires trying to warm chilled hands and feet. Sergeant Peticolas and his friend B.A.

Jones got into one of the old ranch houses. The building was deserted, but they deemed it better than being outside. Taking what comfort they could, the two troopers curled up on the bare floor with a few articles of discarded clothing as bedding. Many were simply too excited to sleep. It had been several weeks since the men of the two commands had seen each other and the men needed to talk. Everyone who was in the fight wanted to tell his story. "Did we go to sleep?" wrote one private, "not a bit of it; we had to talk with the 4th and the 7th and tell them how we had 'set to' the 'Yanks' and how we would have 'whaled' them if the 4th and 7th had only been with us." The story telling and speculating continued well into the dawn. Listening to the chatter, Bill Davidson was reminded of giddy schoolgirls who "if one girl does not see another in two days she will talk to her all night." [11]

The arrival of the reinforcements lifted a huge burden from Pyron's men. "Did we still fear an attack?" recalled a soldier, "not a bit of it." [12] The audacity of Chivington's assault had come as a shock. After the drubbing they served up at Valverde the Texans had not expected the Federals to take the offensive. Before the attack on Pyron, most of them thought the "Abs" unlikely to tangle with a force of that size. Now, with eighteen companies gathered at Canōncito, they again felt secure. Surely, the Yankees were not impudent enough to attack their brigade when so much of it was concentrated in one place. The soldiers wagered that the enemy might whip around and put the rifle to "Gotch" Hardeman's two companies occupying Albuquerque or jump Alf Thurmond and his lone company, still holding Cubrero. They might even lay into Colonel Green and his five companies en route to Santa Fe. What everyone believed Federals would not do was fight again at Apache Canyon. A soldier from the 5th

Regiment later wrote, "We had a good deal to learn yet about what these fellows would do." [13]

Soon after his arrival at Johnson's Ranch, William Read Scurry assumed command of the combined Confederate force. His position was ironic. Disgusted with the inactivity after Valverde, he tried, unsuccessfully, to resign his commission and go home. Now, with General Sibley and Colonel Green far away, Scurry was the Rebels' ranking officer on the field. Known by the sobriquet, "Dirty Shirt," the Colonel was a prominent lawyer and politician before the war. A tireless orator, he frequently rode through small towns, one after another, campaigning for secession. Delivering stormy speeches to the crowds he attracted, he earned his nickname because his clothes were so often road-stained. Born in Gallatin, Tennessee in 1821 the forty-one-year-old Scurry had lived in Texas since 1840. He practiced law in a number of places and served as a member of the House of Representatives of the Republic. At the outbreak of the Mexican War in 1846, he enlisted as a private in Captain Otis M. Wheeler's company in San Augustine. It was immediately obvious that his talents were being wasted. Within a month he was promoted to Major. At that rank, he served with distinction, taking part in the battle of Monterrey. After the war Scurry returned to the law and settled in Clinton, Texas. There he married Janette B. Sutton, with whom he had five children. Later, he was chosen as a delegate to the Secession Convention representing Victoria, DeWitt, Jackson, and Calhoun counties. At the convention, he cast his vote in favor of Texas leaving the Union. A staunch supporter of Southern rights, a battle-hardened veteran, and a natural leader, William Read Scurry was exactly the sort of man General Sibley wanted for his field commanders. On August 23rd, 1861, Sibley appointed him lieutenant colonel of the 4th regiment. At Valverde

Scurry had proved the choice a good one and was promoted to colonel for "gallant and meritorious conduct." Shortly, he would have the opportunity to prove it again. [15]

Lieutenant Colonel (General) William Read Scurry, 4th Regiment, Texas Mounted Volunteers, Courtesy Library of Congress, LC-B8171-8841

As soon as it was daylight on the 27th, the Colonel made a thorough examination of the area. He was pleased to discover that the ground that he had occupied in the dark, was surprisingly good. About

400 yards from Johnson's Ranch the Santa Fe Trail and Galisteo creek turned abruptly and emerged from Apache Canyon. Here at the narrow exit, Scurry formed his troops. "The mountains were so tall on either side that there was chance of attack only to come right down the canion. [sic]" [15] There was a bank at the bend in the road and the Texans set to work raising its elevation. During the Mexican War, New Mexico's governor had fortified the same spot in anticipation of or feigned resistance to the westward advance of General Stephen W. Kearny. The position was naturally strong, but Scurry's men further strengthened the bend to their advantage. By 8 A.M. everything was in readiness. The infantry were secure behind earthworks, and artillery was planted on a small hill where it commanded the gap. The Texans settled down to await the anticipated attack. The wait was to be a long one. [16]

Major Chivington's command was no longer close at hand. After routing Pyron, the Federal troops reassembled at Pigeon's Ranch, but water there proved a problem. Rather than renew the offensive, Major Chivington decided to return to the more accessible water at Kozlowski's Ranch. While Scurry and his men were digging in, most of the Federals were pulling out. Leaving his wounded at Pigeon's, Chivington fell back to regroup and anticipate the arrival of Colonel Slough. [17]

Unaware of their enemy's move, the Texans remained in line of battle throughout the day. Around noon, Scurry's wagon train arrived and was greeted enthusiastically by the men of the 4th and 7th Regiments. The soldiers were exhausted from their previous night's exertions and had been without food and blankets since they left Galisteo. Remembering their unfinished meal of mutton, some of the men began unloading the wagons with the hope that the meat was brought along. No mutton was found, so the soldiers had to be contented with their regular bill of fare: "bread made of flour and cold water." Just the same, refreshments were cooked and the spirits of the men rose considerably. [18] About 3 in the afternoon Company C of the 4th Regiment buried one of its own. Private Theodor Schultz had been ill for five days with pneumonia and died during the forced march the night before. As the men lay him in the ground Sergeant Peticolas wrote in his journal, "Poor boy, a stranger in a strange land, he sleeps the sleep that knows no waking." [19] Little did the onlookers realize that many more would join their friend in his final slumber before the next day was through.

The long cold night passed and the Texans continued to wait. Still, the enemy did not make their appearance. On the morning of March 28th, Colonel Scurry's forbearance came to an end. He could wait no longer. If the Yankees would not bring the battle to him, he would take it to them. [20] Eighteen-year-old Harvey Holcomb, a private in Company F of the 4th Regiment, remembered that "after eating our breakfast we were told to put what we had left in our haversacks, that we would not be back to camp til night, and in a few minutes we were on the march." [21] Believing that his supply train was secure at Johnson's Ranch, Colonel Scurry posted "a small wagon guard" and headed up the canyon toward Pigeon's Ranch with the rest of his command. [22] No record remains of the exact size of the wagon guard or who commanded it, but it is likely that it consisted of men detailed from one or more companies of the 7th. Because Lieutenant John W. Taylor of Company I was in charge of the train on its move from Galisteo, it is possible that he was left in command of the wagon park at Johnson's Ranch. For added security a six-pounder field howitzer, under the command of Sergeant Timothy Nettles, was also left behind to guard the wagons. Although not an artilleryman,

Nettles had demonstrated two days before that he could work the piece with vigor. Besides the guard detail and Nettles' crew, the contingent left at Johnson's Ranch included Scurry's noncombatants: the sick, the wounded, cooks, drivers, and etc. In all nearly 200 men remained at Johnson's Ranch. [23]

Scurry led out with his mounted troops from the 5th and 7th Regiments. Probably for the first time since the start of the campaign Isaac Adair and other soldiers of the 7th found themselves at the head of Sibley's army. Since Major Jordan followed behind with the main body Gustav Hoffman of Company B, the regiment's senior Captain was in command of the battalion's cavalry. [24]

Three days later General Sibley reported that Colonel Scurry marched down the Santa Fe Trail with 1,000 men under his command. The force consisted of portions of at least twenty-three companies, representing nearly all the elements of the Army of New Mexico. The bulk of the command came from the 4th, 5th, and 7th regiments, strengthened by Major Pyron's battalion. In addition to these regular units there were also portions of three independent companies: Captain Phillips's Brigands, the Arizona Rangers and the San Elizario Spy Company. The column was supported by three pieces of artillery and their crews lead by Lieutenant James Bradford of Teel's command. [25]

The number of companies present is deceptive as most were significantly reduced from details and other causes. Although Sibley wrote that Scurry led 1,000 men, the Colonel himself reported that when the units were "(all combined) they did not number over 600 men fit for duty." Scurry's official report of the action does not mention Pyron's command. Assuming that these companies and the 3 companies of "irregulars" included about 100 effectives and that Scurry's total of 600 is otherwise correct, then on the morning of March 28th the Confederates were advancing with a battle ready force of about 700. Scurry's tally almost certainly omits the men left behind to guard his train. Of these, some later joined the action, further swelling the number of Rebel soldiers on the field. The remaining men needed to come near Sibley's total of 1,000 were most likely the sick, the wounded, cooks, drivers, and the other noncombatants, who remained at Johnson's ranch. 26

Morale among the Texans was good and their blood was up. While they broke camp a rumor had circulated that Colonel Green was riding to their aid. According to the grapevine Green received an express explaining the situation and had promised to be on the field by noon. Many of the men believed that his five companies were rushing to join them. The gossip was false. Green was not on his way, but unbeknownst to the Confederates, their enemy was. 27

When news of the fight in Apache Canyon reached Colonel Slough he was still encamped at Bernal Springs. Like Scurry, he reacted quickly and made all possible haste to join his advance. After a forced march in the dark the main body of Union troops eventually reached Kozlowski's ranch. They reunited with Major Chivington's command at about 2 o'clock in the morning on the 28th. Ovando Hollister remembered the reserves arrival. The men with Colonel Slough had heard of the engagement in Apache Canyon and were anxious to have their own chance for glory. In Hollister's words, they "could not be restrained." 28 At about 8 o'clock in the morning the entire Union command, with Captain Charles J. Walker's Company E of the 3rd Cavalry in advance, began to move toward Pigeon's Ranch. Colonel Slough's force numbered about 1,300 strong and was accompanied by two batteries of Federal artillery. Bringing up the rear was a baggage train of nearly 100 wagons. 29

Two miles beyond Kozlowski's Colonel Slough did something risky. Having determined to move against the Texans in two columns, he split his command. Slough knew that Pyron was strongly reinforced and he estimated the Texan strength now lay between 1,200 and 1,400. Nevertheless, in the face of an enemy whose numbers he believed equal to or greater than his own, the Colonel divided his force. Major Chivington was given command of seven companies of infantry numbering about 480 effectives and ordered to strike out for the heights above Apache Canyon. With his main body now numbering around 990 the Union commander continued his movement toward Pigeon's Ranch. About mid-morning Slough dispatched Lieutenant John Falvey of the 3rd U.S. Cavalry with another forty mounted men on a scout toward Galisteo. He was thinking of Sibley and Green and was afraid the Texans might attempt a flanking movement of their own. [30]

Slough planned to surprise the Rebels, who he believed were still encamped at Johnson's Ranch. He would lead a frontal assault and the same time Chivington would fall upon them from the rear. Trapped in the middle, the Confederates would be overwhelmed. Because of Slough's strategy and the Texans' advance, Chivington's command was actually marching away from the coming battle. The two forces about to collide at Glorieta Pass were now almost evenly matched.

Walker's Union cavalry was first to arrive at Pigeon's Ranch. According to the Captain, he halted at the hostelry for about an hour-and-a-half and waited as the rest of the Federal troops arrived. By around 10:30 A.M. all of Slough's command caught up. While most of the men rested, the Colonel directed Captain Gurden Chapin, 7th Infantry, adjutant general, to proceed forward with Captain Walker and Howland's cavalry to reconnoiter the position of the enemy. By this time, the Texans were closing on the ranch and Scurry's advance guard knew the enemy were near in force. Chapin advanced no more than 300 yards before his pickets collided with Scurry's. [31]

Colonel Scurry posted John Phillips "Brigands" to the picket so they were the first contingent of the Army of New Mexico to encounter Slough's "Pike's Peakers." As soon as they met, one of Howland's troopers called out, "Get out of our way you damned sons of b--s, we are going to take dinner in Santa Fe." Equally cocky, Private William D. Kirk of the Brigands hallowed back to them, "You'll take dinner in hell." [32] Sergeant Peticolas heard "the sharp report of a gun and the sharper whistle of a minnie ball," and as Private Bill Davidson put it, "the jig opened." [33]

The Texans were taken somewhat by surprise. One soldier remembered, "We did some of the fastest forming of our lives." [34] The Rebels' mounted troops, including Isaac Adair's company, were "ordered to retire slowly to the rear, dismount, and come into action on foot." [35] At Colonel Scurry's command, Captain Gustav Hoffman, who led the mounted men, "ordered a wheel-aside, dismount and form a skirmish line." [36] As the cavalry moved back Scurry pushed his three pieces of artillery forward. Lieutenant Bradford positioned his guns on a slight elevation in the middle of the trail and the Texan infantry scrambled to deploy. The Confederates formed a line of battle extending from a fence on their left across their cannons and up into the pine forest on their right. By the time Walker's Federal Cavalry pushed past their own pickets, they found Bradford's cannons in the road, ready to receive them. Bradford immediately opened fire. [37]

The suddenness of the encounter was a surprise to the Texans, but it was a severe shock to the Federals. Slough had expected the Rebels to contest every inch of the way to Santa Fe, but he knew nothing of their disposition or intentions. The Union commander had assumed that Pyron and his reinforcements would hold their position in Apache Canyon. At Pigeon's Ranch, the Coloradans and Regulars "were resting - some visiting the wounded in the hospital, others filling their water canteens." [38] Suddenly, their pickets came hurrying in and reported that the Texans were less than half a mile distant and advancing in force. Alexander Vallé described the scene saying, "Gooverment mahns vas at my ranch and fill 'is chnteen viz my viskey (and Gooverment nevaire pay me for zat viskey!); and Texas mahns coom oop, and soorprise zem." [39] Amid a blaring of bugles, Slough hastened his men forward. Before they advanced 500 yards, Bradford's Confederate artillery was cutting the treetops over their heads. Colonel Slough was reacting quickly, but already he had lost the initiative in the battle. The Coloradans would never regain it. Slough planned to drive the Confederates through the canyon into Major Chivington's waiting arms, but as one of his troopers put it, he was about to learn that the Texans "wouldn't drive worth a cent." [40]

Walker's Union cavalry remained in the road just long enough to be sure of the position of Bradford's guns. The Captain then ordered his men into the timber on his left, where they dismounted and began to skirmish on foot. About this same time Captain John F. Ritter's light battery came charging down the trail, accompanied by its infantry support. Ritter quickly unlimbered his four cannon in the road and engaged Bradford's three pieces. Within moments, he was joined by Ira Claflin's battery of four 12-pounder mountain howitzers. Claflin took position on a slight elevation in the trees to Ritter's left and also opened fire with great spirit. [41]

As more and more Federal troops reached the battle, Colonel Slough adopted the same tactics that

Chivington used successfully two days before. Issuing orders in a hoarse voice, he threw part of his force out onto the wings, and attempted to flank the Texans with a pincer movement. Lieutenant Colonel Samuel F. Tappan, who was in immediate command of the first Union battalion to reach the field, deployed according to Slough's orders. One company of Colorado Volunteers was sent to the far left and another to the far right. Others were left straddling the road or positioned left of center where they could support their artillery. The remaining Union cavalry and infantry initially served as wagon train guards and reserves and were positioned nearly a mile to the rear of the first action. 42

The Texan artillery continued to play on the Federals while they deployed. Rebel infantry also began to fire at intervals with their rifled muskets, but their firing was limited by lack of targets. The canyon in this area ran through densely wooded pine country, which much of the time effectively hid the two forces from one another. Sergeant Peticolas complained, "You cannot see a man 20 steps unless he is moving." 43 The brush and timber, however, did not seem an impediment to Colonel Scurry. Standing on the rise next to his cannons, "Scurry pointed to the gunners and told them where to shoot." Corporal Sharp Whitley of the 7th Texas who watched his colonel direct the cannonade wrote, "We couldn't see anything in the world to shoot at, but Scurry must have seen them." 44 Moving toward the Confederate left, Company I of the 1st Colorado Volunteers passed an opening commanded by Bradford's guns. Immediately, the Lieutenant concentrated his fire in that direction with killing effect. Fully exposed, the company composed mostly of German speaking recruits from Denver City suffered severely before they regained the timber. By this time it was obvious to Colonel Scurry that Slough's forces were rapidly advancing in separate columns against both his right and his left. [45]

Acting quickly, Scurry dispatched Major Pyron to the Texan right to check the enemy in that direction. Placing the center in command of Major Henry Raguet, he then hastened with the remainder of his command to the left. Initially well organized, the Confederates were soon scattered. Corporal Whitley remembered; "This is the way the thing started, but the country was so rough, the timber (pine and cedar) so thick, that companies and men all got mixed up." [46]

Nearly a mile to the rear with the Federal reserves, Ovando Hollister could not see the Texans, but he could hear "the deafening roar of artillery, the unceasing rattle of small arms accompanied by all kinds of cheering and yelling from the men." [47]

Jacob Downing and Company D of the 1st Colorado Volunteers may have been the first Federal unit to try and force the Confederate line. Advancing in two columns from the Union left, the company failed to flank the Texans as Colonel Slough intended. Instead Major Pyron's men forced Downing's columns toward the center. Here they came upon the rightmost piece of Bradford's artillery and fell into a trap. Colonel Scurry watched Downing's troopers approach and gave some of his men a curious order. As one soldier recalled, "We were instructed to run like we were scared to death when the cannon fired, as soon as the enemy returned the fire." [48] Bradford's cannon barked and Downing's men tore loose with a volley in response. Just as Scurry had ordered his men leapt to their feet and ran for the rear. The Federals saw the artillery's infantry support fleeing and surged forward. With no one but Scurry and the cannoneers left to defend the piece, Bradford's gun seemed an easy prize. "They came in about twenty steps of the cannon, when a lot of men that Scurry had concealed, and lying down, rose up and began peppering them." [49]

Eighteen-year-old Private Harvey Holcomb remembered that as they leapt up the concealed men gave a "Texas yell" and loosed a volley of rifle fire. [50] By this time the cannoneers reloaded and began firing canister at the stunned Federals. Taken totally by surprise, Downing's company reeled backward and "began getting away from there as fast as their legs could take them." Remembering the ruse, a Texan later mused, "This is the first and only time in the annals of history that anybody ever tricked a Yankee." [51] Seeing the Union troops stagger, Major Pyron's command fiercely counter attacked and began pressing Downing's company back up the flank.

About this same time Major Shropshire realized that the Federals across the canyon were also trying to turn the Texan line. Unwilling to assume that his fellow officers were aware of the threat, he dispatched Private Bill Davidson to warn Major Pyron. With Downing in retreat, Pyron decided the message was important enough that he would personally carry it to Scurry. Wheeling his horse to the left the Major set off down the Texan line at a gallop. As the he passed in front of the battalion of the 7th, he was forced cross a space of open ground. He was riding at full speed when suddenly, "a cannon ball from the enemy cut his horse's head off," and animal and rider crashed to the ground. Neither hurt nor fazed by his narrow escape, Pyron coolly drew his pistols from their saddle holsters and ran off to complete his mission. [52]

Upon receiving the major's report, Colonel Scurry turned to the nearby "Victoria Invincibles", Company C of the 4th Texas. Quickly he ordered "Rube Purcell, Abe Hanna, Jake Henson, [Alexander] Montgomery, Love Bartlett and Tom Fields to the extreme left on the mountain to watch the enemy and report their movements to him." [53] Moving out under the command of Corporal Bartlett the little party soon reached the end of the Texan line. Almost at once they were engaged in a sharp skirmish. Both sides advanced steadily moving from tree to tree, shooting whenever the enemy showed themselves. Having closed to within thirty yards, Abe Hanna was shot through the loins. Jake Henson saw Hanna go down and rushed to his friend's aid. He gave Abe some water and was beginning to pick stones from under him, when kneeling at his friend's side; he too was shot and killed. Henson was struck in the shoulder with the ball ranging towards his heart. He died instantly. Eighteen-year-old Hanna lingered until nightfall. Mercifully, his wound left him without feeling from the hips down. When the end came the young private died easily and without pain. Alexander Montgomery was also killed in the sharp action and Corporal Bartlett was wounded. Despite their terrible losses, the little party accomplished its mission. The Union flankers finding the Texan extreme left fiercely defended, fell back. [54]

  The battle had now raged for nearly an hour and reserves on both sides were anxious to get into action. Near the Union supply train the soldiers could still hear the Texan artillery "playing a lively tune." As the men listened "the thunder reverberated from mountain to mountain." All eleven cannon on the field were firing furiously and Ovando Hollister noted, "We could scarcely tell our guns from theirs - both about equidistant." [55] Private Benjamin Ferris, also waiting in reserve, watched with a mixture of fascination and shock as "some of the wounded being taken to the rear passed in plain sight." [56]

  On the Confederate side Isaac Adair and Gustav Hoffman were hurrying their now dismounted companies toward the front. After Colonel Scurry's order to fight on foot Companies B and H were detailed to return to Johnson's Ranch with all the mounts. When they arrived at Canōncito they left the horses in the hands of the wagon guard and promptly set out on foot back toward Pigeon's Ranch. Marching along, they came upon Private Bill Davidson, now sitting in the road with his breeches off. With his pipe in his mouth, Davidson was "cursing the world and the Yankees by sections ... and tearing up his shirt and tying it around his leg. Captain Adair asked him what was the matter." Shot through the leg, the 18-year-old private gamely replied "that the Yankees had ruined his breeches - tore two big holes in them." [57] Adair then asked Davidson if he knew where his company was. "He said damned if he knowed, Jim Carson had them following Shropshire, but he expected they were on top of the enemy's cannon by that time." [58] Seeing that Davidson could provide little useful information, the late comers left him cursing the Yankees and bandaging his wound, and moved on. A ways further, they reached a gully near an old field. Here in the field to the left of Bradford's cannon, they did their first fighting of the day.

About this same time Colonel Scurry discovered a large body of Union infantry trying to move past his left flank. Availing themselves of a gulch that ran up the center of an enclosed field, Lieutenants Charles Kerber and John Baker had advanced Company I of the 1st Colorado Volunteers to within striking distance of Bradford's guns. With the Rebel artillery close by on higher ground to his left, Lieutenant Baker drew his sword, waved it over his head, and called to his men, "Let's capture the guns!" [59] At that instant he was struck down. A moment later, the ditch was a swirling bedlam as Texans armed with knives and pistols plunged into the midst of the determined Germans. Responding to the threat, Scurry had gathered men from Companies C and E of the 4th Texas and charged the ditch. Amidst heavy fire from the foe the storming party dashed some 200 yards across the open field and fell upon Kerber's men. "For a few moments a most desperate and deadly hand-to-hand conflict raged along the gulch." [60] Charles Buckholts, the Captain of Company E, emptied his pistol at the Federals and then "killed two with his knife." [61] The Germans fought doggedly, using their bayonets, but finally broke "and fled in the wildest disorder and confusion." [62] Private Henry Elliot of Company C reported that when the Texans "plunged into the gully, there were thirteen men still remaining, the rest having fled. Of these, six were killed and five taken prisoners." [63] Another Confederate recalled the Union soldiers "made here the best stand they made during the day." [64]

The arrival of the two companies of fresh dismounted troops added to the Confederates' numerical superiority on the left and with their rout of Kerber's men the Texans began forcing the Federals back. Almost immediately they encountered further resistance. A pocket of the enemy had lodged in another of the many gullies that crisscrossed the battlefield and was making a stand.

> "Here Ben White, of Company C of the 4th, took a handful of powder, poured it into one barrel of his gun, took another handful, poured it into the other barrel, put a little paper on it and rammed it down, and then poured a handful of shot in each barrel, run a little paper down, and turned both barrels loose right down that ravine." [65]

The blast rolled down the gully like an earthquake creating havoc among the Union troops. At least ten of the defenders were either killed or wounded. The rest scrambled away as Rebels swarmed into the ditch. According to Sharp Whitley, "Ben White's old swie-barrel gun did the business, there were ten or twelve in the gully when we took it, but they all had Ben's mark on them." [66]

Now, as Colonel Slough reported, the struggle became an "engagement of the bushwhacking kind." [67]

The Federals stubbornly held their ground, but inch by inch, tree by tree, the superior fire of the Texans slowly drove them back. [68] On the Confederate right Union troops made a determined stand behind a bluff on a little piece of pine covered tableland. Captain Gustav Hoffman's "Company B, of the 7th (what they had together, for by this time [the Texans] were pretty generally jumbled up) assailed it, and at first failed to take it." As Company B fell back, Major Shropshire came up with seven or eight soldiers from his old Company A of the 5th. Assessing the scene, "Shropshire hallooed to Co. B, to come on and help take that position, or stay back and look at men who would take it." In response, everyone sprang forward and B of the 7th and A of the 5th went over the bluff together and routed the Yanks. Corporal Sharp Whitley wrote, that because they had become so scattered "There was not over ten men in those companies at this time." [69]

While fighting raged on the wings, in the center of the Texan line Bradford's battery was fighting a mismatched duel with Ritter and Claflin. As the firing grew hotter, Bradford's infantry support edged away. "The Victoria Invincibles," those who were not sent to the left, were directly in the rear of the cannon. Sergeant Peticolas wrote in his journal, "On our right was an old field fenced in with pine poles. To this field a good many of us repaired when the firing grew hot." [70] In the field the infantry was still exposed to the Union cannon, but at least they were away from the storm exploding immediately around the battery. The shelling from the eight Federal guns was so heavy that the Texan artillerymen could not stand it. In short order one of the men was killed and Lieutenant Bradford himself was grievously wounded. Several of the battery's horses were also shot and collapsed in their traces. With no other officer of artillery present, the remaining gunners decided to withdraw. Cutting out the dead horses they hastily limbered up and departed. Colonel Scurry's attention was elsewhere on the field and he was not immediately aware his artillery had fallen back. Within moments an ominous silence informed the Rebel commander that the center of his line was in trouble. Fuming, Scurry sent to the "rear to have two of the guns brought back to the field." [71] John William Patrick took charge of one cannon. Patrick, who was a sergeant in Teel's artillery, had "deserted" from the 7th Regiment U.S. Infantry to join the campaign. Private Kirk of Phillips' Brigands manned the other piece. Together the two volunteers rallied the cannoneers and gamely wheeled the Confederate artillery back into position. [72]

It was by now about mid-day and the Texans were steadily pressing back their foes equally on both the right and the left. Urging their men forward, Colonel Scurry and the other Texan officers worked back and forth along the line encouraging their men and telling them how it was going at other points. Bill Davidson recalled, "At no time were our lines over eighty yards apart, and frequently in ten steps, and sometimes hand-to-hand. We could see no distance along our line and only knew that we were advancing from the fact that the firing was going back all the time." [73] The Union batteries had given the center of the Texan line a severe pounding, but now they were in danger of being flanked. Colonel Slough correctly recognized the tenuousness of his position and ordered a general withdrawal. So far the inexperience of the Union commander was working to the Confederates' interest. At the start of the battle Slough had enjoyed a slight numerical superiority over his foe. Cautious, he held back a large reserve with his train. He further diluted his strength by attempting simultaneous assaults on the left and the right. The result was that in the hard breast-to-breast fighting on the flanks his men were outnumbered. The success of his cannon in the center only made the situation worse as still greater numbers of Texans flocked to the wings to avoid the storm of shell and case. Outgunned three to one, Slough's troops were being defeated in detail. As the Union troops disengaged and fell back a lull settled over the battlefield. 74

Pigeon's Ranch, Glorieta, New Mexico, June 1880. Courtesy Museum of New Mexico, Neg. No. 15782

On Colonel Slough's orders, the Federal troops retreated 300 or 400 yards, then redeployed into a "new position in front of and near the house of Mr. Pigeon. Claflin's battery took position on an eminence to the [Union] left." 75 A short distance away Ritter's light battery also took position on the left. This was some distance from the road, but between Claflin's position and the house. The Federals' reformed defensive line extended along a rough ledge of rocks to the north, passed below Pigeon's house and across an arroyo near it. To the south, it rested on the summit and nearer slope of a wooded rocky bluff. [76]

To the west, the Rebels also busily redeployed. All morning they fought according to the dictates of the terrain. According to one soldier Texan, "there was and could be no regular order in that place, and where the firing became most rapid we would work our way to help our side." [77] The suddenness of the Union withdrawal left the Confederates somewhat scattered, but Scurry and his officers moved quickly to restore order. Reforming his command Scurry advanced about 1/4 mile to the east. The Texans crossed the ridge previously occupied by the Union troops and moved out onto a flat slope that descended towards Pigeon's Ranch. The eastern face of this eminence, today known as Windmill Hill, became the center of the second Rebel line. Scurry placed Major Henry Raguet to the extreme Confederate left to press the Federal troops on the north ridge. He then shifted Major Pyron from the right and gave him command of the Texan left center from the Santa Fe Trail to the arroyo. Colonel Scurry himself took the right center. Major Shropshire was assigned the Confederate extreme right. Since coming on the field Isaac Adair and his company had fought near Scurry. Now, the three companies of the 7th changed position and joined Major Shropshire on the right. [78]

By the time the Texans finished maneuvering and were ready to advance, Scurry was no longer sure of the enemy's position. Slough's troops had taken cover and it was impossible to tell whether their main body was lying behind an adobe wall, which ran nearly across the canyon, or whether they had taken position behind a ledge of rocks in the rear. To determine the locality of the Union strength, Scurry ordered his cannon back into action. Following the Colonel's instruction, Kirk and Patrick directed their fire against the adobe wall and began "to tear the

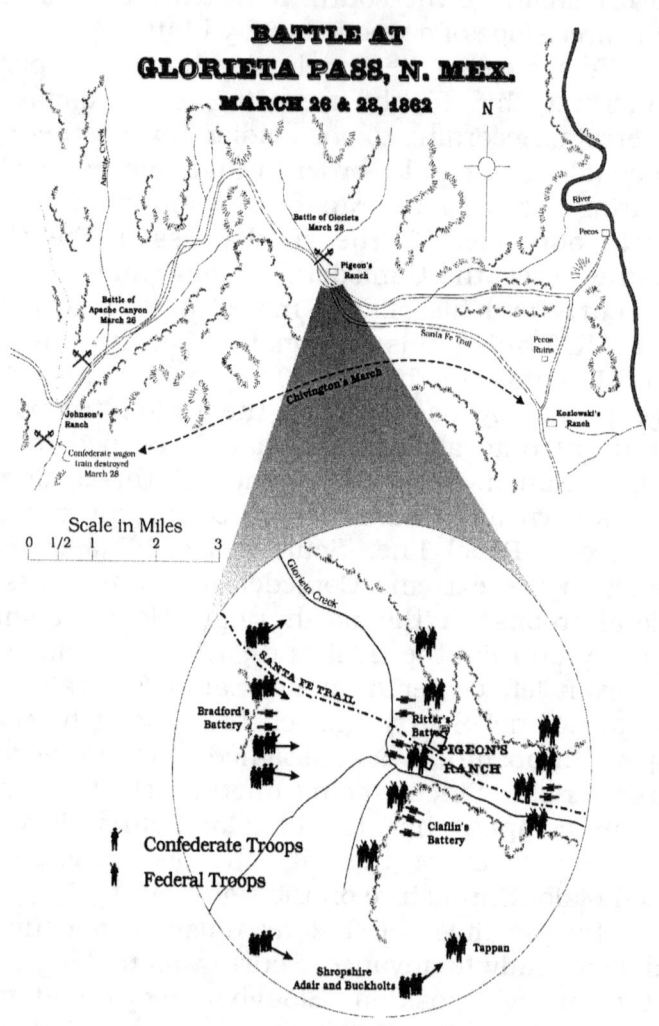

corralls [sic] in pieces." 79 While his cannon probed the Union line with solid shot, Colonel Scurry gathered his officers and prepared to get his advance moving again. In a move that was just as risky as Slough's, Scurry decided to split his force in the face of the enemy. He sent Major Shropshire and his command "to the right, with orders to move up among the pines until he should find the enemy, then he was to attack them on that flank. Major Raguet, with similar orders was dispatched to the left." [80] Scurry remained in the center of the Confederate line, having told the two officers "that as soon as the sound of their guns was heard [he] would charge in front with the remainder of the command." [81]

For several hours, the cannon from both sides pounded away at each other while the infantry consolidated their lines and maneuvered for position. The reverberations of the cannonade rang furiously from the high canyon walls and mesas beyond. The sound was deafening. "Many trees beyond the open space in the battlefield, and particularly in the defile to the east, showed for years the marks of balls, exploding shells and canister." [82] Confederate gunners, Kirk and Patrick, played a lively tune, but it was eventually Ritter's battery that got the upper hand. One of his gunners, Private Kelly of Company E, found the range of the Texan cannon and in a dazzling display of marksmanship quickly disabled both guns. Kelly struck one of the Confederate pieces full in the muzzle with a round shot, knocking it from its carriage. The other was disabled when Kelly blew up its limber box with a case shot. With their two-gun battery destroyed, and Private William Kirk of the Brigands heavily wounded by a gunshot to the leg, the Texan cannoneers withdrew, leaving the Union artillery in command of the field. [83]

Watching the action from an elevated position on the Union left, Lieutenant Colonel Tappan could see not only the batteries, but also the infantry maneuvering below. Majors Shropshire and Raguet were hidden from him as they headed toward the wings, but clearly visible were 200 or 300 Confederates assembling in the center nearly a mile off. Apprehending that they were preparing to charge

Lieutenant Colonel Samuel Tappan, 1st Regiment, Colorado Infantry.
Courtesy Colorado Historical Society, negative F-3467

the Federal batteries, Tappan hurried to communicate his suspicion to Slough. To prepare for the anticipated attack, Colonel Slough's adjutant general, Gurdin Chapin, ordered Ritter's battery to cross the ravine to the other side of the canyon and take position there. Lieutenant Claflin's battery of mountain howitzers was ordered to join Ritter's and in short order all eight Union guns were waiting to receive Scurry's charge. Soon after returning to his assigned location on the hill, Tappan likewise received information from Slough that the Texans clearly intended to charge his position as well. Tappan was now the extreme left of the Union line and his skirmishers extended in a half circle covering nearly three-quarters of a mile. Slough warned the Lieutenant Colonel that if his line on the hill was flanked the enemy could assault the Union battery and provision train. Tappan "was ordered to hold it at all hazards, for all depended upon it." [84]

Around 3 o'clock in the afternoon, Alfred Peticolas, who was on the trailing edge of Shropshire's movement to the right, "saw the Yanks run on the left," Raguet's men pressing them. At the same time he "heard our men in the gully in the old field give a shout and come running down towards the ranch in the valley." [85] As the charge neared the Federal lines, the Union artillerymen depressed their cannon and fired canister into the advancing Texans. According to one Union soldier, "Claflin's battery opened on them like a regiment of Mexican dogs roused by the stranger at midnight. One man shoved in a charge with his arm, another fired her off, and the four pieces played the liveliest Yankee Doodle ever heard." [86] As the storm broke upon them, the advancing Texans faltered and took cover behind the houses corrals and trees.

On the right, Major Shropshire heard the sound of the guns and ordered his men to charge in a right-oblique direction. If possible, he intended to get past the end of the Union line and drive it back. The troops that responded were a mixture of companies from all three regiments. Isaac Adair was there, leading his men from Company H of the 7th. Nearby were his friends and neighbors "The Crockett Boys" of Company I of the 4th, under James Odell. Also from the 4th Regiment were Company E, led by Captain Charles Buckholts, and Company F, commanded by Captain James Murray Crosson. Portions of Company F of the 7th were also present. From the 5th came Shropshire's old Company A, urged forward by its sergeant, twenty-year-old James Carson. [87]

The Texans charged up the hill, sheltering behind every tree and bush, until they came to a wide-open space of ground. Across the clearing invisible in the trees behind a breastwork of logs and rocks waited

Tappan's command. More than two-thirds of the Rebels stopped at the opening fearing to go into it, but thirty-five or forty brave souls, lead by Major Shropshire and the other officers, pushed on. [88] Among Tappan's men, Ovando Hollister patiently watched the enemy approach and waited his opportunity to fire. Afterwards he wrote, "Soon they appeared in front, encouraged and shouted on by as brave officers as live; some in squads, others singly, taking advantage of the timber as much as possible in their approach." [89] To Benjamin Ferris it appeared, "there were so many of them and they made such a noise as they rushed ... the woods were full of them." [90] The Union soldiers waited until the Texans were within about twenty yards of them before they rose up.

Major Shropshire, mounted on his yellow clay bank horse with black mane and tail, was no more than thirty feet from the Yanks when he saw the ambush. "He never faltered, not a muscle moved in his face as he saw the 'Yanks' guns leveled at his head." [91] Straightening himself in the saddle, he raised his arm and prepared to order a charge. At that moment, Private George W. Pierce, of Company F 1st Colorado Volunteers, darted forward and sent a bullet crashing through the Major's skull. The Union line then "delivered volly [sic] after voley at clost range" into the startled Texans. [92] According to Ovando Hollister; "Lieutenant Colonel Tappan sat on his horse during the charge, leisurely loading and firing his pistols as if rabbit hunting." [93] Confederate dead and wounded littered the opening. Both Isaac Adair and Charles Buckholts were cut down in the first moments. Captain Buckholts was killed instantly. Adair fell with a mortal head wound. Captain James Odell was also wounded and the Confederates reeled back. Immediately Colonel Tappan ordered Company F of the 1st Colorado Volunteers to counterattack. As one of the Volunteers remembered, "We followed them a ways to see how well they could run." [94]

When the Federals surged forward, eighteen-year-old Confederate Private J.H. Richardson stood his ground. With his pistol in hand the young private begged his fellows not to run. Nearby, Captain Crosson, one of the few unscathed Rebel officers, likewise drew his pistol and commanded the Texans to hold. Years later Richardson recalled, "Our men, what few were not killed, retreated. [...] Finally we rallied some about 50 yards from where the ambush was, and we shielded ourselves behind trees, rocks, and etc." [95] Here the Texans held, and Company F's counterattack spluttered to a halt.

The fighting on the Confederate right degenerated into pockets of individual skirmishing. Dodging from tree to tree, Benjamin Ferris was suddenly struck by a Rebel ball. As he described it, "ZIP! Something hit my leg. It did not hurt much, but numbed my leg somewhat. I did not feel like advancing, but was not disabled then, but not knowing how soon the company might be ordered back, I thought best to get back while I could." [96]

Lieutenant Phil Clough of the 5th Texas and a Pike's Peaker came suddenly upon each other and both men fired at once. Clough was hit, but not knocked down. The Colorado Volunteer was unscathed. "Here was done some of the fastest loading that was done that day, but Clough got loaded first and the Pike's Peaker threw in the sponge, he had to."[97]

Moving through the trees, Captain Denman Shannon of Company C of the 5th also came suddenly upon the enemy. Confronted by a couple of Yanks, he shot one, who attempted to flee. The other, realizing that Shannon had emptied his pistol, attacked. The

George Hibbard and compadres near the spot where Major Shropshire and Captain Adair were shot. Glorieta, New Mexico, June 1880. Photo by Ben Wittick. Courtesy Museum of New Mexico, Neg. 42922

Texan jumped behind a large tree, but the Yank was right behind. The Union soldier was proceeding to turn the tree and things looked grim for Shannon. Just then James Carson burst from the undergrowth. The Federal trooper "turned on Carson, both fired and the Yank fell." [98]

At another point, Private Richardson looked on in dismay as Private Pierce and three other Union soldiers "came down to Shropshire to take his pair of ivory handled six-shooters and his watch." [99] Upset by the trophy taking, Richardson charged his double-barrel shotgun with buck and ball and left fly with both barrels. The soldiers gathered around Major Shropshire took to their heels, but not before securing their prizes. Richardson was frustrated and angry, but there was little more he could do. The Texans were badly mauled and pursuit was out of the question. Richardson later wrote; "All that saved us on the right; our men in the center charged and beat them back, and the 'Yanks' where we were was afraid of being cut off and they retreated." [100]

Tappan's men threw back Shropshire's Texans, but along the rest of the line Union troops were finding themselves hard pressed. When Colonel Scurry realized that his far right was floundering, he passed in that direction to find the cause. Upon learning that Major Shropshire was dead, he "took command of the right [center] and immediately attacked the enemy who were at the ranch." [101] Despite the fury of the Texan onslaught the Union defenders held and Scurry was momentarily repulsed. Almost immediately, the Confederate commander rallied his men and again hurled them at the Federal line. Again the Union soldiers put up a spirited resistance and again Scurry's Texans were repulsed.

Meanwhile, Majors Raguet and Pyron on the left flank swept the enemy before them until they reached a rocky hill overlooking the Union artillery. Immediately they began "pouring a destructive fire of small-arms in the batteries." [102] One of the cannoneers, Private G.H. Smith, Company E, 5th U.S. Infantry was killed. Privates Raleigh and Woolsey, from the same company, were wounded, as was Private Leddy of Company I, 2nd Cavalry. Two of the artillery horses were shot and fell in their traces. The galling fire from the rocks on the mountainside was making the Union position untenable. Scurry recognized the opportunity and with a yell of, "That ranch, boys; heaven of hell," again sent his men charging down the road. [103] Sizing up the situation, Captain Ritter saw that his cannon were at risk and deemed it proper to pull back. The withdrawal of artillery support, in the face of assaults from both the front and the side, left the Union position too precarious to maintain. Captain Chapin of the U.S. 7th Infantry selected a location for a new line of defense and the Federals at the ranch again retreated.[104]

Now it was Lieutenant Colonel Tappan's turn to find his situation deteriorating. Surveying the field from his position on the hill, Tappan quickly concluded it was time to withdraw while he still could! The Federal batteries had retreated to a position "in front of a deep ravine, where the supports were entirely sheltered from the enemy's fire. The supply train was in the road about 40 yards from the left of the battery." [105] This position was 1/4 to 1/2 mile east of Pigeon's ranch. Tappan wrote in his after action report, "Our column had fallen back from the valley to my right a considerable distance. The enemy occupied the place we had left. Considering it extremely hazardous to remain longer, and thereby enable the enemy to get in my rear and cut me off from support of our battery and protection of our train, I ordered my men to fall back." [106]

About this time a curious experience befell Texan, Alfred Peticolas. During Shropshire's oblique charge, the young sergeant became separated from his fellows. He could hear wild firing away to his right, but because of the dense undergrowth on the hill, he did not know "that Major Shropshire and Captains Buckholts and Adair had been killed, and many of [the] men wounded." [107] The firing near Peticolas' own position was very light, and eventually it dwindled even further. When it ceased altogether he assumed "the enemy had been forced back and that they had taken out towards the hills." What shooting he could still hear, seemed to be coming from the direction of the ranch. Wanting to get back into the fight and thinking he might have "an excellent chance to fire at the artillerymen in the valley on the left," Peticolas started to work his way in that direction. Walking towards the enemy line he began to again take part in the battle at every opportunity firing at the enemy in the valley. He wrote in his journal, "I had fired about a dozen shots and was loading my gun when turning half round I saw, to my astonishment, that I was in two feet of a line of 100 men, all strangers to me." Another glance convinced Peticolas that the men were all "Pike's Peakers." Disoriented and separated from his fellows he had blundered into Tappan and his retiring command. Peticolas was sure he was about to be taken prisoner, but before he "could say or do anything, one of them said, 'Look out! Captain. Those fellows will shoot you.'" In a flash, Peticolas realized that the Federals mistook him for one of their own men. His good fortune was undoubtedly due to the Union overcoat that he picked up on the field at Valverde. Trying to appear unconcerned, he responded, "Who will?" "Those fellows over yonder," came back the Pike's Peaker, pointing in the direction of the Texan line, "there are two or three of them shooting at us." "Are they?" coolly replied the young sergeant, "Then I'll go back and take a shot at them." [108] With that, Peticolas lowered his gun to the charge bayonets position and set off towards his own lines as if advancing towards a real foe. As he moved away, he glanced back over his shoulder, expecting momentarily to be riddled with minie balls or have a bayonet plunged into his back. In a dozen steps, he was safely out of sight in the undergrowth. According to Bill Davidson, "When he got behind those trees that hid him from the enemy that he had just left, he turned and let his gun go off among them." [109]

Shortly after his lucky escape, Peticolas ran into Captain Crosson and informed him of his visit. Gathering his scattered troops, Crosson rallied the Confederate right and began a cautious advance. When the Texans reached their wounded and dead the scene of the ambush was quiet. Tappan and his soldiers were gone. The withdrawal gave Isaac Adair's men the opportunity to help their fallen comrades. The Captain had "a bullet through his head" and there was little his friends could do, except try to make him comfortable. [110] Adair's wound was so severe that later when he was brought into the Confederate camp, some that saw him assumed he was already dead. The assault was a disaster for the men from Crockett. Not only was their captain fearfully wounded, four others from the tightly knit company were killed. Forty-two year old bugler, G.N. Taylor was dead, as was Adair's aide, twenty-year-old private, William Booker. Also dead were eighteen-year-olds, Peter Hail and R.P. Walker. Henry P. Cobb, twenty-five, was wounded. [111]

By this time it was early evening. The battle had raged most of the day. Alexander Vallé, the owner of Pigeon's Ranch, who was an eyewitness to the fighting, later remarked, "zey foight six hour by my vatch, and my vatch vas slow!" [112] The Confederates had driven their foe from the ranch, but the fight was far from over. Abandoning his right and center, Colonel Scurry now concentrated his forces to the left. The Texan drive on that flank was so far successful and Scurry intended to follow it up.

On the extreme left Majors Raguet and Pyron, in close hand-to-hand fighting, had forced the Union defenders to abandon position after position along the rocky ridge. Nevertheless, the Federals held their ground stubbornly, "only yielding, inch by inch, to an overwhelmingly superior fire. When they were outflanked and nearly surrounded they would deliver a stunning volley and fall back a piece." [113] Shortly before 5 o'clock, Colonel Slough's troops made their final and most desperate stands of the day. "The intrepid Raguet and the cool, calm, courageous Pyron had pushed forward among the rocks until the muzzles of the guns of the opposing forces passed each other." [114] Two Union companies "had taken a position among some rocks where they were perfectly protected from the fire of [the Texans]." [115] Advancing toward the entrenched Federals, "Uncle Billy Smith, of Co. I, of the 4th [Texas], got shot in the stomach and his bowels stuck out. Twice he tried to put them back; finding that he could not do it and that he could go no further, he took his gun by the muzzle and looking at [his fellows] said, 'Boys, they shan't have it!' and broke it over a rock." [116]

Faced with stiffened Union resistance, Major Henry Raguet took a party of men and tried to dislodge the Federals. The enemy's fire was so terrible that the Texans faltered. While his men hung back, Major Raguet "rushed on cheering to the boys to follow him." [117] As he neared the rocks he took a direction around to the left. From there he called to his men, yelling that if they joined him they could get behind the Union position. "All this time Henry was within twenty steps of the rocks, and his uniform words and actions attracting the attention of the enemy many of them were shooting at him all the time with their pistols." [118] A ball had passed through his coat sleeves, but so far the Major was unharmed.

Forty rods away a young Union soldier was taking deliberate aim. The "full-grown boy," who was just reaching young manhood, belonged to the Colorado Volunteers. "Early in the forenoon he said to Captain Downing: 'I dreamed last night that I was shot through my heart in battle to-day, and I believe it will come true.'" [119] Captain Downing, good-naturedly, told him it was nothing but a bad dream. All the same, when the battle heated up he detailed the youth to conduct some prisoners back to the Union camp at Kozlowski's Ranch. Believing the young man removed from the fighting, Downing was surprised to later find him back in position in the stack of rocks. Stopping, the Captain remarked, "If you still want to engage in the fight, take a rifle and see if you can hit that Confederate officer." The private let fly and Major Raguet fell, the ball passing through his body. "A Texan sharpshooter, observing this action, instantly discharged at the boy a rifle bullet, which striking his gun, glanced from it and pierced his heart. Turning to [Downing] at his side, he gasped: 'I told you something would happen.'" [120]

Seeing their Major fall, the enraged Texans stormed the Federals head-on. In moments they swarmed over the Union position "and with their pistols filled the rocks with the dead and wounded of the enemy." [121] Leading the assault, it is said; "Major Pyron shot six of them with his six-shooter." [122] "This spot was the scene of one of the most terrible fights of the day." The Union defenders saw that if they tried to run they would be exposing themselves to death, "so they remained behind the rocks to the last, exposing nothing but their heads when they fired upon [the Texans]." The battle on the left closed at this position with the Federals eventually "fleeing in every direction." [123]

When the Union defenders broke before Pyron's onslaught, the Rebels under Colonel Scurry made one last determined attempt to capture the Yankee artillery. Scurry, moved among his troops with a clear understanding of the difficulties to overcome, and animated them to engage in the final desperate encounter of the day. "The officers and men responded with alacrity and grim determination. With the brim of their slouched hats falling over their foreheads, and with deafening yells," the Texans charged towards Ritter's and Claflin's combined batteries. [124] The eight

Union guns responded to the threat with a furious fire of canister and shell. Heedless of the storm, the gutsy Texans pressed on, determined if possible to repeat their success at Valverde. So furious and deadly was the charge that a German officer, among the Colorado Volunteers, shouted to his men near the battery; "Poys, lay down flat dere; does you want to go died?" [125] As the Confederates closed, a heavy body of Union infantry interposed to save the guns. Colonel Scurry wrote, "Here the conflict was terrible. Our men and officers, alike inspired with the unalterable determination to overcome every obstacle to the attainment of their object, dashed among them." [126] The Union supports, rising from the ground, ran forward and shot their deadly rifle bullets fairly into the faces of the Texans. By this time, Scurry's "own cheek was twiced brushed by a minie ball, each time just drawing blood, and [his] clothes torn in two places." [127] The concentration of Federal supports temporarily outnumbered the Texans, and despite their boldness the attackers were thrown back with "great loss and in great disorder." [128]

The Federals won a momentary respite, but it was not enough. With Scurry's men reforming in the trees, a suddenly faint-hearted Colonel Slough decided it was time to abandon the quickly darkening field. The Union commander was not sure his men could withstand another frontal assault, but more importantly he was about to be flanked for a second time and Pyron's troops were enfilading his right. His order to withdraw was met with differing reactions by the exhausted and demoralized Union soldiers. Some greeted it with anger, frustration, and disbelief, and refused to obey. "Never would they turn their backs on those [...] they had faced all day." [129] Alexander Vallé described the men as fairly raging when ordered back, and "they did not hesitate to upbraid their commander." [130] Others, however, "broke ranks and fled from the field." In his after action report, Colonel Scurry wrote, "So precipitate was their flight that they cut loose their teams and set fire to two of their wagons." [131] If there was a moment when a complete rout seemed possible it did not last. Slough and his officers quickly regained control of the situation, and the rest of the supply train along with Claflin's battery headed toward Kozlowski's Ranch in good order.

For a time after Slough's command to fall back, Ritter's battery remained in place. Captain Jacob Downing was among the last soldiers to leave the Federal position on the rocky bluff. As he passed across the field Ritter approached him. "Captain," Ritter said, "you are the only ranking officer left on the field. What are your orders to me?" Downing's terse reply was; "Double-shot your guns and keep firing." [132] Ritter started to follow the Captain's orders, but soon discovered that he was without supports. Realizing it was folly to stand alone the artillery officer limbered up and withdrew.

The men of Lieutenant Colonel Tappan's command were disgusted at the idea of retreating before they were well beaten, but had no choice. The main column in the valley fell back nearly two miles. If the soldiers from the Union left did not hurry and catch up they would be hopelessly cut off. Moving quickly off their hill Tappan's men fell in behind their retiring fellows. [133]

After Major Shropshire fell Captain Denman Shannon assumed command of the Texan forces opposing Tappan. As the Coloradans withdrew the young captain set out boldly in pursuit. "Here Captain Shannon in pursuing them forgot that men on foot could not keep up with a man on horseback." [134] Pressing ahead of his troops Shannon burst from the trees and gained the road, only to find himself directly in among the enemy. Realizing that he was captured the Captain is reported to have looked around and exclaimed, "Ten feet too far, by God." [135]

Colonel Scurry must have felt both disappointment and relief at the Union withdrawal, relief that the battle was over and disappointment that he could not make his victory complete. For six hours the Texans had pushed back the "Pike's Peak miners and regulars, the flower of the U.S. Army" in what Scurry later described as, "the hardest contested fight it had ever been my lot to witness." [136] Now, with the foe driven from the field, the Colonel realized that his own men were spent. Suffering from extreme exhaustion, the Confederate troops were simply in no condition to continue their pursuit.

Looking about the now quiet battlefield the Texan commander decided it was time for an abeyance. Sitting astride his horse, Scurry called to his men for a white handkerchief, saying that, he "wanted to send a flag of truce to tell them damned Yankees to come back and pickup their dead and wounded." No one came forward with a white handkerchief so the wearied Colonel bellowed, "God Damn it, tear off your shirt tail, we have got to have a white flag." [137] Eighteen-year-old, Harvey Holcomb had just picked up a beautiful new white silk handkerchief off of the battlefield. The young private hated to part with his find, but after looking around he decided that "there was not a shirt tail in the crowd that would do for a white flag, they would have suited better for battle flags." [138] Walking up to Scurry, Holcomb handed over his much-prized silk handkerchief. The Colonel said it was just the thing, and promised that it would be returned. Holcomb never expected to get the handkerchief back, and indeed that was the last he saw of it. Scurry gave the makeshift flag to Major Pyron and instructed him to inform the Federals, "he granted them permission to return and bury their dead and take off their wounded, as his men were too tired to do it for them." 139 Pyron set out at once, but pursued the retreating Federals the whole eight miles to Kozlowski's before he found an officer with authority to accept the flag. 140

Colonel Slough's men had fought with desperate courage both individually and in companies, nevertheless they had been forced to withdraw. If responsibility for the Union undoing lay anywhere, it lay with the Federal commander. Colonel Slough started the battle off balance and was later outmaneuvered by a shrewd and aggressive opponent. Indeed, it was too much to expect that the inexperienced Denver lawyer would have handled his large force to great advantage. For the second time during its campaign, a hard-fought battle drew to a close, leaving the Confederate Army of New Mexico masters of the field. 141

Chapter 10

DEFEAT

"Today we have won a hard fought battle, and yet we are whipped, crushed and defeated."
- William Lott Davidson

Throughout the day's fighting one question burned brightly in the mind of every Union officer: where was Major Chivington? Slough's strategy for the battle was to trap the Confederates between two columns. While the main Union force engaged the enemy head-on Chivington and his 480 men were to have circled around and hit the Texans from behind. The Major and his detachment never appeared on the field. Just the same, their actions that day eventually snatched the Union forces from the jaws of defeat.

At about 9:30 in the morning Major Chivington and his seven companies of infantry turned off the Santa Fe Trail. Leaving the main road they headed down a lesser trail that passed through San Cristobal Canyon and led to Galisteo. They followed this road for about eight miles and then set out cross-country to find the Confederate rear. Fortunately for Chivington, Lieutenant Colonel Manuel Chaves of the New Mexico Volunteers accompanied him. After fighting beside Canby at Valverde, Chaves had organized a party of mounted guerrillas and worked his way north to Fort Union. At Santa Fe he assisted Major Donaldson during the evacuation and then escorted his party northward. When about half of his sixty-six Volunteers quit during the retreat the Lieutenant Colonel and his officers stood firm. [1] The forty-year-old Chaves was a brave and skillful officer, an experienced Indian fighter and a veteran of the Mexican War. More importantly he was a former Santa Fe Trail merchant and knew the Sangre de Cristo Mountains around Apache Canyon. Acting as guide, the stalwart Lieutenant Colonel led Chivington's detachment up a steep ascent and then along a difficult path that wound along the summit of Glorieta Mesa. For eight more miles the Union soldiers cut cross-country, working their way through dense thickets of scrub pinon and cedar bushes. Without Chaves to lead them the party would quickly have become lost. The whole time as they marched the troops could hear the distant thunder of artillery and knew that the battle had started without them. [2]

After nearly five hours of arduous marching the Federals came upon their first Texan. Reaching the top of a high ridge they surprised and captured a lone sentinel. The reason for the sentry soon became apparent as Lieutenant Colonel Chaves "pointing over the bluff, said laconically, 'You are on top of them!'" Spread out, some 300 feet below, was Johnson's Ranch and the Texans' supply train of between sixty and seventy wagons. [3]

Colonel Manuel Chaves y Garcia de Noriega, 2nd Regiment, New Mexico Volunteers. Courtesy Museum of New Mexico, Neg. 9833

The ranch house and its surrounding adobe huts were in plain view. Just north was the road leading from Apache Canyon toward Santa Fe. Side ravines led away to the right and left and several low knolls broke up the landscape. On the largest of these Timothy Nettles had placed his six-pounder field howitzer where it commanded the western end of the canyon. The Rebel supply wagons were gathered in a couple of neat clusters toward the center of the ranch.

Nearby were a field hospital and a corral containing horses and mules. 4

Watching from the bluffs, the Federals could see perhaps 200 Confederates moving leisurely about. Unconscious of the threat, the Texans were amusing themselves by "jumping, running foot races & etc." 5 For almost two hours, nothing happened while Major Chivington reconnoitered. Describing Chivington's demeanor during the fight in Apache Canyon, Alexander Vallé said; "'E poot 'is 'ead down, and foight loike mahd bull." 6 Two days later the elder of the church militant was inexplicably cautious. Fearing some kind of a trap the major was reluctant to commit his troops. Finally, taking a last look over the landscape, Chivington took a seat on a log and addressed his officers.

> "'I fear an ambush,' said he. 'What do you say, Captain Lewis?'
>
> 'Well, major, we came here to fight,' said Lewis.
>
> 'What do you say, Captain Carey?'
>
> 'I agree with Captain Lewis.'.
>
> 'And you, Captain Wynkoop?'
>
> 'I agree with Captains Lewis and Carey.'" 7

Still concerned, but no longer hesitant, Chivington gave orders for the attack. He is alleged to have said, "In single file, double-quick, charge!" 8 Whatever his orders, his troops scrambled over the bluff and headed for the unsuspecting camp below, Chivington told Captain Lewis that he was going to remain behind and "that if he saw the party ambushed, he would sound the recall." Lewis who was in immediate command of the assault was disgusted by the Major's trepidation. Turning to fellow officer Asa B. Carey, Lewis remarked quietly that "they would never hear that signal." [9] Chivington had assigned Lewis "the most dangerous duty" of the day and the Captain intended to carry it through, come Hell or high water. [10]

As quickly and quietly as possible the raiding party began a long rough descent towards the ranch. At first the way was so steep that the soldiers used ropes and leather straps to lower themselves down. Holding on with their guns and to each other the men crawled and slid down the talus slope. When they had covered about one fourth of the distance to the camp, the crashing of loosened rocks rolling down the hill and among the scrub trees finally attracted the Texans' attention. With no further reason to keep quiet a Union officer stepped onto a projecting rock and yelled, "Who are you below there?" A Texan officer, who appeared to be in command, yelled back; "Texans g-d d--n you." "We want you," shouted the Union officer. "Come and get us gd d--n you, if you can," yelled the Texan. Charles Gardiner, a private in Chivington's command, recalled that, "in rather unmilitary style," the Union troops were ordered to, "go fur em." [11] Whooping and yelling like wild Indians, Lewis and his men began running and leaping down the lower half of the slope.

Faced with an attack by what appeared to be an overwhelming enemy force, pandemonium broke out among the Confederates. The majority of the men at the encampment were noncombatants, drivers, cooks, the sick and the wounded. Most were either unwilling or unable to fight. Some of the frightened Rebel teamsters and wagon guards grabbed what horses and mules were close at hand and lit out up the road towards Santa Fe. Many others retreated at the double quick up a canyon running eastward. The Texans who were left tried to organize a hurried defense. [12]

Showing the same courage and determination he exhibited two days before in Apache Canyon, twenty-four-year-old Timothy Nettles rushed to man his cannon. Assisted by seven volunteer gunners the Sergeant soon had the six-pounder working. Fortunately for the Federals, Nettles' bravery and enthusiasm were not matched by his skill as a cannoneer. The shots from the cannon fell without effect among the scattered attackers. [13]

Back on the ridge, a party of thirty volunteers under the command of Captain Edward Wynkoop opened fire. Left behind with orders to pick off the artillerymen and silence Nettles' cannon, they delivered a stunning volley into the small party of gunners. Three of Nettles' men were killed outright and several others were wounded. Meanwhile, at the base of the hill Union troops re-formed into two battalions and went into action. Seeing the damage inflicted by Wynkoop, Captain Lewis' and one column charged bravely up the rise toward the Confederate gun. [14]

Nettles, who had fired a total of five shots, realized instantly that he was about to be overrun. Acting without hesitation he grabbed a steel ramrod and spiked his cannon rendering it useless. Before the Federals could reach him he also blew up a caisson containing most of the gun's ammunition. Nettles was standing so close to the explosion that when Bill Davidson saw him later in the day the gutsy cannoneer was "literally burnt all over." [15] During the confusion of the blast, twenty-year-old Confederate 4th Sergeant George H. Little rode up on his horse. Having done all he could, Nettles got up behind his friend and the two men galloped away. Failing to capture the cannon intact, Captain Lewis and Lieutenant B.N. Sanford made doubly sure that the piece could not be used again. They jammed a 6-pound iron ball down its muzzle and tumbled the gun down the eastern side of the knoll, smashing its carriage and wheels. [16]

While Captains Lewis and his column attacked the cannon, the rest of the Union raiders charged and surrounded the Rebel wagon train. During this action the Federals fired on sick and injured Texans, who were housed among the wagons. The Confederate hospital was marked by a yellow flag, but the zealous attackers either failed to see it or, as the Rebels later asserted, failed to respect it. Aghast at what was happening Reverend Lucius H. Jones, the Chaplain of the 4th Texas, grabbed up a piece of white cloth and stood in front of the hospital waving it. The Episcopal Parson continued waving his white flag, until attracting attention to himself, he was shot and dangerously wounded. [17] It is unlikely that Chivington's men intentionally violated the hospital or the Chaplain's flag of truce. The Texans, however, considered the actions deliberate and vehemently condemned them. Colonel Scurry, in his after action report, described the violations as, "acts which the most barbarous savage of the plains would blush to own." [18]

The action around the wagons was sharp, but short-lived. In moments three Confederates lay dead and several more were wounded. Hopelessly outmatched, seventeen Texans, including two officers, threw in the sponge and were taken prisoner. The remaining defenders turned and fled. After only minutes of fighting, Chivington's troops were in complete control of the Rebel encampment. [19]

When Colonel Scurry and his men marched off to battle they left behind everything except their arms and what ammunition they could easily carry. As a result their captured wagons were loaded to capacity with food, ammunition, forage, baggage, clothing, and medical and surgical stores. Everything necessary to sustain Scurry's small army in camp or on the march was now in Union hands. Coloradoan Charles Gardiner reported that the Federal officers allowed their men to "ransack" the camp "and keep whatever valuables they could find." The wagons yielded "a great deal of fine officers clothing, fine Mexican blankets and all kinds of military stores, wines, Brandies, pickles, cand [sic] fruits, oysters, & Navy Revolvers, double barrel shot-guns & etc." [20] Since carrying off most of the captured supplies was out of the question, Chivington immediately ordered their destruction. The heavily laden wagons were overturned and burned on the spot. Flames and smoke leapt skyward as one wagon after another was given the torch. According to Private Gardiner, "Every wagon contained from five to twenty-five kegs of powder. Therefore as soon as the fire would reach the powder the wagons were 'no more.'" [21] "In one, case bacon and cavalry saddles had been piled upon boxes of powder, and the explosion of the latter sent portions of both the former about 200 feet into the air." [22] At another wagon, ammunition exploded, severely wounding Private Simon Ritter, Company A, 1st Colorado Volunteers. The unfortunate Ritter was the only Union casualty during the entire raid. [23] So complete was the destruction that once the flames had died the only thing left of the Texan wagons and their valuable contents was the iron work used in their construction.

    In spite of his complete success Chivington was anxious to withdraw as quickly as possible. While watching the supplies burn, his men had spotted a lone Confederate on horseback. The trooper, riding for all he was worth, had dashed out of a side ravine and spurred his mount towards Pigeon's Ranch. Afterwards, the major again feared a trap. When the Federals overran the camp, they liberated five Union privates who were captured in the fighting between Slough's and Scurry's forces. From these they heard their first intelligence of the general engagement. The five privates painted a gloomy picture. One of them told Chivington; "You had better get away from here quick, the damn Texicans are whipping our men in the canyon like hell, have driven them nearly through the canyon and pretty soon will have them out on the prairie." [24] Adding to Major Chivington's concern was the firmly held conviction among the captured Confederates that Colonel Tom Green and the balance of the 5th Texas were rushing to their relief.

Fearing that if he moved against Scurry's rear his detachment would be crushed between two enemy columns, the Union commander decided to withdraw the same way he came. The Union soldiers rounded up thirty or so captured horses and mules and killed or drove off many others. Then, taking the seventeen prisoners who could walk; they paroled the rest and began the difficult climb back up the mountain. [25]

As the detachment set out, Major Chivington is purported to have given "an order that the prisoners they had taken be shot in case they were attacked on their retreat." [26] When word of this order filtered back to the Confederates it was a deep affront to their sense of honor. Taken together with the wounding of Reverend Jones, it left most Texans with little doubt as to the character of the raiding party. Expressing the commonly held opinion, one Southerner wrote, "Those men sent in our rear to-day certainly are a set of miscreants, they are certainly no part or parcel of the brave men we have been confronting and fighting for the past six weeks, the men who have been fighting us would scorn to do what they did and would scorn them for doing it." [27] Colonel Scurry lamented that, "These instances go to prove that they have lost all sense of humanity in the insane hatred they bear to the citizens of the Confederacy, who have the manliness to arm in defense of their country's independence." [28] Southern bitterness and rhetoric aside, Major Chivington's detachment had just won an important and almost bloodless strategic victory. The schemes and aspirations of General Sibley and the Confederate Army of New Mexico may not have literally gone up in smoke at Johnson's Ranch, but they had been dealt a serious setback.

Before Chivington's men reached the top of the mountain, someone spotted several wagons that had been overlooked. Hidden behind a knoll near the main camp, four wagons loaded with military stores had escaped the destruction. Unwilling to leave anything to the enemy, Chivington sent four volunteers back to burn them. This task took the better part of an hour, during which time the Major and the rest of the detachment waited near the summit of the mountain. [29] While thus engaged, they were met by Lieutenant Alfred S. Cobb bringing urgent and long overdue orders from Colonel Slough. The dispatch from Slough stated that "he had been driven from his position with considerable loss," and requested "immediate aid." As soon as his wagon burners returned, the Major hastened to obey. [30]

The Federals now faced a dilemma. They needed to get back to their own lines as quickly as possible, but Lieutenant Cobb reported that the enemy controlled the trail by which they had come. [31] Lieutenant Colonel Chaves was only familiar with the one route and refused to take responsibility for leading the detachment by another path. Night had fallen and without a reliable guide it would have been difficult for the party to find its way back. Then came a stroke of luck. While waiting on the ridge line, the Federals were joined by Alexander Grzelachowski an ex-Roman Catholic priest, known locally as "Padre Polaco." Grzelachowski, who now owned a business near Las Vegas, was thoroughly familiar with the area. Stepping forward, he saluted the officers in Spanish and began speaking to Colonel Chaves. Through Chaves, Padre

Polaco told Major Chivington that he could lead the party quickly and safely over the mountains alongside the pass and back to Kozlowski's Ranch. As the ex-priest had previously volunteered as the chaplain of the Second New Mexico Volunteers he was well known to Chaves who advised Chivington to accept the offer. In short order Padre Polaco, mounted on his milk white horse, was leading the soldiers along a trackless path through the darkness. [32]

The Confederate messenger, who escaped from Johnson's Ranch, reached Colonel Scurry near the time he was forwarding his flag of truce. The news that their lightly guarded camp was overrun shook the Rebels badly. They heard the cannonading to their rear, but until now had not known what to make of it. [33]

Each Texan started out the morning with a good supply of ammunition, but used it freely all day long. Never thinking that resupply would be a problem, Colonel Scurry had exhorted his men to, "give them Hell boys." As Private Harvey Holcomb put it, "If he called using bullets Hell they were getting plenty of it." [34] Not once had the Rebel commander told his men to conserve their ammunition. Even though Slough's men retreated, the weary Texans must have worried that they were now about to be trapped between the two Union columns. Colonel Scurry's cannon were disabled and his exhausted men were down to less than ten rounds apiece.

Fortunately for the Texans, Slough was well beaten and Chivington was still hours away. Word soon came down from Kozlowski's Ranch that the flag of truce was accepted and both sides set about the gloomy task of caring for their wounded and dead. Like Valverde, the battle of Glorieta Pass was a small affair when measured against the monumental Civil War struggles of the East. Still, the casualties on both sides attest to the intensity with which it was fought.

Contemporary reports of losses are varied and conflicting, but most historians agree that combined losses for the two commands exceeded 250 men. Between ten and fifteen percent of the soldiers, who marched into Glorieta Pass that day, were wounded, dead, or captured. 35

Reports of Union casualties vary, but a good estimate is that Colonel Slough's force sustained losses of about forty-eight killed, seventy wounded, and twenty captured. 36 The only Federal officer killed outright in the melee was Lieutenant Baker of Company I, Colorado Volunteers. As previously noted, Baker was severely wounded in the early part of the battle and later killed by camp followers, scavenging the battlefield. 37 Amazingly, only two other Federal officers were hit. One was Lieutenant Peter McGrath, an U.S. Cavalry regular, who fell defending Ritter's battery. The other was Lieutenant Clark Chambers of the Colorado Volunteers. Chambers' injuries were such that, "Amputation was thought necessary, but he declined being buried in pieces." 38 Noting in his after action report that only three Union officers were hit, Colonel Slough wrote, "Our loss is not great." 39 This was evidently a matter of perspective as Ovando Hollister who spent much of the day in the heat of action confided to his diary, "Our loss had been severe in proportion to the number engaged, amounting in killed, wounded and missing to nearly one fourth of our entire force." 40

With between forty-two and forty-eight killed, sixty wounded, and about twenty-five captured, Texan losses were roughly comparable. Among those killed or mortally wounded, twenty-six were from Colonel Scurry's own 4th Regiment, four were from the 5th Regiment, ten were from the 7th, and one was from the artillery. The high number of casualties among the 4th Regiment was undoubtedly due to the Texans' furious and repeated attacks against the Union artillery. [41]

The Pyrrhic victory of the Confederate Army of New Mexico at Glorieta Pass was partly due to the reckless courage of its officers. Leading by example, Rebel officers were at the front of every action. They consistently drew attention to themselves and inspired their men to greater effort. Following these intrepid officers, the Texans drove the Union troops before them for six hours, but in the end they paid a terrible price for their daring. Compared to their Federal counterparts, a disproportionate number of Confederate officers were casualties. The Union defense was so determined and their fire so hot that, every single Confederate field officer was either killed or touched. Among the killed were the brave and accomplished, Major Raguet, the gallant and impetuous Major Shropshire, the daring Captain Buckholts, and the brave Lieutenant Charles H. Mills. Captain Isaac Adair and Lieutenant James Bradford were fearfully wounded. Major Pyron, Colonel Scurry, and others were all grazed or slightly injured. Denman Shannon along with another captain and three lieutenants were captured. After the fight, Scurry wrote with pride, "This battle proves conclusively that few mistakes were made in the selection of the officers in this command. They were ever in the front, leading their men into the hottest of the fray." [42] Certainly the Confederate officers were brave and impetuous but their recklessness may have cost the Texans more than it gained.

Sometime before 10 o'clock, Major Chivington's raiding party reached the Santa Fe Trail near Kozlowski's Ranch. Their way back had been so demanding that Chivington had dismounted and "stumbled along while leading his horse." [43] Everyone was tired and thirsty, but despite the confusion and difficulty of marching in the dark Grzelachowski had conducted his charges safely.

When the column came within sight of the Union camp fires at Kozlowski's, Major Chivington called a halt. Ignorant of the events of the day, the Major was unsure whether friends or foes waited ahead. Pausing only a few moments, he ordered his men; "Fall in, every man in his place; fix bayonets." When quietly asked whose camp it was, Chivington characteristically replied; "I don't know whose it is, but if it a'nt ours we'll soon make it so. Forward, keep close." Flushed with their earlier success, the command advanced. "On coming within hailing distance of the guard they found it was the Colorados, and reserved their hostility for other occasions." [44]

The raiders were greeted joyously by their comrades, who listened eagerly to accounts of their exploits. Within minutes everyone in the camp knew that Chivington and his men had won an important victory. Cavalryman John D. Miller evaluated the situation promptly and succinctly; "The Texans have possession of the field, but we have possession of their grub." [45]

With Scurry's truce firmly in place Chivington's return buoyed Federal spirits but made little difference to the immediate situation. Both armies had settled back to assess of their condition and details were scouring the battlefield looking for the dead and wounded. This somber work continued throughout the night, as men wandered over the hills and crawled through the underbrush, looking for missing friends. Texan Alfred Peticolas, still wearing his prized Union overcoat, was intrigued that enemy soldiers again took him as one of their own. Twice as he passed over the field, Union troopers who wanted to engage him in conversation stopped him. One was a wounded "Pike's Peak man," the other was a "Sergeant of the artillery who came back to look up the wounded and bury the dead." [46] Just as at Valverde, chivalry held sway on the quiet field and animosity was forgotten in the melancholy presence of the dead and dying. In an act that earned lasting admiration from the Confederates, Union surgeons saw that their enemy was destitute of medical supplies and "divided their medical stores and instruments" with the Texans. As one of Scurry's men recalled; the Federals "then sent back... drew a double supply and divided with us again." [47]

While some of the Confederates gathered the dead and assisted wounded the rest of Scurry's command fell back to Pigeon's Ranch. The men built fires and took what comfort they could in and around the buildings and corrals. It was now well after dark and the Texans were totally without supplies. If they did not carry it with them into battle, it was gone. So desperate was their situation, that they were forced to borrow spades and pick axes from the Federals to bury their dead. None of Scurry's men had blankets and the last food they had eaten was breakfast that morning. Harvey Holcomb reported that some men were so hungry that they gathered corn in the corral that the horses and mules had wasted. [48] Those lucky enough to find any, roasted the ears in the ashes of their campfires. Captain Julius Giesecke summed up their tenuous situation in his diary with the succinct phrase, "we remained on the battlefield without food, near a fire, but froze no little." [49]

The Texans knew their train had been attacked, but on the night of the 28th few if any of them knew the full extent of the damage. Huddled around their fires some of the men speculated about their situation. Others laughed and cracked jokes just as merrily as they had at their camps on the Salado. The Texans' morale was bolstered by their apparent victory and spirits were high. Just the same, there was an undercurrent of apprehension around the fires. Twenty-year-old Private Fred Tremble of Company D of the 5th Regiment, leaned over to Bill Davidson, who was lying nearby, and "whispered confidentially, that [they] were in a hell of a fix." [50] Davidson suspected that Tremble was right. It seemed to the wounded private that, "Leaving our train without a heavy guard was a terrible blunder. At Valverde although we were harder pressed than we have been any time to-day, yet a heavy guard was continually kept with the train." [51] As the seriousness of their situation set in the Texans became subdued. Expressing feelings which were on the minds of many, Davidson, wrote "Today we have won a hard fought battle, and yet we are whipped, crushed and defeated." [52]

At some point during the evening rumors circulated that Colonel Green had arrived at Johnson's Ranch and had engaged the cart burners. Ostensibly to cut off the enemy's retreat, but more probably to guard against surprise, Scurry ordered part of his command back up the canyon toward their old encampment. Moving with this group was twenty-one-year-old Henry C. Wright. At a small ranch about a mile down the road from the pass, Wright, who was foraging for food, got lucky. Rummaging through the place he found "a lot of baled buffalo meat ... and a number of sacks of flour." [53] The buffalo meat was a curiosity to Wright and others who had never before seen any. Some of the men suggested that it must "have been put up by Indians," others believed "the Abs had it stored." [54] Whatever its source, the soldiers were grateful for the find and soon their haversacks were bountifully lined with the meat. Pickets were sent farther up the road and everyone settled down to wait.

Before morning a mountain storm arose. Temperatures in the pass plummeted and snow began to fall. The night turned icy and terrible and the Texan wounded suffered intensely from the cold. The medical supplies provided by the Union surgeons were godsends, but they did not include tents or blankets.

Without shelter and supplies there was little the destitute Texans could do to help their injured comrades. Lying among the fallen Isaac Adair was cared for by his friends and survived to see the dawn. Others were not so fortunate. By morning, several of the Confederate wounded had frozen to death. Looking back with anguish, Bill Davidson wrote, "All that we could do to save them we did. We took off our coats an I piled them upon them; we built the best fires we could build for them; we rubbed their limbs and bodies but all to no avail, they died in spite of all we could do." [55]

On the morning of the 29th, both armies remained in camp and continued to attend to their dead and wounded. Slough's confidence was shaken by his fight with the Texans and he had no intention of renewing the conflict. By bringing on a full-scale battle he had overstepped his authority and placed himself in disobedience to Colonel Canby's direct orders. His "reconnaissance in force" towards Santa Fe very nearly met with disaster. Only the return of Major Chivington's raiders secured his position. The Union commander was still rattled and had yet to realize the full strategic importance of the Major's attack. The Texans were now hungry and cold, without artillery, and perilously low on ammunition, but Slough had no way of knowing it. He was driven from the field by a determined foe and he fully expected them to resume the engagement when the truce expired. At this critical juncture, he received "some reports that General Sibley was moving by another road upon Fort Union with the balance of his forces." [56] Rather than risk a second battle with Scurry's troops, the possible imperilment of Fort Union, and further disobedience to his orders, Colonel Slough decided to withdraw. In so doing, he unwittingly passed up the Union's best opportunity to destroy or capture the bulk of the Army of New Mexico. [57]

Once the decision was made, the Federal force prepared to pull back. "Teams were busy until noon, bringing in the wounded," and "thirty-five dead were buried on the field." [58] Meanwhile, Colonel Scurry forwarded a second flag of truce and requested that the cessation of hostilities be extended until 8 o'clock the next morning. Colonel Slough quickly agreed. Most Union soldiers were half-glad to escape a renewal of the day before, yet many were revolted at the idea of backing out before they were well whipped. Resigned to the retreat, Ovando Hollister wrote, "After granting the first truce it made but little difference how many more were consented to, especially as our command was about to start on its backward movement to Union." [59] By early afternoon everything was in readiness. With their dead interred and a crowded hospital established at Kozlowski's Ranch, Slough's soldiers turned their backs on Glorieta Pass and set out toward Fort Union.

For the Texans, the 29th was a day of worry and restless anticipation. It was rumored that the Yankees still controlled their old camp at Johnson's Ranch and were guarding the pass at Apache Canyon. If this was true, then the Rebels were cut off from Santa Fe. Believing themselves trapped between two forces, the Texans were in a quandary. They were too weak to launch an attack and there seemed to be no other way out of their predicament. Confiding his worries to his diary one officer wrote, "What was going to become of us we hardly knew." [60] Desperate for better intelligence, Colonel Scurry ordered an advance party down the canyon to reconnoiter.

The other Texans remained in camp and buried their dead. As bodies were collected, they were laid out on the earthen floor of Alexander Vallé's ranch house. While the cadavers were prepared, a great trench was excavated just west of the ranch. The site was on a level spot across the arroyo, close to a high ledge of rocks. [61] When the common grave was ready the dead were piled into the trench three layers deep. In all, 31 soldiers were laid to rest, "the dead men's arms folded across their chests, personal items like a 'Jews harp' or a clay pipe clutched in their lifeless hands." [62] In later years, a long slight depression was all that marked the Texans final bivouac. Eventually, with the passage of years, even this disappeared and the site of the grave was lost entirely.

While the work of the burial progressed word came back from the scouts. Alfred Peticolas reported, "We learned certainly before noon that our baggage train had been all burnt." [63] Adding insult to injury, Mexican scavengers subsequently stole everything that the flames did not consume. The Texans also learned, once and for all, that Colonel Green had not come as reported. It was at this point that Colonel Scurry sent Colonel Slough his request to extend their truce. Scurry claimed that the extension was needed because it would consume that period of time to provide for the wounded. It is more likely that the Confederate commander now wanted time to formulate a plan of escape.

Ignorant of Slough's impending withdrawal, the hungry Texans spent the afternoon organizing and searching for food. One fortunate group of foragers found a "flock of sheep belonging to someone in the Canion." [64] The sheep were so few in number and so puny that it prompted a soldier to comment; they were "the smallest things of the sheep kind we ever saw." Despite the sheep's picayune size, the men quickly slaughtered the flock and broiled them on the coals. Without salt or bread, the army made short work of the mutton. Remembering the sheep twenty years later, Private Davidson wrote, "There were not enough of them for fifty men but we made them supply the whole six hundred." [65]

Just at dark the strident sound of a bugle called the Texans into line. Colonel Scurry looked out over the anxious faces of his men and made a short speech. He told his assembled soldiers that the rumors about their train were confirmed. All their wagons and all the supplies they contained had been burnt. The hospital at Johnson's Ranch was captured and all the sick taken prisoners. The nearest and only place to resupply was Santa Fe twenty-eight miles away, but only if the Yankees did not get there first. Scurry told his men to prepare for marching orders. Determined to reach Santa Fe, they were going to try to force their way past the unknown enemy said to be holding Apache Canyon. At about 10 o'clock with the canyon buried in darkness, the army was given orders to shoulder their arms and take up the line of march.[66]

Leaving behind Isaac Adair and the other sick and wounded, the Texans trudged grimly down the canyon. The men were ready to fight or die, but soon their worst fears were dispelled. The pass at Apache Canyon was clear. Major Chivington and his command were long gone and the enemy was nowhere about. All that now lay between the Confederates and their goal was a forced march of twenty-two miles on empty stomachs. Fortunately for the exhausted army, the road was good. Passing through tall stands of pine, it ascended gradually for fourteen miles until it reached the height of a range of hills. There it began a gradual descent to a small creek about four miles from Santa Fe. By 4 A.M. most of the retreating Texans reached the banks of this creek and stopped to rest. Campfires sprang up here and there as soldiers waited for friends, who had given out on the road. Everyone was hungry and bleary-eyed with fatigue. Many who intended to stop only briefly found that they were too exhausted to go on. Describing a scene played out over and over again a weary soldier wrote, "I expected to stop at these fires, get a nap, and wait for day to make the rest of the distance. I was perfectly worn out and soon fell asleep and slept by the fire till day." [67]

March 30, 1862 was a Sunday and the streets of Santa Fe were still dark as the first Confederates stumbled into the city. Mother Madgalen Hayden, awake in the convent of Loretto noted, "We could hear them passing all night, our convent being on the street through which they had to pass, but we did not know to which side they belonged until morning when we saw by their clothes that they were Texans." [68] A few men were on horseback, but most were on foot. Others were so used up that they were practically dragged into the city. The forced march left haggard soldiers spread out for miles along the road, and it was nearly noon before the last of them straggled in. Watching the procession, Mother Hayden wrote, "All were in a most needy and destitute condition in regard to the commonest necessities of life." [69]

"Santa Fe, Looking North," From: Ladd, Horatio O. The Story of New Mexico. Copyright: D. Lothrop Company, 1891

As the careworn advance of the Army of New Mexico shuffled into Santa Fe, sixty miles south in Albuquerque its erstwhile commander received his first word of the battle. Brigadier General Henry Hopkins Sibley was delighted with the news. Provided with what was probably a garbled and overly optimistic account of the fight, Sibley decided to celebrate. Troops present in Albuquerque were assembled in the main plaza, and Major Alexander M. Jackson, Sibley's Assistant Adjutant General, read them the report of the battle. [70] When he finished, the army's brass band struck up "Dixie" and the men gave a rousing cheer. Everyone was euphoric and in no time word of mouth embellished the news. Events became so distorted that later in the day Private William Henry Smith, Company I, 5th Regiment, exulted to his diary, "We this morning received glorious news, Colonel Scurry with the [4th] regiment whipped five regiments of Kansas soldiers, whipped the Kansas fellows greatly." [71] This news would most certainly have come as a surprise to the determined Colorado Volunteers and Union Regulars engaged in Glorieta Canyon. To the Confederates in Albuquerque the details were irrelevant. What was important was that Colonel Scurry had apparently whipped somebody.

Even in Santa Fe the weary Texans were cautiously optimistic. Colonel Scurry knew that the destruction of his supplies left him hard pressed, but he did not believe the blow was mortal. Writing his first official report of the action on the afternoon of the 30th, he told General Sibley, "The loss of my supplies so crippled me that after burying my dead I was unable to follow up the victory. My men for two days went unfed and blanketless unmurmuringly. I was compelled to come here for something to eat." [72] Despite the burden of this setback, the aggressive

Scurry still considered himself master of the field and wanted to get back into action as quickly as possible. Sanguinely his report continued, "Lieutenant [George H.] Bennett writes for more ammunition [artillery]. Please have it sent. As soon as I am fixed for it I wish to get after them again." The dispatch ends with the note, "P.S.-I do not know if I write intelligently. I have not slept for three nights, and can scarcely hold my eyes open." [73]

The depth of Scurry's conviction that he had won a glorious victory is evident in the following proclamation. Written on the battlefield, and issued as one of his first actions upon reaching Santa Fe, the message read,

"Headquarters Advance Division
Army of New Mexico,
Canõn Glorieta, March 29, 1892

General Order
No. 4

Soldiers - You have added another victory to the long list of triumphs won by the Confederate armies. By your conduct you have given another evidence of the daring courage and heroic endurance which actuate you in this great struggle for the independence of your country. You have proven your right to stand by the side of those who fought and conquered on the red field of San Jacinto. The battle of Glorieta - where for six long hours you steadily drove before you a foe of twice your numbers - over a field chosen by themselves, and deemed impregnable, will take its place upon the rolls of your country's triumphs, and serve to excite your children to imitate the brave deeds of their fathers, in every hour of that country's peril.

Soldiers - I am proud of you. Go on as you have commenced, and it will not be long until not a single soldier of the United States will be left upon the soil of New Mexico. The Territory, relieved of the burdens imposed on it by its late oppressors, will once more, throughout its beautiful valleys, 'blossom as the rose,' beneath the plastic hand of peaceful industry.

By order of
Lieut. Col. WM. R. SCURRY, Commanding" [74]

Many citizens of Santa Fe were terrified by what was happening. The Texans were in full possession of the city and had placed their cannon in a defensive position should Slough pursue them from the north. Watching the preparations, Mother Madgalen Hayden wrote, "I feared they were going to have a battle here and that our house would be burned or thrown down by the cannon balls." [75] Despite the good Mother's worries, the greatest concerns of Scurry's men were food and rest. To the footsore and worn soldiers Santa Fe's multitude of one-story adobe buildings looked neat, comfortable, and inviting. As the Texans walked through the capital's well laid out streets, some of the men stopped at stores along the way. Alfred Peticolas reported that he and his friend W.T. Davis bartered for some bread and whiskey, using coffee that they recovered from the ashes at Johnson's Ranch. Eventually the troops found quarters in ruined buildings belonging to the government. Hay, gathered from the government corrals, was brought inside and the Texans slept on the straw covered floors. [76]

Meanwhile in Albuquerque, General Sibley acted on the strength of Scurry's first battlefield dispatch and put Green's regiment on the march. With orders to reinforce Santa Fe, Colonel Green broke camp immediately. By 3 o'clock in the morning companies E, F, G, H, I, and K were on the road with all the supplies they could carry. As it headed for the capital Green's cavalry was joined by a two-gun section of Reily's battery. General Sibley remained in Albuquerque with his staff, Major Teel's Light Company B Confederate States Artillery, and some other units, making plans and final arrangements. [77]

On the 31st, Teel prepared his artillery for action. He ordered his men to "have the horses shod, limber chests filled, and cannon and caisson's wheels greased." [78] When all was in readiness the battery headed for Santa Fe. Sibley and his staff tarried a while longer, leaving Albuquerque on either the 31st or the 1st. To protect his supply depot, the General left behind Company A, of the 4th Regiment and Company D of Baylor's Second Texas. Reily's remaining six-pounder field piece and three twelve-pounder mountain howitzers supported these troops. Command of the rear guard was given to forty-four-year-old Mexican War veteran and Indian fighter, William "Gotch" Hardeman. Two days earlier Hardeman had been promoted to Lieutenant Colonel for his gallantry at Valverde. [79]

Captain Bethel Coopwood and twenty-five members of his San Elizario Spy Company, who arrived from the Mesilla Valley, joined the troops left in Albuquerque on the 1st. Coopwood and his men had avoided Canby's Federals at Fort Craig by taking an arduous route through the foothills of the San Mateo Mountains, west of the Magdalena Mountains and the Rio Grande. The route of their trek would shortly prove significant to the Rebel army. [80]

After departing Albuquerque General Sibley and his staff quickly overtook Teel's artillery. As the combined party moved north a courier carrying Scurry's first official report of his engagement met them. When Sibley read the message, "He was very much surprised at the intelligence." In contrast to the Colonel's optimistic battlefield dispatch the new report gave the General cause for concern. Confiding to his staff Sibley said, "he was afraid that Col. Scurry had suffered himself to be surprised." [81]

Although the elements of the Army of New Mexico had moved slowly toward Fort Union, their advance was part of an overall plan. Sibley had intended Pyron to move from Santa Fe, draw the Yankees out of the fort and engage them. In the meantime Colonel Green, moving by the most easterly road to Union, would get between the enemy and the fort and attack them from the rear. Scurry, moving by the middle road was supposed to fall on their flank. Private Davidson noted sarcastically, "Of course, the enemy would be asleep and walk into the trap." [82] The plan was shaky at best, but it fell apart completely when Scurry advanced into Glorieta Pass. Scurry's move brought on a fight before Green could be positioned and dashed Sibley's hopes of a coordinated attack. Lieutenant Phil Fulcrod of Sibley's party later stated; Colonel Scurry was instructed to hold the gap, and his decision to advance was "more than he should have done." Not wanting to go so far as to accuse Scurry of disobeying orders, Fulcrod suggested that the General's instructions might have been unclear. Still he wrote, "It was a great misfortune to us that they were not carried out, as it was [Scurry] won the fight but lost his train, which was a great disaster to us." [83]

When the General's party reached the capital Green's companies were already there. As Sibley described the scene, he "found the whole exultant army assembled." To his critical eye, things looked well under control. "The sick and wounded had been comfortably quartered and attended," and "the loss of clothing and transportation had been made up from the enemy's stores and confiscations." Praising Scurry for his management of the situation, Sibley reported to Richmond; he found "everything done which should have been done." [84]

The situation of Scurry's troops had stabilized since the battle, but the time did not pass without hardship. The soldiers who suffered the most were the wounded left at Pigeon's ranch. Commenting on their plight, Union Private Alonzo Ickis noted in his diary; "[Scurry] retreated to Albuquerque in the night leaving his wounded at ranches near the battlefield without food and poor surgeons ... [Scurry] done the best he could under the circumstances unless he would surrender he had no food to leave with his wounded it had all been burned." [85] Governor Connelly of New Mexico wrote on April 6th, the Confederate "wounded are in a hard condition on the late field of battle, without medicine, medical aid, or the necessary subsistence, and are said to be near 200 in numbers." [86]

Connelly's estimate of 200 undoubtedly includes a large number of healthy Texans who remained behind to care for their sick and wounded comrades. One of these was Henry Wright. Wright spent the day after the battle searching for a friend who had been shot down at his side. The wounded soldier dragged himself off the field and it was not until much later that Private Wright found him huddled on the dirt floor of a small shack. Piled on the floor with him were another dozen wounded men all helpless and forgotten. Wright immediately took charge of the situation and made the men as comfortable as possible. In a little dugout or potato house he found a hen just beginning to sit on 13 eggs. According to Wright, "that hen made into soup and those eggs fed those fellows nearly a week until the last of them (that lived) was hauled into Santa Fe." [87]

As soon as he reached the capital Colonel Scurry made arrangements to retrieve his wounded. He was severely hampered, however, by a lack of appropriate transportation. He was able to confiscate conveyances in Santa Fe, but these were not designed as ambulances. Weakened by injury and exposure many of his men would certainly have died if subjected to the rigors of harsh wagon rides over bumpy roads. Help came from an unexpected quarter. Among the wives of Union officers, who remained in the capital when their husbands evacuated, was Louisa Canby. Hearing the plight of the Texan wounded, Mrs. Canby "invented a way in the absence of ambulances to bring the wounded to town. She had tent cloths nailed across the rough wagon beds, so as to form hammocks, on which wounded could ride in comparative comfort, thus doubtless saving many lives." [88]

Suggesting the hammocks was only one of the many ways that Louisa Canby's compassion led her to aid the Texans. When Pyron and Shropshire first marched their commands toward Apache Canyon, Mrs. Canby urged the Union ladies in Santa Fe to make preparations to care for the wounded of any impending struggle. When some of the women objected that it might be Confederates that were brought in Louisa snapped, "No matter whether friend or foe, our wounded enemy must be cared for and their lives saved if it is possible; they are sons of some dear mother." [89] As good as her word, the day after Scurry's Texans arrived, Mrs. Canby appeared at the Confederate hospital, accompanied by a young girl and carrying two baskets of delicacies for the wounded. James Carson, of Company A 5th Regiment, remembered, "Colonel Scurry met her at the door and told her about the burning of our train, clothing and bedding, the suffering of the boys and freezing of some of our wounded." [90] At the description of so much anguish, Mrs. Canby began to cry. Then recovering herself, she told Scurry, "These men must not suffer any more, there are a large number of government blankets hidden where you never could find them, but I will tell you where they are." [91] The kindhearted Mrs. Canby then revealed the location of a large cache of property belonging to the local Indian agency. The supplies were gathered for distribution to the Navajo, but because of hostility from the tribe had never been delivered. Before he abandoned Santa Fe, Superintendent James L. Collins had placed the goods in a storeroom and ordered the doors sealed and plastered over. Once breached, the store yielded enough blankets so that the Texans had at least two for every three men.

In the following days, Mrs. Canby, who was living in a large house, "threw open her door and invited in all [the] sick and wounded and nursed them like they were her own sons." The whole time the Texans remained in Santa Fe, "she had her house full of sick and wounded boys." [92] At one time she was caring for as many as fourteen wounded at once. The wounded, who could not be brought into town, became her special charges. "Her carriage could be seen every day on the road bearing either her, or some needed items for the men at the field hospital." [93] Mrs. Canby's compassion was so great and her love so genuine that she earned the Texans' adoration for the rest of their lives. As much as sixty-five years later Sibley's veterans could not write of the time in Santa Fe without expressing their devotion. In 1927 Harvey Holcomb reflected; "I will say this that Mrs. Camby [sic] captured more hearts of Confederate soldiers than the old general [Canby] ever captured Confederate bodies." [94] Another soldier wrote in 1888, "Twenty-six years have passed and gone, but her features, her kindness is still fresh in our hearts, and so long as one of that old brigade lives or their children live Mrs. Canby will be loved and her memory cherished." "Mrs. Canby was an angel ... The brigade would have voted her queen." [95]

Sometime between April 1st and April 6th, Isaac Adair was laid in the back of one of the improvised ambulances and carried over the rugged road to the capital. Once in Santa Fe, he joined the other sick and wounded convalescing in the makeshift hospital. Between the casualties from the fighting and those who fell prey to disease several hundred of Sibley's men were unfit for duty. Adair's regimental commander, Major Powhatan Jordan, a physician before the war, was chief surgeon at the hospital. [96] Assisted by other doctors and a large staff of volunteer attendants, Jordan ministered to his charges as best he could. Although he had plenty of manpower, he was severely limited by serious shortages of food and medicine. The physicians examined their charges and wrote prescriptions for drugs and treatment, but unless friends could procure the medicines in town, most prescriptions went unfilled. [97] Private Henry C. Wright remembered that the medical staff lacking other recourse employed "cold water applications, under which treatment the wounded and fever stricken rapidly recovered." Isaac Adair's wounds were beyond "nature's remedies," and he continued to decline. [98]

Chapter 11

ALBUQUERQUE AND PERALTA

"For the first time in my life, I saw cannon balls rolling along the ground like a parcel of marbles."
- William Lott Davidson

During their occupation the Texans scoured the New Mexican capital looking for supplies. Captain John Phillips company of "Santa Fe Gamblers", who "fought gallantly and desperately at Glorieta," were of immense service in this undertaking. [1] Knowing everything there was about the city, Phillips men assisted the quartermasters and commissary department with the foraging. The eating was poor, "no bacon nor pork and very little coffee." Most of the soldiers were "living on corn meal," but no one was starving. [2] In all, nearly $30,000 worth of government property was recovered. Between these supplies and confiscations from local merchants, losses of clothing and transportation were partially replaced. Cooking utensils were very scarce, but "the equipping had succeeded to the point where each man at least had one blanket." [3] A quantity of shoes were also gathered and distributed to those companies in need. With hard work, and the help of Louisa Canby, the Confederates in Santa Fe made themselves reasonably comfortable. Most recovered quickly from their hard marches. Those who did not have other responsibilities wrote letters home or wandered the town sightseeing. First Sergeant Robert Thomas Williams reported that the regimental band even played a concert in the public plaza. [4]

Plaza, Santa Fe, New Mexico, ca. 1866-68. Photo by Nicholas Brown. Courtesy Museum of New Mexico, Neg. 38005

Despite these modest successes Sibley and his officers found their situation precarious. By April 6th, the gravity of Scurry's loss was finally apparent to all. The first elements of the brigade entered the territorial capital back on March 10th. After occupancy of nearly a month the forage and supplies obtainable in Santa Fe were exhausted. Something had to be done. General Sibley evaluated the situation, conferred with his staff, and determined to abandon the city. Since the capital could no longer support his troops, he decided to move the whole army to the village of Manzano. [5]

Manzano, located on the eastern side of the Manzano Mountains, was strategically attractive to the Texans. The village was well situated, lying at a point roughly intermediate between Albuquerque and Fort Craig. By marching there, Sibley's army could keep an eye on Federal movements and possibly prevent

Slough and Canby from uniting their forces. Manzano also lay on the road to Fort Stanton. Occupying it meant that a clear line of communication with Texas and the Mesilla Valley could be held open. Most importantly, Sibley believed that the area was sufficiently abundant that his army could forage and live off the land. Another factor weighing into his decision was the possibility of reinforcement. Just days before, he wrote to both Richmond and Texas appealing for additional troops and supplies. In Manzano, the Texans could recuperate and safely await their arrival. Sibley believed that once reinforced he would again be able to launch an offensive against Fort Union and bring his campaign to its ultimate and glorious conclusion. If such aid did not arrive and retreat to the Mesilla Valley became a necessity, an evacuation from Manzano carried little risk of Federal attack. [6]

The move never occurred. No sooner was the plan agreed upon than it was disconcerted by a series of "rapid and continuous expresses" from "Gotch" Hardeman's command in Albuquerque. [7] A reanimated Edward Richard Sprigg Canby was again in the field. On April 1st, Canby had sallied from Fort Craig with a force of 860 regulars and 350 volunteers and was rapidly closing on Albuquerque. [8] Aware that most of the Texans' remaining supplies were their responsibility, and that any further loss would ruin the Confederates, Hardeman's small force determined to hold the city at all hazards. Faced with overwhelming odds, they needed immediate reinforcement. Once again General Sibley had expected the enemy to sit idly by while he maneuvered and once again events were moving beyond his control. This oversight was not lost on Sibley's men. Sergeant Frank Starr wrote to his father in disgust, Canby "had arrived within twenty-five miles before it was known - in such a manner are our affiars [sic] managed." 9

Around March 31st, Colonel Canby had received a communication from Colonel Slough describing Chivington's engagement in Apache Canyon and "announcing his intention to move against the enemy with his entire force." 10 Canby was upset by the message. He felt that Slough's action was premature and at variance with his own instructions. Worried that the move would involve serious consequences, Canby was galvanized into action. Charging "Kit" Carson and ten companies of New Mexico Volunteers with the duty of holding Fort Craig, he ordered 1,210 men under his immediate command to be ready to march at first light. With these soldiers, he planned to rush northward and effect a junction with the troops under Colonel Slough and Gabriel Paul. Two routes lay open, one by Abo Pass and Anton Chico, the other along the Rio Grande to Albuquerque and thence by San Antonio and Galisteo. Either road would be contested if the Texans got wind of his advance. Canby opted for the bold move against Albuquerque. Being the least expected, he believed it would carry the greatest element of surprise. He would make a demonstration against the city; and, if possible, without serious loss, capture and occupy it. Even if Albuquerque could not be taken, Canby reasoned that his attack would draw the bulk of Sibley's army back from Santa Fe, allowing his own soldiers to slip north without opposition. Once he linked up with the troops in the northern part of the department, he planned to assume command of the combined force and drive the Texans from the territory. 11

As Canby's soldiers moved slowly northward a road that was increasingly soft and sandy hampered them. The column's supply train was fully laden and it was only with the greatest difficulty that the men were able to keep the heavy wagons and field pieces moving. "To avoid wearing out the draft animals, they made frequent stops." [12]

The command had barely reached the outskirts of Socorro when a messenger named "Doc" Stracham met them. Stracham had ridden hard from the north to bring Canby and his men their first word of the battle of Glorieta Pass. Canby was elated by the news. Ordering the column to halt, he formed his men into open square and read them the dispatch. When these veterans of Valverde heard of the destruction of the Confederate train and Scurry's subsequent retreat to Santa Fe, every man from Canby himself down to the lowliest private joined in three rousing cheers. [13]

The Rebel hospital that was established after Valverde lay in nearby Socorro. Within earshot the small detachment of Sibley's army watched and listened nervously. Hearing the cheers and seeing the Federal troops drawn up before the town, the Texans assumed they were about to be attacked. While some of the men hurriedly burned dispatches, others hoisted a hospital flag. Dr. Hal Hunter, surgeon of the 7th Texas and commander of the post, sent a delegation to Canby to explain that the only able-bodied soldiers in the town were the few left to guard and care for the sick and wounded. After assuring the Texans that their hospital would not be molested, the Federals made camp. The next day, April 3rd, Dr. Hunter reported that he had the honor of seeing the Union commander pass through town in an ambulance. His impression was that, "Canby is a very ordinary looking man." As the beleaguered Texans watched their enemy march away, they felt sure that their comrades in Albuquerque were in for a fight. [14]

It was late on April 6th when Hardeman's frantic messages for help began arriving in Santa Fe. Bill Davidson remembered, "Immediately upon receiving the news we were ordered to march." [15]

About daylight the next morning Colonel Green set out for Albuquerque with the army's cavalry. He was followed a day later by Colonel Scurry with the 4th regiment and dismounted units of the 5th and 7th. The Texans' entire supply and baggage train accompanied Green. Many of the wagons were drawn by oxen and moved so slowly as to be an encumbrance. Green, seeing finally that he could make no time hindered by the train, cut it loose. Leaving a guard of "two pieces of artillery, ten men with good horses, and the lame men who could not keep up the march," he began a race for Albuquerque.[16]

The Confederate sick and wounded who could walk set out with the supply train. The march would be difficult, but most preferred "that to staying in Santa Fe and being captured."[17] After the exodus, the Rebel hospital was still filled to overflowing. Approximately 100 soldiers were simply too weak to make the trek. Despite their apprehensions they were forced to stay behind. Of these, a total of 34 were from Houston County. Eleven of the convalescents were men from Isaac Adair's Company. Another 23 were from James Odell's "Crockett Boys." Knowing full well that they would eventually fall into enemy hands, Chief Surgeon Major Powhatan Jordan and a handful of attendants, including Adair's sergeant James Macintosh Porter, remained to care for the patients. The departing Texans did everything in their power for the comfort of the sick and wounded, leaving behind sufficient funds in Confederate paper for their needs and what little specie there was available. Just the same, all those departing were distressed to abandon their comrades. Near the end of the expedition General Sibley wrote that his "chief regret" of the entire campaign "was the necessity of leaving hospitals at Santa Fe, Albuquerque, and Socorro."[18]

Amidst of the hubbub of the withdrawal Isaac Adair slipped toward oblivion. The Captain was a strong man, but his wound was grievous and after months of hardship and exposure his physical reserves were exhausted. At 4 P.M. on April 9th, 1862, with his friend James Porter by his side, Captain Adair surrendered his life for the Confederacy. [19]

Ironically, as Adair passed away, a young Colorado Volunteer was writing in his diary why the enemy had to die.

> "Death must come to all once," he wrote. "A nobler cause in which to meet it can never come. What signifies whether it comes a few days sooner or later? Then let them hate and scorn us. We will teach them reason by killing them off as fast as possible. They have left us no alternative. We may as well submit to it gracefully. It is a sure cure. The patient is never taken with a relapse. Dead men never put on the airs of the 'hereditary lords of the manor,' nor seek paltry excuses for 'venting the venom of their spleen' on their brethren. The history of Joseph and his brothers might teach them a useful lesson - or might have taught. It is now too late - there is nothing left for them but death or submission." [20]

On Thursday April 10, Captain Adair was buried in Santa Fe's Masonic cemetery. It snowed all day. [21]

Adair's men certainly knew that he was dying, but they were not immediately aware of his death. The able-bodied men of Company H, led by 1st Lieutenant Charles Q. Haley and 2nd Lieutenants B.B. Arrington and James M. Daniel, had departed with Colonel Scurry earlier in the day. Like most of the Army of New Mexico, they were hurrying toward Albuquerque. Dismounted since losing their horses at Johnson's

Ranch, Company H was part of a massive foot race to see who would control the city.

After leaving Socorro, Canby's column continued to be hampered by deep sand. The element of surprise was on his side, but his mules were very weak and the going was slow. If General Sibley had kept better tabs on his enemy, the delays might have given the Texans an upper hand. As it turned out, the Federal head start was insurmountable. Colonel Canby and his troops won the race, "arriving before Albuquerque on the afternoon of the 8th." [22] Drawing up his entire force before the town, the Union commander immediately made a demonstration "for the purpose of ascertaining its strength and the position of the enemy's batteries." [23] Early on, this took the form of a cannonade, "which was replied to with spirit" by Reily's one section of artillery. [24] "Canby had his two 24-pounders up and threw two or three bombs into the town, but did no damage." [25] For their part, Reily's Texans skillfully shuffled their four cannon from place to place making it difficult for Canby to assess their actual numbers. Evaluating the Rebel response, one Union volunteer wrote, "The enemy are firing round shot at us but the boys laugh at them they seldom do much harm." [26]

The artillery duel continued for a short time then the Federals began to test the Texan perimeter. They did not make any determined assaults, but throughout the rest of the day they made feints, first at one spot and then at another. By evening this experimental probing led Captains Hardeman and Coopwood to believe that the Union troops intended a full-scale night attack. As the beleaguered Rebels could do little except wait, "a sleepless night was spent by the little garrison watching the enemy." [27]

The Texan fear of a night attack proved groundless, but at first light Canby renewed his probing. Occasionally heavy long distance skirmishing developed between Texan outposts and the Federal advance; still much of the fighting was desultory. Nearly one-half of the Rebels were armed with shotguns and in these brief exchanges the short-range weapons were of little use. All morning the skirmishing continued, first at one part of town and then at another. "Gotch" Hardeman and Captain Coopwood rushed their defenders from place to place, "always concentrating their little force of less than two hundred men at the point threatened and repulsing or driving back every advance of the foe." [28]

Towards afternoon, several citizens of Albuquerque, including some of the town's more prominent women, slipped out and petitioned Canby to desist his shelling. They told him that the Confederates were not allowing them to take cover and that his cannons were doing more damage to their homes than they were to the enemy. Canby was well aware that over forty men in his command had families in the city. Rather than risk injury to innocents, he ordered a halt to the bombardment. Afterwards, "he sent a man in under a flag to see if the Texans would not allow the women and children to leave." [29] Knowing that they were badly outnumbered Hardeman and Coopwood shrewdly declined. The refusal angered the Union troops, who roundly cursed their enemy. Alonzo Ickis wrote in his diary, the "Texans would not let them go G-- D--- such men and the cause for which they are fighting." [30]

Plaza and Church, Albuquerque, New Mexico, 1857. Courtesy Museum of New Mexico, Neg. 71389

Canby planted his artillery in a large irrigation ditch to the southeast of town. At about 3 o'clock in the afternoon, in clear sight of the Confederates, a heavy force of Federals massed nearby. Assuming that an assault from that quarter was imminent, "Old Gotch quickly concentrated his force at the point threatened and made his arrangements to repel the attack."[31] Reily's four cannon were placed so as to command the approach and every available man was called to the defense. Captain James Walker of Company D was very sick, but along with many other invalids he left the hospital and took a place in the Texan lines. Counting both the sick and well, Hardeman's total force numbered 226.

Soon Graydon's Spy Company and a heavy column of Union cavalry, led by Major Thomas Duncan, advanced upon the town. As the Federals came within range, the Texan cannon opened fire. Although enthusiastic, the Rebel cannonade was again largely ineffective and the mounted Federals continued their advance. At about 300 yards, those Texans who were armed with rifles opened fire. As the cavalry continued to close, Major Duncan "was cut down by a cannon shot, this threw [the attackers] into confusion and they retreated in disorder." [33] By the time the attack was repelled, it was quite late in the day. Canby sent forward a flag of truce and, according to a Texan writing twenty-five years later, the Federals spent "the balance of the evening ... in collecting their dead and wounded." [33]

With night once again approaching the Union commander "ordered his men to fall back about two miles to some temporary entrenchments which had been thrown up." [34] The skirmish, that would later be called the "Battle of Albuquerque," was drawing to a close. Two days of stubborn Confederate resistance had convinced Canby that the town was too strongly defended to take by direct assault. Falling back on his other plan of action, he prepared to slip away and effect his juncture with Colonels Slough and Paul. While Hardeman and Coopwood waited nervously for the Federals to try them again, Canby prepared a ruse to cover his withdrawal. In a stentorian voice, clearly audible to Confederate pickets, he made a speech in which he ostensibly "begged" his troops "to charge the city and dig down the adobie [sic] walls if necessary." [35] Under cover of darkness, the Union troops then quickly loaded their wagons and quietly slipped away. To conceal the move, a few soldiers remained behind, and fires were kept burning brightly throughout the abandoned camp. Completing the illusion were buglers, drummers, and fifers, who at 8 o'clock played the usual evening "tattoo." Immediately afterwards, the musicians and those tending the fires mounted their horses and rode after their retreating column. [36]

Before the deceptive "tattoo," the besieged Confederates heard a lot of commotion from the Union camp. The Texans knew something was afoot, but they had no idea what it was. Looking out into the darkness the only thing they could see were the fires of the Union host. At about 10 o'clock the proverbial cavalry arrived. "Daddy" Tom Green came dashing into town at the head of the brigade's mounted troops. So successful was Canby's deception that Hardeman's men went wild with joy and relief. At the sight of their own cavalry the little garrison gave a loud cheer. Everyone was excited, yelling and shouting. "Even 'Old Gotch' for one time in his life forgot to be cool, calm and deliberate, and actually pulled off his hat, threw it in the air and whooped." [37]

Green was ordered to relieve Albuquerque with all possible haste. "His marches will attest to the manner in which this order was obeyed." [38] Traveling more than thirty miles a day, his cavalry had pushed hurriedly down the Rio Grande. Driven by concern for their comrades they covered the last fifty miles non-stop. As prodigious as these marches were, they paled in comparison with those of Scurry's foot soldiers. Thinking back on their efforts Theophilus Noel wrote, "such marches as they made are not to be found in the annals of modern history." [39] Close behind the cavalry, Scurry's dismounted troops marched both day and night, covering twenty-five to thirty miles at a stretch. Footsore and weary, the determined Texans pushed beyond the limits of endurance. Numbers of soldiers simply gave out and stretched out flat on the ground as their fellows hurried by. Trying to record the events in his journal Alfred Peticolas found himself at a loss as he wrote, "Oh the suffering of this march words can never tell." [40] Both hard rain and heavy snow fell on the lightly equipped Confederates. When they lay down to rest, it was on damp ground. Blankets were soaked and shoes were wet. With tired sore legs and empty stomachs Scurry's advance reached Albuquerque on the morning of the 10th. So close behind Green's cavalry were these foot soldiers that one Texan wrote, the cheers had barely died away when "another shout arose and more hats went into the air ... This was caused by the arrival of the gallant Scurry with the foot of the brigade." [41]

Albuquerque was relieved, but the enemy was already gone. On the morning of April 10th, Canby's troops were marching to the east. Already well away from the Texans, they moved unmolested along the road towards Tijeras Canyon, San Antonio, and Galisteo. This was the same road that Scurry's forces took to Glorieta barely one month earlier. Canby's intent at Albuquerque was to draw the bulk of Sibley's forces away from Santa Fe. If he could get them to move south, the Texans would not threaten his planned linkage with the troops at Fort Union. He was almost too successful. While making his feints against Hardeman's command it is unlikely the Union commander knew that Green and Scurry were already on the march. If he had, he probably would have disengaged much sooner. Canby came dangerously close to a premature battle with Sibley's whole army. Had Green arrived in time to prevent the Federal withdrawal, Canby would have been forced into a major clash where he was badly outnumbered. "Victory for the Texans would have meant the capture of Canby's train of desperately needed commissary and ordinance supplies." As it was, Canby's timely departure tolled the death knell for Sibley's campaign. [42]

By the morning of the 11th the entire Army of New Mexico was concentrated at Albuquerque. Although their limited cache of supplies was secure from capture, the Texan position was precarious. "With few exceptions," the population was "indifferent or hostile," and "resources of food and forage extremely limited." Their "hold on the country" was "bounded by the range of their guns." [43] Their "ammunition was nearly all gone, not having enough left for a days fight," and their "supplies would last but 20 days." [44] It was clear to the Confederates that they could not remain in Albuquerque, but "to move away from there was difficult also." The majority of the brigade was now on foot and their transportation was almost nonexistent. Things had reached such a state that they were down to "but one wagon to the company and the mules were poor & week [sic]." [45] In these "straightened circumstances the question now arose in [General Sibley's] mind whether to evacuate the country or take the desperate chances of fighting the enemy in his stronghold (Union), for scant rations at the best." [46] Faced with the specter of starvation or a fight with a larger and better-equipped army, Sibley and his officers knew that a crisis was at hand. After careful consultation, they decided that their only option was to retreat to the Mesilla Valley, where Colonel William Steele and the balance of the 7th Regiment could supply some measure of relief. As General Sibley nonchalantly put it, "The course adopted was deemed the wisest." [47] With a mixture of disgust and relief, the Texans promptly began preparations to abandon the territory.

Back in Santa Fe George W. Howland's Federal cavalry cantered into the city. Howland's entry into Santa Fe was a low point for Major Jordan and the other Texans forced to remain in the capital. Until the Union cavalry actually clattered down its streets, there were possibilities. From that point on surrender and capture were inevitable. Although Howland and his men had free rein of Santa Fe, they kept their distance and left the Texan hospital alone. Henry Wright, who remained behind as one of its attendants wrote, "It was fully a week after the troops entered S.F. before we were aware of it." [48] At Colonel Canby's orders, not a man was allowed to come near the hospital. It was not until the Texans' small store of supplies and provisions entirely failed that they had any dealings with the Federals. At last, with sick and wounded still to care for and his resources exhausted, Major Jordan was forced to appeal to Canby for help. After Jordan and his assistants stated their case, Canby replied, "Gentlemen, I had no intentions of interfering with the hospital in any way. But the only way I can assist you would be as prisoners of war." [49] Major Jordan told him that was expected, and on April 20th reluctantly surrendered the hospital. [50] After the Texans lay down their arms, Canby had their names, commands, etc. recorded and then, as promised, issued them full supplies of everything needful. Months later, when the sick and wounded were well enough to travel, the Union commander paroled them, furnished them with mules, wagons and provisions and sent them back to Texas. Canby's chivalrous treatment of the hospital won undying admiration from the Confederates, and led Henry Wright to proclaim; "A nobler man never lived." [51]

On April 12th, the Confederates at Albuquerque began their evacuation in earnest. Supplies were apportioned for another hospital and what remained was loaded on to the available wagons. Hampered by inadequate transportation, the Texans discarded everything of questionable value. Among the items abandoned were eight of the brigade's mountain howitzers. The ammunition for these small guns was exhausted and mules to pull them were in short supply. Consequently, Major Teel ordered the barrels of the pieces removed from their carriages and Lieutenant Phil Fulcrod supervised their burial in a secret location. [52]

While the work proceeded, elements of the 5th Regiment continued to search Albuquerque and its surroundings for badly needed supplies. Colonel Green received intelligence of provisions and forage twenty-five miles north along the river and acting on this information, he dispatched a detail of forty men and fourteen wagons to capture it and bring it in. Command of this party was placed in the hands of William Lott Davidson. Davidson, who was still recovering from the thigh wound he received at Glorieta, was a Quartermaster Sergeant at the beginning of the campaign and was again serving in that capacity. "At sundown two companies of Federal cavalry passed" the foragers "along the foot of the mountains going in the direction of Albuquerque." [53] Davidson assumed that his party was about to be cut off. Immediately, a soldier from Company I of the 5th was dispatched to carry the news to Colonel Green. Davidson later learned that his courier was mortally wounded and never made it back.

    The Union cavalry disappeared and by 11 o'clock that night the Rebel detail reached its goal. The fourteen wagons were loaded with "corn in the shuck" and quickly started back. Davidson "knew that the Mexicans would take the news to the Federal army" and that "his train's "safety depended on the speed with which [...they...] traveled." [54] Despite the urgency, the heavily loaded wagons moved slowly through the darkness. At daylight the train crossed a high ridge that ran to the river some twelve miles above Albuquerque. From this prominence Davidson got a clear view of the surrounding country. Remembering the scene he wrote, "I could see about sunup a heavy dust arising far in our rear, which told me they were in pursuit." The ad hoc commander ordered his men to hurry up their mules, which they did. Swiftly, a new threat presented itself. As Davidson put it, "the mules were doing some pretty tall traveling, when pretty soon I saw a heavy dust in our front." "They are in front of us," was repeated throughout the little band. [55] Rushing toward the oncoming dust, Bill Davidson urged his men to even greater speed. He believed that if he could get close enough to Albuquerque, before his command was overtaken, Colonel Green would hear the firing and come to their relief.

The detail pushed their small train another two miles before they stopped. The dust to their front was almost upon them. Intending to make a fight of it, Davidson circled his wagons. The foraging party took positions behind them and prepared to resist an attack. When all was in readiness the men from below got close enough to be recognized. Suddenly everyone in Davidson's party was cheering and throwing their hats in the air. The "attackers" turned out to be Lieutenant James A. Darby, of Company I of the 5th, and 100 mounted Texans. Colonel Green, concerned for the train, had dispatched Darby to bring them in safely. The pursuit to the rear was indeed Federal cavalry, but "upon seeing Darby, their desire to come further south was entirely appeased." [56] Davidson's escorted wagons returned to Albuquerque without further incident and their cargo of corn was ground into meal for the troops. By the time they made it back, the evacuation was in full swing.

At dawn on the 12th, Colonel Scurry, leading the dismounted elements of the army and the remainder of Major Teel's artillery, had moved down the Rio Grande about three miles and begun crossing his troops to the west bank. The crossing, which was made near the village of Atrisco, took the entire day. Ferrying all the company wagons across was particularly tedious and nightfall found Captain Hardeman's wagons still waiting on the east bank. [57] Many of the sick and wounded chose to accompany their departing fellows, "preferring to go along and take their chances to staying here and become prisoners." [58] One of those who left the hospital and joined the evacuation was the diarist, Private William Randolph Howell. Among those too weak to leave was Isaac Adair's friend, John W. Murchison. Murchison was related by marriage to Captain Adair's sister-in-law, Mollie Smith. Like so many others from Company H, he never made the long march back home to Crockett. Left behind sick, Private Murchison died on April 20, 1862. [59]

Colonel Green and the brigade's cavalry tarried in Albuquerque another day, but on the 13th they also abandoned the city. Instead of crossing the Rio Grande like Scurry the mounted elements of the 5th Regiment, Pyron's command, and Fulcrod's battery of artillery began their retreat by moving down the river's east bank. [60] At nightfall they once again made camp at Judge Baird's ranch. The Judge, who greeted the Texans so warmly on their advance, was packing to leave. Baird knew that if he remained in New Mexico he would be persecuted for his support of the Southern cause. Consequently, he and his family intended to accompany the brigade back to Texas. Baird was only one of a number Southern sympathizers, who having cast their lot with the invaders, now felt compelled to leave. When the Texans left Santa Fe, William Pelham and Alexander P. Wilbar accompanied them. Both men were ex-surveyors-general of the territory. Sibley is reported to have established an occupation government and appointed Pelham as governor. The Armijo brothers, Rafael and Manuel, "abandoned luxurious homes and well-filled storehouses to join their fate to the Southern Confederacy." Referring to these worthies at the end of the campaign, General Sibley wrote; "I trust they will not be forgotten in the final settlement." [61]

While Sibley's army moved slowly down both sides of the Rio Grande, the Federal forces to the northeast rushed to make their long-awaited juncture. Immediately after the battle at Glorieta the Union troops under Colonel Slough had fallen back to the village of San José. Continuing on to Bernal Springs, they were met by a messenger carrying dispatches from Colonel Canby. At that time Canby was still at

Fort Craig and ignorant of Slough's tactical situation. Fearing a disaster he had ordered the whole force to immediately return to Fort Union. [62] Colonel Slough read Canby's dispatch with dismay. By that time his entire command knew the full significance of Chivington's raid. They were well aware of Scurry's precipitous retreat to Santa Fe and they had ascertained that the rumors of a threat to Fort Union were false. Although there were reports of Texan foragers in the area, the Texans no longer held any terrors for Slough's men. They were "flushed with an honorable and complete victory," and were "eager to complete the destruction of the enemy." Colonel Slough was in a predicament. "He could not destroy the order; it had been too openly delivered to leave any room for evasion. To obey it was to let the enemy, broken and disheartened, escape; to refuse was to subject himself to court-martial and disgrace." [63] The next day, a frustrated Slough took the only option open to him, and ordered his regiment to march for Fort Union.

While riding back Colonel Slough decided to resign his commission in protest. On reaching the fort he made good on his intent and turned over command of the garrison to the more prudent and experienced Gabriel Paul. Slough was unpopular with his regiment and his personal contact with his men was never of a kind to make him beloved. Still, Ovando Hollister described him as "a man of undoubted ability and bravery," and the troops supported his position. To a man, the Colorado Volunteers felt that the order to retreat to Fort Union had been a disgrace. Hollister wrote, Colonel Slough "obeyed it as became a subordinate officer. He resigned as became a gentleman and a man." [64]

A couple of days later Colonel Paul received word that Canby had sallied from Fort Craig and that the forces from Fort Union were needed in the south to divert the enemy's attention or assist in driving him out of the country. On the morning of April 5th, Paul issued orders for the volunteers and regulars to pack up and be ready to leave in one hour. Between the 6th and the 11th Paul's troops retraced their steps back to Glorieta Pass and soon afterwards went into camp at their old stamping ground at Kozlowski's ranch. While encamped, the Colonel learned of Canby's demonstration before Albuquerque and his subsequent nighttime move to Carnuel Pass. [65] Informed that Canby was awaiting his arrival, Paul gathered his forces and marched rapidly to join him.

After camping briefly at Galisteo Creek Paul's men followed the road towards Carnuel Pass, retracing Scurry's route in reverse. The trek through the Sandia Mountains passed without incident and just before dark on the 13th the column found Canby's camp, nestled in the dense timber at Tijeras. After a predawn departure from Galisteo, Paul's command was on the road nearly fourteen hours without food. Describing their arrival at Tijeras, a Colorado Volunteer wrote, "Some of the horses had to be led into camp, and they will probably never leave it." [66] The forced march took a toll on the Federals, but it put the Union forces in their strongest strategic position since Sibley's army first entered the territory.

Canby had been promoted to brigadier general of volunteers on March 31 and he was now in command of a superior force. Well aware that the Texans were leaving Albuquerque and moving down the Rio Grande, he ordered an immediate pursuit. The morning after Paul's arrival the combined command moved about six miles down the pass, halted, and took a slight lunch. From that vantagepoint "by the aid of a spyglass," the Union troops could "see the river like a silver thread glistening under the slanting beams of the setting sun." [67] Striking out along the foothills to their left, the column took a southwestward course almost parallel to the Rio Grande. The sky was clear, the weather mild, and the moon full. General Canby kept his troops moving both day and night. On the 14th and after a hard march, they struck the wooded river bottom about eighteen miles below Albuquerque. By midnight, they were about a mile from the hamlet of Los Pinos on the outskirts of Peralta. [68]

Completely ignorant of the approaching danger, Colonel Green and his command were camped in and around a nearby hacienda. On April 14th Green's column had departed Judge Baird's and taken up the line of march with a view of crossing the river nearby. "On trying, the ford was found to be an impracticable one, on account of quicksand, which rendered it even dangerous." [69] Green was informed that the ford between villages of Peralta and Los Lunas was good and at once determined to move down to that crossing. As the 5th Regiment and Pyron's command rode down the east bank of the Rio Grande, they were shadowed by Scurry's dismounted force, making for Los Lunas along the west bank.

Alfred Peticolas reported that on occupying Los Lunas Scurry's advance guard fought a sharp skirmish with a company of New Mexico Volunteers. There were no casualties, but the Texans captured one prisoner and two horses. The vastly outnumbered New Mexicans retreated rapidly in the direction of Fort Craig. [70] The reason for the defense was that Los Lunas contained a large storehouse of goods and many other supplies valuable to the Rebels. Foragers in the village collected everything from ristras of red peppers to kegs of molasses. One prominent citizen, Toribio Romero, later reported that he suffered losses totaling more than $4000 when the Texans relieved him of twelve barrels of whiskey, stocks of wheat, corn, tobacco, wine, and a variety of other foodstuffs. [71] With Los Lunas' defenders routed and its goods confiscated, Scurry's men settled down to await Green's crossing.

When the last elements of Scurry's command wandered in, word arrived that locals had killed two stragglers. Emboldened by the Texans' retreat, citizens of the town of Los Padillas had reportedly attacked a small party of men as they passed through. The Texans were outraged at the duplicity and immediately sent back a company with orders to demolish the town. Fortunately for Los Padillas the real culprits were another company of "Kit" Carson's volunteers. Captain John Philip's Brigands trailed the New Mexicans and in a brief fight killed two and captured twenty-five. [72]

Across the river Colonel Green was stuck near Peralta. He had not planned to stop, but his train had encountered a bed of heavy sand. The sand was two or three miles wide and stretched for five miles. On reaching it the wagon teams could hardly travel. Private Bill Davidson, who was on special duty and in charge of the trains, "made Sam Delaplain, the [civilian] wagonmaster of the lighter train of wagons, double teams." In this manner, Delaplain was able to "leave one half his train, take the other half through to hard ground, and then go back and get the other half." [73] Since the light wagons were making good progress, Davidson ordered the wagonmaster of the heavier commissary wagons to do the same. This wagonmaster stubbornly refused, "and insisted on moving each wagon fifty or sixty yards and then bring up another." [74]

Leapfrogging along, the train of heavy wagons moved so slowly that Green's advance and the lighter wagons were forced to wait at Los Pinos on the outskirts of Peralta. Ultimately it was reported that one of the heavy commissary wagons had broken down. Governor Henry Connelly's large residence was immediately north of the village and the Confederates decided to bivouac in and around its fields and grounds. While the column made camp, Colonel Green ordered his acting quartermasters to take their light conveyances and bring in supplies to lighten the loads of the stranded commissary wagons. [75]

Gathering up a small party Bill Davidson and 2nd Lieutenant Phil Clough went back to see to the task. The damaged wagon and six others were located about three miles above Peralta in the sand bed. Green "sent positive orders" that, after the supplies were off-loaded, the lightened train was to be brought in to safety. The wagonmaster in charge once again had other ideas. Davidson and Clough told him the Colonel's orders, but "he had turned his teams loose and refused to move." [76] It would shortly prove a costly mistake. The stores were loaded onto the lighter wagons and sent to Connelly's along with word about the condition of affairs. Davidson and Clough remained with the stuck train until about 2 A.M. on the 15th when they were relieved by Lieutenant Darby and an escort of thirty men.

Meanwhile the rest of Green's troops made themselves free with Governor Connelly's rancho and all it contained. When in the wee hours of the morning Canby's men arrived within hearing, their "ears were saluted with the 'sound of revelry by night.' The violin was in full blast, accompanied by other and more noisy instruments." [77] To the Federals' surprise, "The Texan officers were carousing at a fandango." [78] It was apparent to everyone that Green's men were unconscious of their approach. Colonel Green was normally a vigilant commander, but he believed Canby's force was still in Tijeras Canyon. Accordingly he took no precautions against surprise. One Union lieutenant wrote incredulously that during their march they did not encounter a single Texan outpost, "not even a vidette." [79] With the party in full swing, the Texans' security was so lax that one Union scout actually "passed their lines and stood unobserved outside of one of the windows, through which he had a full view of the festivities." [80] Colonel Chivington believed that a golden opportunity was at hand and urged an immediate attack. Canby was reluctant, deeming it better to wait until morning. Chivington's blood was up and when he saw that Canby was not going to order an assault, he "offered to capture or disperse them with the Coloradans alone." Prudently Canby refused. The overeager Colorado troops thought him either "afraid of the result, or jealous." [81]

Next to Fort Union, Connelly's rancho was one of the strongest positions in the territory. According to the Governor, his residence was

> "surrounded by quite a dense forest of trees, extending in every direction for at least half a mile, and the only approach for vehicles is by the main road. The ditches (acequias), for the purpose of irrigation, running across and parallel with the road, offer no small impediment to the operation of artillery." [82]

Henry H. Connelly, Territorial Governor of New Mexico, 1861-1866, ca. 1865. Courtesy Museum of New Mexico, Neg. 9846

Making the Texan position even more formidable were a series of high adobe walls that served as enclosures for Connelly's farmlands. Fandango or not, Canby knew it would be foolhardy to attack such a position, unreconnoitered and in darkness. While the sounds of a waltz and "the hilarious shout of some over-excited participant" carried into the morning hours, Canby positioned his troops. [83] Wheels of the artillery were muffled. Lieutenant Joseph Bell afterwards reminisced that, "quietly, unmolested, the whole command with cautionary silence took position within a few hundred yards of the place, the infantry and heavy field battery on the north, my light battery and mounted troops on the east. No fires were lighted, no noise to apprise the enemy of our presence; and troops quietly lay down in their tracks for a little much-needed sleep before the morning's work." [84]

At sunrise on the 15th, an advance guard of Union regulars moved into the woods surrounding the rancho. Quietly, they overwhelmed and captured Green's unsuspecting pickets. Abruptly the stillness of the New Mexico morning was shattered. Colorado Volunteers from Company F listened in disbelief, as the first sounds they heard were "a thrilling reveille from Canby's bugles." [85] To their further consternation, this was "followed up by the stirring strains of Dixie thrust upon the deathly quiet by the brazen throats of Sibley's Brass Band." Rather than fall upon an unsuspecting enemy as Colonel Chivington suggested, Canby had revealed the Union presence! Both camps were instantly in commotion. In the words of Ovando Hollister, "All thoughts of surprise were at an end." The reveille was a signal to Canby's artillery and in answer "the three great guns" of the heavy battery "hurled their iron surprise into the midst of the revelers." "Boom! Boom! Boom!" "Three more guns, with short-fused shell and round shot, ploughed the ground into furrows that just before was smooth with dancing feet." [86]

With no further reason for stealth, "Captain Graydon's independent company of New Mexico Volunteers galloped [toward] town and exchanged a few shots by way of challenge." [87] Still nearly a mile away, the New Mexicans and Union pickets opened fire on the Texan camp with their long-range rifles. Some of the Confederates were still slumbering; others had fires going and were preparing breakfast. Benton Bell Seat, recently elected Captain of Company F of the 5th Texas, recalled, "I was sitting down at our fire with a frying pan in my hand frying bacon when the enemy opened fire." "One ball struck in the center of the pan and knocked its contents into the fire." [88] Fast asleep, Bill Davidson was startled awake by the volley. "This," wrote Davidson, "was very rude and ungentlemanly yet a very effectual way of waking a fellow up." [89] The nearness of the Federal force shocked the unwary Texans, but they recovered quickly. "The trumpet sounded 'Boots & Saddles'," and everywhere men jumped to their feet and rushed to meet the foe.

About this same time, the Texans' overdue commissary wagons hauled into view. Lieutenant Darby finally had the stalled train moving. Unaware of what was transpiring, he was marching straight toward the enemy. When Canby's men first spotted the wagons, the train was coming from the direction of Albuquerque and was about equidistant between the Union and Confederate positions. Observing through a spyglass, the Federals could see that the train was lightly escorted. Immediately Company F of the Colorado Cavalry was ordered forward and charged out in pursuit. As the Coloradans galloped toward the wagons, Darby's men realized their predicament and prepared to make a defense. With the cavalry thundering down upon them, Ovando Hollister thought the Texans "fluttered like birds in a snare." [90] If Darby's men had abandoned the ponderous wagons and fled, they might easily have reached their own lines. Instead they unlimbered and loaded their little 12-pounder mountain howitzer and took cover around the train. Ignorant of the size of the Union force, Darby probably believed that Colonel Green would hear the firing and come to his aid.

At 200 yards the Coloradans dismounted, deployed as skirmishers, and advanced. As the Volunteers drew within range, Darby's men loosed a volley. Quick as thought, the Coloradans dropped to the ground and returned the fire. Then it was up and forward, and then down again as Darby's men fired a second volley. Among the attackers was John Ferris, brother to Ben Ferris, who was wounded at Glorieta. When Ben was carried away in a hospital wagon John had told him, "If we ever find them Texans, I intend to make them suffer for shooting you." [91] At fifty yards Ferris made good on his promise by leading the Coloradans in a final charge. With a yell, Company F rushed upon the Texans. For a moment there was chaos among the wagons while the two small forces fought at close quarters. A dozen or so of the Texans immediately "dropped their arms and hoisted a dirty handkerchief on a ramrod, in token of surrender." Others continued to fight on or ran. "Some of them were shot down, some captured, and a few escaped." [92] Two companies of Union infantry arrived on the scene in time to witness Darby's surrender. Their rapid approach was undoubtedly one reason for the short-lived Texan defense.

    The brief skirmish was costly for the wagon guard. Six of Darby's men were killed, three wounded, and twenty-two captured. By contrast, the Coloradans suffered only one casualty. [93] Private J.H. Hawley was severely wounded and died a few days later. John Ferris was promoted to sergeant for his valor. Since most of the commissary supplies were unloaded the day before, the Federals were soon disappointed to learn that the wagons contained "nothing of any great value." [94] Still, the assault was a rousing success. The seven wagons were themselves a prize and in addition the Coloradans snared the mountain howitzer, ten to fifteen horses, seventy mules, and a variety of equipment. Everything was gathered up, and in short order the train was put in motion for the Union lines. The victorious Federals added insult to injury by limbering up the little howitzer and forcing the Rebel prisoners to haul it by hand. [95] By the time the

Coloradans got back to their lines, other Texan cannon were booming across the field.

When Canby's bugles alerted the Texans to their danger, Colonel Green immediately organized his force to meet the threat. Los Pinos was completely surrounded by adobe walls and Green ordered his men to positions behind these fortifications. By this point in the campaign the 5th Regiment was short of field officers. Its lieutenant colonel, Henry C. McNeill, was across the river with General Sibley at Los Lunas. Major Lockridge was killed at Valverde and Major Shropshire had fallen at Glorieta. The 5th's senior captains Denman Shannon and Dan Ragsdale had both been captured. Green placed Bethel Coopwood and his independent San Elizario Spy Company in command of his right center. Captain Hugh A. McPhaill from Company E, of the much-reduced 5th, was given charge of his far right. Major Pyron, with the four companies of his command, was posted to anchor the left. In all, Colonel Green had about 550 men and four pieces of artillery. [96]

The woods that encircled Los Pinos offered protection to the Texans, but they also hid Canby's forces from Green's view. To rectify this situation he handed Bill Davidson a field glass and sent him up to a church belfry to observe and report the enemy's movements. Along the way Davidson scooped up Private Fred W. Tremble of Company D of the 5th. The height of the cupola gave the two men a fine view of the surrounding country. More importantly, they could see Canby's army, which Davidson "thought to be about three thousand strong." [97] With the help of his observers, Colonel Green soon put his four howitzers into action.

"The first ball the Texans fired fell short, bounced over the enemy, and buried itself in loose sand behind. The next, after making a high arc in the air, came whizzing in, and crashed among a pair of battery wheel mules." [98]

Both animals were struck in the head and died instantly. Finding that Canby's baggage train was within range, the Texan gunners were soon killing Union mules "three or four at a shot." [99] Federal artillerymen responded and the distraction they caused allowed Union teamsters to move their train to safety. With few worthwhile targets in sight, the artillery on both sides shortly ceased fire. This brief exchange set the tone for the rest of the engagement. Long range, mostly ineffective cannonading would be the order of the day.

Directly, Colonel Canby reorganized his force and hunted for a weakness in the Texan line. Troops under his personal command engaged in heavy, but bloodless, skirmishing with Coopwood's soldiers near the Confederate center right. Meanwhile, Colonels Paul and Chivington split their force into two columns, each with a section of artillery, and headed for the Texan left. Their intent was to move into the heavy timber along the river. From there, they could swing past Los Pinos towards Peralta and control the ford. Slowly, the columns swung around the hamlet in a great arc. [100]

From his vantage point in the cupola, Private Davidson, saw plainly that the enemy was trying to get between the river and the town. Colonel Green immediately dispatched Phil Fulcrod with a 2-gun battery to reinforce Major Pyron. The Lieutenant swung his cannons around behind the church and brought them into line on Pyron's left. Acting quickly, Fulcrod's men tore down a section of adobe wall to get a free field of fire and opened on the advancing Union columns. Paul and Chivington ordered their four pieces of artillery unlimbered and in short order the two batteries were having a lively conversation. The Texans had expended their explosive shell and case in earlier engagements, so Fulcrod pounded the Federal lines with ineffective solid shot. The Union gunners responded in kind. Watching from his perch in the cupola, Bill Davidson "saw cannon balls rolling along the ground like a parcel of marbles." [101] At Valverde, the Federals fired some solid shot, but it flew high overhead and disappeared from sight. At Glorieta the Texans used some round shot against the corrals, but the Union artillery fired only shell and canister. At Peralta, wrote Davidson, "the things were just rolling along without the least respect for persons." [102] "Colonel Chivington and one of his captains barely escaped a cannon ball, which, after skipping along the ground directly toward them, bounded a few inches over their heads." [103] Immediately after clearing the two officers, the shot plowed into two enlisted men to their rear, killing them instantly.

Fulcrod's battery and the four Union cannon, under Lieutenant Claflin, "conversed with each other for about an hour." [104] Meanwhile Canby's other artillery played on Coopwood, who responded with his two cannon, commanded by Lieutenant Joseph H. McGinnis. Despite heavily outnumbering the Confederates, the Federals were at a tactical disadvantage. Green's men were snug behind their adobe walls and his gunners had the enemy's range. The Federals knew that the Texans would not resign until forced. Since they were not making any headway against Fulcrod and Pyron, Paul and Chivington sent about two-thirds of their force back toward the center to search for weakness in that area.

It was just at this time that someone spotted Davidson and Tremble in their cupola. In the center of the Union lines, a cannon was run out on to a small mound and immediately opened fire. At first, the shooting was wild and provided a source of amusement for the two Texans. While Tremble waved his hat at the enemy, Davidson jeered and ridiculed the gunners. Then the Federal aim improved. There was a puff of smoke and a ball screamed directly over the tower and landed about twenty feet in the rear of the church. Now, the two observers became serious. Davidson, thinking that the enemy mistook him for an officer, "bawled out to them that [he] was nothing but a private and lame at that." The Federal reply was another ball that went ripping by closer than the last. Watching from the ground, friends could see the two men trying to smile at each other. "It was a very ghastly affair," remembered a trooper, "more like two opossums grinning at each other." [105] The next shot smashed though the old tower just under the observers' feet, tearing a good deal of it away. Both men's faces were white as sheets. Colonel Green, who was busy directing his troops, now, looked toward his sentinels in the watchtower. Spying the gaping hole under their feet, he instantly yelled, "Come down from there d--d quick!" The Colonel's words were wasted because Tremble was on the ground before he got them out. Davidson was so close on his friend's heels that most of those watching felt it was only his lameness that kept him from winning the race. "Such a getting down stairs you never did see." [106]

About this time the weather turned ugly. Everywhere there was water, it froze thick and a biting wind blew at nearly fifty miles per hour. "The enemy's round shot were tearing and rolling round and as thick as hops, and things were looking gloomy" for the Texans. [107] The Union troops kept marching and maneuvering around Green's beleaguered men, making demonstrations first at one point and then at another. Despite the lack of a general engagement, the Union posturing unnerved the outnumbered Texans.

According to a Rebel Private, "We were beginning to think that the time had come when we were to pass in our checks." [108] Suddenly, a loud cheer from Coopwood's men, down on the extreme right, announced that something was afoot. Green's other men looked down that way to see what was transpiring and then hats went up, along with yell after yell. Coming up from the river at the double quick was Colonel Scurry, with the 4th and 7th Regiments at his heels!

One of Colonel Green's first actions, upon finding Canby's army at his doorstep, was to send an express rider across the river to Los Lunas to locate General Sibley. On being notified of the critical situation of Green's command, the General had quickly dispatched Scurry to his relief, along with the whole disposable force at Los Lunas. The men of the 4th and 7th, who had already begun their day's march, turned their wagons around and countermarched to Los Lunas. Reaching their late place of encampment, they left the wagons and all with a light guard, and rushed to their comrades assistance. Despite the severe cold, Scurry and his men broke the ice on the edges of the Rio Grande and waded in. While more slush ice floated by, the soldiers crossed in muddy water, which swirled around their waists and sometimes reached their armpits. By the time they reached Peralta, "their clothes were actually frozen upon them." [109] It was only 11 A.M.

Mindful of the calamity that overtook Scurry at Glorieta, General Sibley remained in Los Lunas for a short time to organize a proper defense for his supplies. Major Teel, who also remained behind, gathered together the remaining troops and saw to their disposition. Lookouts were placed on the rooftops and mounted pickets were thrown out around the town's perimeter. The rest of the rear guard formed a line and settled down to await news from across the river. [110]

With his supplies relatively secure, General Sibley, accompanied by Major Teel, Captain Willis L. Robards, and Captain Henry E. Loebnitz galloped for the battlefield three miles away. Planning to assume immediate command of his forces, the General hurried across the ford. He later reported in dismay, "having crossed the river, I was notified by several officers who had preceded me some hundred yards of the rapid approach of a large number of the enemy's cavalry." [111] Canby's troops had pushed the Texans out of the bosque on the far left and now controlled a portion of the ford. Finding themselves completely cut off, General Sibley and his staff had no alternative, but to plunge back into the icy water and return to Los Lunas. When part way across, the Federals opened fire and the little party continued "amid a shower of balls." [112] Except for a few minutes at Valverde, this was the only time Henry Sibley was under fire during the whole campaign. Moments later, the General and his staff clambered safely onto the west bank. Once again the Confederate Army of New Mexico was involved in a significant life or death struggle and its commander would never make it to the field.

After Scurry and his men emerged wet and dripping from the river, there were enough Confederates in Peralta to contest the field. Ironically, their "ammunition was too scarce to hazard a fight." In a letter to his father, Sergeant James Franklin Starr, complained that because of the shortage, "We were obliged to act on the defensive and not bring on the battle as we usually did by attacking." [113] Just the same, the action now began to heat up on the Texan center right. A battery that withdrew from in front of Pyron joined Canby's other artillery across the field and began to pound Coopwood's position. At the same time, Federal troops began massing in that direction.

Colonel Green quickly shifted his strength to counter the threat by ordering Lieutenant Fulcrod to limber his two cannon and join McGinnis. When after some time the battery failed to make its appearance, Green detailed Bill Davidson to go see what had become of it. Racing back to the left, Davidson found Fulcrod "stalled in a deep bed of sand right in front of the old church." One of his horses had a bad shoulder, and instead of pulling forward, was pulling backwards and would not budge. "The tears were running down [Fulcrod's] cheeks and he was in a terrible stew." To make matters worse the Federal artillery had discovered his predicament and were beginning to drop shells around him. "As a shell would burst near him, he would shake his fist at them and exclaim, 'I'll give you h--l for this!'" [114] Fortunately, Davidson was mounted on a large fine mule. The two animals were soon exchanged, and Fulcrod was on his way.

On reaching McGinnis, Fulcrod unlimbered. With the help of sergeants Timothy Nettles and Peyton Hume, he then commenced another lively duel with the Federals. Many of the Texans found satisfaction that their gunners were using some of the cannons they captured at Valverde. Theophilus Noel wrote, "Here it was that the Valverde Battery was first tried by us. Such shots as were made by it on this occasion are but rare occurrences in the history of artillery firing. Every man belonging to it proved himself a hero." [115]

The enthusiasm and perseverance of the Confederate gunners notwithstanding, the cannonade was a very one-sided affair. Hunkered down under cover, Bill Davidson estimated that, the Texans' four guns were countered by at least eighteen Federal pieces, booming away across the field. [116] Fulcrod and McGinnis had nothing to fire except solid shot, which although impressive did little damage. Alonzo Ickis, lying behind one of the Union batteries, watched the solid shot "coming thick and fast." It seemed to the twenty-six-year-old Private that the cannon balls "whistle Secesh [secessionist] very loud as they pass over our heads." [117] Quickly tiring of the game of giant marbles the Federal gunners switched to explosive shell. For the next two hours the Union guns pounded the Confederate positions, while Federal troops massed on the right.

Lying behind an adobe wall, a young Texan private watched in horror as an enemy shell fell right behind his position. "The fuse was burning 'chew, chew'." Recalling his fearful wait for the ensuing explosion he wrote, "I was spread out as thin as I could, but it still seemed to me that I was nineteen feet-thick and forty-eight feet long, and when the thing exploded it was bound to hit me." [118] At the last moment, Benjamin Slater of Company A of the 5th Texas, ran forward, scooped up the spluttering shell, and hurled it into water filled ditch, extinguishing the fuse. Reflecting on his brave but foolhardy act, Slater said, "It was better for it to kill [me] than the whole company." [119]

Lacking explosive or antipersonnel rounds of their own, Fulcrod and McGinnis tried firing a few rounds of glass bottles. This unconventional barrage served only to enrage the Federals. The bottles contained some liquid and a rumor quickly circulated among the Union troops that it was poison. Seething with anger Colonel Chivington sent a messenger to the Texans, under a flag of truce, with the promise that "if they fired another bottle or any other poisonous substance" he "would kill and scalp every 'S of a B' of them." [120] The Texan gunners took the threat to heart and switched back to solid shot.

Waiting near the Union center, Colonel Paul was anxious to bring on an engagement. He could see that Lieutenant Colonel Roberts had massed Canby's troops and artillery and seemed to be gaining the other side of the town. The troops from Fort Union expected that at any moment a signal would be given and both wings would "assault and take the place by storm." [121]

Everything seemed in readiness for a final onslaught, when Colonel Canby rode up and put a stop to the plans. His subordinates were flabbergasted. Lieutenant Colonel Roberts even begged Canby to let his men charge. Roberts argued that Sibley was already beaten, the Texans demoralized, and but few men would be lost in an assault. Canby ended the discussion by saying, "Even if I could take it, I don't want to lose the men necessary to do it, when I can accomplish the same object without losing a man." [122] The Union commander was by nature a cautious man and he felt no reason to hurry. Canby knew that hunger and exposure were his allies and that if he did not defeat the Texans by force of arms, victory would soon lie with the Union just the same. At about 2 P.M. Canby ordered a halt to his cannonade and the Federals fell back to wait. "They withdrew to a safe distance," noted one Texan, "leaving us in quiet possession of the field. Their encampments, however, were within full view of the garrison." [123] About this same time the high wind, that had howled all day, became a veritable storm. "The air was one solid cloud of moving sand and dust in which one could scarcely breathe. Further operations were impossible while it continued." [124]

So ended the "Battle of Peralta." Considering the number of troops involved and the amount of ordnance expended, it was one of the most harmless battles on record. Soldiers from both sides made light of the fighting. Julius Giesecke wrote in his diary, "When the Yankees found out that the First regiment had waded the river and were advancing for the attack, they retreated and a few cannon shots only were exchanged." [125] A Colorado Volunteer described the action saying, it put him "in mind of two gamblers colleagued to do a greeny, betting and bluffing together with perfect recklessness to bait him, but suddenly finding their judgment when he put his foot into it." 126 These opinions may accurately portray the results of the fighting, but they do not necessarily reflect the action's intensity. On the day of the battle, another Colorado Volunteer wrote in his diary, "The enemy had neither shell, grape, or canister. Their loss cannot fall much short of 200 killed & wounded for we played the shell into them all day from 8 to 6." 127

Actual Confederate losses were only six killed, three wounded, and twenty-two captured, all incurred during the capture of the wagon train. 128 In Los Pinos itself, they "lost not a man." 129 Reflecting on the fighting, one Texan remembered, "We had no men killed or wounded, and why we did not seems a miracle, for their round shot and shell fell all around and about us." 130 Reports of Union casualties conflict somewhat, but they were also very light. Colonel Canby reported that losses during the morning skirmish in the woods were "one killed and three wounded." 131 Another Colorado Volunteer was killed during the charge upon the wagon train and Ovando Hollister noted the "loss of two men (killed by round shot)." 132

Following the Federal withdrawal, the Texans regrouped and waited to see what would develop. Captain Seat, who had the frying pan knocked from his hand during breakfast, related that "Very soon the camp fires were started and supper prepared." 133 "After night-fall," General Sibley, still in Los Lunas, "gave orders for the recrossing of the whole army to the west bank of the river." 134 Colonel Green knew that for the evacuation to succeed, it would need to be completed before dawn and without the enemy's knowledge. To cover his withdrawal, he readied the same ruse that Canby used effectively at Albuquerque.

A detail was made up from each company and a string of bright fires were lit all along the Texan front. Green ordered that the fires be kept going all night and that a guard be posted visibly in front of each. In the meantime, preparations were made to leave. [135]

Colonel Green ordered Bill Davidson to gather the command's remaining wagons and get them ready to move. Teamsters were admonished about the need for silence and secrecy, and promptly set about the work. Supplies that could not be easily moved were abandoned or destroyed. "One of the wagons loaded with captured rifles, was emptied of its contents and the rifles broken up and some thrown into the river." [136] At around 8 o'clock, Davidson quietly moved the wagons down to the ford and began the crossing. Straightaway, there were problems. The brigade's mules were worn down, the river was swollen, and the quicksand deep. Soldiers and teamsters alike were left with little choice, except to wade into the water, "take hold of the wheels and push to enable the mules to pull through." [137] It proved an all-night job. The weather was extremely cold and the river was running with slush ice, yet many of the Texans remained in the water from 8 P.M. on the 15th until 6 A.M. on the 16th. Bill Davidson and Captain Hardeman of the 4th "were in the river nearly all the time, pushing at the wheels." [138]

Just before dawn Colonel Green ordered his soldiers to abandon their positions. Leaving their campfires burning, the men of brigade marched into the river and headed for Los Lunas. For the men of the 4th and 7th, this was their second crossing in 24 hours. It was a miserable affair. "The river was nearly eight hundred yards wide; that night ice had frozen four inches thick; 'mush' ice was running in the river, which was fast rising; the water on the ford was on an average of four feet deep." [139] Wading in water up to their armpits, the Texans crossed, holding rifles over their heads with one hand and cartridge boxes with the other. William Howell noted in his diary; "We get into Los Lunas at 4 A.M. wet and sleepy." [140] Despite their early start, the Texans' slow moving supply wagons were the last elements of the Army of New Mexico to finish the crossing. At sun-up, the weary teamsters "rolled the last wagon up the west bank of the river, just as the enemy's advance guard reached the east bank." [141]

When the Union troops discovered the Texans, across the river, "snapping their fingers" in disdain, they were outraged. Grumbling was rampant. Ordinary soldiers, chiefly the Coloradans, castigated Colonel Canby unmercifully for allowing their enemy to escape. "Of what avail our forced marches?" railed a volunteer. "Our regiment has made great efforts and sacrifices to meet the vile traitors and see them escape when actually within our grasp, from the stupidity or treachery of our General, effectually kills enthusiasm if it goes no farther." In the following days, Canby was accused of everything from cowardice to collusion. After all wrote Ovando Hollister, "Canby and Sibley are comrades of old." [142]

Chapter 12

THE LONG WALK HOME

"We beat the enemy whenever we encountered them. The famishing country beat us."
- General Henry Hopkins Sibley

The Texans narrowly escaped from Peralta, but with the river between themselves and their enemy they felt adequately secure. General Sibley reassumed command and they proceeded at a leisurely pace to Los Lunas where they made breakfast and dried their clothing. While the men were eating and drying out, the General ordered the brigade's remaining heavy baggage destroyed. Nearly everything except foodstuffs and ammunition was either burnt or discarded. The only things the Texans kept were one suit of clothes per man, their blankets and overcoats, and some cooking utensils. Sibley's goal was to further lighten his supply wagons so that the teams could move more rapidly. If the Texans marched quickly enough, it was just possible that they could beat Canby to Fort Craig and overwhelm its reduced garrison, before he could arrive. [1]

With everything in readiness the brigade set out in a body down the river. Colonel Scurry with the 4th and 7th Regiments took the advance. Tom Green followed with the 5th Regiment, the wagon train and the artillery. Major Pyron's men, who were still well mounted, took up position as the column's rear guard. April 16th was no more pleasant for the weary Confederates than the long night before. All day, they trudged slowly through heavy sand while the wind blew unabated. The dust and sand were extremely distressing; swirling around the men in clouds that threatened to blind them as they struggled along. [2]

Colonel Canby did not start an immediate pursuit, but neither did he let the Texans just walk away unmolested. An advance guard of cavalry, under command of Captain Robert M. Morris, was sent down the east bank to shadow the Confederates' movements. Whenever the Texans looked across the river, there was "that confounded cavalry of the enemy right opposite." [3] A soldier of the 5th Regiment wrote; all day long, they watched "the enemy's advance guard halting when we halted, and moving when we moved." [4] Two or three companies of Union cavalry also crossed the river and dogged the rear of the Texan column, trying to pick up stragglers. This party, possibly Captain Graydon's company reinforced by some regular cavalry, cautiously followed the Confederates, always there, always just out of range. [5]

After covering about 15 miles, the Texans reached the area of Belén. Wood was plentiful in the area so they halted for the night. Since leaving Los Lunas, there had been no sign of the enemy in force. [6]

Canby had tarried at Peralta. Although well assured that the Texans were on the other side of the river and some distance below, Canby did not rush his troops into the town. Instead, to the annoyance of the more hotheaded among his command, he spent the morning reorganizing his forces. As Ovando Hollister put it, "We maneuvered round Peralta something like a dog round a rattlesnake. Courage having swelled to the requisite degree, we entered the town." [7] It was around noon when the "cavalry and infantry charged into the deserted plaza, followed by the racket of moving batteries." [8] The debris of the previous day's clash was scattered everywhere. In their stealthy flight the Texans discarded everything that was a hindrance. Wheelless ambulances, broken wagons and other impediments littered the town. Sick and wounded Confederates, who remained behind, without medicine and almost without food, demanded attention.

Evidence of destruction was on all sides. The havoc caused by the Union artillery barrage was extensive, but Green's men did considerable damage themselves. Governor Henry Connelly wrote in a letter to W.H. Seward that the Texans inflicted $30,000 damage on his estate, "much of this through a pure vandalic spirit." [9]

In 1862, Peralta was "for two miles a succession of adobe houses, thick heavy walls of the same material, raised acequias equal to common field works and patches of large cottonwood timber." On entering the place, the Union soldiers were astonished, that the Texans ever decided to leave. If defended with spirit, the town could scarcely have been taken. Sibley's choice to abandon it was proof to everyone that the Texans were "irreparably lame somewhere." [10] For the first time, ordinary Union soldiers realized that, the Confederates were too far from their base of supply and were probably destitute of the stores necessary to wage war.

It was obvious to the Union commander that Sibley's army was trying to abandon the Territory. No longer anticipating battle, Canby detached "staff officers attached to departmental headquarters to make arrangements for future operations." [11] Most importantly, Canby detached his Senior Quartermaster, Captain J.C. McFerran. McFerran was ordered to take all the wagons the army could spare and return to Fort Union. Once there, he was to gather supplies and forward them as soon as possible. Canby's army, like Sibley's, was running low on food. Since Fort Craig alone could not support the force he was marching down the Rio Grande, Canby knew immediate resupply was critical to any future action.

With Peralta secure and his arrangements in order, Canby divided his remaining command into three columns and set out after his advance. Colonel Paul commanded one column, Colonel Chivington another, and Captain Morris with all the cavalry the third. Rather than cross his force and pursue Sibley directly, Canby chose to remain on the left bank. This road was supposedly shorter and he believed he would eventually overtake the Texans. Once ahead of the enemy, Canby intended to cross his force at La Joya, Polvadera, Sabino, or Fort Craig. [12]

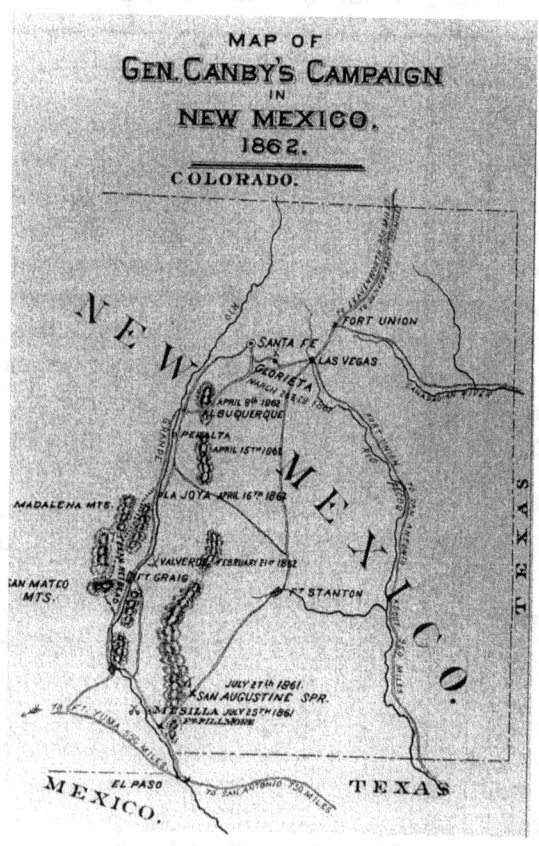

"Map of Gen. Canby's Campaign in New Mexico 1862." From: Anderson, Latham. "Canby's Campaign in New Mexico." In Sketches of War History 1861-1865, Papers Read Before the Ohio Commandry of the Military Order of the Loyal Legion of the United States 1886-1888. Copyright: Cincinnati, OH: Robert Clarke & Co., 1888

Below Los Lunas, the Federals looked across the river and saw the smoking remains of Sibley's heavy baggage. For some, this conjured up annoying images of their enemy, "two or three hours ahead, proceeding at their leisure." The weather did nothing to improve the soldiers' disposition. "The wind blew tremendously all day and the air was moving sand." [13] After covering about ten or twelve miles, Canby ordered a halt. The Texans were still five miles ahead.

That night there was more grumbling in the Union camp. Ovando Hollister's diary for April 16th, 1862 contains the entry, "Sixty miles per day to catch the traitors and ten to let them go. Of course it is all right. We do not want to take any unfair advantage of them." [14] Such expressions of dissatisfaction found voice most often among the Coloradans and other troops from Fort Union. These soldiers were still excited by their serendipitous success at Apache Canyon and wanted to gloriously finish the job they had begun. They suspected that Canby intended to let the Texans slip away without a fight.

This assessment was probably correct. In field reports from this period, General Canby wrote that he was pursuing the Confederates with "hopes of intercepting them." [15] It is likely that this was simply martial bravado for the benefit of superiors in Washington. The moment the Texans abandoned Peralta, Canby probably decided to let them go. At the time, few of the well-fed soldiers from Fort Union understood their commander's motives. They were no doubt clearer to Canby's own troops. These men were "on half rations or less since the 21st of Feb." "Kit" Carson's command, waiting at Fort Craig, was subsisting "on 8oz of flour" per man per day "and very little of anything else." [16]

Suspicions to the contrary aside, Canby's decision had nothing to do with courage or past associations. It was strictly a matter of logistics. His troops were under-supplied. With barren country and little else stretched before them they would face hunger until Captain McFerran returned with supplies from the north. Canby knew that if he overtook and defeated Sibley, he would have to provide for his enemy's army as well as his own. Always a cautious officer, he probably felt it was more expedient to simply let Sibley escape.

    Even if he made a decision to avoid further engagement, Canby still intended to hurry the Confederate Army of New Mexico on its way. When the Texans awoke on the morning of April 17th, they found that the Federals had gained on them while they slept. Captain Morris with the Union cavalry was across the river, directly opposite their camp. Not far away, the enemy "with all his paraphernalia of war, was in full view," moving down the far shore. "In this way the two armies marched the entire day, frequently within one mile of each other - all the time in full view." [17] Colonel Canby remarked that, for most of the day, the two forces were "almost within cannon range." [18] "When one halted, no matter how short the halt, the other did likewise." [19] Men from both sides found the situation novel. Here were two hostile armies with only a narrow river between them, "Marching together, halting together, one imitating every move of the other, neither seeming anxious to bring on a battle, yet neither trying to avoid it." [20]

    The proximity of the enemy was "inviting to those fond of fight." [21] For some of Sibley's men the temptation to provoke the Federals was just too great. In one instance Joe Bowers, from the "Arizona Guards", made his way down to the river bank and shouted at the top of his lungs, "Say, I want to know whether you fellows have gone crazy, or whether you are a set of d--d fools, naturally." [22] A couple of pieces of Union lead quickly chased him back to his company. At intervals throughout day Texan pickets skirmished with Union cavalry across the river and "sharpshooters exchanged compliments." [23]

The Confederates expected an attack by the superior Union force, but it never came. Time and time again Texan pickets tried to entice the Federals to cross the river, "but the enemy would never take up the gauntlet thus thrown down." [24] Some of Sibley's men assumed their enemy was afraid. Canby's command was nearly 2,000 strong and included a splendid train of nearly 100 wagons, but the Texans were not impressed. Sibley's men knew that the army across the river consisted of the "Pikes Peakers" they fought at Glorieta and troops from Fort Craig that they bested at Valverde. Expressing a general contempt, Alfred Peticolas wrote, "These forces opposite us we have whipped some of them twice, and we are all confident that we can clean them up again." As for Carson's New Mexican troops, waiting at Fort Craig, "we despise rather than dread them." [25]

Around 1 o'clock in the afternoon the Texans crossed the mouth of the Rio Puerco and called a halt. It was early, but they had already covered fifteen miles. With Canby shadowing their every movement decisions needed to be made before they went any farther. In full view of the enemy Sibley's army made camp on the open prairie. While the men lounged, the General called a council of war. With a two-day head start on Canby out of Albuquerque, Sibley's original intention was to push down the river, attack the weak garrison at Craig, and demolish the fort as a parting insult. Colonel Green's inability to find a convenient point to cross the river and Canby's sudden appearance defeated that plan. Seemingly divining their object the Union commander had managed to unite his scattered forces and intercept the Texans' march. Reproachfully, one of Colonel Green's men later wrote, "The events of Paralto [sic] have disclosed the fact to our leaders, which they ought to have known at first, that we have a wise and vigilant foe, who is keeping a close watch on our every move." 26

A collision appeared unavoidable. With Canby snapping at his heels, Sibley's failure to subdue Fort Craig was back to haunt him. The next day the Texans' passage would surely be contested in the narrows around Polvadera. Carson's regiment from the fort would be in their front, and Canby would be at their rear. The Union forces would occupy the heights with their artillery and crush Sibley's army or compel surrender. Despite the confidence of their men, the Rebel officers knew that they lacked the ammunition and other resources necessary for a general action. Not over 1,000 men of the brigade were fit for duty. Each man had less than forty rounds of ammunition and only twenty rounds remained for each of their nine cannon. If forced to fight, the Texans were going to loose. 27

At this critical point, Colonel Green and Colonel Scurry with several practical officers stepped forward and proposed a desperate gamble. Since Fort Craig was sitting astride the Camino Real, guarding both the level Chihuahua road across the Jornada del Muerto and the river channel route to the south, the only uncontested road lay southwest toward the craggy Magdalena Mountains. Green and the others reasoned that if they abandoned everything, except their food, small arms, and artillery, they might elude their pursuers in the rugged canyons. Making a detour of 100 miles, the brigade could bypass Craig entirely and strike the Rio Grande near Amilla, some thirty miles below the fort. 28

Bethel Coopwood, who because of his recent ascent from Mesilla, was familiar with the area, offered to undertake "the difficult and responsible task of guiding the army through this mountainous, trackless waste." Colonel Scurry pledged that his regiment would see that the brigade's artillery were "put over every obstacle, however formidable." [29] Everyone understood the impending danger, yet some of the brigade's officers still "wanted to go on to Polvadera, make a glorious battle and an honorable surrender." [30] Sibley "was in favor of going down the river. Green, Coopwood, and McNeill preferred the mountain route, and Scurry was silent." [31] The council turned heated and contentious. Captain Alfred Thurmond became so disrespectful that General Sibley threatened him with arrest. "Scurry was called on for his opinion but refused to give it at all." [32] Captain Coopwood got so mad, that he hopped up and left. Colonel Green, who originally proposed the mountain route, "became sullen and would not express himself in favor of either side, but seemed to think one course was death in a northern prison; the other death in the mountains." [33] Eventually, the determination was made to try the mountains. General Sibley, afterwards, wrote of the decision, "The arguments presented in favor of this course were potent. Besides having the advantage of grass and a firm road, with very little difference in distance, the enemy would be completely mystified." [34]

With a course of action settled, the council broke up and orders were swiftly issued. "Wear what you can, provide seven days rations, destroy the remainder, and carry your guns and ammunition if nothing more." [35] The orders were well received among the men. Although faced with an uncertain journey of 100 miles through an almost waterless wilderness, most preferred that to the prospect of pining away the war in a northern prison. Even before the decision was made, some of the men started to make preparations on their own. While the council was still in full swing, Bill Davidson came upon his friend Fred Tremble and several of Pyron's men "strapping their grub to their saddles." When he asked them what they were about, "they replied that there was talk of going down to Pulvedeer [sic] making a fight and then surrender;

they would go down, fight as long as Gen. Sibley said fight, but the moment he said surrender, they were going with Coopwood into the mountains and make their way to Texas." 36

Everyone prepared to follow Coopwood. Having completed their suppers, Sibley's men packed their blankets and remaining food onto the brigade's mules and started destroying everything else which was not essential. Once valued possessions were scattered everywhere. Wagons, clothing of all descriptions and a great amount of baggage were all consigned to the flames. Despite blowing sand, the Federals, across the river could see the huge bonfires burning brightly with the liberal admixture of pieces and parcels. Alonzo Ickis wrote laconically in his diary, "Enemy is burning wagons this evening." 37

By dark everything was in readiness. All that remained was to take leave of those forced to remain behind. Eighteen-year-old John Wesley Shiflett had joined Isaac Adair's company in Crockett Texas. He had marched more than a thousand miles and fought beside his fallen captain at Glorieta Pass. Like many sick and invalid soldiers, he avoided capture at Albuquerque by joining his fellows on their retreat. On the night of April 17th, Shiflett knew that he was too weak to continue. With the rigors of the mountains ahead all his efforts came to nothing. Alfred Peticolas wrote, "It was affecting to see the brave companions in arms of these sick men grasping them by the hand and bidding them an affectionate farewell. 'Good bye,' said one as he squeezed his companion's hand, 'The abs will take me in tomorrow morning.'" 38 As their friends marched off into the darkness the men left behind huddled around their campfires to await their fate. From the corner of a remaining wagon a yellow hospital flag fluttered above their heads.

It was about 7 P.M. when the brigade took up the line of march. The 4th and 7th regiments took the lead with most of the artillery and caissons. Colonel Green and the 5th regiment brought up the rear with another section of artillery and a few supply wagons. Green maintained that it was a mistake to destroy all of the brigade's transport, so he retained three heavy wagons and several lighter conveyances. These he "thought could be taken through, and would be of service in hauling the sick and men who gave out." [39] The brigade continued west-southwest toward the southern slopes of Ladron Peak until it "reached the hilly cedar country of the mountains." [40] It was well after midnight when the men spread their blankets on the ground and "made a dry camp, without any water or anything to eat." [41]

At sunup Colonel Scurry roused the regiments and told the soldiers, "Come, boys, its only four miles to breakfast; let's go and get it!" [42] Taking a bite of bread and a swallow from their canteens the men repacked their mules and set out down a sandy canyon. As the columns crawled along their pace slowed and hours slipped by. Scurry's four miles eventually proved closer to eight or ten and it was 10 A.M. before the first tired and thirsty soldiers reached the brackish waters of Salado Creek. Gratefully they threw themselves down to rest. A good many of the men were worn down from illness and exposure and the morning's exertions nearly finished them. The march through the mountains had only begun and already it was taking its toll. [43]

The creek's salty water drew mixed reactions from the Texans. "How refreshing!" exclaimed a thirsty trooper. "None can tell, save those who, like myself, were feeble from the effects of sickness and compelled to make the long marches from one point to another on foot." [44] For most of the men it was a different story. Voicing the common opinion, Sergeant Peticolas wrote, "This water we found extremely unpalatable and salty, and the coffee made from it was hardly fit to drink at all, and as we had nothing but coffee and bread, we had pretty hard fare." 45 Faced with a march of fully twenty-five miles to the next available water, the Texans were compelled to stay and drink their bitter coffee.

It was still early, but Scurry's men made camp along the creek and settled down to wait. Colonel Green's command was fettered by its supply train and was spread along the length of the morning's march. His three heavy wagons were at the end of the column and were moving at a snail's pace. "The road was deep, heavy sand, the mules so poor that they could hardly pull." Bill Davidson, who was again in charge of Green's train, was reduced to moving the wagons one at a time. He "would have all the mules put to one wagon and by pushing at the wheels, take it a short distance and then go back and bring up the others." 46 Because of the delay, everyone suffered for water. Around 2 P.M. the column's mounted rear guard had enough and went trotting off toward the Salado. Davidson and the teamsters were the only troops still on the trail. Realizing the futility of their efforts, Davidson sent word to Colonel Green.

Promising the other regiments that he would leave his train if they waited for him, Green took a detachment of men and went back for his wagoneers and supplies. Everything of use was unloaded from the stalled conveyances and packed onto horses and mules. Abandoning the useless wagons where they sat, Green's detachment and the teamsters arrived at the brigade's camp at about 5 o'clock. Almost everyone was exhausted for wont of water. 47

Back on the Rio Grande, Union troops awoke on the morning of the 18th to find the Texans gone. A soldier looking across the river noted, "This morning there is nothing to be seen of our foe but nine wagons, which it seems he was compelled to leave." 48 As General Sibley predicted, his move mystified the

Federals. Officer and enlisted man alike could not believe that the Texans were foolhardy enough to trust their fates to the barren and near waterless mountains. Suddenly, it was obvious to the Union soldiers that they were winning. While avoiding a bloody confrontation, they were driving the invaders from New Mexico.

"Paddy" Graydon and his spy company were the first Federals across the river. Reconnoitering the abandoned camp, they discovered that the nine wagons contained the Texan sick and disabled and little else. These they left untouched. When Graydon reported the situation, Colonel Canby immediately issued orders to have the prisoners collected and properly cared for. "After making arrangements for securing the property abandoned by the enemy the march was continued to Polvadera." [49] As the main body of Federals trudged off down the east bank of the river, Graydon's spy company set out to dog the Texans' trail.

The fruitless struggle with Colonel Green's wagons made it clear that they were more of a hindrance than they were worth. On the morning of the 19th, near Salado Creek, the Texans burned or blew up most of their remaining wheeled vehicles. Six, one-hundred-pound barrels of gunpowder were also burnt along with one hundred rounds of cannon ammunition. Reconnoitering in the Texans wake, Paddy Graydon reported that he found the remains of nineteen wagons, ten ambulances, and six caissons. To further reduce their load, the Texans also destroyed the carriages for two mountain howitzers and one 12-pounder field howitzer. The tubes of the three cannon, along with seventy-eight artillery shells were secretly buried. [50] The Texans' train, which once numbered more than 100 wagons, was reduced to almost nothing. All that remained were the carriages of some private citizens and a few conveyances belonging to Sibley's regimental staff.

According to Private Sharp Whitley, the lightened column was preparing to march when "a rumpus was raised about Davidson's mule, which he loaned to Fulcrod at Peralta." With the wagons gone, Bill Davidson discovered himself on foot. Finding the situation disagreeable, he went to Fulcrod and requested the return of his steed. The Lieutenant said that "he had pledged his honor to return it, and told him to take it." Others disagreed and demanded that the mule remain with the artillery. Tempers flared and a considerable dispute broke out. Davidson and Fulcrod were on one side and good many on the other. To cut the matter short, Davidson took the mule. The aggrieved artillerymen petitioned General Sibley. Taking their side, Sibley issued a special order to press the mule for the artillery. Next, Colonel Green waded into the altercation. Indignant over Sibley's action, Green said that "the mule belonged to a crippled soldier who had risked his life to get it, and they would have to whip the 5th regiment before they should take it." As no one wanted to take the tempest in a teapot to the next level, this pronouncement settled the matter. Davidson got to take his animal. With his anger mollified he quickly thought better of the ruckus he had caused. Magnanimously, he walked "the mule back over and loaned it to the artillery till they got to the Rio Grande." [51] Before the sunset, Davidson probably regretted his decision.

The Texans' trek on the 19th was one of the most difficult of the entire campaign. There was no road to follow and little order to the march. Alfred Peticolas mused,

"The brigade presents a singular appearance this morning. A great many of the infantry, tired of marching through heavy sand, have picked up mules, little poor scrawny things, upon which they tie a fold of blankets for a saddle, and with a rope for a bridle strike out, every man for himself." [52]

For the first couple of miles the procession wound through a narrow canyon between vertical walls of rock. The salt creek seeped or crawled down the narrow valley floor and the going was boggy. After marching about five miles the troops paused at a small spring near the junction of the Rio Salado and La Jencia Creek. Here they filled their canteens and got a bite to eat. From this spot, it was a full twenty miles to the next available water. [53]

Continuing southward, the Texans began an arduous ascent out of the canyon. The slopes they needed to climb to reach the tablelands above were extremely steep and high. The 4th Regiment's artillery gained the hill first and was immediately stalled. Jumping down from his horse, Colonel Scurry laid hold of one of the cannon ropes and called for volunteers to help the guns up the slope. "Men flocked to the pieces and the whole six were soon drawn safely to the top." [54] In the coming days, the brigade would worm its way through the precipitous, deeply canyoned San Mateo Mountains and this performance would be repeated time and time again. Sergeant Frank Starr wrote of the 4th Regiment's heroic efforts,

"Whenever they came to one of those hills up which a horse could scarcely go, the men would take hold where ever they could and by pushing and pulling with ropes they would get them up - Colonels, Captains and all working alike - everyone determining that those guns should go through." [55]

After gaining the canyon rim Captain Coopwood assumed his role as pilot and guide and struck out to the southwest. With a vast plain stretching before them, the rest of the brigade strung out in his wake. The troops plodded four or five miles when suddenly three antelope burst from the grass beside the column. Trying to get past, the panicked animals ran at full speed up the line of men. Alfred Peticolas recalled that as they sprinted by "a hundred guns discharged at them." [56] All the antelope were killed, but one managed to round the head of the column. Despite the veritable barrage this last animal nearly made its escape before it was brought down. Later in the day a bear was killed, which was described as weighing 400 pounds. The fresh game from these two encounters was a welcome addition to the Texans' larder. By this time their supplies were nearly exhausted and the men were surviving on a diet of bread and coffee. Unfortunately, the windfalls did not stretch very far when, as Private Sharp Whitley noted, "the boys tried to divide equally among them all." Other than a few wild turkeys and one or two broken down oxen "that the weakest and nearest starved were permitted to eat." This was the only meat the brigade ate during the entire retreat. [57]

After the brief excitement caused by the antelope, several miles of marching brought the column to their second obstacle of the day. The upper canyon of La Jencia Creek swung westward and once again and lay across the Texans' path. Although not particularly steep sided, to the weary soldiers the declivity appeared "a tremendous canyon 500 feet deep." [58] With no choice but to continue the men again attached ropes and began the strenuous chore of crossing their remaining wagons and artillery. It was late in the evening before the task was complete. Everyone was exhausted and thirsty, but water was still many miles ahead on the other side of a mountain pass. Slowly, the men began the long gradual ascent toward the summit.

Private Howell, who was spending his first day on foot and who was feeling very feeble, described their path as "an awful rocky mountainous track." [59] As exertion and thirst took their toll both men and animals alike began to break down. When the brigade's advance finally gained the pass the sun was setting and water was still six miles off. The men's' throats were parched and those who were strong enough hurried forward. "No order was observed," wrote one soldier. "No company stayed together. The weary sank down upon the grass regardless of cold to rest." Despite encouragement from their fellows, many despaired of ever reaching water, stopped, built fires, and slept. "Packs slipped off the bare backed mules, and mules gave out and refused to move farther." [60] Those, who were able, pressed on. It was well after dark when the first of the men finally entered a canyon, abundant with oak, cedar and fir, and reached a spring of good water. This large spring, which is called Ojo del Pueblo after the ruins of a nearby Indian village, is located about one-mile northwest of present-day Magdalena, New Mexico. [61] "The column, which on first setting out in the morning, was perhaps scarcely one mile in length" was by this time "at least ten miles long." [62] Among those still on the road, the cry became more intense and universal for water. At every fire, exhausted soldiers would stop, inquire the distance to water, and then with hopes blasted stumble on.

Alfred Peticolas, who was leading a packhorse, was so tired that when he "lost blankets, overcoats and everything that was under the pack," he failed to even notice. [63] Others discarded belongings intentionally, unwilling to lug the burdens a step further. Scouting the Texans' route a couple of weeks later, Paddy Graydon reported that the road was "strewn with old harness, iron ovens, and in fact everything but small ammunition." 64

The Texan camp that night was a scene of utter confusion. The supply of water from the spring was plentiful, but thirsty horses and men rushing to drink soon muddied it. Troops, who arrived first, camped without any regard for their units. As each new man or group of men straggled in, they added their voices to the clamor of those halloing for lost companies and regiments and those shouting at their animals. The din "rendered the place a perfect babel." 65

After slaking their thirst, many soldiers were lucky enough to find their messmates and eat a meal of bread before falling quickly to sleep. Others were not as fortunate. William Howell stumbled into camp around 10 P.M. only to discover that most of the brigade had already gone to bed. Unable to find his company the unhappy private was forced lay by a fire all night without his blanket. The day's march had began before sunup, but it was after midnight before the last spent soldiers threw themselves down and gratefully sought the oblivion of sleep. 66

The trek on the 19th had taken the brigade across twenty-five or thirty miles of what Frank Starr described as, "some of the worst country for wheeled vehicles that I ever saw." 67 The next morning the men awoke heartily exhausted and looked for further encumbrances to cast off. They burned three more wagons and equipment from their hospital department, including unneeded medicines and supplies. Another caisson was blown up and a few shells and some round shot were discarded. 68 There was even talk of spiking the artillery. After the struggles of the previous day, Colonel Green and the 5th Regiment were fed up with hauling their battery and were ready to leave the guns behind. Colonel Scurry flatly refused. Scurry saw the artillery, captured at Valverde, as the only tangible proof of the brigade's courage and heroism. He would not consent to abandon these trophies by the wayside. Now in command of the 4th Regiment, Baylor's men, and the fragment of the 7th, Scurry again pledged his men to see the pieces through and requested that all the artillery be turned over to his care. [69]

At 9 A.M. most of the brigade left the springs at Ojo del Pueblo and pushed deeper into the trackless waste. Men, too weak to continue, remained behind and departed when their strength permitted. Private Howell, still haggard and unrefreshed after his blanketless night by the fire, lingered among the pine and cedar until nearly 4 P.M. [70]

The line of march, away from the springs, led up a mountain and down into another valley, "and then by a gradual ascent, passing through a chain of hills, through a rough canyon." After this, the Texans' path "lay across a broad, stretch of rolling country destitute of timber, but affording a pretty good road." [71] Already worn down, the best the men could manage was about half the distance of the day before. Stopping around sunset, they camped at some inadequate springs or water holes near the southern end of the Magdalena Mountains. Sharp Whitley wrote, "There was hardly enough water for the men to drink and cook, so our horses and mules had to do without." [72] Once again, men continued to wander in until long after dark.

The 5th Regiment made a late start and never got to the water at all. After accomplishing only eight miles, Green's men gave it up and settled for a dry camp. Despite their short march, Private Howell, who was by now quite sick, straggled behind. Unable to keep up, he appeared destined for another miserable cold night. His luck changed, when a friend, eighteen-year-old William Perry, rode up and loaned him his horse. [73] Once mounted, Howell was able to make good time and reach the regiment's camp. Howell's experience was not unique and young Perry was only one of many good Samaritans among the cavalry portion of the caravan. Throughout the retreat, those on horseback did all they could to help their unmounted companions. Theophilus Noel wrote,

> "The mounted men ... will ever be gratefully remembered by many of us, who very feeble from the effects of sickness, on foot, feet blistered and in many instances bleeding, parched tongues and broken-down from fatigue, and lying by the roadside" ... "were kindly requested to mount some friend's horse and ride to camp while he trudged over rocks and mountains on foot in our stead." [74]

On April 21st, all elements of the Army of New Mexico got an early start. While the 5th regiment, anticipating breakfast and a chance to refill their canteens, covered the 5 miles remaining to the water holes, Scurry's men set out for their next objective. Continuing to move toward the southwest, Coopwood led the way up a narrow valley separating the Magdalena and San Mateo Mountains. From there, the Texans began to climb the lower slopes of the San Mateos themselves. Crawling along the side of the mountain, the men could see for miles and miles. In the distance, to their left, lay the river valley and the glistening waters of the Rio Grande. Beyond that, clearly visible to every man, lay the table top of the Mesa Del Contadero and Fort Craig. The 21st was a Sunday and by coincidence it was exactly two months since the Confederate victory at the ford. Alfred Peticolas mused, "We traveled along in full view of this rather (to us) noted place for two hours." [75] One can only imagine the swirl of emotions the Texans experienced, as near ruination, they gazed upon the site of their prior success.

Continuing to climb, the men of the brigade entered the mountains proper. The going was rocky and steep, and vast craggy pinnacles arose in the distance, with peaks "so high as to make one giddy to look up at them." 76

Quite a number of women accompanied the retreating Texans. For the most part these were the wives and daughters of New Mexican citizens like the Armijo brothers, who because of their support of the Southern cause felt it prudent to leave when Sibley withdrew. These people drove light wagons and ambulances and many were carting sundry possessions. 77 As these worthies and Sibley's regimental staff rode along in the relative comfort of their conveyances, the broken down soldiers of the Army of New Mexico watched with a mixture of envy and contempt. Private Howell complained to his diary, "My health is very bad yet. I am compelled to walk while mean Mexican women ride." 78

Here in the mountains near Fort Craig, two men, who were too sick to be moved could not find places in the wagons and were abandoned along the road. According to Alfred Peticolas, "They were thrown out of the wagons by Major [Richard T.] Brownrigg and one out of [the] end of Sibley's wagon." General Sibley evinced little leadership during the retreat and was "heartily despised by every man in the brigade for his want of feeling, poor generalship, and cowardice." Venting his feelings to his diary, Sergeant Peticolas scrawled, "Several Mexican whores can find room to ride in his wagons while the poor private soldier is thrown out to die on the way." 79 By now, the widely held opinion among the troops was that they would never come to this land again unless they were well mounted and commanded by a different general.

Just before dusk on the 21st, Scurry's command pulled its artillery up one last steep grade and pitched camp in a narrow canyon. The brigade had again covered nearly twenty miles without water and the nearest source was still a mile away at the bottom of a steep gully. Unable to get any closer with their wheeled vehicles, the soldiers took their "pack mules over the hill, almost too steep for any four-footed animal to go down, and stopped at the water at the bottom." [80] Towering pines shot up among the rocky cliffs and the little mountain stream was as cold as ice. That night some of the men slept near the water. The rest remained at the dry camp with the artillery and wagons.

Over the course of the next three days, the Army of New Mexico struggled through the mountains. There was nothing to eat except bread, baked in a frying pan or on a stick and washed down with a little coffee. The dough was made without salt or shortening of any sort and was cooked first on one side and then the other. Frequently the cakes were burnt. When the soldiers remembered "the sacks of flour, cans of lard, sacks of sugar and coffee, barrels of pork and boxes of bacon," that were left in Albuquerque or discarded along the way, it was almost more than they could stand. [81]

Bethel Coopwood knew little about the trackless area through which he was leading the Sibley Brigade, nonetheless he "proved himself a good mountaineer." [82] Scouting ahead, he always managed to find at least some water supply as an objective for the next day's march. Often this meant that the hearty Alabaman spent his nights out exploring while others slept. Unfortunately for the Texans, water sources in the rugged mountains were few and far between. Those which existed were not always adequate for such a large party and in several cases lay at the bottom of steep ravines. Coopwood's best efforts were not enough to keep the men from the ravages of thirst.

April 22nd, was a particularly bad day. The next source of water for the Texans was the small stream issuing from Nogalita Spring. Located in Nogal Canyon, the water was fully twenty-five miles away.

All day long the men tramped steadily under a hot sun. Retracing their steps for a couple of miles, they turned southward along the base of the mountains and then crossed the "seemingly impassible" barrier of East Red Canyon. [83] Down one steep side they scrambled and then up the other they toiled. Up another mountain and up and down they tramped. With the creek still ten miles ahead, canteens were empty and the men, reeking with sweat, were already parched. As the march dragged on, the suffering for water became appalling. Describing the scene Sharp Whitley wrote, "The stronger rushed frantically forward to gain water, before being consumed by thirst, while many of the sick and weak laid down to die, and the weary would lie down and rest, and get up and limp on and then lie down and rest, and then limp on." The head of the column reached the creek about dark, "but from that time until 12 o'clock men were frantically rushing to the water as they reached camp." [84]

The creek lay at the bottom of a canyon. Heedless of the risk, the thirsty soldiers scrambled wildly down. Those who went first were forced to watch out as men above carelessly dislodged loose stones that thundered past. Describing his own desperate weaving descent, Alfred Peticolas wrote, "With lips black and parched, and throats swelled and dry, and breath hot and voice husky, we dashed recklessly down the steep sides of the canion." Those going down jostled roughly against men who were climbing up satiated. Reaching the bottom, the thirsty soldiers threw themselves upon the rocks and "regardless of the crowding horses and mules, regardless of the swearing men, regardless of everything" drank. "Oh, the water, the good water!!" [85] That night the exhausted army camped without a guard, their artillery half a mile away.

Canby's spy captain, James Graydon, estimated the distance of the march to Nogal Canyon at twenty-nine miles and described the road as "very rough." He wrote that along the way the Texans "deserted one wagon and a camp and left three dead bodies half buried." "In another place," Graydon "found bones of a man's arm, half-eaten by wolves." [86] The Union officer ordered all buried. Pondering the tribulations of their journey, William Howell mused, "Surely such a march over such a country and made by men mostly on foot, not accustomed to walking, was never surpassed." The brigade's exertions reminded the young private of stories he once read of "Bonaparte's celebrated march over the Alps." [87] Unquestionably, the perseverance and determination shown by Sibley's men, during this "second Napoleon's crossing of the Alps," was nothing less than remarkable. [88]

The exertions of the men in charge of the brigade's artillery were especially impressive. After pledging to see the guns through on the 20th, Colonel Scurry summoned his men and placed each company in charge of a single cannon. This, he informed his boys, was so they could "go straight on without so many halts." [89] He told the assembled soldiers that he committed the guns to their care and that each company was responsible for the safe passage of their piece. Throughout the remainder of that grim retreat, regardless of thirst and hunger, the men of Scurry's command kept the artillery moving. With wheels locked, the cannon were lowered down sheer slopes. Groaning and weary, the men strained back on long ropes only to reverse the process at the bottom of each hill and, like Sisyphus, toil upwards once again. If one company's gun should stall, Scurry would holler out and other men would spring to the ropes to get it moving again. In his after-action report General Sibley heaped praise on the men of the 4th and 7th. "Not a murmur escaped the lips of these brave boys," he wrote. "Descents into and ascents out of the deepest canyons, which a single horseman would have sought for miles to avoid, were undertaken and accomplished with a cheerfulness and ability which were the admiration and praise of the whole army." [90] This undertaking was so extraordinary that it even earned the respect of northern observers. Among those it impressed was Colonel Latham Anderson, who served with Canby as a lieutenant. In later years Anderson honored his onetime enemies saying, "The energy and devotion these men displayed in carrying their artillery over apparently insurmountable obstacles was phenomenal." [91]

At about 5 P.M. on April 23, 1862, the brigade reached the meager water source at Penasco Spring. There, the men drank heartily. Since there was not enough water for the stock, a decision was made to keep moving. Walking in the dark, the Texans continued southward. The next water was reported to be about seven and one and one half miles away, but the distance turned out to be farther. The exhausted soldiers marched on until about 9 o'clock and then gave up and made a dry camp. Without water to mix with their flour, they could not make bread and so the men also went without supper. Private Howell's journal for the 23rd reads; "I go to bed hungry and thirsty, but being completely broken down, I sleep soundly." [92]

The next morning the Confederates "shelled out early for water and grub." Captain Coopwood had pressed ahead during the night and now the whole command knew that the long promised Alamosa River lay only five or six miles ahead. "With bodies unrefreshed, and both hungry and thirsty," the men hurried forward. [93] A couple of hours later the column reached the rim of Monticello Canyon. Eight hundred to one thousand feet below the Texans could see the small rapid stream that coursed through its bottom.

Fortunately for the weary troops, a long side canyon was located that led to the valley floor with relative ease. By noon everyone had finished the descent and reached the river.

After satisfying their thirst, the men' first order of business was to do some cooking. Many of the soldiers had gone over twenty-four hours without anything to eat. A few broken-down work oxen were slaughtered and soon the hungry Texans were browning "flap jacks" and broiling beef. Following breakfast, the Confederates lay down to rest. Men were haggard and the artillery teams were worn out, so the brigade stayed put for the remainder of the day. In the early evening Colonel Scurry roused his men and they worked their cannons up a steep hill on the south side of the canyon. After supper the whole brigade filled their canteens and went up the hill to camp. [94]

It was about 9 P.M. and nearly dark when Sibley's men were unexpectedly joined by the 4th Regiment's long absent commander, Colonel James Reily. Up from the south, the Colonel rode into camp with a number of other men and the exciting news that Colonel William Steele and the balance of the 7th Regiment were encamped no more than six miles away. Although excited to see their friends, the newcomers were daunted by the condition of their once proud army. Putting pen to paper twenty years later, one of Reily's party wrote, "Such sights as I there saw are yet fresh in my memory. It would be impossible for me to give anything like a graphic account of what I saw ... where suffering in all its types was to be seen." [95] Colonel Reily was so moved that his eyes streamed tears as he grasped the hands of Colonels Scurry and Hardeman and greeted them with a warm "How are you?"

The knowledge that a scant day's march would reunite the two columns was an immediate solace to

Sibley's veterans. Better still was Reily's assertion that a large provision train was en route for their relief. If this glorious news was not enough reason for "a grand hallelujah of a time," the Colonel also brought dispatches and letters from home. It was many months since most of the men had heard from loved ones, so there was a great jubilee in the camp. "Messes sat up late reading letters and discussing their contents and talking with the men who had come in." [96] "At the hour of midnight many, many a weary and sick soldier could have been seen sitting around a little blaze of fire - forced to blaze by some friend 'fanning' with his hat - reading letters from his mother, sister, sweetheart or friend. This was truly a night of rejoicing with the Army of New Mexico." [97] "There was a great and general stir in camp, which did not calm down until 2 o'clock at night." [98]

In the morning, with lighter hearts, the Texans set out across the flat plain between Monticello Canyon and Cuchillo Negro Creek. On reaching the stream, they found Colonel Steele's campfires still burning, but his command had moved on toward the Rio Grande. Sibley's men followed. Near the head of Sheep Canyon, Steele paused and the Confederates formed a junction. One can only imagine the joy of that reunion. The veterans of the Army of New Mexico were ragged, footsore, and weary, but they were now together with their friends and provisions were on the way. Colonel Steele's troops "had four days full rations with them at the time which they divided to the last mouthful with the boys before reaching the river." [99]

After pausing briefly to eat and rejoice the Texans pushed on. A Yankee cavalry patrol had been seen near Sibley's camp on the morning of the 23rd, so it was certain the Federals were about. The mouth of Sheep Canyon was only about twenty-five miles below Fort Craig and the Texans knew that if Canby planned to contest their passage, it would be somewhere along that stretch. With the Rio Grande still twelve to fifteen miles away, the brigade pressed steadily on. Sibley's veterans were rundown, but the condition of their draft animals was even worse. Rough usage and the rugged mountainous terrain had killed between fifty and sixty horses and mules. Bodies of these animals littered the road in the Texans' wake. Teams hitched to Scurry's artillery were lucky to have lasted as long as they did and those that remained were near collapse. To hurry the column along, Colonel Steele provided the guns with fresh horses. Still the march to the river took the rest of the day. Steele's six companies, who were in their saddles all of the night before, took up a screening position as a rear guard. At every moment the Confederates expected Canby to make his appearance. [100]

Theophilus Noel, believing himself as able to walk as anyone, generously loaned his horse to a young friend, seventeen-year-old Burwell Collier Allen. As the day wore on Noel's feet became blistered, and his perspective changed considerably. "I would have 'caved'," he wrote, "had it not been that hundreds were still going forward who had traveled for many days at that rate, and who were by odds in much worse plight than myself when it came to sores, to say nothing of hunger." [101] Eventually, the broken down "foot pad" hove in sight of the river and its fertile valley. With many exclamations of "How beautiful!" and "No more suffering on account of water," the column reached the Rio Grande just south of present-day Truth Or Consequences. [102] In short order, the Rebels made camp and prepared to stay the night. Their supply train was still three days away, but at least there was plenty of water to drink and their ordeal in the mountains was over. With scant provisions and inadequate transportation, the men had marched nearly 100 miles in eight days through some of the most unforgiving country in the Southwest. Many of

Sibley's veterans later came to view the mountainous retreat as among their most remarkable achievements.[103]

The place the Confederates struck the river was about thirty-eight miles below Fort Craig. Despite their relief at being free of the mountains, it was a consternation to the Texans that no Federal force contested their passage. In its weakened condition the Army of New Mexico was particularly vulnerable. Since Canby could easily have moved down the river, the Texans took his failure to appear as evidence of how badly the Union forces were whipped. Felix Collard, a private in Steele's command, noted years afterwards, "Canby never followed up his victory, nor has not to this good day." [104]

The Union commander knew that the Texans were already defeated and believed that further pursuit was neither feasible nor warranted. Just the same the Confederates barely escaped. While Sibley's men crawled through the mountains, the Federal forces concentrated at Fort Craig. On April 23rd Chivington's Colorado Volunteers had set off with flags flying and a brass band playing Yankee Doodle and moved several miles down the Rio Grande. Excited by the proximity of the enemy, "Captain Morris in command of the cavalry wished to pursue and fall on their rear." Colonels Paul and Chivington were also anxious to bring on an engagement. Canby, however, kept his own council and the next morning the Coloradans were ordered back to the post. [105] Nervously encamped on the banks of the Rio Grande, Sibley's Texans did not know it, but their enemy had lost interest. The shooting part of the Civil War in New Mexico was already over.

After the battle at Valverde and the subsequent failure to secure the supply depots at Albuquerque and Santa Fe, Lieutenant Colonel Scurry tried to resign his commission. At the time, his appeal was rejected. Colonel Reily was far away in Mexico and General Sibley needed experienced officers. Instead of accepting Scurry's resignation, the General had promoted him to full colonel and required him to remain in New Mexico. Scurry's ensuing leadership and personal courage made him the most respected officer in the brigade. Even the Federals were aware of his daring. As Alfred Peticolas told it, "The Pikes Peak men know Scurry and dread him accordingly." [106] The return of James Reily changed things. Despite his sterling record, Scurry's immediate services were no longer required. With Reily once again in command of the 4th Regiment, the hero of Glorieta was told he was free to leave.

On the evening of April 25th, Colonel Scurry informed his troops that "he had been ordered to return to Texas to raise a new regiment." [107] He then made an affecting speech to his men. "Dirty Shirt" Scurry was an orator of some renown and his farewell address was later described as "the most eloquent of his life." He praised the men for what they accomplished and, "in a most touching manner," reminded them of the "green graves" of "companions and brothers left behind." [108] Shedding tears, he referred to their trials and tribulations, and "said that it was like taking leave of wife and children to take leave of" comrades "who had fought with him so bravely and been with him so long." [109] Scurry closed by telling his men that if they wanted to write letters home, he would carry them back to Texas. After the speech, the soldiers drifted away to their campfires.

Nearly a month had passed since Isaac Adair was killed at Glorieta. During that time Company H had operated without an official captain. Now reunited with the rest of the 7th Regiment, the men decided it was right and proper to reelect officers. The outcome was no surprise. Charles Haley, from Trinity County, moved from 1st Lieutenant to Captain and 2nd

Lieutenant Bennett Arrington was elected to fill Haley's vacant spot. Several other men also advanced including twenty-two-year-old George Hennis, who moved from Private to 2nd Lieutenant, and twenty-five-year-old William A. Carlton, who was chosen by his fellows to become 1st Sergeant. [110] That same night, Bethel Coopwood was promoted to major. This promotion was well received by the men. They thought Coopwood "a brave man and a good fighter" and deserving of recognition "for successfully guiding the brigade through the mountains around Craig." [111]

At daybreak, Colonel Scurry took a small escort and departed for Texas and home. Watching him leave, Alfred Peticolas mused, "Thus we lost the best officer, most polished gentleman, most sociable gentleman, and the most popular Col. in the whole outfit." [112] As the brigade marched along in Scurry's wake a growing number of men did so on empty stomachs. Some messes still had a little flour, but the rations brought by Colonel Steele's command were exhausted and many had again eaten their last bread. Soldiers with something left counted themselves lucky, while their fellows tightened their belts. Marching by the river was quite a change from their strenuous path through the mountains, but many Texans were almost beyond caring. Only the expectation that they would meet Colonel Steele's supply train the next day kept the men plodding along. [113]

The smallpox and pneumonia that were prevalent among the veterans exacerbated suffering. Because of inadequate transportation two soldiers were again left by the side of the road too sick to be moved. Colonel Canby later reported to Washington, "The [Confederate] sick and wounded have been left by the wayside, without care and often without food. Many of them have been collected and are properly cared for." [114] Edward Canby's humanity and compassion were not lost on his enemies. In mid-May, a council of the commissioned officers of the 5th Regiment adopted and published the following resolution, "That the 5th Regiment T.M.V., appreciate the kindness shown to the sick, wounded and prisoners of this regiment by Gen. Canby, commanding the Federal forces in New Mexico." [115] In later years veterans of the brigade frequently wrote of Canby with more reverence than they accorded to Sibley.

Gamely the Texans covered thirty-six miles in two days and reached a point about seven miles above Fort Thorn. There on the evening of April 27th they finally met the seven loaded wagons of Colonel Steele's provision train. Captain Julius Giesecke noted, "We immediately pitched camp and cooked, baked, and ate." [116] William Howell, who was among the sick, got "a little pickle pork" to eat with his "bread baked in a frying pan." [117] Healthier soldiers like Alfred Peticolas, had to content themselves with the usual staples. "We all ate heartily of bread and coffee," wrote the sergeant, "but got nothing else brought us." [118] The provisions lacked variety but their quantity was sufficient. In the words of Theo Noel, "The hunger was duly appeased." [119]

Following a night of rest, the men tramped through Fort Thorn and camped a mile below. The weather had turned warmer and the brigade planned to wade the Rio Grande at the San Diego. The ford was about twelve miles away and the bulk of the army did not reach it until afternoon on the 29th. As the column approached, there was a sudden flurry of excitement. The brigade's artillery, which was marching ahead, arrived at the crossing considerably in advance. While waiting for the "footpads" to appear, those in charge of the guns prepared them to cross. The army was traveling in a state of constant readiness so the cannons were all loaded. Since wet charges might swell and become lodged in the barrels it was decided to unload before the crossing. The gunners tried the "pullcans," but as it turned out, the charges were already stuck fast. It was decided that the best way to get them out was by force. "Headquarters' consent was received to fire away, and boom! boom! half a dozen times thundered artillery." [120] The sound of the cannon created a sensation among the advancing troops. Men and officers alike assumed that the Yankees had somehow gotten ahead of them. Rushing forward to save their battery, more than one soldier was heard to swear, "He'd rather fight twenty Yankees than try another one of Coopwood's cutoffs." [121] The excitement was short lived. Once the true situation was learned, the commotion quickly died. This was the last time that anyone in New Mexico would hear the roar of Confederate cannon.

The brigade built rafts to ferry across their ammunition and "archives," and crossed the Rio Grande without further incident. On the morning of April 30, 1862, with his troops out of danger, General Sibley again turned command over to Colonel Green. Together with Colonel Reily and Judge Baird and his family, the General then set out for Fort Bliss. Henry Sibley's army was still 1,000 miles from home, but his campaign was finished. [122]

Chapter 13

SHATTERED DREAMS

"We all think that our operations out here will all be lost in history."
- Sergeant Frank Starr

The Mesilla Valley into which the Texans returned was just as lacking in provisions as it had been on their outward march. Since no one part could support the entire brigade, it was decided to quarter the regiments in separate camps. From the ford at San Diego, the Texans made a series of easy marches down the valley splitting up as they went. The 7th Regiment stopped at its old bivouac above Doña Ana and was charged "to remain in camp where it [was] till further orders." [1] Colonel Green then sent the foot soldiers from the 5th to lodge near Las Cruces. His cavalry proceeded further south to seek out the better grass and forage near Fort Fillmore. The 4th Regiment continued all the way to Fort Bliss and took up quarters in and around El Paso. By the time they arrived, General Sibley had already established himself a comfortable headquarters at the residence of James Magoffin. [2]

Musters were held at the various camps and the brigade settled down to rest and recuperate. On May 4th, Henry Sibley prepared an after action report for Samuel Cooper, the Confederate Inspector General. After describing the salient events of the past months, he told Cooper, "As for the results of the campaign, I have only to say that we have beaten the enemy in every encounter and against large odds; that from being the worst armed my forces are now the best armed in the country. We reached this point last winter in rags and blanketless. The army is now well clad and well supplied in other respects. The entire campaign has been prosecuted without a dollar in the quartermaster's department." [3] Sibley continued his report by stating that his soldiers "manifested a dogged, irreconcilable detestation of the country and the people." The Brigadier wrote that there was a "prevailing discontent" among his troops, but in light of "the distinguished valor displayed on every field " the men were entitled "to marked consideration and indulgence." He warned Cooper that because of this attitude, some "considerations, in connection with the scant supply of provisions," and a tendency of the local citizens to discount Confederate currency that he might have to evacuate the territory without waiting for instructions. He concluded, "Trusting that the management of this more than difficult campaign, entrusted to me by the Government, may prove satisfactory to the President, I have the honor, general, to be, your obedient servant, H.H. Sibley, Brigadier General, Commanding." [4]

These statements are so outrageous that one must assume that General Sibley was intentionally misleading his superiors to protect his career. The expedition to New Mexico was an unmitigated failure. Captain William Lee Alexander, of the 4th Regiment, summed up the situation in a letter home. "After all our toils and losses of good and noble officers & men, and of wagons and in fact everything save our guns, we have to return to Texas without having benefited our country one dime's worth." [5] By anyone's estimation the Confederate Army of New Mexico was a wreck. Of the nearly 2,525 combat ready soldiers, that marched out of the Mesilla Valley, barely 1,800 effectives remained. The Army's wake was littered with abandoned equipment, dead draft animals, charred wagons, and the sick and wounded who were too weak to keep pace. Hospitals, established at Socorro, Albuquerque, and Santa Fe, were filled to capacity with other casualties, awaiting an uncertain fate. At a minimum, 119 of Sibley's men were killed in battle or died from wounds. Disease and exposure killed another sixty-seven, while no less than 532 were taken prisoner. With nothing tangible to show for its efforts except, 1,800 to 2,000 stand of small arms and the artillery it captured at Valverde, Sibley's army had suffered nearly thirty percent casualties. Among the three companies raised in and around Houston County casualties were even higher. Besides their captain, Isaac Adair's company lost another thirty-four men. Redden Pridgen's lost thirty-three, and the Nunn/Odell company a whopping fifty-four. Of the 268 effectives in these three companies on the eve of the invasion, only 134 marched back into the Mesilla Valley. The casualty rate for the Houston County companies was a staggering fifty percent. [6]

The dissatisfaction of those who survived the campaign went far beyond the "prevailing discontent" alluded to by General Sibley. The Army of New Mexico had advanced upon their enemy's country poorly prepared and poorly equipped. Nevertheless, what little they had was gone. During the course of the offensive the Texans lost their wagons, half their horses, and everything else save the clothes on their backs. "Worse than all," wrote Frank Starr, "We have left behind us the graves of many, many of our brave soldiers, everyone has to mourn for the loss of some dear friend or relative." [7]

The consensus among the troops was that bad management had been their ruin and the angry veterans lay the blame directly at Sibley's feet. In every camp ridicule and curses were heaped upon his head. Many disgruntled soldiers called him a coward. "Which appears very plausible too," noted one, "for he has never been in an engagement or where there was any appearance of there going to be one." [8] The Texans held every confidence in each other but little or none in their leadership. "I can say this," complained a captain of the 4th, "that the men did their duty. You surely see or have some notion where I think the fault lies." [9] Echoing the same sentiment, Frank Starr wrote, "It can never be said that the unfortunate result of this campaign was caused by any failure on the part of the soldiers in the performance of their duty, they have in every instances shown themselves to be true Texians." [10]

The failures to capture supplies at Albuquerque and Santa Fe were the turning points in Sibley's campaign. From then on, no matter what happened on the battlefield, it was only a matter of time until hunger and privation forced the Texans into retreat. After the invasion and for years to come, General Sibley was widely condemned for letting the Union stores slip away. It was said, "He was too slow in his movements; by his victory [at Valverde] he appeared to think the country conquered; so, instead of acting quickly, he consumed more than a month in marching to Santa Fe, which he could have easily accomplished in ten days." [11] Captain William Lee Alexander, from Company H of the 4th regiment, wrote, "although a party of 500 men might have been sent up the river with dispatch and taken the entire Territory including Ft. Union (for there were not 500 men in arms above Ft. Craig at that time) such was our masterly inactivity that large reinforcements from Denver City came in & so we got neither Ft. Craig nor Ft. Union." [12] A Union observer commented wryly, "Less time spent in attending balls and other amusements would have enabled [General Sibley] to attack Fort Union before reinforcements reached that post." [13]

Many attributed Henry Sibley's lack of generalship to his excessive drinking. "It is to be hoped," seethed Captain Alexander, "that there will be some courts-martial and Courts of Inquiry, and let the people of Texas see whether certain persons can be any longer be allowed to play-off when the bullets begin to whistle, and stay in comfortable quarters in towns soaking themselves with rum and whiskey while others are doing the work." [14] "General Sibley was not a good administrative officer," wrote Trevanion Teel, "He did not husband his resources, and was too prone to let the morrow take care of itself. But for this the expedition never would have been undertaken, nor would he have left the enemy between him and his base of supplies." [15] According to Bill Davidson, "This old brigade never saw the day that they would not have swapped Sibley for Canby." [16] In a more vengeful mood, another soldier wrote simply, "I hope the day is not far distant when Gen. Sibley will be hung." [17]

From early May through early June of 1862, the brigade languished in the Mesilla Valley. Much of the time was spent simply "lying in camp eating scant rations and wishing for a change of clothes." [18] While the army waited, a paymaster arrived from the south and began to pay off the troops. The men were glad to receive the money, but Captain Giesecke noted that when his company was paid, it was only through Dec. 30th. The practical Giesecke used his windfall, such as it was, to buy "a horse from a Mr. J. Sturdevant of Company B, First Artillery." He also bought "a saddle, bridle, horse blanket and five pounds of chocolate." [19] All this cost Giesecke the sum of $180. Beyond the confines of the camps the Confederate notes were virtually worthless. A merchant on the Mexican side of the river at El Paso wrote at the time, "The Confederate money (paper) is selling at 20 cents on the dollar, and large amounts could be bought for less if there were any purchasers." [20] With lots of money and little to spend it on, the men gambled heavily. Large sums daily changed hands over impromptu gaming tables.

The weather remained warm, which was opportune, as everyone was more or less unwell. Alfred Peticolas recorded in his journal, "It is distressing to notice how general is the debility in camp." [21] In William Alexander's company no one was dangerously ill, but all the lieutenants were down with the measles and everyone else was either sick or on the mend and complaining. "I have scarcely 10 men in my Co. fit for duty," grumbled the captain. [22] Frank Starr, working as a clerk in Sibley's headquarters, wrote to his father, "There are many soldiers now here who have disease planted in their systems, which will hereafter reveal itself, caused by the exposure and hardships they have undergone in this disastrous campaign." [23] Many soldiers, like Private William Howell, were so broken down that they were discharged because of their bad health. [24]

Fueled by their general's apparent inaction and lack of concern, morale in the brigade reached its lowest ebb in early May. The prevailing opinion in the camps was that New Mexico was "not worth the loss of lives and money necessary for its conquest." "I do not think it is worth the life of a single Texian," wrote Frank Starr. [25] The campaign seemed to be over, but no one was certain about their future. While his men dealt with illness and short rations, a traveler noted, "We left Gen. Sibley enjoying the comfortable quarters, the delectable society, the comforts and luxuries of Magoffinsville." Assisted by his Aides, Major Dwyer and Major Sam Magoffin, the General, to all appearances, "was in excellent health." [26]

Things came to a head on May 12th when the commissioned officers of the 5th Regiment assembled at a hotel in Las Cruces to discuss removal of the regiment to Texas. Conspicuously absent from the council were the regiment's commander, Tom Green, and anyone from brigade headquarters. The officers took pains to declare that there was nothing mutinous about their gathering. Nonetheless, their avowed purpose "was to determine upon some course of action in regard to their future movements." The object, as briefly stated by Captain Hugh A. McPhaill of Company E, "was to determine whether we should quietly see this fine army of ours remain idle, waste away by disease and sloth, and worse than all, with gradual starvation." [27] The officers did not intend any conduct that was rash or rebellious, but neither did they intend allow the current state of affairs to continue.

Walking on dangerous ground, the impromptu council prepared a carefully worded justification for its position. Reports were presented by the regiment's Commissary, Quartermaster, and Surgeon's Departments, all three of which painted a gloomy picture of the brigade's circumstances. Captain Joseph H. Beck, Assistant Commissary, informed the gathering that all the wheat and corn that could be gathered was being ground in mills at Mesilla but at best it amounted to breadstuffs for 800 men for ninety-three days. Beef in possession of the Commissary was only enough for fifteen days and what existed was "very poor and almost unfit for use." "Under ordinary circumstances," wrote Beck, "it would be condemned as unwholesome food for troops." [28] Supplies of soap and candles were inadequate. Salt was abundant, but only at an exorbitant cost. Pork, bacon, sugar, coffee, lard, tallow, and rice could not be found in the territory at any price. The only provision that could be obtained in tolerable amounts was vinegar.

Thomas G. Wright, Assistant Quartermaster, reported that the 5th Regiment had only 170 mules remaining and that all were "in a bad condition." All feed corn was exhausted and the animals were surviving on "corn hay of inferior quality." Only 12 of the unit's wagons were complete and serviceable.

About clothing, Wright declared, "None on hand, and none to be found." 29

Assistant Surgeon John M. Bronaugh delivered the most vehement and damning report. Bronaugh was with the brigade since its organization and was the 5th Regiment's only qualified medical officer. Without hesitation he told his fellow officers that the rations issued to their men were "of an unwholesome character" and that the prevailing "indigestion, diarrhea, dysentery, & etc." were the results. He also swore that the troops were "almost in a state of nudity, and that from the organization of the regiment to the present time it has had an inadequacy of clothing and blankets. Much of the mortality of the past winter," stated Bronaugh, "was attributable to these causes." 30

After listening to the various reports, the officers of the 5th resolved to request that Colonel Green "use speedy means" to remove the regiment's sick and wounded from New Mexico. They also agreed to petition General Sibley to move the regiment to some other scene of action. To ensure that their requests carried weight, the council took a riskier and more rebellious course of action. They bypassed the chain of command and went over their commanders' heads. Along with their various reports, the officers wrote a carefully prepared statement of facts and sent it directly to George W. Randolph, the Confederate Secretary of War. Several pages long, the statement described the prominent events of the campaign and divulged how little was achieved. It also made it clear that the burden of failure did not lay with the average soldier.

"In every contest with the enemy," stated the officers, "we have vanquished them, and always contending against vast odds. We have achieved several victories, either of which would have immortalized us in any other field of action; but we have necessarily sacrificed many brave Texians to secure them." The statement concluded, "We respectfully ask that this report receive your favorable consideration, and that we be transferred to some other field of operation, where our services may be rendered more efficient, and our efforts in the great struggle for independence may result more profitably to the cause, than they have in this remote region, where there is nothing to stimulate the heart of the patriot or to nerve the arm of the soldier." [31]

For good measure the council forwarded additional copies of their statement and reports to the Governor of Texas and the Houston Telegraph for publication in the popular press.

There is no record of General Sibley's reaction to the council and its actions, but certainly they contributed to what happened next. On April 14th, just two days after the council's final meeting, Sibley ordered the following address printed and distributed to his troops.

"Soldiers of the Army of New Mexico
It is with unfeigned pride and pleasure that I find myself occupying a position which devolves upon me the duty of congratulating the army of New Mexico upon the successes which have crowned their arms in the many encounters with the enemy during the short but brilliant campaign which has just terminated.
Called from your homes almost at a moment's warning, cheerfully leaving friends, families and private affairs, in many cases solely dependent upon your presence and personal attention, scarcely prepared for a month's campaign, in the immediate defense of your own firesides, you have made a march, many of over a thousand miles, before ever reaching the field of active operations.
The boasted valor of Texans has been fully vindicated. Valverde, Glorieta, Albuquerque, Paralto [sic], and last, though not least, your successful and almost unprecedented evacuation, through mountain passes and

over a trackless waste of a hundred miles through a famishing country, will be duly chronicled, and form one of the brightest pages in the history of the second American revolution.

That I should be proud of you - that every participant in the campaign should be proud of himself - who can doubt?

During the short period of inaction which you are now enjoying, your general indulges the hope that you will constantly bear in mind that at any moment you may be recalled into activity.

God and an indulgent Providence have guided us in our councils and watched our ways; let us be thankful to Him for our successes, and to Him let us not forget to offer a prayer for our noble dead.
H.H. SIBLEY
Brig. Gen. Commanding" [32]

In later years the address was a source of pride for Sibley's veterans, but at the time it was received with some indifference. Alfred Peticolas pasted a copy into his journal, but only as he put it, because "It is a curious specimen of literature in some respects." [33] Better received were orders, issued on the 18th, "to take up the line of march for San Antonio." [34]

Inadequate resources and near rebellious officers were reasons enough to evacuate, but the immediate catalyst for Sibley's decision was probably news arriving from farther west. During the time the brigade campaigned in New Mexico, a detached company of "Arizona Rangers" had operated in the vicinity of Tucson. This small unit, under the command of a captain named Sherod Hunter, was originally sent west to escort Colonel Reily on his second diplomatic mission to Mexico. According to General Sibley, he also ordered Hunter "to take post at Tucson," "with a view to the protection of the important and growing interest, chiefly mineral, in Western Arizona, and for the further purpose of opening communications with Southern California." [35]

For several months Hunter's company protected the white citizenry of Western Arizona, stepping into a vacuum left by the withdrawal of federal troops. At the same time, the Rangers pursued Confederate interests. They drove suspected Union sympathizers out of Tucson, confiscated a few mines and a mill, and disrupted Union supply activities along the Overland Mail route to the west. All the while, Hunter heard persistent rumors of a large Federal force advancing from California. On April 15th while Sibley's army was engaged at Peralta, a ten-man picket from Hunter's command was attacked by the Union column's advance guard. The skirmish, which took place at Picacho Pass, is generally regarded as the westernmost land action of the Civil War. After an hour and a half of desperate fighting the Federals withdrew, carrying off several wounded. Behind them, dead on the field, were a lieutenant and two other men. Confederate losses were three captured. Badly overestimating the strength of the force that it encountered, the "California Column" retreated nearly 100 miles back up the Gila, before cautiously renewing its advance. Although the Rangers got the best of the skirmish, Hunter knew his tenure in Arizona was over. Abandoning the "Post at Tucson" in mid May, he started back for the Mesilla Valley. Proceeding him came the unwelcome news that close on his heels were General James H. Carleton and a Federal brigade consisting of "ten companies of infantry, five of cavalry, and one field battery of four pieces." 36

Whatever General Sibley's immediate reasons for ordering his brigade back to Texas, the approach of nearly 2,500 well equipped Union troops must certainly have played heavily into his decision. By May 20th, most Texans knew they were soon going home. Talk in the camps was all of going down to San Antonio and the impending march across the plains.

William Howell's diary for that period reads succinctly, "Get a horse and prepare to go home, GLORIOUS THOUGHT!" 37 For many, who rode on the outward journey, no mount was available. Ill-equipped and on foot, these soldiers were now faced with the daunting prospect of crossing 650 miles of arid waste.

Major Pyron and his battalion of the 2nd Regiment Mounted Rifles left for San Antonio almost immediately. These soldiers came to the Territory with Colonel Baylor and were away from their homes longer than any others. They were also serving under twelve-month enlistments that were set to expire within the week. On the morning of June 5th, the rest of the army began its retreat. Colonel Hardeman and a battalion, consisting of companies A, B, D, E, G, I, and K of the 4th Regiment, were the first to strike out for home. Before they departed, the companies were ordered into line and Hardeman made a brief speech. He told his men "he would not have them marching under false impressions," rations were short and although he expected they would be met by a resupply train near Fort Lancaster, nothing was certain. Hardeman encouraged the troops to "bear up under the disadvantageous circumstances," and then finished somewhat lamely by assuring the men the "trip might not prove to be so bad as [they] had every reason to fear it would be." 38 The speech making complete, the soldiers faced Texas and took up the line of march.

The next morning Major George J. Hampton departed with the remaining companies of the 4th regiment. General Sibley and his staff pulled up stakes on June 10th. Two days later, Colonel Green followed with the 5th Regiment and the veteran battalion of the 7th. By June 20th, less than 600 Confederates remained in the Mesilla Valley. 39

The march across the desert to San Antonio lasted seven weeks and from the moment it began it was a struggle. The outward trek was made during winter. Now it was summer and the weather was oppressively hot. Weakened by their ordeal in the mountains of New Mexico, the Texans had to inure themselves to hardship all over again. "The sickness occasioned by the first day or two's march was truly painful to behold." According to one trooper, "it was not an unusual sight to see our poor boys giving out along the road, when but a few miles of the days journey had been performed." [40] On one particular morning, before 10 A.M., Theophilus Noel remembered counting twenty-three soldiers exhausted and unable to go any farther.

    The worst part of the journey was between Fort Quitman and Fort Davis. Sources of water on this stretch were scarce and in some cases lay more than thirty miles apart. The days were oppressive. "Hot! Hot! and no shade, vine or cloud to hide the sun," exclaimed a weary soldier. [41] At Eagle Springs, the first watering place after leaving Fort Quitman and the Rio Grande, the men baked two days rations and filled their water barrels. Those who were mounted went five miles further to camp near better grass. While there, Indians visited the mounted party, stole one horse and shot two mules with arrows.

    The foot soldiers left Eagle Springs after sundown. Traveling at night to avoid the summer sun, they set out for Van Horn's well, twenty miles away. The column's advance reached the well at daybreak, but only to discover that the water was foul. Indians had filled the well with carcasses and dirt. The natives did their work thoroughly. The water hole was in such bad shape that the Texans did not try to clean it out. Unable to fill their canteens or go back, the exhausted and thirsty foot soldiers were left with no choice but to continue on. The sun was now well up and the next water thirty-eight miles away. [42]

Many of the men were already broken down, and the brigade's teams were "fast caving." No order was maintained by the "footpads" instead, it was "every man for himself and the wagons take the hindmost." 43 At about 11 o'clock A.M. a short halt was made and the Texans drank the last of their water. The next source, the aptly named Dead Man's Hole, was still twenty-eight miles away. From this point on the foot soldiers' suffering was as intense as any yet experienced during the campaign. "Many there were who gave completely out, and threw themselves down by the side of the road to die. Many kept on forward with their tongues so swollen that they could not articulate a word; more crazed than rational, they looked like frantic mad men." 44

"Great God have mercy upon us," cried soldiers as they dropped by the roadside to await their fate. Before the withdrawal from El Paso, Burwell Collier Allen, a seventeen-year-old private, was sick with dysentery. Eight miles from Dead Man's Hole, he could go no farther, and his soul "was called from hence to the God who gave it." 45 Alone, many leagues from civilization and home, his body was left under a large pile of stones anointed with the tears of his friends. More Texans would certainly have joined young Collier if not for the efforts of their advance party. Lieutenant John Barnes, and others who went ahead, loaded barrels of water onto a wagon and returned to help their friends. By the time the water reached him, Theophilus Noel had almost resolved to give up. "No one, save those who have experienced it," he wrote, "has any just conception of how refreshing that first quart was that restored life to many." 46

The diaries of Julius Giesecke and William Howell for this same period are not nearly as sensational. Captain Giesecke says, there was a heavy rainstorm after leaving Eagle Springs and that for fifteen miles there was water standing in the road.

Both men noted that water was short at Van Horn Wells, but that some was obtained. Howell wrote "one bucket water to a horse and none for the mules." [47] The march from Van Horn Wells to Dead Man's Hole is barely mentioned by either man. It may be that Theophilus Noel embellished his narrative for dramatic effect. It is more likely however, that these are the different perspectives of soldiers who were mounted and those who had to walk. Giesecke and Howell both had horses!

After resting at Dead Man's Hole for a day, the brigade proceeded to Barrel Springs and the next day to Fort Davis. At the fort, relief supplies including "some good fat beef" met the Texans. [48] Many of the men had not eaten in thirty-six hours, so as one described it, here they "gormandised sumptuously." [49] While at Dead Man's Hole, Indians stole three of General Sibley's ambulance mules that were out grazing.

Water continued to be scarce and food was always in short supply, but morale was improving. A traveler who passed the 4th Regiment on the road below Fort Davis, sent the following account to the San Antonio Weekly Herald.

> "The men were suffering terribly from the effects of heat; very many of them are a-foot, and scarcely able to travel from blistered feet. They were subsisting on bread and water, both officers and men; many of them were sick, many ragged, and all hungry; but we did not see a gloomy face - not one! They were all cheerful, for their faces were turned homewards. 'We are going home!' How many pale, sick, hungry faces, have we seen brighten as they repeat the glad sound." [50]

Drawing some coffee and sugar at Fort Stockton, the brigade continued past Escondido Springs and down the Pecos River toward Fort Lancaster. The Pecos was a "narrow, long, deep, crooked and muddy stream," with "rattlesnakes and gnats in abundance," but from this point on, things began to ease up. [51] Hurrying in advance, Colonel Reily reached San Antonio well ahead of the main body of Sibley's troops. Quickly, he issued a heartfelt public appeal "To the Patriots of Callwell, Austin, Gonzales, Victoria, Guadalupe, Milam, Nacodoches, Angelina, Cherokee, Polk, Houston, and other Counties." Reily described the courage and patriotism of his soldiers and declared to their friends and relatives, that the men deserved and needed sympathy and assistance. He urged that supplies and transportation wagons "be sent to meet these returning heroes as far on the road as possible." "Immediately take steps to prepare clothing" and supplies, he wrote. "They need everything their fellow citizens can furnish." [52]

Early on the morning of July 7th, twenty-two miles above Beaver Lake and the head of the Devil's River, Sibley's veterans were surprised to see six wagons hove into view. The soldiers were still some 240 miles above San Antonio; nevertheless, they were being met by friends come to their relief. Driven by two patriotic gray-haired gentlemen and a few younger men, the wagons were packed with supplies. The family and friends of Company A of the 4th Regiment had collected the trove of provisions. To the joy and happiness of those soldiers, the train contained stores of all descriptions. "Clothing, soap and other cleansing articles, such as combs, &c., were by them received, to say nothing of the good, fresh corn meal, sugar, salt, bacon, and some little of the 'creter,' together with some tobacco." The lucky men of Company A were "in no way disposed to be selfish or closed fisted with what they received." [53] "Old Ned," tobacco, and everything else was divided to the last with companions from other companies. [54]

The Texans now covered the remaining distance to San Antonio with relatively little discomfort. Passing through the increasingly settled area below Fort Hudson, San Felipe Springs and Fort Clark, they were able to supplement their dwindling supplies and additional provision trains came to their relief. From Uvalde and D'Hanis eastward, many friends and relatives met their loved ones along the way and escorted the weary soldiers the final miles. The first detachments of the returning brigade reached San Antonio in early July. General Sibley, with the majority of his command, arrived around the middle of the month and other units continued to trail in until early August. [55]

As the soldiers straggled in, many citizens of San Antonio were distressed by their appearance. R.H. Williams, a transplanted Englishman, now a member of a company of "Partisan Rangers," wrote, "It was in the end of October in the previous year that [the brigade] had marched out, three thousand strong, the flower of Texan youth, with high hopes of victory; and now it was a broken, disorganized rabble, ragged and half starved. The horses had nearly all died, and such of the men as returned had tramped hundreds of miles with scarce a whole boot amongst them." [56]

As the various squads and companies arrived, the townsfolk did everything in their power to make the returning soldiers feel welcome. One private remembered that as he walked in, dressed in rags, his small party was met by a brass band and escorted into the city. Everywhere, "there were ladies on front porches and at up stairs windows, and on verandas, waving handkerchiefs." "When we got into the city proper," he wrote, "all hotels were open and free, so were the livery stables and saloons. We got new clothes, new shoes, under-wear, and all." [57] Almost home at last, many of the soldiers got drunk.

The final elements of the Army of New Mexico to evacuate their theater of operations were the six "fresh" companies of the 7th Regiment. During the general pullout, Sibley ordered Colonel Steele and his men, who were encamped at Doña Ana, to remain behind "for the purpose of holding Arizona." [58] Steele's command was augmented by Major Teel's three-gun battery of six-pounders and four local ranger companies, but he was plainly faced with a hopeless task. The locally raised ranger companies, including Sherod Hunter's men, were reorganized remnants of Baylor's old command. Nominally called the 1st Arizona Battalion Mounted Rifles, this unit never amounted to much more than a paper organization. [59]

Soon after General Sibley withdrew from the country with the greater portion of his command, Colonel Steele began to have difficulties. "The Mexican population, justly thinking [the Texans'] tenure very frail and uncertain, showed great unwillingness to sell property of any sort for Confederate paper." If Steele and his men were compelled to retire, "which was at any time probable," the Confederate notes would be valueless. [60] Since the Colonel did not have specie, with which to make purchases, his only alternative was to seize upon whatever supplies his men needed. This policy occasioned so much ill feeling on the part of the Mexicans that in many instances armed resistance was offered to the Confederate foraging parties.

In one such encounter, word reached the Texans that a small bunch of cattle could be procured at Ysleta and San Elizario. Situated just below El Paso, these were two little settlements with mixed populations of Mexicans and Pueblo Indians. A squad of six men including Private Felix R. Collard of Company G, was detailed to go down the river and collect the animals. The Texans found the cattle, and as they had nothing to pay for them, they simply rounded them up and drove them into a corral. Private Collard remembered, that about the time they got the animals penned "the alcalde came out and said his people would fight if we took the cattle." [61] Words quickly escalated to actions, and soon guns were blazing in both directions. The Texans took cover behind the adobe corral and the locals among a little cluster of adobe houses. At the height of the skirmish a lone Mexican horseman sped off from the village. Apparently riding for reinforcements, he skirted the river and ran within 200 yards of the corral. The lieutenant in command of the foraging party "said to one of his men, who was a sharp-shooter, 'You had better stop that fellow." The Texan "laid his gun up on the wall, and when it fired the horse ran off riderless." The foragers cut out the best of the cattle and waited in the corral for nightfall. When the time was right, the lieutenant said, "Now boys, make them pant," and the party escaped under cover of darkness. [62]

The Texans got the better of the encounter at Ysleta and San Elizario, but that was not always the case. On July 1st, a lively skirmish took place in the Mesilla Valley in which Captain William H. Cleaver and five other men from Company D were killed. In all, ten Texans lost their lives while foraging. Breadstuffs for Steele's command dwindled to less than a thirty-day supply. If something were not done quickly, the troops would be in a state of starvation. The men were "so disgusted with the campaign and so anxious to return to Texas that in one or two instances they were on the point of open mutiny, and threatened to take matter in their own hands unless they were speedily marched back to San Antonio." [63] On July 6, the advance of Carleton's California Column reached Fort Thorn. The previous day, troops from Fort Craig were reported moving towards the same point. "Knowing this," wrote Steele, "and that the enemy, after leaving competent garrisons behind, would be able to bring 3,000 troops against me [...], the necessity of moving my force became imperative." [64] Two days later, Colonel Steele abandoned the Mesilla Valley and marched for Fort Bliss.

For the area's southern sympathizers, the heady days of Confederate Arizona were at an end. Most civilians who actively supported the Rebel cause or who held posts in the provisional government had already seen the writing on the wall and left. There were many Americans, some with families, however, who having taken no part in the struggle, chose to remain in their homes. Because the occupation had caused so much ill feeling among the valley's Mexican population, Colonel Steele feared for these peoples' lives. Just before leaving, he made an attempt to secure their safety, by striking a covenant with the principal Mexican citizens of Mesilla. Under the terms of the deal, the Mexicans bound themselves to protect the Americans remaining in the country. In return, Steele released one Domingo Cebeno, who he was holding under sentence of death. Even so, the Colonel was uneasy about the situation. In one of his last official acts as commander of Arizona, he wrote to the "Commanding Officer United States Forces," and requested, that "for the sake of humanity," he "inquire into the manner in which the agreement has been kept." [65]

Steele and his men lingered at Fort Bliss only long enough to hold a fire sale of public property that was too bulky to remove or not worth transporting. A considerable quantity of stores horse shoes, cannon ammunition, tents, etc. could not be sold, and were simply abandoned. Still, the sale, which was held for specie and breadstuffs, raised $850 in hard cash. William Steele turned the $850 over to Dr. Malek A Southworth, who was left in charge of the general hospital in Franklin. After arranging a line of credit for the hospital with parties in Mexico, the Colonel put his troops on the road to San Antonio. [66]

Steele's transportation was limited and his supplies of breadstuff and beef were insufficient for the journey ahead. In many instances, his troops were almost naked. Trusting that relief supplies would meet him, the Colonel split his battalion into detachments and headed home. With but a few bushels of unsifted cornmeal, mixed with spirits of turpentine to keep the bugs out, the six companies strung out along the road. According to Private Collard, some of the men were sick, some with festering wounds. Their clothes were worn to rags and there were no commissary stores. Some were on foot and many of these were bare-footed. What horses and mules there were left, were so thin and poor that one could count their ribs. The going was extremely slow. Many days the companies covered no more than ten miles. When the command finally reached Fort Quitman, Steele allowed those who wished to "club up" into small parties and strike out on their own. [67] The hope was that by traveling in smaller groups, they might get something to eat for themselves and their horses. The Colonel's only stipulation was that there be at least seven men together so that they would not fall prey to Indians. After many hardships and tribulations, the last of Steele's men reached San Antonio in late August. Marking the end of the Army of New Mexico, one observer wrote, "I saw that gallant force march away, with drums beating and flags flying, and every man from, from the General downwards, confident of victory." "Alas! A few months after, I saw the [...] remnant come straggling back on foot, broken, disorganized, and in an altogether deplorable condition." [68]

In the fall of 1861, while trying to organize his defense of the New Mexico territory, Colonel Canby sent his superiors repeated pleas for reinforcement.

After Valverde, other Union officers added their voices to the appeal. Major James Donaldson "urgently recommended that four regiments of infantry, some cavalry, and a battery of rifled cannon be at once put in route for [Fort] Union." [69] Colonel Paul petitioned Washington three times, urging "the absolute necessity for a re-enforcement of 4,000 men, two batteries of rifled cannon, and six siege pieces." [70] As the campaign progressed, the Confederates likewise requested additional troops. After Valverde, Henry Sibley wrote to Richmond that he needed reinforcement, "at as early a day as possible." [71] After the fight at Glorieta Pass, his pleas read; "I must have re-enforcements. Send me re-enforcements." [72] The appeals from both sides were largely ignored. Except for the volunteers from Colorado, and the belated appearance of General Carleton's column, neither command saw any of the troops they requested.

In early May of 1862, with the fighting over and done, both Colonel Canby and General Sibley got wind that the eyes of their respective governments were finally turned to the West. Canby learned through newspapers that five regiments of volunteers were ordered to reinforce him from the East. In response, the Union commander fired off a brief note to Washington that read, "If this force is intended only for the defense of New Mexico and the reoccupation of Arizona, the whole of it will not in my judgment be necessary." [73] Canby made it plain to Washington that two regiments were the most that he could accommodate and only if they brought their own food and provisions.

At nearly the same time, General Sibley learned through unofficial sources that his government was also sending reinforcements and that New Mexico and Arizona were "to be held at all hazards." Henry Sibley probably did not know whether to laugh or cry. In the end, he responded like his Union counterpart. In a candid letter to General Hamilton Bee, commanding the Western District of the Department of Texas, Sibley wrote that his army was subsisting on a limited supply of "poor meat and bread." They were down to 100 rounds for their cannons and ammunition could be said to be "completely exhausted." Clothing was also "exhausted, with no means of renewing the supply." New Mexico and Arizona were already lost so reinforcements were no longer needed. Sibley closed bitterly, "I have made report after report to the Government, but up to this date, have received not a single line of acknowledgement or encouragement." [74]

Ironically, back on April 16th, just before the brigade began its near disastrous retreat into the mountains, the Confederate government in Richmond passed the following resolution,

> "Resolved by the Congress of the Confederate States of America, That the Thanks of Congress are hereby tendered to Brigadier General H.H. Sibley, and to the officers and men under his command for the complete and brilliant victories over our enemies in New Mexico.
> Approved, April 16, 1862." [75]

On May 31st, 1862, writing from Confederate Headquarters in Richmond, Virginia, General Robert E. Lee told the commander of the Department of Texas that he was "perfectly right" in diverting two regiments of cavalry to General Sibley's relief. Further, Lee ordered, "You will also cause to be sent to the western frontier of Texas all the supplies you can for the use of General Sibley's forces. The very remote and isolated position of General Sibley's command makes it necessary that you should promptly afford him all the aid you can in men and supplies." [76] If Lee's and Sibley's letters had been addressed to each other, they would have crossed in the mail.

Belated attention of both governments made no difference to the outcome of events in the West. Still, it suggests the latent significance of the campaign had finally sunk home. When Henry Sibley convinced Jefferson Davis to let him raise an army, it was not conquest of the remote and unimportant territories of New Mexico and Arizona that swayed the Confederate leader. It was dreams of the gold fields of Colorado and California and the deep-water ports of the Pacific. If the Sibley Brigade had managed to capture the garrisons and supplies at Fort Craig and Fort Union, and had held New Mexico until reinforced, the course of the Civil War may have been very different. Southerners and Southern sympathizers were scattered throughout the Western mountain regions. If a heavily reinforced and victorious Confederate army of battle-hardened veterans had pushed westward out of New Mexico, armed with an additional 6,000 to 8,000 stand of arms and twenty-five to thirty pieces of captured artillery, Henry Sibley's extravagant scheme might actually have succeeded. For much of the war, European recognition of the Confederacy hung by a thread and President Lincoln himself described the current of gold flowing from the Pacific as the "life-blood" of the Union's financial credit. [77] One cannot help but speculate, what might have been the outcome if that flow had been cut off and Richmond had shown the world a Southern Confederacy that stretched from sea to sea. As it was, the dreams were shattered. Instead of being one of the most consequential campaigns of the war, history has relegated the invasion to obscurity. Despite untold suffering and sacrifice, the campaign amounted to little more than "a series of insignificant skirmishes, devoid of military or political significance." [78] Henry Sibley, himself, gave the campaign its most fitting epitaph when he wrote; "The Territory of New Mexico is not worth a quarter of the blood and treasure expended in its conquest." [79]

NOTES

CHAPTER 1 - ISAAC ADAIR

1. Smith-Arrington, Civil War letters.
2. Adair, Will of Isaac Adair; Houston County Probate Records.
3. Aldrich, History of Houston County, p.121; Diary of Elizabeth Smith, p.49; Hall, The Confederate Army of New Mexico, p.267. Sources conflict about Isaac Adair's year of birth, some say 1823, others say 1825. The 1850 census lists his age as twenty-five, lending credence to the later date.
4. Adair, Adair History, p.147.
5. Ibid, pp.147-148.
6. Adair, Adair History, p.173; Census 1850; Lannie Walker Sr.; Carter, Territorial Papers, p.196. The Federal Census of 1850 lists Isaac's father as Zadock. Other sources, however, list his name as Zadox, Zadoux, and even Zedie. One source places the year of his birth as 1766 and his marriage as 1796.
7. Carter, Territorial Papers, p.196.
8. Texas Land Grant Records.
9. Ulrich, Crockett Newspapers.
10. The muster in San Antonio occurred on May 3, 1847. Hall, The Confederate Army of New Mexico, p.267; Spurlin, Texas Veterans; Diary of Elizabeth Smith, p.49; Muster Rolls, War with Mexico.
11. Census 1850.
12. Biography of Augusta Louise Smith, Houston Cty. Hist. Commission; Bishop, History of Houston County, p.574. The community of Alabama no longer exists.
13. Aldrich, History of Houston County, p.31; Smith-Arrington, Family Bible; Bishop, History of Houston County, p.574. Augusta Louise Smith was born in Georgia, Jan. 1, 1837. She is purported to have been the great-grand daughter of Revolutionary War general, Nathaniel Greene.

14. Aldrich, History of Houston County, p.121; Diary of Elizabeth Smith, p.49. The marriage took place about 1852, but its exact date and location have been lost.

15. Diary of Elizabeth Smith, Oct. 31, 1859; Texas Land Grant Records; Bishop, History of Houston County, pp.445 & 574. In later years, John T. Smith operated several steamboats on the Trinity River, including the "Ida Reese" and the "Indian No.2."

16. Diary of Elizabeth Smith, January 31, 1858, April 21, 1858, December 22, 1858, April 23-28, 1859, and November 17, 1859.

17. Ibid, p.1, April 30, 1858, March 19, 1858, and March 27, 1858.

18. Ibid, February 10, 1858, March 3, 1858, February 8, 1858, February 23, 1858, June 11, 1858, June 25, 1858, September 2, 1858, and April 1, 1859.

19. Ibid, Aug. 3, 1858; Houston Co. Tax rolls, May 24, 1855; Aldrich, History of Houston County, p.121; Bishop, History of Houston County, p.224.

20. Biography of Augusta Louise Smith, Houston Cty. Hist. Commission; Smith-Arrington, Family Bible; Adair, Adair History, p.173; Diary of Elizabeth Smith, p.52. Some researchers have stated that Isaac and Augusta Adair had five children: John b.1854, Ben b.1856, Isaac Jr. b.1856, Ada b.1859, and Emma born after 1860. This seems to be a case of name confusion. When Isaac wrote his will in 1861, he made provisions for only three children: John, Ben, and Emma. It is extremely unlikely that he would purposely have excluded two children. There is no record of what became of Ben, but "Isaac Jr." died in 1870 at the age of thirteen. Since both boys are supposed to have been born in 1856, they were almost certainly one and the same. In the case of Emma, her middle name was Ada, and her family called her by both names. "Ada" appeared on the 1860 census, but not "Emma" giving the impression that "Emma" came along later. The birth certificate of Emma Ada's daughter, Antoinette, clearly states that the Emma was born in 1859 prior to the census.

21. Ibid, p.iii, various entries.

22. Census 1860. It is likely that the Wilkensons were tutors, hired to teach the Adair children. This was a

common practice before the establishment of public schools.

23. James Madison Hall, Diary, February 23, 1861.

24. Aldrich, History of Houston County, p.156; Mainer, Houston County in the Civil War, p.4.

25. James Madison Hall, Diary, April 6, 1861. The other three men were; Charley Lund, Sam Sharps, and Ed Jones.

26. Bishop, History of Houston County.

27. Muster Abstracts, Texas; James Madison Hall, Diary, May 17, 1861.

28. Muster Abstracts, Texas.

29. Thompson, Westward the Texans - Journal of Private William Randolph Howell, pp.54-66.

30. Texas Land Grant Records; Muster Abstracts, Texas. The Texas Militia was organized into brigades which (with one exception) were geographically the same as the senatorial districts for the legislature. Anderson, Houston, and Trinity counties were in the same district so they formed the 11th Brigade. The "Beat" was an administrative subdivision of the county. The term today is "Precinct."

CHAPTER 2 - PLANS AND AMBITION

1. Thompson, Henry Hopkins Sibley, pp.27-32.
2. Hall, The Confederate Army of New Mexico, p.43; Thompson, Henry Hopkins Sibley, pp.56-57.
3. Ibid.p.44; Thompson, Westward the Texans, p.1; Frazier, Blood and Treasure, pp. 46-48. Sibley also fought in the battles of Cerro Gordo, Contreras, Churubusco, Molino del Rey, and took part in operations before Mexico City.
4. Thompson, Henry Hopkins Sibley, p.68.
5. Ibid, pp.162-167.
6. New Orleans Daily Picayune, July 16, 1861.
7. Thompson, Henry Hopkins Sibley, pp.130-133.
8. Ibid, p.43; Thompson, as quoted.
9. Westward the Texans, p.1; Frazier, Blood and Treasure, pp.46-48; H.H.Sibley to D.H.Maury.
10. Kerby, Confederate Invasion, p.30.
11. Teel, Sibley's New Mexico Campaign, p.700.
12. The War of the Rebellion: A Compilation of the Official Records of the Union and Confederate Armies, hereafter cited as "OR," I,IV,p.93.
13. Teel, Sibley's New Mexico Campaign, p.700.
14. Ibid, p.700.
15. OR,I,IV,pp.141-143.
16. Thompson, Westward the Texans, pp.54-55.
17. Hall, The Confederate Army of New Mexico, p.113.
18. Austin State Gazette, September 7, 1861.
19. Mainer, Houston County in the Civil War, p.45. James Stephen Hogg, the mustering officer, later became governor of Texas.
20. Hall, The Confederate Army of New Mexico, p.267; Census 1860; Frazier, Blood and Treasure, p.86.
21. McPherson, What They Fought For, p.47, as quoted.
22. Adair, Adair History, p.150. The Adair family was holding slaves well before 1800.
23. McPherson, What They Fought For, p.48., as quoted.
24. Mainer, Houston County in the Civil War, p.95; Hall, The Confederate Army of New Mexico, p.194.

25. Ulrich, Crockett Newspapers, p.28. Frank Edens became sick in San Antonio and was left behind when the brigade marched to New Mexico.

26. McPherson, What They Fought For, p.9., as quoted.

27. Muster Abstracts, Texas; Service Record of Isaac Adair; Muster Roll Company H, 7th TMV; Hall, The Confederate Army of New Mexico, pp.267-273; Mainer, Houston County in the Civil War, pp.65-70; Wood, Leon County CSA Sketches, p.48; Ralph A. Wooster, Lone Star Blue and Gray, pp.53-54. The median age for Company H's privates was twenty-four. Noncommissioned officers were older with a median age of twenty-nine. The median age for his commisioned officers was thirty-six. The median ages for Sibley's entire brigade were: privates twenty-two, noncommissioned officers twenty-six and commissioned officers twenty-seven.

28. Ralph A. Wooster, Lone Star Blue and Gray, pp.48, 52.

29. Smith-Arrington, Civil War letters; Frazier, Blood and Treasure, p.83; Houston County Probate Records; Ralph A. Wooster, Lone Star Blue and Gray, p.50. Charles Stokes, the soldier who received the flag in Crockett, refused to be mustered for the duration of the war and subsequently resigned and returned to Crockett.

30. Smith-Arrington, Civil War letters; Service Records of B.B. Arrington; Muster Roll Company H, 7th TMV; Service Record of Isaac Adair.

31. Noel, Campaign from Santa Fe, pp.12-13.

32. Hall, Sibley's New Mexico Campaign, p.38.

33. OR,I,IV,p.17, Report of John R. Baylor, C.S. Army, of skirmish at Mesilla; Thompson, Henry Hopkins Sibley, p.225; Frazier, Blood and Treasure, p.119.

34. Josephy, The Civil War in the American West, p.45.

35. OR,I,IV,p.17, Report of John R. Baylor, C.S. Army, of skirmish at Mesilla.

36. Ibid,pp.4-17.

37. Ibid, pp.6-7.

38. Ibid,pp.11, 19.

39. OR,I,IV,p. 19, Report of John R. Baylor, C.S. Army, of skirmish at Mesilla. Lynde's subordinates complained so violently about the surrender that Colonel Baylor asked who was in command of the Federal force and responsible for its

action. For his conduct Major Lynde was dropped from the army. Later in 1866 his commission was restored and he was placed on the army's retired list.

40. D'Hamel, Adventures of a Tenderfoot, p.11.
41. Frazier, Blood and Treasure, pp.58-61; Alberts, Rebels on the Rio Grande, p.12; Thompson, Westward the Texans, p.23; Josephy, The Civil War in the American West, pp.45-48; OR,I,IV, p.23.
42. OR,I,IV, p.133, Baylor to Sibley, Oct 25,1861.
43. OR,I,IV, pp.128-129, John R. Baylor to Judge S. Hart, October 24, 1861; OR,I,IV, pp.132-133, John R. Baylor to Brigadier-General Sibley, October 25, 1861; Frazier, Blood and Treasure, p.110; Hall, Sibley's New Mexico Campaign, p.42.

CHAPTER 3 - ON TO FORT BLISS

1. Noel, Campaign from Santa Fe, p.15.
2. Ibid, p.15.
3. Ibid, p.15.
4. Ibid, p.16.
5. Frazier, Blood and Treasure, pp.117-118.
6. Benton Bell Seat Memoirs, pp.89-90. This incident took place near the Frio River some seventy-five miles west of San Antonio.
7. Noel, Campaign from Santa Fe, p.17.
8. Ibid, p.17.
9. [William Lott Davidson], "Reminiscences of the Old Brigade on the March - In the Front of the Field - as Witnessed by the Writers during the Rebellion," Overton Sharp-Shooter, Oct. 27, 1887.
10. Hall, Sibley's New Mexico Campaign, p.38.
11. Thompson, Westward the Texans, p.55.
12. Thompson, Henry Hopkins Sibley, p.226.
13. Austin State Gazette, September 7, 1861, "Attention Volunteers!"
14. Thompson, Westward the Texans, p.112, Randolph to Home Folks, Gonzales, Texas, Wednesday, August 28, 1861.
15. Noel, Campaign from Santa Fe, p.13.
16. Compiled Service Record of Isaac Adair, 7th Regiment Texas Mounted Volunteers, Civil War. Confederate Adjutant General's Office, Record Group 109, National Archives, Washington, D.C.. The assumption that the men in Company H supplied their own weapons is supported by the amount of ammunition Captain Adair requested. For the three Colt Navy revolvers on his requisition, he asked for 800 rounds, or 133 full cylinders at six shots each. He also requested twenty-five cylinders, 150 rounds, for two .44 caliber Colt Army Revolvers. To have needed that much ammunition, the volunteers must have arrived at San Antonio packing six-shooters from home. Besides the pistol rounds, Captain Adair requested 1,700 musket-size cartridges for smoothbore guns. This worked out to about three-quarters of a cartridge box or forty rounds per man in the company. Since only about

twenty of the guns on the ordnance request were smoothbore, the men from Crockett must have planned to throw musket cartridges out of their shotguns, both those they requested and those they brought from home. If all this ammunition was not enough, the company also intended to "roll their own" along the way, and Adair also requisitioned seventy-five powder flasks, eighteen-and-one-half pounds of loose powder, and twenty pounds of loose shot.

17. Heartsill, Fourteen Hundred and Ninety-one days in the Confederate Army, p.59, The item appeared in the January 17th, 1862 issue of the Camp Hudson Times.

18. Service Record of Isaac Adair, Major S. Maclin, the CSA Acting Ordnance Officer, issued Captain Adair a cavalry sabre, a cavalry sabre belt, and a cavalry sabre belt plate. Adair paid $7.00 for the sabre, $1.35 for the belt, and $0.50 for the buckle.

19. [Davidson], "Reminiscences of the Old Brigade," Oct. 27, 1887.

20. OR,I,IV,p.128, Baylor to Sibley.

21. Smith-Arrington, Civil War letters. Company H's first lieutenant, Charles Q. Haley, led this detachment. Haley was a forty-one year-old farmer from Leon County. During the War with Mexico, Lieutenant Haley and Captain Adair saw brief service together, along the Rio Grande with Colonel "Jack" Hays First Regiment of Texas Mounted Volunteers.

22. Wright, Texas in the War, p.93.

23. Noel, Campaign from Santa Fe, p.18; Smith-Arrington, Civil War letters.

24. Hall, Sibley's New Mexico Campaign, p.53.

25. Smith-Arrington, Civil War letters.

26. Benton Bell Seat Memoirs, p.88.

27. Haas, "The Diary of Julius Giesecke," November 21, 1861.

28. Thompson, Westward the Texans, p.71.

29. Ibid, p.71.

30. Haas, "The Diary of Julius Giesecke," November 8, 1861.

31. Hall, Sibley's New Mexico Campaign, p.47.

32. Thompson, Westward the Texans, p.71; [Davidson], "Reminiscences of the Old Brigade," Nov. 10, 1887.

33. Thompson, Westward the Texans, p.71.
34. Collard, Reminiscences, p.2.
35. Ibid, p.2.
36. Haas, "The Diary of Julius Giesecke," December 8, 1861.
37. Westward the Texans, p.73.
38. San Antonio Herald, December 12, 1861.
39. Haas, "The Diary of Julius Giesecke," December 8, 1861.
40. Noel, Campaign from Santa Fe, p.21.
41. Smith-Arrington, Civil War letters.
42. Thompson, Westward the Texans, p.78.
43. OR,I,IV,p.167, H.H. Sibley to General S. Cooper. Sibley wanted Reily to address three principal points. First, the Colonel was to determine whether or not the Mexican Government had "conceded to the United States the right of transit" for its troops, and whether or not any such troops were on the move. Second, he was to try to obtain permission for Sibley's troops to conduct operations in Mexico when in hot pursuit of "savage Indians." And third, Reily was to arrange for the purchase of supplies and provisions. After meeting with Don Louis Terrazas, the governor of Chihuahua, Reily wrote to Sibley, "Permit me to congratulate you, general, in having obtained the first official recognition of the Government of the Confederate States by any foreign power." While it was true that Colonel Reily was always fully uniformed when he met with Governor Terrazas, and that the Governor negotiated with him as an officer in the Confederate army, calling the meetings "official recognition" was a little farfetched. Terrazas treated Reily with the traditional Latin respect accorded an honored guest, but conceded nothing. At this early stage of the war it was still possible the Confederacy might be a permanent neighbor and courtesy cost Terrazas nothing. He told Reily that the U.S. had not been given right of transit. He apologized, but said it would be impossible for Texan troops to chase Indians into his country. As for provisions, he wrote to General Sibley that established agents and contractors already existed along the border, who could sell provisions and that official intervention was unnecessary. Despite Reily's claims of success, the meetings changed little. His trip to Sonora was

no more successful, securing only "the privilege of buying for cash anything the citizens had to dispose of," and then only for specie, not Confederate paper. OR,I,IV,p.168 H.H. Sibley to His Excellency Governor of the State of Chihuahua; OR,I,IV,pp. 170-171, James Reily to General H.H. Sibley; OR,I,IV,pp.171-172, Louis Terrazas to H.H. Sibley; OR,I,IX,p.677, J.M. Chivington to E.R.S. Canby.

44. Haas, "The Diary of Julius Giesecke," December 26, 1861.

45. Shropshire to Carrie, December 26, 1861.

46. Collard, Reminiscences, p.3.

47. Heartsill, Fourteen Hundred and 91 days in the Confederate Army, p.49.

48. OR,I,4,p.157, General Orders No.10 Hdqrs. Army of New Mexico, Fort Bliss, Tex., December 14, 1861.

49. OR,I,4,p.159, General Orders No.12 Hdqrs. Army of New Mexico, Fort Bliss, Tex., December 20,1861.

50. Teel, "Sibley's New Mexico Campaign," p.700.

51. OR,I,4,p.90, Proclamation of Brig. Gen. H.H. Sibley, Army of the Confederate States, to the people of New Mexico.

52. Ibid, p.90.

53. General Order No. 2 Hdqrs. Army of New Mexico, Fort Bliss, Tex., January 9, 1862 as quoted in Hall, Sibley's New Mexico Campaign, p.51. Sibley congratulated his men by proclamation, rather than addressing them in person.

54. Teel, "Sibley's New Mexico Campaign," p.700.

55. Thompson, Henry Hopkins Sibley, pp.337-339.

56. Noel, Campaign from Santa Fe, p.19.

57. OR,I,4,p.89, E.R.S. Canby to the Adjutant-General of the Army, Wash. D.C.

58. Noel, Campaign from Santa Fe, p.22.

59. OR,I,4,p.133, Crosby to Sibley Oct. 27, 1861. The three principle secessionists that offered support were Josiah Crosby, Simeon Hart, and James Magoffin. Crosby was a district judge and a prominent figure in El Paso. Hart was a wealthy mill owner and contractor, who operated a number of businesses also around El Paso. Magoffin was a successful contractor who was the sutler at Fort Bliss.

60. OR,I,4,p.134, Hart to Sibley Oct. 27, 1861.

61. New Orleans Daily Picayune, March 27, 1862.

62. Collard, My War Horse Pete, pp. 1-2

63. Noel, Campaign from Santa Fe, p.20.

64. Austin, State Gazette, February 15, 1862;Thompson, Westward the Texans, p.82; Hall, The Confederate Army of New Mexico, p.270; Heartsill, Fourteen Hundred and 91 days in the Confederate Army, p.65. An equally plausible speculation is that Private Dickey was a victim of his own carelessness. Volume 1 Issue No 2 of the Western Pioneer, Fort Lancaster, Texas for February 8th, 1862 carried the following item; "A few days since, a Gentleman belonging to the 3rd Reg't of Sibley's Brigade, accidently shot himself, a Minnie [sic] ball passing directly through his hand. This is the second accident of this kind happened in the last month."

65. OR,I,4,p.89, E.R.S. Canby to the Adjutant-General of the Army, Wash, D.C.

66. Frazier, Blood and Treasure, p.141.

67. Benton Bell Seat Memoirs, p.90.

68. Austin, State Gazette, January 18, 1862.

69. Noel, Campaign from Santa Fe, p.18. On January 6, 1862, Company E of the 7th Regiment was left at Fort Clark while the measles ran their course.

CHAPTER 4 - A GATHERING STORM

1. OR,I,IX,p.507, H.H.Sibley to General S.Cooper Adjutant and Inspector General.
2. William Keleher, Turmoil in New Mexico, p.143.
3. Noel, Campaign from Santa Fe, pp.18-19, 24.
4. OR,I,IX,p.507, H.H.Sibley to General S.Cooper Adjutant and Inspector General
5. Taylor, Bloody Valverde, pp.9, 19-20; Marchand, "News From Fort Craig New Mexico, 1863,", pp.37; Josephy, The Civil War in the American West, p.61. Plans for the fort called for an outer ditch to slow attackers. This ditch may or may not have existed at the time of the Texan invasion. Private Alonzo Ickis a Colorado Volunteer stationed at Craig recorded in his diary that none existed, but another chronicler, Frank Starr, wrote that "the fort was very strongly fortified, having a deep wide ditch all around." Ickis, "Diary,", Feb. 1, 1862; Gracy, "New Mexico Campaign Letters of Frank Starr," p.175.
6. Hall, The Confederate Army of New Mexico, p.25; Josephy, The Civil War in the American West, pp.39-40; Thompson, Henry Hopkins Sibley, p.178, 297
7. OR,I,IX,p.488, E.R.S.Canby to Adjutant-General of the Army, Washington, D.C. Unlike Canby's regular's, most of the 2,600 volunteers and militia who stepped forward to defend their homes were native New Mexicans of Hispanic descent. Spanish was the first language for these soldiers and some companies included as few as one man capable of functioning with facility in English. Only a handful of Anglos, like the bilingual "Kit" Carson, understood the Hispanics or appreciated their value as soldiers. Carson had married into a Spanish-speaking family and was familiar with the New Mexicans' generations of guerrilla warfare against the Indians. Edward Canby and the rest of the Anglo military hierarchy exhorted the New Mexicans to join the army and in some cases conscripted them by force. Nevertheless, they held little confidence in the natives' ability to fight. Too much cultural baggage existed. Most Union regulars held a "well-entrenched race and class prejudice, which precluded much tolerance in evaluating the local people." This became a serious problem when the

two groups were thrown into intimate contact in Canby's army. Meketa, Legacy of Honor, pp.7, 121-123.

8. Mumey, Bloody Trails, p.30.
9. Hall, Sibley's New Mexico Campaign, p.73; Frazier, Blood and Treasure, p.70; Josephy, The Civil War in the American West, p.63.
10. OR,I,IX,p.488, E.R.S.Canby to Adjutant-General of the Army, Washington, D.C.; Josephy, The Civil War in the American West, pp.42, 63; Frazier, Blood and Treasure, p.70; Meketa, Legacy of Honor, p.125.
11. OR,I,IX,p.644, Henry Connelly to Secretary of State, Washington D.C.
12. Ibid, p.644.
13. Noel, Campaign from Santa Fe, pp.18-19, 24; Frazier, Blood and Treasure, p.147; Hall, Sibley's New Mexico Campaign, p.77.
14. Thompson, Westward the Texans, p.85
15. Ibid, p.85.
16. [Davidson], "Reminiscences of the Old Brigade," Nov. 24, 1887.
17. Faulkner,"With Sibley in New Mexico," pp.129-130.
18. Thompson, Westward the Texans, p.86. Texan scouting parties sighted their Union counterparts on February 11 and 12. On the 14th, several companies out skirmishing captured twenty-one of Canby's New Mexico Volunteers.
19. Faulkner,"With Sibley in New Mexico," p.133.
20. Thompson, Westward the Texans, p.86.
21. Hall, Sibley's New Mexico Campaign, p.74; Frazier, Blood and Treasure, p.150.
22. Ickis, "Diary," Feb. 13, 1862. The term "Greasers" was used freely by Anglo troops both Union and Confederate. Racism was deeply rooted in the Anglo colonization of the Southwest and native New Mexicans were frequently subjected to insults and treated as inferiors by the Anglo officers and men. Meketa, Legacy of Honor, p.121-145.
23. Faulkner,"With Sibley in New Mexico," p.134.
24. Thompson, Westward the Texans, p.86.
25. Ickis, "Diary," Feb. 13, 1862.
26. Alberts, Rebels on the Rio Grande, p.36.

27. Haas, "The Diary of Julius Giesecke," February 14, 1862.

28. Hall, Sibley's New Mexico Campaign, p.76

29. Josephy, The Civil War in the American West, p.59; Alberts, Rebels on the Rio Grande, p.31; Frazier, Blood and Treasure, p.148.

30. Hall, Sibley's New Mexico Campaign, p.76; OR,I,IX,p.487, E.R.S.Canby to the Adjutant-General of the Army, Wash, D.C.; Frazier, Blood and Treasure, pp. 95, 138; Noel, Campaign from Santa Fe, p.24. General Sibley organized the mountain howitzer batteries, under the command of Lieutenants John Reily and William H. Woods. Reily was the son of Colonel James Reily, commander of the 4th Regiment and William Woods was a private who Sibley promoted to the rank of acting first lieutenant. The crews for the guns were men drawn from companies throughout the 4th and 5th regiments.

31. Noel, Campaign from Santa Fe, p.13.

32. [Davidson], "Reminiscences of the Old Brigade," Dec. 26, 1888.

33. Peterson, Round Shot and Rammers, pp.93-96. The barrels of mountain howitzers were only 32.9 inches long and weighed only 220 pounds each. Unlike regular field pieces, the guns did not require limbers and could be pulled by a single horse. More significantly they could to be disassembled and transported on mules or horses. The barrel was loaded onto one animal, the four-piece carriage onto another, and the ammunition chests on a third. Although easily transported the guns were not intended to fire solid shot and their short barrels limited their effective range. By 1861, it was common to equip mountain howitzers with so-called "prairie carriages" and limbers, that allowed the little cannon to be pulled more efficiently. Since this was the norm, Sibley's mountain howitzers were probably never broken down and carried by mule. Because of his western service, General Sibley was undoubtedly familiar with mountain howitzers. It is unlikely, however, that he specifically requisitioned them. It is more probable that the small cannon were part of the Federal arms surrendered by General David E. Twiggs and they they were all that were available.

34. Hall, Sibley's New Mexico Campaign, p.76; Josephy, The Civil War in the American West, p.59; OR,I,IX,p.487, E.R.S.Canby to the Adjutant-General of the Army, Wash, D.C.; Hall, The Confederate Army of New Mexico, pp.268-270. The soldiers discharged in San Antonio were Sergeant J.M. Davis, Corporal Henry McKenzie, and Corporal James Henry Pool. The two who died on the march were Quartermaster Sergeant W.S. McMorris and Private J. P. T. Dickey. The others left sick along the way were Privates M.A. Dickey, Edmond Hill, and N. Ben Whitley.

35. Noel, Campaign from Santa Fe, p.24. Despite the flowery description Noel was actually sick in Mesilla with smallpox and never saw the camp.

36. Taylor, Bloody Valverde, pp.25-29; Thompson, Henry Hopkins Sibley, p.252.

37. Thompson, Henry Hopkins Sibley, p.252.

38. Ibid, p.252.

39. Hall, Sibley's New Mexico Campaign, p.77; Hall, The Confederate Army of New Mexico, pp.114, 268; Taylor, Bloody Valverde, p.26.

40. Thompson, Westward the Texans, p.86.

41. Ibid, p.86.

42. Faulkner,"With Sibley in New Mexico," p.134.

43. OR,I,IX,p.488, E.R.S.Canby to Adjutant-General of the Army, Washington, D.C.

44. Ibid, p.488.

45. Meketa, Legacy of Honor, p.165.

46. Thompson, Westward the Texans, p.86.

47. Ickis, "Diary," Feb. 16, 1862.

48. Meketa, Legacy of Honor, p.165.

49. Haas, "The Diary of Julius Giesecke," Feb. 16, 1862.

50. Ickis, "Diary," Feb. 16, 1862.

51. OR,I,IX,p.507, H.H.Sibley to General S.Cooper Adjutant and Inspector General, Richmond, VA; Hall, Sibley's New Mexico Campaign, pp.78-79; Alberts, Rebels on the Rio Grande.

52. OR,I,IX,p.507, H.H.Sibley to General S.Cooper Adjutant and Inspector General.

53. Hanna Diary, Feb.17-19,1862; Haas, "The Diary of Julius Giesecke," Feb. 17-17, 1862; Faulkner, "With Sibley in New Mexico," p.134;

54. Noel, Campaign from Santa Fe, p.27. The ford and Texan camp were near the village of Fra Cristobal.

55. Harris, "A Tale of Men Who Knew Not Fear," pp.27-28, 30; Hall, The Confederate Army of New Mexico, p.220. Isaac Adair and his men were probably positioned with the wagons. The 7th Regiment was originally mustered for garrison duty in the areas captured by the brigade, and often drew support assignments. While Company H and the battalion of the 7th, under Lieutenant Colonel Sutton, campaigned with Sibley, the other five companies of the 7th remained with Colonel Steele as a rear guard and occupation force in the El Paso-Mesilla area.

56. Noel, Campaign from Santa Fe, p.28.

57. Ibid, p.28.

58. [Davidson], "Reminiscences of the Old Brigade," Jan. 5, 1888, Phil Fulcrod.

59. Gracy, "New Mexico Campaign Letters of Frank Starr," p.172.

60. Frazier, Blood and Treasure, p.154.

61. OR,I,IX,p.489, E.R.S.Canby to the Adjutant-General of the Army, Wash. D.C.

62. "Diary of D.A. Nunn," The Crocket Courier, July 12, 1928.

63. Gracy, "New Mexico Campaign Letters of Frank Starr," p.172.

64. Barr, Charles Porter's Account, p.14; Frazier, Blood and Treasure, p.154; Taylor, Bloody Valverde, p.37.

65. [Davidson], "Reminiscences of the Old Brigade," Jan. 5, 1888, Phil Fulcrod.

66. OR,I,IX,p.489, E.R.S.Canby to the Adjutant-General of the Army, Wash. D.C.

67. Hanna Diary, Feb.20,1862.

68. [Phil Fulcrod], "Reminiscences of the Old Brigade," Jan. 5, 1888.

69. Ibid. Since the Texans crossed the river on the 19th they had in reality been away from water less than a day and a half.

70. [Davidson], "Reminiscences of the Old Brigade," Jan. 5, 1888; Hall, Sibley's New Mexico Campaign, p.80.

71. [Davidson], "Reminiscences of the Old Brigade," Jan. 5, 1888, Phil Fulcrod.

72. Alberts, Rebels on the Rio Grande, p.40.

73. [Davidson], "Reminiscences of the Old Brigade," Jan. 5, 1888, Phil Fulcrod. Two of the men who went for water were Sergeant Major James S. Ferguson of the 7th and Quartermaster Sergeant William L. Davidson of the 5th.

74. Bell, "The New Mexico Campaign", p.58.

75. Ibid, p.58. The story of Graydon's fireworks first found its way into print when J.M. Bell, who served in New Mexico, related the tale in a paper read before the Commandery of Wisconsin M.O.L.L.U.S.. Not too surprisingly, it does not appear in any offical reports. The story has been retold many times and is frequently embellished. George H. Pettis, another New Mexico veteran, wrote that, Graydon had two mules loaded with twenty-four pound howitzer shells. After the fuses are lit, the old mules refuse to leave and then chase Graydon and his terrified men as they try to escape. Needless to say, the mules in this version are also blown to kingdom come.

76. Ibid, p58.

77. The Crocket Courier, July 12, 1928, Diary of Captain D.A. Nunn.

78. OR,I,IX,p.489, E.R.S.Canby to the Adjutant-General of the Army, Wash, D.C.; The Crocket Courier, July 12, 1928. Colonel Canby placed the number of captured horses and mules at between 200 and 300.

CHAPTER 5 - BLOODY VALVERDE

1. Faulkner, "With Sibley in New Mexico," p.135
2. OR,I,IX,p.508, H.H. Sibley to General S. Cooper Adjutant, Richmond, Va.
3. The Crockett Courier, July 12, 1928. Alfred Peticolas states that "the wagons without teams were burned to keep them from falling into the hands of the enemy." Apparently some were also simply abandoned as later on the 21st Major Charles E. Wesche, 2nd New Mexico Militia reported that his command had located and destroyed an abandoned camp consisting of partially loaded wagons. Alberts, Rebels on the Rio Grande, p.41n1.
4. [Davidson], "Reminiscences of the Old Brigade," Jan. 5, 1888, Phil Fulcrod.
5. OR,I,IX,p.508, H.H. Sibley to General S. Cooper Adjutant, Richmond, Va.
6. Ibid.
7. OR,I,IX,p.519, Report of Col. Thomas Green, Fifth Texas Cavalry.
8. Major Charles Pyron OR,I,IX,p.512, C.L. Pyron to Assistant Adjutant-General, Army of New Mexico.
9. Hall, Sibley's New Mexico Campaign, p.84.
10. Major Charles Pyron OR,I,IX,p.512, C.L. Pyron to Assistant Adjutant-General, Army of New Mexico.
11. OR,I,IX,p.489, E.R.S. Canby to the Adjutant-General of the Army, Wash, D.C.; Taylor, Bloody Valverde, pp.42-44.
12. OR,I,IX,p.497, Report of Major Thomas Duncan, Third U.S. Cavalry.
13. Ibid.
14. OR,I,IX,p.512, Report of Major Charles L. Pyron.
15. [Davidson], "Reminiscences of the Old Brigade," Jan.19, 1888.
16. OR,I,IX,pp.513-514, Report of Lieutenant Colonel William R. Scurry, Fourth Texas Cavalry
17. OR,I,IX,p.512, Report of Major Charles L. Pyron
18. OR,I,IX,pp.513-514, Report of Lieutenant Colonel William R. Scurry, Fourth Texas Cavalry; Taylor, Bloody Valverde, pp.47-48.
19. Alberts, Rebels on the Rio Grande, pp.41-42.
20. The Crockett Courier, July 12, 1928.

21. OR,I,IX,p.489, E.R.S.Canby to the Adjutant-General of the Army, Wash, D.C.; OR,I,IX,p.500, Report of Major Thomas Duncan, Third U.S. Cavalry; OR,I,IX,p.494, Report of Colonel Benjamin S. Roberts, Fifth New Mexico Infantry.

22. OR,I,IX,pp.494, 501, Reports of Colonel Benjamin S. Roberts, Fifth New Mexico Infantry; Taylor, Bloody Valverde, p.51. Roberts felt that had Duncan secured the bosque "the subsequent misfortunes of the day would not have occurred."

23. [Davidson], "Reminiscences of the Old Brigade," Feb. 9, 1888.

24. The Crockett Courier, July 12, 1928.

25. Ibid.

26. Ibid.

27. OR,I,IX,p.514, Report of Lieut. Col. William R. Scurry, Fourth Texas Cavalry.

28. The Crockett Courier, July 12, 1928. Earlier, Lieutenant John Reily's twelve-pounder mountain howitzers were driven from the lower bosque by the heavier Union artillery on the far shore. One of the light pieces continued to fire intermittently at Federal troops in the wood, but the other, on Lieutenant Colonel Scurry's orders, disengaged and fell back.

29. OR,I,IX,p.514, Report of Lieut. Col. William R. Scurry, Fourth Texas Cavalry; OR,I,IX,p.524, Report of Capt. Trevanion T. Teel, Texas Light Artillery. After the duel, Teel limbered up his guns and moved to support Major Pyron on the Confederate left.

30. OR,I,IX,p.489, E.R.S. Canby to Adjutant-General, Washington D.C.; Taylor, Bloody Valverde, p.52. The troops sent to the ford consisted of Captain Henry Seldon's eight companies of regular infantry-640 men; Theodore Dodd's Colorado Volunteers, and "Kit" Carson's seven companies of New Mexico Volunteers-460 men. The detachments left patrolling the mesa and for defence of the fort were under the command of Major Wesche and Colonel Pino.

31. OR,I,IX,p.519, Report of Col. Thomas Green, Fifth Texas Cavalry.

32. OR,I,IX,pp.516-517, Report of Major Henry W. Raguet, Fourth Texas Cavalry.

33. Anderson, "Canby's Campaign in New Mexico," pp.377-378.

34. OR,I,IX,p.495, Report of Col. Benjamin S. Roberts, Fifth New Mexico Infantry.

35. Meketa, Legacy of Honor, p.167; Alberts, Rebels on the Rio Grande, p.43.

36. Alberts, Rebels on the Rio Grande, p.43.

37. The Crockett Courier, July 12, 1928.

38. The Crockett Courier, July 12, 1928; Alberts, Rebels on the Rio Grande, p.43; Mainer, Houston County in the Civil War, p.53; Hall, The Confederate Army of New Mexico, p.116. The story of Private Gossett's death comes from the A.B. Peticolas journal. Strangely, Captain Nunn's diary says Zeb Gossett was "slightly wounded." Based on muster rolls, Hall says Gossett died two weeks later at Socorro.

39. Alberts, Rebels on the Rio Grande, p.44.

40. [Davidson], "Reminiscences of the Old Brigade," Jan. 2, 1888.

41. The Crockett Courier, July 12, 1928.

42. Hall, Sibley's New Mexico Campaign, p.90; Anderson, "Canby's Campaign in New Mexico," p.378; Taylor, Bloody Valverde, p.68 The Texans held little respect for the native levies and Scurry may have given his permission to charge, believing that Lang faced a foe who could be easily intimidated. Alonzo Ickis wrote, "The Texans saw from our dress we were not regulars (they have since told me this) and they mistook us for Mexicans." Mumey, Bloody Trails, p.38.

43. [Davidson], "Reminiscences of the Old Brigade," Jan. 5, 1888.

44. Ibid.

45. Mumey, Bloody Trails, p.31

46. Anderson, "Canby's Campaign in New Mexico," pp.378-379.

47. Mumey, Bloody Trails, p.31. Canby's map of the action shows a small rectangle at this position, suggesting that Plympton and Dodd actually formed "squares."

48. Bloody Trails, pp.32, 76. "Buck and ball" was a musket load consisting of several pieces of buckshot placed in the same cartridge with a regular musket ball.

49. [Whitley], "Reminiscences of the Old Brigade," Dec. 8, 1887. Latham Anderson states that only about six or eight lancers passed around the flanks of the rallied troops.

He also notes the lancers' use of their pistols. Anderson, "Canby's Campaign in New Mexico," p.379.
   50. Bloody Trails, pp.32, 76.
   51. [Davidson], "Reminiscences of the Old Brigade," Jan. 2, 1888.
   52. OR,I,IX,p.514, Report of Lieutenant Colonel William R. Scurry, Fourth Texas Cavalry.
   53. [Davidson], "Reminiscences of the Old Brigade," Jan 2, 1888; Alberts, Rebels on the Rio Grande, p.44; OR,I,IX,p.514, Report of Lieut. Col. William R. Scurry, Fourth Texas Cavalry.
   54. Alberts, Rebels on the Rio Grande, p.44.
   55. OR,I,IX,p.514, Report of Lieut. Col. William R. Scurry, Fourth Texas Cavalry.
   56. [Davidson], "Reminiscences of the Old Brigade," Dec. 8, 1887 and Jan. 26, 1888
   57. OR,I,IX,p.495, Report of Colonel Benjamin S. Roberts, Fifth New Mexico Infantry.
   58. OR,I,IX,p.508, H.H. Sibley to General S.Cooper. Mr. A. Mennet, of Las Vegas, New Mexico, who was in the fight on the Confederate side, stated that General Sibley "remained in his ambulance near the battlefield." Twitchell, Leading Facts, p. 376 n.300.
   59. OR,I,IX,p.523, Report of Capt. Powhatan Jordan, Seventh Texas Cavalry. Jordon's report actually says companies A and F were left with the train, but all other evidence points to A and H. Most significantly, at the battle's end company F of the 7th reported four men killed and thirteen wounded. Neither company A or H reported any casualties.
   60 Thompson, Westward the Texans, pp.88
   61. Ibid,p.118.
   62. OR,I,IX,p.523, Report of Capt. Powhatan Jordan, Seventh Texas Cavalry; OR,I,IX,p.489, E.R.S. Canby to the Adjutant-General of the Army, Wash, D.C. To garrison his post, Canby left nearly 1,000 men commanded by Colonels Manuel Armijo and Gabriel René Paul. The bulk of these troops were from the 1st New Mexico Militia, but included two companies of volunteers and some detachments from the regular troops. Colonel Canby was accompanied to the ford by Miguel Pino's regiment of the 2ndNew Mexico

Volunteers, Company G, 1st U.S. Cavalry, and the remaining section of McRae's battery.

63. Alberts, Rebels on the Rio Grande, pp.45, 51.

64. OR,I,IX,p.489, E.R.S. Canby to the Adjutant-General of the Army, Wash, D.C.; Gracy, "New Mexico Campaign Letters of Frank Starr," p.174. Colonel Canby reported that the Union losses from the morning's fighting were ten killed and sixty-three wounded. The Texans did not record their initial casualties, but it is safe to assume that they were equally heavy.

65. OR,I,IX,p.489, E.R.S. Canby to the Adjutant-General of the Army, Wash, D.C.

66. Alberts, Rebels on the Rio Grande, p.46.

67. Ibid.

68. The Crockett Courier, July 12, 1928.

69. Ibid, July 12, 1928. Nunn is referring to Captain Reddin Smith Pridgeon. After the campaign, Colonel Tom Green was promoted to General. Veterans writing years after the fact frequently used this rank when talking about the events in New Mexico.

70. [Davidson], "Reminiscences of the Old Brigade," Dec. 8, 1887.

71. Alberts, Rebels on the Rio Grande, p.46.

72. OR,I,IX,p.717, Report of Maj. Henry W. Raguet, Fourth Texas Cavalry; Taylor, Bloody Valverde, p.113.

73. OR,I,IX,p.489, E.R.S. Canby to the Adjutant-General of the Army, Wash, D.C.

74. OR,I,IX,p.517, Report of Maj. Henry W. Raguet, Fourth Texas Cavalry; OR,I,IX,p.499, Report of Major Thomas Duncan, Third U.S. Cavalry.

75. Meketa, Legacy of Honor, p.169.

76. Taylor, Bloody Valverde, p.84, from an unpublished letter. Charles R. Scott to Mr. C.A. Dupree, dated April 10, 1929.

77. OR,I,IX,pp.513-514, Report of Lieutenant Colonel William R. Scurry, Fourth Texas Cavalry.

78. Alberts, Rebels on the Rio Grande, p.48.

79. [Davidson], "Reminiscences of the Old Brigade," Dec. 15, 1887.

80.. OR,I,IX,p.524, Report of Capt. Trevanion T. Teel, Texas Light Artillery.

81. OR,I,IX,p.515, Report of Lieutenant Colonel William R. Scurry, Fourth Texas Cavalry. Participants in the campaign often incorrectly refer to cannons firing "grape." Grape was a naval ammunition. Cannister was actually the ammunition in use.

82. [Davidson], "Reminiscences of the Old Brigade," Dec. 15, 1887.

83. Alberts, Rebels on the Rio Grande, p.48.

84. Ibid, p.65.

85. OR,I,IX,p.489, E.R.S. Canby to the Adjutant-General of the Army, Wash, D.C.

86. Ibid, p.490.

87. [Davidson], "Reminiscences of the Old Brigade," Dec. 8, 1887.

88. Alberts, Rebels on the Rio Grande, p.65.

89. The Crockett Courier, July 12, 1928.

90. Hall, The Confederate Army of New Mexico, p.219.

91. Bell, "The Campaign of New Mexico," p.64.

92. [Davidson], "Reminiscences of the Old Brigade," Dec. 15, 1887.

93. Collins, "A Texan's Account of the Battle of Valverde," pp. 33-35.

94. OR,I,IX,p.491, E.R.S. Canby to the Adjutant-General of the Army, Wash, D.C.

95. [Davidson], "Reminiscences of the Old Brigade," Dec. 15, 1887.

96. OR,I,IX,p.638, Henry Connelly to Secretary of State, Washington, D.C.

97. Bell, "The Campaign of New Mexico," p.64.

98. [Davidson], "Reminiscences of the Old Brigade," Dec. 15, 1887.

99. Gracy, "New Mexico Campaign Letters of Frank Starr," p.175

100. Alberts, Rebels on the Rio Grande, p.48.

101. Ickis, "Diary," Feb. 21, 1862.

102. [Davidson], "Reminiscences of the Old Brigade," January, 26, 1888.

103. Alberts, Rebels on the Rio Grande, p.48. B.B. Seat recorded in his memoirs that, "Lockridge's blood spurted out on the [cannon] and was visible on it for two years afterwards." Benton Bell Seat Memoirs, p.95.

104. Ibid, p.48.

105. [Davidson], "Reminiscences of the Old Brigade," Dec. 15, 1887.

106. OR,I,IX,p.492, E.R.S. Canby to the Adjutant-General of the Army, Wash, D.C.

107. Alberts, Rebels on the Rio Grande, pp.48, 51. Peticolas exaggerates losses among the Union artillerymen, still fully half the gunners were killed or wounded. Like McRae's cannoneers, Captain Dodd's Colorado volunteers fought to the end, suffering casualties above fifty percent.

108. Taylor, Bloody Valverde, p.90.

109. Lord was later exonerated of any wrong doing, see OR,I,IX,p.504, Findings of Court of Inquiry on Conduct of Capt. R.S.C Lord, First U.S. Cavalry.

110. OR,I,IX,p.491, E.R.S. Canby to the Adjutant-General of the Army, Wash, D.C. The fire from Wingate's troops and that of the men on the battery's left was the crossfire that drove Lord back.

111. Ibid.

112. [Davidson], "Reminiscences of the Old Brigade," Dec. 15, 1887.

113. Ibid.

114. OR,I,IX,p.491, E.R.S. Canby to the Adjutant-General of the Army, Wash, D.C.

115. OR,I,IX,p.515, Report of Lieutenant Colonel William R. Scurry, Fourth Texas Cavalry. Lieutenant Raguet was the twenty-seven-year-old brother of Major Henry Raguet.

116. OR,I,IX,p.520, Report of Col. Thomas Green, Fifth Texas Cavalry.

117. [Davidson], "Reminiscences of the Old Brigade," Dec. 15, 1887.

118. Alberts, Rebels on the Rio Grande, p.51. Union casualties incurred crossing the river were significant, but probably not the horrific slaughter described in Confederate accounts. Alberts states that "No more than a dozen Federal soldiers were killed in crossing the Rio Grande, and probably that many more wounded." (Alberts, Rebels, p.51n) According to John Taylor, Dr. Alberts "subsequently stated that, based on Meketa's casualty analysis, this number may be low." (Taylor, Bloody Valverde, p.163n13)

119. Daniel Robinson Collection, p.20

120. Mumey, Bloody Trails, p.33. Navies refers to Colt navy revolvers.
121. Meketa, Legacy of Honor, p.169.
122. OR,I,IX,pp.517-518, Report of Maj. Henry W. Raguet, Fourth Texas Cavalry; Hall, The Confederate Army of New Mexico, pp.87, 106. The mounted companies were E and H of the 4th Regiment, commanded by Captains Charles Buckholts and William Lee Alexander.
123. OR,I,IX,p.491, E.R.S. Canby to the Adjutant-General of the Army, Wash, D.C.
124. Ibid.
125. [Davidson], "Reminiscences of the Old Brigade," Jan. 5, 1888. Clough also states that the wagon guards "were charged several times by the brave and heretofore invincible "Kit" Carson but every charge was repulsed." It is certain that Carson's regiment never attacked the train in force, but this may indicate that the Texan guards skirmished lightly with New Mexico militia patrolling the mesa.
126. OR,I,IX,p.508, Report of Brig. Gen. Henry H. Sibley
127. Thompson, Westward the Texans, p.118. Company A of the 7th was commanded by its lieutenant Alfred Thurmond. Company C of the 5th was commanded by Captain Denman W. Shannon.
128. OR,I,IX,pp.517-518, Report of Maj. Henry W. Raguet, Fourth Texas Cavalry.
129. OR,I,IX,p.515, Report of Lieutenant Colonel William R. Scurry, Fourth Texas Cavalry.
130. OR,I,IX,p.521, Report of Col. Thomas Green, Fifth Texas Cavalry
131. OR,I,IX,p.508, Report of H.H. Sibley Commanding.
132. Thompson, Westward the Texans, p.89.
133. Hall, "A Confederate officers letter...," p.332.
134. OR,I,IX,p.508, Report of H.H. Sibley Commanding. There is little question that the Federals took full advantage of the truce and avoided further conflict by their hasty flight to Fort Craig. The question of whether the Texans could have mounted an effective pursuit and completed their victory is another matter entirely. Private Theophilus Noel made a more realistic appraisal of the situation when he wrote, "Many were disposed at the time to censure Colonel Green for receiving the flag. Yet, as the enemy lost the day

by crossing the river with their artillery, we would doubtless have lost much of our gains had we have crossed over our cavalry." Notwithstanding that Canby's troops retreated from the field, they were far from crushed. In his report of the battle, Canby stated optimistically, "Although defeated, my command is not dispirited. All feel that greater injuries have been inflicted upon the enemy than we have sustained ourselves, and that what we have lost has been without loss of honor." If Lieutenant Colonel Scurry had continued his pursuit, the Federal command would certainly have turned and fought. Duncan's and Carson's troops withdrew practically unscathed after their repulse of Raguet, and the temporary numerical advantage that helped the Texan's overrun McRae's guns evaporated as the Union forces regrouped on the west bank. With the bulk of his troops exhausted and scattered and with night fast approaching, Green's decision to accept Canby's truce was really his only option. Noel, Campaign from Santa Fe, p.29; OR,I,IX,p.492, Report of Col. E.R.S. Canby.

135. Taylor, Bloody Valverde, pp.102-104, 133-135; Meketa, Legacy of Honor, p.179. B and E of Baylor's command and the Brigands also reported no casualties.

136. Mumey, Bloody Trails, pp.33-34.

CHAPTER 6 - MASTERLY INACTIVITY

1. Alberts, Rebels on the Rio Grande, p.65.
2. Ibid, p.49.
3. Ibid.
4. Ibid.
5. Noel, Campaign from Santa Fe, p.30.
6. Alberts, Rebels on the Rio Grande, p.66.
7. Ickis, "Diary," Feb. 22, 1862.
8. Meketa, Legacy of Honor, p.171.
9. Thompson, Westward the Texans, Randolph Howell to W.S. Howell, near Mesilla, Arizona, Friday May 2, 1862.
10. Alberts, Rebels on the Rio Grande, p.50.
11. Hanna Diary, Feb. 22, 1862.
12. Meketa, Legacy of Honor, pp.170-171.
13. Ibid.
14. Mumey, Bloody Trails, p.82; Thompson, Westward the Texans, p.89.
15. Harris, "A Tale of Men Who Knew Not Fear, p.39.
16. Hall, The Confederate Army of New Mexico, p.219.
17. H.J. Hunter, Letter to Jettie Word dated April 4, 1862.
18. OR,I,IX,p.492, E.R.S.Canby to the Adjutant-General of the Army, Wash, D.C.
19. Noel, Campaign from Santa Fe, p.30.
20. Alberts, Rebels on the Rio Grande, pp.49-51.
21. OR,I,IX,p.508, Report of H.H. Sibley Commanding.
22. Ibid.
23. Ibid.
24. OR,I,IX,p.522, Report of Col. Thomas Green, Fifth Texas Cavalry.
25. Gracy, "New Mexico Campaign Letters of Frank Starr," p.175. Scurry was promoted to full Colonel on the 21st, for his conduct during the battle.
26. Meketa, Legacy of Honor, p.170.
27. OR,I,IX,p.508, Report of H.H. Sibley commanding.
28. Ibid.
29. Teel, "Sibley's New Mexico Campaign."
30. Ibid.
31. Alberts, Rebels on the Rio Grande, p.52.
32. Ibid.

33. Taylor, Bloody Valverde, p.102; Hall, The Confederate Army of New Mexico, pp.94, 145, 152.
34. [Davidson], "Reminiscences of the Old Brigade," Dec. 15, 1888.
35. Ibid, Feb. 9, 1888.
36. Alberts, Rebels on the Rio Grande, p.52.
37. OR,I,IX,p.633, ED.R.S. Canby to Adjutant-General of the Army, Washington, D.C.
38. Ibid.
39. Ibid.
40. Ibid.
41. Alberts, Rebels on the Rio Grande, p.52.; Thompson, Westward the Texans, p.89; Noel, Campaign from Santa Fe, p.30.
42. Alberts, Rebels on the Rio Grande, p.52.
43. Thompson, Westward the Texans, p.89; Sanders, FAQ, Q2.7.
44. OR,I,IX,p.605, Report of Maj. Charles E. Wesche, Second New Mexico Militia. After leaving Fort Craig on the night of the 22nd, Pino's detachment set out to secure a supply depot at Polvadera north of Socorro. Major General O.P. Hovey of the New Mexico Militia, who was stationed somewhere north of Polvadera, sent a dispatch to Pino with counter orders telling him to drop back and defend the town.
45. Ibid. According to Taylor, the bulk of the militia "joined the army because of promises of money (much of which had not been forthcoming) and to protect their homes from the depredations of marauding Indians." Taylor, Bloody Valverde, p.115.
46. Ibid,p.605. These visits occurred after Colonel McNeill's warning shot, but before Lt. Simmons arrived with the demand to surrender.
47. OR,I,IX,p.607, Report of Maj. Charles E. Wesche, Second New Mexico Militia . Colonel Pino and Major Wesche were also paroled and released.
48. Noel, Campaign from Santa Fe, p.30.
49. Alberts, Rebels on the Rio Grande, p.53.
50. [Davidson], "Reminiscences of the Old Brigade," Feb. 16, 1888; Alberts, Rebels on the Rio Grande, p.53.
51. [Davidson], "Reminiscences of the Old Brigade," Feb. 16, 1888.

52. Hanna Diary, Feb. 26, 1862.
53. Thompson, Westward the Texans, p.92.
54. [Davidson], "Reminiscences of the Old Brigade," Feb. 16, 1888.
55. Hanna Diary, Feb. 27, 1862.
56. Noel, Campaign from Santa Fe, p.30.
57. OR,I,IX,p.515, Report of Lieutenant Colonel William R. Scurry.
58. Alberts, Rebels on the Rio Grande, p.55; Hall, The Confederate Army of New Mexico, pp.113, 117. David Nunn returned to Crockett where he quickly raised another cavalry company for action in Arkansas. Nunn, who is respected in Houston County to this day, continued to serve the Confederacy until the end of the war, ultimately rising to the rank of Colonel. After the war, the popular Odell became a county judge in Crockett and later settled in Cleburne, where he was elected mayor for two or three terms. Mainer, Houston County in the Civil War, pp.58, 62.
59. OR,I,IX,p.509, Report of H.H. Sibley Brigadier General Commanding; Noel, Campaign from Santa Fe, p.31; Alberts, Rebels on the Rio Grande, p.55. The decision to dismount the 4th was made on the 24th, but horses were actually appraised and turned over on the 27th.
60. Alberts, Rebels on the Rio Grande, p.55.
61. Ibid.
62. OR,I,IX,p.509, Report of H.H. Sibley Brigadier General Commanding.
63. Alberts, Rebels on the Rio Grande, p.55; service record of Isaac Adair; service record of B.B. Arrington; service records of J.M. Porter.
64. Noel, Campaign from Santa Fe, p.31.
65. Ibid, p.33.
66. Hanna Diary, Feb. 28, 1862
67. Alberts, Rebels on the Rio Grande, p.56.
68. [Davidson], "Reminiscences of the Old Brigade," Feb. 16, 1888.
69. Ibid.
70. Hanna Diary, Feb. 28, 1862.
71. [Davidson], "Reminiscences of the Old Brigade," Feb. 16, 1888.
72. Alberts, Rebels on the Rio Grande, p.56.
73. Thompson, Westward the Texans, p.92.

74. Haas, "The Diary of Julius Giesecke," Mar. 1, 1862.
75. Hanna Diary, Mar. 1, 1862.
76. Alberts, Rebels on the Rio Grande, p.56.
77. Haas, "The Diary of Julius Giesecke," Mar. 2, 1862; Hanna Diary, Mar. 2, 1862.
78 Alberts, Rebels on the Rio Grande, p.57.
79. Noel, Campaign from Santa Fe, p.33.
80. OR,I,IX,p.527, Report of Capt. Herbert M. Enos.
81. Ibid.
82. Ibid.
83. Noel, Campaign from Santa Fe, p.33.
84. [Fulcrod], "Reminiscences of the Old Brigade," Feb. 16, 1888.
85. Ibid.
86. Ibid.
87. OR,I,IX,p.527, Report of Maj. James L. Donaldson, Quartermaster, U.S. Army, commanding District of Santa Fe, N. Mex.
88. Ibid, p.527. Major Donaldson evacuated Santa Fe on March 4, 1862.
89. [Davidson], "Reminiscences of the Old Brigade," Feb. 16, 1888, Fulcrod.
90. Noel, Campaign from Santa Fe, p.34.
91. OR,I,IX,p.529, Report of Capt. A. S. Thurmond, Third Regiment, Sibley's Brigade.
92. Ibid.
93. Hall, Sibley's New Mexico Campaign, p.115.
94. Noel, Campaign from Santa Fe, p.34.
95. OR,I,IX,p.529, Report of Capt. A. S. Thurmond, Third Regiment, Sibley's Brigade. Captain Aragon and his men were paroled and told to return to Albuquerque. Since the route back led past the realm of hostile Navajos, Thurmond gave them transportation and 20 muskets, with 40 rounds each. In return, Aragon promised that on their arrival in Albuquerque the arms and wagons would be turned over to the Confederate States Army officer commanding there. The journey was made safely and, true to his word, Aragon returned the wagons and weapons.
96. Noel, Campaign from Santa Fe, p.34.
97. OR,I,IX,p.509, H.H. Sibley to General S. Cooper. Supplies taken at Santa Fe were included in Sibley's "three months" estimate.

98. Haas, "The Diary of Julius Giesecke," Mar. 2, 1862.
99. Hanna Diary, March 3, 1862.
100. [Davidson], "Reminiscences of the Old Brigade," Feb. 16, 1888.
101. Hanna Diary, March 3, 1862.
102. Faulkner,"With Sibley in New Mexico," p.136.
103. Alberts, Rebels on the Rio Grande, p.57.
104. Thompson, Westward the Texans, p.92.
105. [Davidson], "Reminiscences of the Old Brigade," Feb. 16, 1888.
106. Thompson, Westward the Texans, p.153n85.
107. Thompson, Henry Hopkins Sibley, p.273 from Confederate Depredation Claims, March and April 1862, Adjutant General's Records, New Mexico State Archives.
108. Ibid.
109. Miller, "Hispanos and the Civil War," p.111.
110. Ibid; Division Order No.5 and Order No.7, January 25, 1862. Annual Reports of Adjutant General, Territorial Archives of New Mexico, Microfilm Edition, roll 84; Thompson to Nicodemus, February 7, 1862.
111. Alberts, Rebels on the Rio Grande, p.58.
112. Ibid, p.58.
113. Ibid, p.58.
114. Ibid, p.61.
115. Thompson, Westward the Texans, pp.92-93; Haas, "The Diary of Julius Giesecke," Mar. 4, 1862.
116. Alberts, Rebels on the Rio Grande, p.59.
117. Ibid, p.59.
118. Haas, "The Diary of Julius Giesecke," Mar. 5, 1862.
119. Hanna Diary, Mar. 5, 1862.
120. Ibid.
121. Ibid.
122. Alberts, Rebels on the Rio Grande, p.61.
123. Ibid.
124. Thompson, Westward the Texans, p.93.
125. Ibid.
126. Alberts, Rebels on the Rio Grande, p.63.
127. Haas, "The Diary of Julius Giesecke," Mar. 7, 1862.
128 OR,I,IX,p.511, H.H. Sibley to General S. Cooper; Meketa, Legacy of Honor, p.378. Manuel Armijo was a colonel in the territorial militia and actually commanded a garrison regiment at Valverde. When proclaiming his

sympathy for the Southern cause, he protested that he was pressed into the militia and forced to be present at the battle. Sibley clearly identifies the Armijo brothers in his field report, but later writers often confuse Manuel Armijo with Miguel Antonio Otero. Otero, another prominent New Mexican, served as the Territory's delegate to Congress during the late 1850's. In Washington Otero married a southern belle and aligned himself with the South on most issues. When the territorial legislature passed its slave code in 1859, Otero's influence was an important factor. "In a letter to the Territorial Secretary, Otero pointed out that the laws of the United States, as well as the Dred Scott decision, established slavery beyond a question in all of the territories and that it would be in New Mexico's best interest to recognize the fact." This pro-southern stance is undoubtedly why Otero is frequently mistaken for Armijo. Beck, New Mexico, A History of Four Centuries, p.145.

129. Thompson, Westward the Texans, p.93.
130. Hanna Diary, Mar. 7, 1862.
131. Ibid.
132. Hall, Sibley's New Mexico Campaign, p.116; Alberts, Rebels on the Rio Grande, p.67; Thompson, Henry Hopkins Sibley, p.275.
133. Santa Fe Gazette, April 26, 1862.
134. OR,I,IX,p.511, H.H. Sibley to General S. Cooper.
135. Alberts, Rebels on the Rio Grande, p.67; Hall, Sibley's New Mexico Campaign, p.121; Frazier, Blood and Treasure, p.199.
136. Alberts, Rebels on the Rio Grande, p.66.
137. Haas, "The Diary of Julius Giesecke," Mar. 8, 1862.
138. Hanna Diary, Mar. 8, 1862.
139. Alberts, Rebels on the Rio Grande, p.67.
140. Haas, "The Diary of Julius Giesecke," Mar. 9, 1868; Alberts, Rebels on the Rio Grande, pp.67.
141. Houston Tri-Weekly Telegraph Aug. 27, 1862.
142. Thompson, Westward the Texans, p.93.
143. Alberts, Rebels on the Rio Grande, p.67.
144. Thompson, Westward the Texans, p.93.
145. Hanna Diary, Mar. 10, 1862.
146. Hall, Sibley's New Mexico Campaign, p.120; Josephy, The Civil War in the American West, p.75. This anecdote comes entirely from Ellen Williams book, "Three

Years and a Half in the Army; or History of the Second Coloradans." Hall notes that no record of a Captain or Lieutenant Battles appears in existing muster rolls, however, the roll for Phillips Brigands has been lost.

147. Thompson, Henry Hopkins Sibley, pp.276-277; Hall, Sibley's New Mexico Campaign, pp.120-121; Josephy, The Civil War in the American West, pp.74-75.

148. Haas, "The Diary of Julius Giesecke," Mar. 12, 1862. By contrast, Benton Bell Seat wrote that the men had "but little of anything to eat that could be regarded as wholesome." Houston Tri-Weekly Telegraph Aug. 27, 1862

149. Alberts, Rebels on the Rio Grande, p.68.

150. Faulkner, "With Sibley in New Mexico," p.138.

151. Thompson, Westward the Texans, p.95.

152. Ibid.

153. [Davidson], "Reminiscences of the Old Brigade," Feb. 16, 1888.

154. Mainer, Houston County in the Civil War, p.69; Hall, The Confederate Army of New Mexico, p.268. While the number of Texans who fell ill far exceeded those injured in battle, the brigade's eventual death toll from disease was 69 compared to 119 from combat.

155. Haas, "The Diary of Julius Giesecke," Mar. 13, 1862. These villages were Tijeras and San Antonio. Tijeras is at the gateway to the north-south route along the eastern face of the Sandia Mountains. San Antonio is near the top of Route 14.

156. Hanna Diary, Mar 13, 1862.

157. [Davidson], "Reminiscences of the Old Brigade," Feb. 16, 1888.

158. Alberts, Rebels on the Rio Grande, p.70.

159. Haas, "The Diary of Julius Giesecke," Mar. 14, 1862.

160. Ibid, Mar. 15, 1862.

161. Alberts, Rebels on the Rio Grande, p.70.

162. Benton Bell Seat Memoirs, p.96.

163. Alberts, Rebels on the Rio Grande, p.70.

164. Hanna Diary, Mar. 16, 1862.

165. Ibid.

166. Alberts, Rebels on the Rio Grande, p.70.

167. Hanna Diary, Mar. 16, 1862.

168. Hall, The Confederate Army of New Mexico, p.225; Hanna Diary, Mar. 16, 1862.

169. Alberts, Rebels on the Rio Grande, p.72.

170. Haas, "The Diary of Julius Giesecke," Mar. 16-19, 1862.

171. OR,I,IX,p.509, H.H. Sibley to General S. Cooper; [Davidson], "Reminiscences of the Old Brigade," Feb. 23, 1888, Sharp Whitley; Hall, Sibley's New Mexico Campaign, pp.121-123

172. Hall, Sibley's New Mexico Campaign, p.121; Faulkner, "With Sibley in New Mexico," pp.138-139; Hanna Diary, Mar. 20, 1862.

173. Alberts, Rebels on the Rio Grande, p.72.

174. Ibid, p.73.

175. Hanna Diary, Mar. 25, 1862.

176. Alberts, Rebels on the Rio Grande, p.72; Haas, "The Diary of Julius Giesecke," Mar. 24, 1862.

177. Alberts, Rebels on the Rio Grande, p.74.

178. Ibid, p.75.

179. Williams Diary, Mar. 25, 26, 1862

180. [Sharp Whitley], "Reminiscences of the Old Brigade," Feb. 23, 1888.

181. Bloom, "Confederate Reminiscences," p.316. Private Harvey Holcomb, Company H, 4th Regiment.

182. Ibid, p.317.

183. [Fulcrod], "Reminiscences of the Old Brigade," May 17, 1888.

184. Haas, "The Diary of Julius Giesecke," Mar. 26, 1862. Giesecke's count of 250 effectives is probably a little low for Major Pyron's command, 280 is considered more accurate. The Union force he faced consisted of 180 infantrymen and 238 cavalrymen for a total of 418. This figure however does not include thirty men of the Second New Mexico who were there as well. Edrington and Taylor, The Battle of Glorieta Pass, Appendix pp.126-128; OR,I,IX,p.530, Report of Maj. John M. Chivington, First Colorado Infantry; Meketa, Legacy of Honor, p.183, 382n37, 383n38.

185. Alberts, Rebels on the Rio Grande, p.75.

186. Haas, "The Diary of Julius Giesecke," Mar. 26, 1862.

187. [Davidson], "Reminiscences of the Old Brigade," Feb. 23, 1888. Major Jordan's role in these events is unclear. It appears that he was with his battalion at Galisteo but did not accompany them on the advance to Apache Canyon. In his report of May 4 Sibley states that "the battalion of Colonel Steele's regiment, under Maj. Powhatan Jordan, was pushed forward in the direction of Galisteo." Subsequent reports by Scurry fail to mention Jordan and the Gustav Hoffman diary states that he himself was in command.

CHAPTER 7 - PIKE'S PEAKERS

1. Gilpin may have been involved with a city named Linnton that predated Portland on the same site. Most historians agree that Portland was founded in 1845 by Lovejoy and Pettygrove. Josephy, The Civil War in the American West, p.292; Whitford, Battle of Glorieta Pass, pp.36-38; Karnes, William Gilpin, pp.5 & 114.

2. OR,I,IV,p.73, William Gilpin to E.R.S. Canby; Karnes, William Gilpin, p.272.

3. Whitford, Battle of Glorieta Pass, p.39.

4. Ibid, pp.38-39; Karnes, William Gilpin, p.273.

5. Karnes lists McKee as head of the Confederate gun buying effort, but doesn't site a source. In the Official Records, Gov. Gilpin to Col. Canby writes; "you will learn that a guerrilla party has been captured by Captain Otis near Fort Wise; the captain of this band, McKee, has been in jail for several weeks in this city. Ovando Hollister says; "Capt. McKee...had been arrested on the point of leaving with about forty partizans to join Sibley's forces..., Whitford, Battle of Glorieta Pass, p.41; Karnes, William Gilpin, p.274; OR,I,IV,p.73, William Gilpin to Col. E.R.S. Canby; Hollister, Boldly They Rode, p.26.

6. Hollister notes that, Miller later attempted to push a train of supplies through Kansas to the Texans in New Mexico. The train was captured, but Miller escaped. Karnes, William Gilpin, p.274; Hollister, Boldly They Rode, p.26.

7. OR,I,IV,p.73, William Gilpin to Col. E.R.S. Canby.

8. OR,I,IV,pp.53-54, ED.R.S Canby to Governor of Colorado Territory.

9. Hollister, Boldly They Rode, p.6; Whitford, Battle of Glorieta Pass, pp.45 & 48.

10. Dorsey, The Journal of Mollie Dorsey Sanford, p.158; Hollister, Boldly They Rode, p.2; Ferris, Civil War, p.1.

11. Hollister, Boldly They Rode, p.2; Ferris, Civil War, p.1.

12. Hollister, Boldly They Rode, p.3; Ferris, Civil War, p.1.

13. Hollister, Boldly They Rode, p.3; Ferris, Civil War, p.1.
14. Dorsey, The Journal of Mollie Dorsey Sanford, p.158; Hollister, Boldly They Rode, pp.4-5; Ferris, Civil War, p.1; Karnes, William Gilpin, p.282.
15. Whitford, Battle of Glorieta Pass, p.47; Scott, Glory Glory Glorieta, pp.46-47.
16. Boyd, "Thunder on the Rio Grande," p.4; Whitford, Battle of Glorieta Pass, p.47; Hall, Sibley's New Mexico Campaign, p.132; Scott, Glory Glory Glorieta, p.47.
17. Hollister, Boldly They Rode, p.6; Williams, Three years and a half in the Army, p.3; Whitford, Battle of Glorieta Pass, p.45.
18. Dorsey, The Journal of Mollie Dorsey Sanford, p.158.
19. OR,I,III,p.496, William Gilpin to Simon Cameron.
20. OR,I,III,p.466, Fremont to Gilpin; Whitford, Battle of Glorieta Pass, p.43.
21. Whitford, Battle of Glorieta Pass, p.43; Scott, Glory Glory Glorieta, p.58.
22. In his letter Gilpin referred to Companies A and B under then captains Slough and Tappan. OR,I,IV,p.68 William Gilpin to Col. E.R.S. Canby; OR,I,IV,pp.68-69, ED.R.S.Canby to His Excellency Governor of Colorado Territory.
23. Ibid.
24. OR,I,IV,p.72, ED.R.S. Canby to William Gilpin; OR,I,IV,p.73, William Gilpin to Col. E.R.S. Canby.
25. Whitford, Battle of Glorieta Pass, pp.43-p50.
26. Ibid, p.53; Karnes, William Gilpin, pp.278-279.
27. Ibid, p.279.
28. Scott, Glory Glory Glorieta, p.51, as quoted from the Rocky Mountain News; Whitford, Battle of Glorieta Pass, p.45; Hollister, Boldly They Rode, p.6.
29. Karnes, William Gilpin, p.279; Hollister, Boldly They Rode, p.6; Scott, Glory Glory Glorieta, p.51.
30. Whitford, Battle of Glorieta Pass, p.53; Karnes, William Gilpin, p.279; Scott, Glory Glory Glorieta, p.52.
31. Dorsey, The Journal of Mollie Dorsey Sanford, p.163; Scott, Glory Glory Glorieta, pp.52-53, as quoted in.
32. Karnes, William Gilpin, p.281-284.

33. Whitford, Battle of Glorieta Pass, pp.43-44; OR,I,IX,p.527, Report of Maj. J.L. Donaldson; Williams, Three years and a half in the Army.
34. Hollister, Boldly They Rode, pp.31 & 33; Ferris, Civil War, p.2.
35. Hollister, Boldly They Rode, pp.34-35; Ferris, Civil War, p.2.
36. Hall, Sibley's New Mexico Campaign, p.66; OR,I,IV,p.82, ED.R.S. Canby to William Gilpin.
37. Whitford, Battle of Glorieta Pass, p.50.
38. Scott, Glory Glory Glorieta, p.115.
39. OR,I,IX,p.630, D.Hunter to His Excellency Acting Governor of Colorado; Twitchell, The leading facts of New Mexico History, p.381, from the journal of Major Downing.
40. OR,I,IX,p.632, Lewis Weld to Brig. Gen. E.R.S. Canby.
41. Scott, Glory Glory Glorieta, p.116; Whitford, Battle of Glorieta Pass, p.77; Hollister, Boldly They Rode, p.47.
42. Ibid, p.45; Whitford, Battle of Glorieta Pass, p.77.
43. Hollister, Boldly They Rode, p.47.
44. Ibid, pp.47-48.
45. Ferris, Civil War, p.3; Hollister, Boldly They Rode, p.48.
46. Ibid, pp.48-51.
47. Ibid, p.52; Ferris, Civil War, p.3.

CHAPTER 8 - APACHE CANYON

1. OR,I,IX,p.653, ED. R. S. Canby to Colonel Paul.
2. OR,I,IX,p.646, G.R. Paul to Adjutant-General U.S. Army.
3. Gaither, "Pet Lambs at Glorieta Pass," p.32.
4. Hall, Sibley's New Mexico Campaign, p.129; Whitford, Battle of Glorieta Pass, p.81. Slough's command consisted of his own 1st Colorado Regiment, Captain James Ford's Independent Company, a battalion of the U.S. 5th Infantry, three detachments of Cavalry, two light artillery batteries, and one company from the 4th Regiment of New Mexico Volunteers.
5. Belville Countryman, June 7, 1862; Edrington and Taylor, The Battle of Glorieta Pass, Appendix pp.126-128; Alberts, Rebels on the Rio Grande, p.75n40.
Since there are no official enumerations of Major Pyron's force, the exact number of effectives that he lead into Apache Canyon will always be a matter of speculation. Estimates from knowledgeable authorities range between a low of 250 and a high of 440. I feel the Edrington and Taylor proposed figure of 280 is about right. See Edrington and Taylor, The Battle of Glorieta Pass, Appendix pp.126-128. For an accounting of the high estimate see Alberts, The Battle of Glorieta, p. 49.
6. [Davidson], "Reminiscences of the Old Brigade," Feb. 23, 1888. The reference to being barefoot is probably an exaggeration. Later forensic evidence suggests that the Texans were well shod. Alberts, Rebels on the Rio Grande, p.167
7. Greer, "Historical Facts about Battlegrounds," p.3.
8. Hollister, Boldly They Rode, pp.58-59; OR,I,IX,p.530, Report of Maj. John M. Chivington, First Colorado Infantry. The main body of Slough's command encamped at Bernal Springs, a strategically located village that the colonel planned to make his base of operations in the area. Situated near a tip of the mountains, it was in a position to control access to Fort Union, both along the Pecos River and through Glorieta Pass.
9. Hall, Sibley's New Mexico Campaign, p.132.
10. Mallory, "Ferris - Civil War Memoir," p.5.

11. Whitford, Battle of Glorieta Pass, p.84. Kozlowski's Ranch was situated on the Santa Fe Trail near the old Pecos Indian ruins.

12. Mallory, "Ferris - Civil War Memoir," p.5; OR,I,IX,p.530, Report of Maj. John M. Chivington, First Colorado Infantry.

13. Hayes, "The New Mexico Campaign of 1862;" Hall, Sibley's New Mexico Campaign, pp.145-146; Bloom, "Confederate Reminiscences." It has also been postulated that Alexander Valle received his nickname because he spoke "pidgin" English. Whatever the origin the name Pigeon's Ranch has passed into local history.

14. Hollister, Colorado Volunteers, p.59. Hollister's assertion that McIntyre held a Union commission and was on Colonel Canby's staff at Valverde is uncorroborated by other sources.

15. [Davidson], "Reminiscences of the Old Brigade," February 23, 1888, Davidson; Hall, The Confederate Army of New Mexico, p.375; Mallory, "Ferris - Civil War Memoir," p.5.

16. Hollister, Colorado Volunteers, p.59.

17. Ibid, p.61. The unusual marching order comes from Hollister who states "We left camp about 8 o'clock, the infantry detachment immediately in advance." He also states that "The cavalry number 210 and marched in the order of their rank."

18. Emmett, Fort Union, p.266 from Ft. Union; Thompson, Henry Hopkins Sibley, p.280; Whitford, Battle of Glorieta Pass, appendix pp.3-4. The identities of the two lieutenants involved are unknown. Although this incident is accepted by many authorities, both Alberts and Edrington/Taylor suggested that it is an exaggeration taken from Chivington's memoirs of the earlier capture of Lieutenant John McIntyre and his three companions at Pigeon's ranch. Since Chivington describes the capture of an advance guard and two lieutenants in his after action report as separate from the capture of the pickets and Hollister also describes the capture of "the lieutenant in command of their artillery" as distinct from the capture of McIntyre and his cohorts, I choose to take the story at face value.

19. Hollister, Colorado Volunteers, p.61.

20. Ibid.

21. [Davidson], "Reminiscences of the Old Brigade," May 17, 1888, February 23, 1888; Mallory, "Ferris - Civil War Memoir," p.6; Whitford, Battle of Glorieta Pass, p.87.

22. [Davidson], "Reminiscences of the Old Brigade," May 17, 1888; OR,I,IX,p.530, Report of Maj. John M. Chivington, First Colorado Infantry; Hall, The Confederate Army of New Mexico, pp.146-147.

23. [Davidson], "Reminiscences of the Old Brigade," May 17, 1888.

24. Mallory, "Ferris - Civil War Memoir," p.6.

25. Hollister, Colorado Volunteers, p.62.

26. Ibid.

27. Emmett, Fort Union, p.264, from Ft. Union, 1862 file.

28. Boyd, "Thunder on the Rio Grande," p.4. John M. Chivington was born in Warren County Ohio in 1821. He migrated to Illinois where he joined the Illinois Conference of the Methodist Episcopal Church. He later joined the Missouri Conference and became a missionary to the Wyandotte Indians. In 1860 he moved to Colorado and became the presiding elder of its large Methodist congregation. When the 1st Regiment Colorado Volunteers formed, Chivington was tendered the position of regimental chaplain. He would have none of it. Every bit as rough and tumble as the miners to whom he preached, he told the governor of Colorado Gilpin, "If there's fighting to be done, I want to fight." "There is no force more evil on earth than the Confederacy and its people." Chivington was subsequently appointed a major. Craig, The Fighting Parson: A Biography of Col. John M.Chivington.

29. [Davidson], "Reminiscences of the Old Brigade," February 23, 1888.

30. OR,I,IX,p.531, Report of Capt. Charles J. Walker, Second U.S. Cavalry; Mumey, Bloody Trails, p.96; Hollister, Colorado Volunteers, p.62; Hall, Sibley's New Mexico Campaign, p.135; Whitford, Battle of Glorieta Pass, p.89; Houston Tri-Weekly Telegraph Aug. 27, 1862.

31. [Davidson], "Reminiscences of the Old Brigade," February 23, 1888. According to Benton Bell Seat, the cannon were nearly two miles ahead the main body of Texans when Chivinton struck. While an exaggeration,

Seat's report does support the notion that the Texan's were spread out and unprepared.

32. Ibid.

33. Mallory, "Ferris - Civil War Memoir," p.5; Hollister, Colorado Volunteers, p.63; OR,I,IX,p.530, Report of Maj. John M. Chivington, 1st Colorado Infantry; Hall, Sibley's New Mexico Campaign, p.136.

34. Craig, The Fighting Parson: A Biography of Col. John M.Chivington, p.19.

35. OR,I,IX,p.530, Report of Maj. John M. Chivington, 1st Colorado Infantry; OR,I,IX,p.531, Report of Capt. Charles J. Walker, Second U.S. Cavalry.

36. [Davidson], "Reminiscences of the Old Brigade," February 23, 1888. Dr. Don Alberts notes that artifact evidence confirms that the 2 guns accompanying Pyron were 6-pounders. See Alberts, Don E., The Battle of Glorieta, p.189n.14.

37. Mallory, "Ferris - Civil War Memoir," p.6. The wounded trooper was Mort A. Patterson.

38. Hollister, Colorado Volunteers, p.63.

39. Ibid, p.64.

40. Chivington, "The First Colorado," p.149; Whitford, Battle of Glorieta Pass, p.91. In recent years authors have questioned the veracity of the arroyo jumping incident as described by Chivington and retold by Whitford, pointing to its lack of corroboration by other participants. The narrow road's unsuitability for a cavalry charge and low casualty rates are also strong arguments that the charge did not occur as described. While it is certain that Chivington embellished the tale and that it has grown with the retelling, I believe it also contains a nugget of truth. Benjamin Ferris who rode in the charge described "a ditch across the wagon road about 5 feet deep and 10 to 15 feet wide." He also wrote, "Capt. Cook soon fell some ten feet ahead of me, about the time we crossed the ditch." Company F may not have leapt Chivington's 18-foot chasm replete with burning bridge, but it is reasonable to assume their galloping "column of twos" handily negotiated a 10-foot "ditch." Mallory, "Ferris - Civil War Memoir," p.6. See also Alberts, Don E., The Battle of Glorieta, p.62 and Edrington and Taylor, The Battle of Glorieta Pass, p.51.

41. Hollister, Colorado Volunteers, p.167. The excerpt about "regular demons" and "flying devils" is part of a letter which Ovando Hollister included in his book and attributed to a Confederate prisoner named George M. Brown. Because no soldier of that name appears on any of the Army of New Mexico's muster rolls and because of the letter's overall tone and lavish praise of the Colorado troops, later historians have considered the letter suspect.

42. Ibid, p.64. See also OR,I,IX,p.530, Report of Maj. John M. Chivington, 1st Colorado Infantry and OR,I,IX,p.531, Report of Capt. Charles J. Walker, Second U.S. Cavalry. The other Federals that rushed down from the hillsides were Jacob Downing's Company D, 1st Colorado Volunteers and Companies A and E, under Captains Edward Wynkoop and Scott Anthony.

43. [Davidson], "Reminiscences of the Old Brigade," February 23, 1888.

44. Ibid.

45. Ibid.

46. Hollister, Colorado Volunteers, p.64. Private Hopkins M. Boon, Company C, 1st Colorado Volunteers, was killed two days later in the fighting at Glorieta Pass.

47. [Davidson], "Reminiscences of the Old Brigade," February 23, 1888 and April 15, 1888, Love Tooke.

48. Hollister, Colorado Volunteers, p.65.

49. OR,I,IX,p.531, Report of Capt. Charles J. Walker, Second U.S. Cavalry; Whitford, Battle of Glorieta Pass, p.92.

50. OR,I,IX,p.530, Report of Maj. John M. Chivington, 1st Colorado Infantry.

51. OR,I,IX,p.530, Report of Maj. John M. Chivington, 1st Colorado Infantry; OR,I,IX,p.531, Report of Capt. Charles J. Walker, Second U.S. Cavalry.

52. OR,I,IX,p.530, Report of Maj. John M. Chivington, 1st Colorado Infantry; Hanna Diary, March 27, 1862; Alberts, Rebels on the Rio Grande, p.76.

53. Hollister, Colorado Volunteers, p.65.

54. Mallory, "Ferris - Civil War Memoir," p.7.

CHAPTER 9 - THE ROAD TO GLORIETA

1. OR,I,IX,p.542, Report of Col. W.R. Scurry, Fourth Texas Cavalry. The order to march was given within ten minutes but it took about an hour before all in Scurry's command were under way.
2. Alberts, Rebels on the Rio Grande, p.76.
3. OR,I,IX,p.542, Report of Col. W.R. Scurry, Fourth Texas Cavalry; Hanna Diary, March 26, 1862; Alberts, Rebels on the Rio Grande, p.76.
4. Alberts, Rebels on the Rio Grande, p.76.
5. OR,I,IX,p.542, Report of Col. W.R. Scurry, Fourth Texas Cavalry.
6. [Fulcrod], "Reminiscences of the Old Brigade," May 17, 1888.
7. Ibid.
8. [Davidson], "Reminiscences of the Old Brigade," February 23, 1888. Although Pyron assumed a defensive posture and his men were nervous, there was little chance of attack during the night. Shortly after sundown Pyron sent a white flag to Chivington requesting a temporary truce to tend to the wounded and bury the dead. The Union commander agreed, so there was actually a formal cessation of hostilities in effect until 8 o'clock the next morning.
9. Ibid.
10. Ibid, See also Alberts, Rebels on the Rio Grande, p.76.
11. Ibid.
12. Ibid.
13. Ibid. On the night of March 26th, Green may or may not heve been on the road to Santa Fe. There is some indication that he moved about twenty miles northeast of Albuquerque on the 25th, but after a day or so turned around to protect the town from a rumored advance by Canby. See also [Davidson], "Reminiscences of the Old Brigade, "May 17, 1888, Fulcrod and Hall, Sibley's New Mexico Campaign, p.165.
14. Webb, The Handbook of Texas, p.584; Hall, The Confederate Army of New Mexico, p.53; Frazier, Blood and Treasure, p.78; Taylor, Bloody Valverde, p.18.
15. Hanna Diary, March 27, 1862.

16. OR,I,IX,p.543, Report of Col. W.R. Scurry, Fourth Texas Cavalry; Hanna Diary, March 27, 1862; Alberts, Rebels on the Rio Grande, p.77. The significance of 8 o'clock is that this was the time Pyron's truce with Chivington expired.

17. Hollister, Boldly They Rode, p.67; Mallory, "Ferris - Civil War Memoir," p.8. The water supply at Pigeon's ranch came from a well twelve feet across, forty feet around; twenty-six feet to bottom. Although the it contained between six and eight feet of water, raising a sufficient amount for the Union horses was an onerous task. See also Greer, "Historical Facts about Battlegrounds," p.9.

18. Bloom, "Confederate Reminiscences," Harvey Holcomb, p.317; Hanna Diary, March 27, 1862.

19. Alberts, Rebels on the Rio Grande, p.77.

20. OR,I,IX,p.543, Report of Col. W.R. Scurry, Fourth Texas Cavalry. Scurry's decision to advance may have been contrary to General Sibley's orders. According to Lieutenant Phil Fulcrod, the General instructed Scurry to remain at the gap and hold until Colonel Green could take his command and assail the enemy rear. See [Davidson], "Reminiscences of the Old Brigade," May 17, 1888.

21. Bloom, "Confederate Reminiscences," Harvey Holcomb, p.317.

22. OR,I,IX,p.543, Report of Col. W.R. Scurry, Fourth Texas Cavalry.

23. [Davidson], "Reminiscences of the Old Brigade," March 1, 1888; Edrington and Taylor, The Battle of Glorieta Pass, pp.140, 141. Private Davidson reported that Nettles' cannon was left behind because there were no horses to move it. Scurry's command had plenty of available horses, so Davidson's assertion may indicate that the cannon was damaged in some manner that made it awkward to move.

24. New Braunfels Herald, Aug. 22, 1961. Major Jordon may actually have been with the advance, but it seems unlikely, as Hoffman states clearly that he was in command of the cavalry. There is also no record of the position of Captain Adair or his Company, but based on the presence Hoffman's Company B, it is safe to assume that they were also with the advance.

25. OR,I,IX,p.541, Report of Brig. Gen. Henry H. Sibley, C.S. Army; OR,I,IX,p.543, Report of Col. W.R. Scurry,

Fourth Texas Cavalry. As he was still in Albuquerque, Sibley's knowledge was second-hand. When he reported that Scurry's command numbered 1,000 he may not have been aware of Pyron's losses in Apache Canyon.

26. OR,I,IX,p.541, Report of Brig. Gen. Henry H. Sibley, C.S. Army; OR,I,IX,p.543, Report of Col. W.R. Scurry, Fourth Texas Cavalry. The exact number of effectives that Scurry lead into battle is a topic of some controversy with estimates from respected authorities ranging between a low of 600 to a high of 1,285. Although one can see how the higher number could be reached, Scurry clearly stated that his combined force from the 4th, 5th, and 7th regiments numbered no more than 600. Lacking strong new evidence that he understated the size of his force, I think we must take his report at face value. See also Edrington and Taylor, The Battle of Glorieta Pass, pp.132, 133; Alberts, The Battle of Glorieta, pp. 78, 79.

27. [Davidson], "Reminiscences of the Old Brigade," March 1, 1888. According to Davidson, Green first heard about the engagements in Apache and Glorieta Canyons on the night of the 29th.

28. Hollister, Boldly They Rode, p.68.

29. OR,I,IX,p.534, Report of Col. John P. Slough, First Colorado Infantry; Hall, Sibley's New Mexico Campaign, p.145. Nine-hundred-and-sixteen men came from the 1st Colorado Volunteers. One-hundred-and-fifty were from Captain George W. Howland's detachments of U.S. 1st and 3rd Cavalry. Another one-hundred-and-ninety-one were a mix from Captain W.H. Lewis' battalion, U.S. 5th Infantry, the 4th New Mexico Volunteers, and Ford's Independent Company; the remaining eighty-three were crews assigned to the two batteries. One battery consisted of four twelve-pounder mountain howitzers and was commanded by Lieutenant Ira W. Claflin. The other battery included two twelve-pounder and two six-pounder field pieces. It was commanded by Captain John F. Ritter.

30. OR,I,IX,p.534, Report of Col. John P. Slough, First Colorado Infantry; OR,I,IX,p.538, Report of Major John M. Chivington, First Colorado Cavalry; Hollister, Boldly They Rode, p.63; Hall, Sibley's New Mexico Campaign, p.131. Chivington's detail consisted of companies A and G of the U.S. 5th Infantry, in charge of Lieutenants Samuel Barr and

Stephen Norvell; companies A, B, E, and H of the 1st Regiment Colorado Volunteers, under their respective Captains Edward Wynkoop, Samuel Logan, Scott Anthony, and George Sandborn; Captain James Ford's Independent Company of the 2nd Colorado; and a detachment of New Mexico Volunteers commanded by Lieutenant Colonel Manuel Chaves.

31. OR,I,IX,p.532, Report of Captain Charles J Walker, Second U.S. Cavalry; OR,I,IX,p.534, Report of Col. John P. Slough, First Colorado Infantry.

32. [Davidson], "Reminiscences of the Old Brigade," March 1, 1888.

33. Alberts, Rebels on the Rio Grande, p.77; [Davidson], "Reminiscences of the Old Brigade," March 1, 1888.

34. [Davidson], "Reminiscences of the Old Brigade," March 1, 1888.

35. OR,I,IX,p.543, Report of Col. W.R. Scurry, Fourth Texas Cavalry.

36. New Braunfels Herald, Aug. 22, 1961.

37. OR,I,IX,p.532, Report of Captain Charles J Walker, Second U.S. Cavalry. It was long thought that all Scurry's guns were six-pounders. Compelling artifact evidence gathered by Dr. Don Alberts now suggests that the battery consisted of one six-pounder and two twelve-pounder field howitzers. Since the Confederates brought no twelve-pounders with them into New Mexico the two pieces with Scurry were almost certainly part of McRaes Battery captured at Valverde. See Alberts, The Battle of Glorieta, pp. 79, 197n25.

38. Hollister, Boldly They Rode, p.68.

39. Hayes, "An Unwritten Chapter of the Late War," p.144.

40. Gaither, "Pet Lambs at Glorieta Pass," p.33.

41. OR,I,IX,p.532, Report of Captain Charles J Walker, Second U.S. Cavalry; OR,I,IX,p.536, Report of Lieutenant Colonel Samuel F. Tappan.

42. OR,I,IX,p.536, Report of Lieutenant Colonel Samuel F. Tappan; Whitford, Battle of Glorieta Pass, pp.48-49, also Appendix, Burt Schmitz maps and commentary; Hall, Sibley's New Mexico Campaign, p.147; Hollister, Boldly They Rode, p.68. Captain Jacob Downing and Company D of the 1st Colorado Volunteers were placed to the far left.

Captain Samuel Robbins' Company K took position on the brow of a small hill, left center, where they supported Claflin's four guns. Richard Sporis and Company C of the 1st Colorado Volunteers straddled the road and supported Ritter's battery. Company I, composed mostly of German's recruited in and around Denver City, was placed on the Union right under the command of lieutenants Charles Kerber and John Baker.

43. Alberts, Rebels on the Rio Grande, p.78.

44. [Davidson], "Reminiscences of the Old Brigade," March 1, 1888, Whitley. In Sharp Whitley's narrative of the battle, his description of Scurry directing the cannon comes, as I've included it here, near the start of the action. It is likely, however, that he was remembering a time later in the day when the Texans lost track of the main enemy force and Scurry used the cannon to probe for its position.

45. OR,I,IX,p.536, Report of Lieutenant Colonel Samuel F. Tappan, First Colorado Infantry.

46. [Davidson], "Reminiscences of the Old Brigade," March 1, 1888.

47. Hollister, Boldly They Rode, pp.68-69.

48. [Davidson], "Reminiscences of the Old Brigade," March 1, 1888, Whitley.

49. Ibid, March 1, 1888, Whitley.

50. Bloom, "Confederate Reminiscences," Harvey Holcomb.

51. [Whitley], "Reminiscences of the Old Brigade," March 1, 1888. Whitley describes this incident, but does not identify the direction of the attack or the Federal troops involved. I have assumed it was Downing's men, as they were the only Union force reported to have approached a Texan cannon. Implying an element of surprise, Whitford says that Bradford's cannon was "masked." He does not, however, mention Scurry's ruse. In his excellent book "The Battle of Glorieta" Dr. Don Alberts questions the whole ruse story attributing it to a misinterpretation of events by "participants who were not able to see what actually happened." True or false the story is a fine one and as Dr. Alberts later notes, "even if it is not true, it should have been!" See Whitford, Battle of Glorieta Pass, p.108; Alberts, Battle of Glorieta, pp.102, 200n17.

52. [Davidson], "Reminiscences of the Old Brigade," March 1, 1888.
53. Alberts, Rebels on the Rio Grande, p.86.
54. Ibid. Abe Hanna's diary ends abruptly with his entry for the 27th, but in another hand is the notation; "This is the end of this little memorandum Journal kept by Ebenezer Hanna, who faught [sic] and died on the Battle Field of Glorietta[sic]." Hanna Diary.
55. Hollister, Boldly They Rode, p.69.
56. Mallory, "Ferris - Civil War Memoir," p.8.
57. [Davidson], "Reminiscences of the Old Brigade," March 8, 1888. The idea that Companies B and H returned to Johnson's Ranch with all the Texan horses is conjecture, but it is supported by available information. We know that Scurry's cavalry was in the lead on the morning of the 28th and that it was ordered to dismount and fight on foot. We also know that Chivington claimed that later in the day his men found 1,100 horses and mules in a side canyon near Johnson's Ranch. All four companies of the 7th were mounted and possibly Pyron's two companies and Shropshire's four companies of the 5th. This means that with each trooper leading three or four horses, at least two companies must have been assigned to return the horses. This is supported by Hollister's and Whitford's assertion that Scurry was reinforced by two companies of "fresh" troops early in the battle. I have assumed Adair's Company H was one of the two because there is evidence from Whitley's account that the fight was well under way before Company H reached the front. My reason for picking Hoffman's Company B, is based on Whitford's assertion that two companies of Germans were assigned to guard the Confederate train. According to Whitford, an aging Texas Captain told him that the Germans declared they had "enlisted to get glory by fighting, and not in guarding mules and provisions," and that they deserted their posts and rushed to the sound of the fighting. Whitford's anecdotal account seems unlikely, but probably contains a kernel of truth. There were only two companies of Germans in the Sibley Brigade, Hoffman's and Captain Julius Giesecke's Company G of the 4th. Giesecke's company was afoot and according to his diary, was several miles from camp when the combat began. This means that if there were Germans

at Johnson's Ranch they must have been Hoffman's men. When Hoffman and Adair appeared with the horses, it is likely that hearing the sounds of battle, the wagon guard urged them to stay. It is unlikely that anyone shirked an assigned duty. See also service record of Isaac Adair; service record of B.B. Arrington; service records of J.M. Porter; Whitford, Battle of Glorieta Pass, p.119; Hall, Sibley's New Mexico Campaign, p.157.

58. [Davidson], "Reminiscences of the Old Brigade," March 8, 1888. Davidson is refering to James Carson, a twenty-year-old 5th sergeant with Company A of the 5th Regiment.

59. Whitford, Battle of Glorieta Pass, p.107. Lieutenant Colonel Tappan wrote about Baker's death in his after action report stating, "Lieutenant Baker, of Company I, was severely wounded during the early part of the engagement, and afterward beaten to death by the enemy with the butt of a musket or club and his body stripped of its clothing. He was found the next morning, his head scarcely recognizable, so horribly mangled. He fought gallantly, and the vengeance of the foe pursued him after death." Although Tappan clearly believed the Confederates responsible for this atrocity, others blamed native scavengers. Ovando Hollister wrote of the incident; "It was laid to the miserable Greasers who followed the Texans." OR,I,IX,p538, Report of Lieutenant Colonel Tappan; Hollister, Boldly They Rode, p.73.

60. OR,I,IX,p.543, Report of Col. W.R. Scurry, Fourth Texas Cavalry.

61. [Davidson], "Reminiscences of the Old Brigade," March 8, 1888, Whitley. The exploits of Captain Buckholts with his knife is one of several stories of the campaign that has grown with each retelling. Peticolas stated in his diary that, "Buckholts killed one with his bowie knife." Sharp Whitley wrote that he "killed two with his knife." Noel wrote of "three dead Federals who had undoubtedly been killed by his knife." See Alberts, Rebels on the Rio Grande, p.79; Noel, Campaign from Santa Fe, p.36.

62. OR,I,IX,p.543, Report of Col. W.R. Scurry, Fourth Texas Cavalry.

63. Alberts, Rebels on the Rio Grande, p.79. By the end of the day's fighting total losses for Company I reached

fifteen dead, fifteen wounded, and five captured, a third of their effective strength. See Whitford, Battle of Glorieta Pass, pp. 144-150.

64. [Davidson], "Reminiscences of the Old Brigade," March 8, 1888.
65. Ibid, Whitley.
66. Ibid, .
67. OR,I,IX,p.533, Report of Col. John P. Slough, First Colorado Infantry.
68. Hollister, Boldly They Rode, p.70.
69. [Davidson], "Reminiscences of the Old Brigade," March 8, 1888, Whitley.
70. Alberts, Rebels on the Rio Grande, p.79.
71. OR,I,IX,p.543, Report of Col. W.R. Scurry, Fourth Texas Cavalry. Because of a shortage of gunners, the third cannon was not returned to the field.
72. Hall, The Confederate Army of New Mexico, p.341.
73. [Davidson], "Reminiscences of the Old Brigade," March 8, 1888.
74. Hollister, Boldly They Rode, pp.69-70; Hall, Sibley's New Mexico Campaign, p.148.
75. OR,I,IX,p.536, Report of Lieutenant Colonel Samuel F. Tappan.
76. OR,I,IX,p.540, Report of Capt. John F. Ritter, Fifteenth U.S. Infantry; Whitford, Battle of Glorieta Pass, p.108; OR,I,IX,p.532, Report of Captain Charles J. Walker, Second U.S. Cavalry.
77. [Davidson], "Reminiscences of the Old Brigade," March 8, 1888.
78. OR,I,IX,p.543, Report of Col. W.R. Scurry, Fourth Texas Cavalry; Whitford, Battle of Glorieta Pass, Appendix, Burt Schmitz maps and commentary; Hall, Sibley's New Mexico Campaign, p.149; Alberts, Rebels on the Rio Grande, p.81.
79. Rebels on the Rio Grande, p.81.
80. OR,I,IX,p.544, Report of Col. W.R. Scurry, Fourth Texas Cavalry.
81. [Davidson], "Reminiscences of the Old Brigade," March 8, 1888.
82. Whitford, Battle of Glorieta Pass, p.108.
83. OR,I,IX,p.540, Report of Capt. John F. Ritter, Fifteenth U.S. Infantry; Frazier, Blood and Treasure, p.220.

84. OR,I,IX,p.537, Report of Lieutenant Colonel Samuel F. Tappan.

85. [Peticolas], "Reminiscences of the Old Brigade," March 8, 1888.

86. Hollister, Boldly They Rode, p.71.

87. [Davidson], "Reminiscences of the Old Brigade," March 1 and 15, 1888; Hall, Sibley's New Mexico Campaign, pp.87, 93.

88. [Davidson], "Reminiscences of the Old Brigade," March 1, 1888.

89. Hollister, Colorado Volunteers, p.114.

90. Mallory, "Ferris - Civil War Memoir," p.9.

91. [Davidson], "Reminiscences of the Old Brigade," March 8, 1888.

92. Mallory, "Ferris - Civil War Memoir," p.9. Confederate eyewitness accounts of Shropshire's death differ as to whether he was mounted or leading his horse when he was shot. All, however, agree that he was shot in the head while urging his men forward.

93. Hollister, Boldly They Rode, p.70.

94. Ibid, p.71. See also OR,I,IX,p.536, Report of Lieutenant Colonel Samuel F. Tappan;1888.

95. [Davidson], "Reminiscences of the Old Brigade," March 8, 1888, J.H. Richardson.

96. Mallory, "Ferris - Civil War Memoir," p.9.

97. [Davidson], "Reminiscences of the Old Brigade," March 8, 1888.

98. Ibid.

99. Ibid, J.H. Richardson.

100. Ibid, March 8, 1888. See also OR,I,IX,p.536, Report of Lieutenant Colonel Samuel F. Tappan.

101. OR,I,IX,p.544, Report of Col. W.R. Scurry, Fourth Texas Cavalry.

102. OR,I,IX,p.540, Report of Capt. John F. Ritter, Fifteenth U.S. Infantry.

103. Alberts, Rebels on the Rio Grande, p.121. According to one estimate, Scurry may have charged down the Santa Fe Trail against the combined battery as many as five times before Ritter and Claflin withdrew. See Whitford, Battle of Glorieta Pass, Appendix, Burt Schmitz maps and commentary.

104. OR,I,IX,p.540, Report of Capt. John F. Ritter, Fifteenth U.S. Infantry; OR,I,IX,p.544, Report of Col. W.R. Scurry, Fourth Texas Cavalry.
105. OR,I,IX,p.540, Report of Capt. John F. Ritter, Fifteenth U.S. Infantry.
106. OR,I,IX,p.537, Report of Lieutenant Colonel Samuel F. Tappan.
107. [Peticolas], "Reminiscences of the Old Brigade," March 1, 1888.
108. Ibid.
109. Ibid, Davidson.
110. Ibid.
111. Hall, The Confederate Army of New Mexico, pp.269-272; Mainer, Houston County in the Civil War, pp.69-70.
112. Hayes, "An Unwritten Chapter of the Late War," p.144.
113. Hollister, Boldly They Rode, pp.69-70.
114. OR,I,IX,p.544, Report of Col. W.R. Scurry, Fourth Texas Cavalry.
115. Gracy, "New Mexico Campaign Letters of Frank Starr," p.177.
116. [Davidson], "Reminiscences of the Old Brigade," March 8, 1888. The story of "Uncle Billy" is probably a tall tale or an event of some other campaign. Company I of the 4th was the Nunn/Odell company from Crockett and there were no Smiths on its muster roll. According to Hall's enumeration there was only one William Smith at Glorieta, but since he was eighteen it is unlikely that he would have been called "Uncle Billy."
117. Gracy, "New Mexico Campaign Letters of Frank Starr," p.177.
118. Ibid.
119. Whitford, Battle of Glorieta Pass, p.112.
120. Ibid.
121. Gracy, "New Mexico Campaign Letters of Frank Starr," p.178.
122. [Davidson], "Reminiscences of the Old Brigade," March 8, 1888.
123. Gracy, "New Mexico Campaign Letters of Frank Starr," p.178.
124. Whitford, Battle of Glorieta Pass, p.111.

125. Harris, "A Tale of Men Who Knew Not Fear, p.49. Anecdotes, such as this one are frequently difficult to place in time. Although I have chosen to include it here, the incident could just as easily be placed during any of the Texans' other four charges against the Union artillery.

126. OR,I,IX,p.544, Report of Col. W.R. Scurry, Fourth Texas Cavalry.

127. Ibid.

128. OR,I,IX,p.540, Report of Capt. John F. Ritter, Fifteenth U.S. Infantry. Union and Confederate reports disagree at this point. Union reports say the Texans were thrown back, Texan reports make statements like, "We charged them and they broke in confusion." See [Davidson], "Reminiscences of the Old Brigade," March 23, 1888.

129. Harris, "A Tale of Men Who Knew Not Fear, p.50.

130. Hayes, "An Unwritten Chapter of the Late War," p.144.

131. OR,I,IX,p.544, Report of Col. W.R. Scurry, Fourth Texas Cavalry.

132. Whitford, Battle of Glorieta Pass, p.115, as quoted.

133. OR,I,IX,p.537, Report of Lieutenant Colonel Samuel F. Tappan.

134. [Davidson], "Reminiscences of the Old Brigade," March 8, 1888.

135. Ibid. Davidson's timing of this anecdote is at odds with Tappan's after action report that states that Shannon was captured at the moment Shropshire was killed.

136. OR,I,IX,p.544, Report of Col. W.R. Scurry, Fourth Texas Cavalry. These were wagons whose teamsters had been ordered away to carry ammunition to Claflin's battery. See Alberts, Battle of Glorieta, p.121.

137. Bloom, "Confederate Reminiscences," p.318, Harvey Holcomb.

138. Ibid, p.318, Harvey Holcomb.

139. Alberts, Rebels on the Rio Grande, p.86.

140. Hall, Sibley's New Mexico Campaign, p.153. William Whitford asserts that the truce flag was carried by Sibley's assistant adjutant-general, Major Alexander M. Jackson. He says that Jackson, who was riding in an ambulance, was intercepted by Captains Downing and Ritter, who led him blindfolded to Kozlowski's. This is

probably confusion with Jackson's later appearance at San José on April 9th. Whitford, Battle of Glorieta Pass, p.115.

    141. Hayes, "An Unwritten Chapter of the Late War," p.144.

CHAPTER 10 - DEFEAT

1. OR,I,IX,p.527 Report of Maj. James L. Donaldson, Quartermaster, U.S. Army, commanding District of Santa Fe, N. Mex.; Meketa, Legacy of Honor, p.383. Major Donaldson reported that Chaves' men deserted, but later investigations proved that this was not the case. The volunteers' six-month enlistments expired during their march north and many simply decided to go home.

2. Hayes, "The New Mexico Campaign of 1862," pp.179-180; OR,I,IX,p.538, Report of Maj. John M. Chivington, First Colorado Infantry; Whitford, Battle of Glorieta Pass, p.116; Thompson, Henry Hopkins Sibley, p.289.

3. Hayes, "The New Mexico Campaign of 1862," p.180. The number of wagons in the Confederate train varies from report to report. Estimates range from a low of 60 to a high of 80.

4. Whitford, Battle of Glorieta Pass, p.118; Hall, The Confederate Army of New Mexico, p.213; OR,I,IX,p.538, Report of Maj. John M. Chivington, First Colorado Infantry.

5. Gaither, "Pet Lambs at Glorieta Pass," p.33.

6. Hayes, "The New Mexico Campaign of 1862," p.179.

7. Ibid, p.180. William H. Lewis and Asa B. Carey were both captains in the U.S. 5th Infantry. Hayes does not directly attribute this conversation, but his article implies that the source was Carey.

8. Whitford, Battle of Glorieta Pass, p.118. Chivington's order to "charge" is quoted from William Whitford's excellent book, unfortunately Whitford fails to cite his own source. The alleged command seems inappropriate for the situation, but Major Chivington's after action report uses similar wording.

9. Hayes, "The New Mexico Campaign of 1862," p.180.

10. OR,I,IX,p.538, Report of Maj. John M. Chivington, First Colorado Infantry.

11. Gaither, "Pet Lambs at Glorieta Pass," p.34.

12. Whitford, Battle of Glorieta Pass, p.118; Thompson, Henry Hopkins Sibley, p.289; Hall, Sibley's New Mexico Campaign, pp.156-157.

13. Whitford, Battle of Glorieta Pass, p.118; Thompson, Henry Hopkins Sibley, p.289; Hall, Sibley's New Mexico Campaign, pp.156-157.

14. Whitford, Battle of Glorieta Pass, p.119; Thompson, Henry Hopkins Sibley, p.289; Hall, Sibley's New Mexico Campaign, pp.156-157; Alberts, The Battle of Glorieta, pp.132, 203n8. During the 1970's Dr. Don Alberts located the position of Wynkoop's thirty volunteers evidenced by a subsurface line of discarded percussion caps found with a metal detector.

15. [Davidson], "Reminiscences of the Old Brigade," March 1, 1888 and March 8, 1888. This account of the destruction of the Confederate cannon is at odds with often repeated Union reports, that assert Captain Lewis spiked the gun and destroyed the ammunition. It is, however, supported by Colonel Scurry's after action report which states, "The men at the train blew up the limber-box and spiked the 6-pounder I had left at the train, so that it was rendered useless, and the cart-burners left it." See OR,I,IX,p.538, Report of Maj. John M. Chivington, First Colorado Infantry; OR,I,IX,p.544, Report of Col. W.R. Scurry, Fourth Texas Cavalry.

16. Whitford, Battle of Glorieta Pass, p.119.

17. [Davidson], "Reminiscences of the Old Brigade," March 1, 1888.

18. OR,I,IX,p.544, Report of Col. W.R. Scurry, Fourth Texas Cavalry.

19. OR,I,IX,p.534, Report of Col. John P. Slough, First Colorado Infantry; OR,I,IX,p.657, Henry Connelly. Major Chivington's detachment actually captured many more of the Texans, but sick and wounded were not included in the enumeration. New Mexico Governor, Henry Connelly put the total at forty.

20. Gaither, "Pet Lambs at Glorieta Pass," p.34.

21. Ibid.

22. Whitford, Battle of Glorieta Pass, p.120.

23. OR,I,IX,p.539, Report of Maj. John M. Chivington, First Colorado Infantry.

24. [Davidson], "Reminiscences of the Old Brigade," March 8, 1888. Major Chivington only speaks of freeing five Union prisoners in his report, but there may have been more. Colonel Scurry's after action report says, he sent "a

party of prisoners" to the rear, who arrived while Union troops held the camp. Writing twenty years later, W.L. Davidson numbered this party at eighty. See OR,I,IX,p.539, report of Maj. John M. Chivington, First Colorado Infantry; OR,I,IX,p.544, report of Col. W.R. Scurry, Fourth Texas Cavalry; Whitford, Battle of Glorieta Pass, p.120; Alberts, Rebels on the Rio Grande, p.77.

    25. Whitford, Battle of Glorieta Pass, p.122; OR,I,IX,p.539, Report of Maj. John M. Chivington, First Colorado Infantry; Bloom, "Confederate Reminiscences," p.322. If Major Chivington's party had marched back by way of the pass, they might well have trapped Scurry's command between the two Union columns. This probably would have resulted in a decisive Union victory. Almost certainly the battle's toll in dead and wounded would have increased. Writing years later Major Chivington claimed that his men found 1,100 horses and mules in a side canyon near Johnson's Ranch and bayoneted them all. Despite frequent repetition, this story is probably badly exaggerated. Charles Gardiner, in a letter to his mother, wrote, "three hundred killed with our bayonets." If Chivington had indeed destroyed 1,100 animals it seems exceedingly unlikely, that it would have been omitted from all official records, both Union and Confederate. Confederate veteran Henry C. Wright, Private, Company F, 4th Texas wrote of Chivington's tale, "Your account says they killed 1100 mules. At the outside we did not have over 500, and I for one never saw or heard of a dead one." Undoubtedly, many rebel mounts and draft animals were captured, killed, or simply shooed away during the raid. Evidence includes the muster roll for Isaac Adair's Company H, which is littered with notes such as: "Lost Horse battle Glorieta. - Captured by enemy", "Horse, equipments captured by enemy.", and "Dismounted March 28th 1862."

    26. OR,I,IX,p.544, Report of Col. W.R. Scurry, Fourth Texas Cavalry. Because there is no Union corroboration that Chivington ordered his prisoners be shot if his column was attacked, some historians have declared the tale "sheer nonsense." It is not, however, out of character for Chivington and seems less farfetched in light of his later

actions at Sand Creek. See Carroll, The Sand Creek Massacre, pp.1-84.

27. [Davidson], "Reminiscences of the Old Brigade," March 1, 1888.

28. OR,I,IX,p.544, Report of Col. W.R. Scurry, Fourth Texas Cavalry.

29. Whitford, Battle of Glorieta Pass, p.122.

30. Gaither, "Pet lambs at Glorieta Pass," p.34; OR,I,IX,p.539, Report of Maj. John M. Chivington, First Colorado Infantry; Hall, Sibley's New Mexico Campaign, p.158.

31. Gaither, "Pet lambs at Glorieta Pass," p.35; Hall, Sibley's New Mexico Campaign, p.159; Whitford, Battle of Glorieta Pass, p.122. Gardiner states that a second messenger brought word that the way back was blocked and that Slough had been completely driven from the canyon.

32. Kajencki, "Was the Guide Ortiz or Grzelachowski," pp.47-54. In an newspaper article, that appeared in the Denver Republican on April 27, 1890, Colonel Chivington wrote: "I wish to say of this priest - I wish I had his name - that he was the only native priest that I saw during the entire campaign and our stay afterward in New Mexico who was loyal to the Federal Government." In many subsequent accounts the priest was called Padre Ortiz. Although the story was often retold, the name Ortiz does not figure in any contemporary reports. It is only in later accounts that the name makes its appearance. A persuasive study, published in 1987 by Francis C. Kajencki, makes the case that the name Ortiz was anecdotal, and that the actual guide was "Padre Polaco," the Rev. Alexander Grzelachowski. Grzelachowski, a Polander by birth, was the Spanish speaking Chaplin of the Second New Mexico Volunteers, and was serving with Colonel Chaves. He is credited as the guide by a 1881 newspaper article, and it is certain he was with Chivington during the trek. Church records of the time fail to list a Father Ortiz anywhere in the area.

33. [Davidson], "Reminiscences of the Old Brigade," March 1, 1888; Alberts, Rebels on the Rio Grande, p.86. Colonel Scurry may have known about the attack on his train before calling for a truce. This is certainly implied as his motive by Union sources. On the other hand, the point

is by no means obvious. Scurry's field report does not address the question and other sources are ambiguous. For instance, Alfred Peticolas, who clearly states that word had arrived about the train's destruction, later writes, "They [the Federals] had run clear off. 3/4 of an hour had elapsed since all firing had ceased, and they made no effort to get permission to bury their dead. So Col. Scurry sent Maj. Pyron back with a flag of truce, informing them that he granted them permission to return and bury their dead and take off their wounded."

    34. Bloom, "Confederate Reminiscences," p.318.

    35. Hall, The Confederate Army of New Mexico, pp.1-381; Hollister, Boldly They Rode, pp.74-76; Whitford, Battle of Glorieta Pass, pp.123-125; Hall, Sibley's New Mexico Campaign, pp.157-158; Alberts, Rebels on the Rio Grande, p.85. I believe the combined strength of the two forces at Glorieta Pass was about 1,650.

    36. OR,I,IX,p.534, Report of Col. John P. Slough, First Colorado Infantry; Hollister, Boldly They Rode, pp.74-76; OR,I,IX,p.538, Report of Lieut. Col. Samuel F. Tappan, First Colorado Infantry. Colonel Slough reported his losses at twenty-eight killed, forty wounded, and fifteen taken prisoner. These figures were undoubtedly understated. Hollister lists the names of forty-six men who were killed and sixty-four wounded and his figures do not include losses among the U.S. regulars. See also Alberts, The Battle of Glorieta, pp.138-139, 204n28; Edrington, Taylor, "The Battle of Glorieta Pass, pp.130-131.

    37. Hollister, Boldly They Rode, p.73. Hollister wrote of Lieutenant Baker's death, "Lieut. Baker of I, was severely wounded in the side. He dragged himself to a small hollow and built a fire to soften the chilly atmosphere. In the morning he was dead and stripped. A bullet-hole through his head told his sad story - murdered and robbed."

    38. Ibid, p.72.

    39. OR,I,IX,p.534, Report of Col. John P. Slough, First Colorado Infantry.

    40. Hollister, Boldly They Rode, p.72.

    41. OR,I,IX,p.544, Report of Col. W.R. Scurry, Fourth Texas Cavalry. Hall, The Confederate Army of New Mexico. Scurry reported his losses as thirty-six killed and sixty wounded. Tallys made made from Hall's invaluable work

adjusted by contemporary sources yield the higher figures. See also Edrington, Taylor, "The Battle of Glorieta Pass," p.137.

42. Report of Col. W.R. Scurry, Fourth Texas Cavalry. Henry Connelly, the Governor of New Mexico, wrote that three Confederate captains and eight lieutenants were captured. He identifies the Captains as; Shannon, Wells, and Scott. Scott was probably John J. Scott, who gained the captaincy of Company B of the 5th Regiment after Willis Lang and Demetrius Bass were left at the hospital in Socorro. Wells was Stephen Wells Monroe, who was captured at the head of Major Shropshire's old company, A of the 5th. Since Scurry reported that Company A was led by Lieutenant Pleasant J. Oakes on the morning of the 28th, it is likely that Wells was actually captured at Apache Canyon on the 26th. This probably also accounts for the "extra" five lieutenants enumerated by Connelly. See OR,I,IX,p.542, Report of Col. W.R. Scurry, Fourth Texas Cavalry; OR,I,IX,p.660, Henry Connelly; OR,I,IX,p.545,.

43. Hall, Sibley's New Mexico Campaign, p.159

44, Hollister, Boldly They Rode, p.72.

45. Emmett, Fort Union, p.266 from Ft. Union, 1862 file; Hall, Sibley's New Mexico Campaign, p.72. Colonel Slough's after action reports tout the raid on the Texan rear guard while barely mentioning his own action. He maintains that; "Hearing of the success of Major Chivington's command, and the object of our movement being successful, we fell back to our camp." This seems highly unlikely. It is much more probable, that Colonel Slough was trying to disguise the fact that, despite Canby's orders to the contrary, he had engaged the Texans in a full scale battle, and lost.

46. Alberts, Rebels on the Rio Grande, p.86.

47. [Davidson], "Reminiscences of the Old Brigade," March 8, 1888.

48. Bloom, "Confederate Reminiscences," pp.317-318, Holcomb. The loan of these tools was another act that garnered Slough's soldiers the lasting respect of the Texans. See also [Whitley], "Reminiscences of the Old Brigade," March 8, 1888.

49. Haas, "The Diary of Julius Giesecke," March 28, 1862.

50. [Davidson], "Reminiscences of the Old Brigade," March 1, 1888.
51. Ibid.
52. Ibid.
53. Bloom, "Confederate Reminiscences," p.322.
54. Alberts, Rebels on the Rio Grande, p.86.
55. [Davidson], "Reminiscences of the Old Brigade," March 8, 1888. There is no question that the wounded of both armies suffered and died during the long cold night of the March 28, 1862. There is some question, however, whether a foot of new snow fell on the field and added to their plight. This may simply be another cherished myth of the campaign. Davidson was writing twenty years after the battle when he asserted that it snowed, and Theophilus Noel, who also wrote of snow, was not actually present. Diarists who were on the field, Alfred Peticolas, Julius Giesecke, and Ovando Hollister make no mention of snow, although they all made note of it at other times. Snow is not mentioned in any official after action reports. See also Noel, Campaign from Santa Fe, p.35.
56. OR,I,IX,p.657, Henry Connelly to W.H. Seward, Secretary of State. The reports of Sibley's movement were false.
57. Hall, Sibley's New Mexico Campaign, p.161; Whitford, Battle of Glorieta Pass, pp.126-127; Hollister, Boldly They Rode, p.73; OR,IX,p.660, Henry Connelly to W.H. Seward, Secretary of State.
58. Hollister, Boldly They Rode, p.73.
59. Ibid, p.74.
60. Haas, "The Diary of Julius Giesecke," March 29, 1862.
61. Whitford, Battle of Glorieta Pass, pp.125-126. This description of the gravesite location is erroneous, but for many years, until the actual site was rediscovered, it was accepted as fact. See also Mitchell, "The 2nd Battle of Glorieta." p.26.
62. Frazier, Blood and Treasure, p.227. Thirty soldiers were laid in the common grave and the body of Major Shropshire was interred nearby. The bodies of Majors Shorpshire and Raguet were held for several days until coffins could be sent for them from Santa Fe. "The coffin made for Maj. Shropshire was too short and he still sleeps

at Glorieta where he fell." See also [Davidson], "Reminiscences of the Old Brigade," March 1, 1888.

63. Alberts, Rebels on the Rio Grande, pp.86-87.
64. Ibid, p.87.
65. [Davidson], "Reminiscences of the Old Brigade," March 1, 1888.
66. Bloom, "Confederate Reminiscences," p.318, Harvey Holcomb; Haas, "The Diary of Julius Giesecke," March 29, 1862; Alberts, Rebels on the Rio Grande, p.87.
67. Alberts, Rebels on the Rio Grande, p.87. See also Haas, "The Diary of Julius Giesecke," March 29, 1862.
68. Straw, Loretto, p.36.
69. Ibid, p.38.
70. Frazier, Blood and Treasure, p.329n49. There is no record that Jackson addressed the men, but Frazier makes the case and it is a reasonable assumption based on his position as Adujant. See also Thompson, Westward the Texans, p.96; Thompson, Henry Hopkins Sibley, pp.290-291.
71. Faulkner,"With Sibley in New Mexico," p.140.
72. OR,I,IX,p.542, Report of Col. W.R. Scurry, Fourth Texas Cavalry.
73. Ibid, p.542.
74. Noel, Campaign from Santa Fe, p.36.
75. Straw, Loretto, p.38.
76. Haas, "The Diary of Julius Giesecke," March 30, 1862; Alberts, Rebels on the Rio Grande, p.88.
77. Thompson, Westward the Texans, p.96; [Davidson], "Reminiscences of the Old Brigade," March 1, 1888 and May 17, 1888; Hall, Sibley's New Mexico Campaign, p.165. According to Davidson, Green's men were encamped fourteen miles east of Albuquerque at the time of the move.
78. [Fulcrod], "Reminiscences of the Old Brigade," May 17, 1888.
79. Hall, Sibley's New Mexico Campaign, p.166; Hall, The Confederate Army of New Mexico, p.61; OR,I,IX,p.509, H.H. Sibley to General S. Cooper. Frank Starr in a letter to his father, dated May 4, 1862, states Captain James Walker of Baylor's command was the officer left in charge. See Gracy, "New Mexico Campaign Letters of Frank Starr," p.179.

80. [Fulcrod], "Reminiscences of the Old Brigade," May 17, 1888; Sibley's New Mexico Campaign, p.166; Thompson, Westward the Texans, p.97. Howell's diary notes that Coopwood brought the first news the Texans had received from the outside world in six weeks. Julius Giesecke noted that Coopwood brought him a letter dated December 24th.

81. [Fulcrod], "Reminiscences of the Old Brigade," May 17, 1888. Fulcrod's account of this incident is questionable as Sibley may still have been in Albuquerque on the afternoon of the 1st, when he penned a letter to Governor Francis R. Lubbock of Texas, describing the loss of Scurry's train and petitioning for reinforcement. Most certainly he was still in Albuquerque on the 31st when he wrote to the Adjutant General in Richmond, reported the action, and pleaded; "I must have re-enforcements ... Send me re-enforcements."

82. [Davidson], "Reminiscences of the Old Brigade," March 1, 1888. Whether or not such a plan existed is a matter of debate. Evidence suggests that Sibley simply muddled along.

83. [Fulcrod], "Reminiscences of the Old Brigade," May 17, 1888.

84. OR,I,IX,p.509, H.H. Sibley to General S. Cooper.

85. Ickis, "Diary," March 28, 1862. Misinformed, Ickis wrote Sibley instead of Scurry.

86. OR,I,IX,p.660, Henry Connelly, the Governor of New Mexico.

87. Bloom, "Confederate Reminiscences," p.323, H.C. Wright.

88. Ibid.

89. Williams, Three Years and a Half in the Army, p.20.

90. [Davidson], "Reminiscences of the Old Brigade," March 15, 1888.

91. Ibid; See also Hall, Sibley's New Mexico Campaign, p.165.

92. Bloom, "Confederate Reminiscences," p.320, Harvey Holcomb.

93. Hall, Sibley's New Mexico Campaign, p.164.

94. Bloom, "Confederate Reminiscences," p.320, Harvey Holcomb.

95. [Davidson], "Reminiscences of the Old Brigade," March 15, 1888, Davidson.

96. Hall, The Confederate Army of New Mexico, p.222. Major Jordan remained at the hospital and was captured on April 20. He was paroled at Fort Union ten days later and sent to Camp Douglas. He was eventually exchanged at Vicksburg on Sept. 22, 1862.

97. As a young man, the author saw a one page prescription that was written for Captain Adair by Major Jordan. Unfortunately, after surviving for more than a century, this fragile document has since been lost.

98. Frazier, Blood and Treasure, p.232, as quoted.

CHAPTER 11 - ALBUQUERQUE AND PERALTA

1. Alberts, Rebels on the Rio Grande, p.88.
2. Ibid, p.91.
3. Haas, "The Diary of Julius Giesecke," April 1, 1862.
4. Robert Thomas Williams diary, April 4, 1862. Twenty-three-year-old Williams remained in Santa Fe to nurse a sick friend. He was taken prisoner April 20 and paroled April 30. Afterwards he was sent to Camp Douglas and later exchanged at Vicksburg September 22, 1862.
5. OR,I,IX,pp.509-510, H.H. Sibley to General S. Cooper; Hall, Sibley's New Mexico Campaign, p.167; Thompson, Henry Hopkins Sibley, p.293.
6. OR,I,IX,pp.509-510, H.H. Sibley to General S. Cooper; Hall, Sibley's New Mexico Campaign, p.167; Thompson, Henry Hopkins Sibley, p.293; Frazier, Blood and Treasure, p.236. Reinforcements were never sent to the Army of New Mexico, but no less a strategic thinker than Robert E. Lee felt they should have been. In a message on May 31, 1862 to the commander of the Department of Texas Lee wrote, "Communications have been received by the President [Jefferson Davis] reporting the very destitute and critical condition of General Sibley's command now operating in New Mexico. ... The very remote and isolated position of General Sibley's command makes it necessary that you should promptly afford him all the aid you can in men and supplies." OR,I,IX,p.716, R.E. Lee to Brigadier General Herbert, Commanding Department of Texas.
7. OR,I,IX,p.510, H.H. Sibley to General S. Cooper.
8. OR,I,IX,pp.549-550, Report of Col. Edward R.S. Canby.
9. Gracy, "New Mexico Campaign Letters of Frank Starr," p.179.
10. OR,I,IX,p.658, ED. R.S. Canby to Adjutant-General of the Army.
11. Ibid, p.658.
12. Hall, Sibley's New Mexico Campaign, p.171.
13. Stanley, Fort Union, p.176; Hall, Sibley's New Mexico Campaign, p.171.
14. Frazier, Blood and Treasure, p.229, as quoted from Hunter Diary. Left behind enemy lines, the hospital at

Socorro eventually ran short of food and was forced to petition Colonel Carson at Fort Craig for help. Carson required a negotiated surrender in return for supplies and the starving Texans had no choice but to agree. One-hundred-and-sixteen Texans at Socorro then took an oath that they would avoid any connection with their army and not do anything against the U.S. as long as they remained at the hospital. Rather than submit to this indignity thirty-three men fled northward hoping to find Sibley. See Hall, Sibley's New Mexico Campaign, p.171.

15. [Davidson], "Reminiscences of the Old Brigade," March 29, 1888.

16. Ibid. See also Thompson, Westward the Texans, p.99; Robert Thomas Williams diary, April 7-9, 1862.

17. [Davidson], "Reminiscences of the Old Brigade," March 29, 1888.

18. OR,I,IX,p.511, H.H. Sibley to General S. Cooper, Adjutant and Inspector General, Richmond, Va. See also [Davidson], "Reminiscences of the Old Brigade," March 29, 1888; Hall, The Confederate Army of New Mexico, pp.114-119, 269-272; OR,I,IX,p.662, Henry Connelly to W.H. Seward.

19. Robert Thomas Williams diary, April 9, 1862; Aldrich, History of Houston County, p.121.

20. Hollister, Boldly They Rode, p.82.

21. Robert Thomas Williams diary, April 10, 1862.

22. OR,I,IX,p.550, E.R.S. Canby to Adjutant General of the Army. Canby's transportation was nearly as bad as Sibley's. Draft animals were in such poor shape and such short supply that Captain James Graydon's independent company of cavalry were forced to range ahead of the Union column, confiscating replacement animals as they went. On April 7, Graydon and Captain Robert Morris, 3rd U.S. Cavalry, brought in ninty-four mules they took from around Armijo, only five miles from Albuquerque.

23. Ibid.

24. [Davidson], "Reminiscences of the Old Brigade," March 29, 1888.

25. Alberts, Rebels on the Rio Grande, p.99.

26. Mumey, Bloody Trails, p.93.

27. [Davidson], "Reminiscences of the Old Brigade," March 29, 1888, Davidson.

28. Ibid. Alfred Peticolas notes in his journal that, "The boys told us that the fighting was done almost entirely with Artillery." Alberts, Rebels on the Rio Grande, p.99; See also Noel, Campaign from Santa Fe, p.37.

29. Hall, Sibley's New Mexico Campaign, p.173; See also Thompson, Henry Hopkins Sibley, p.294.

30. Mumey, Bloody Trails, p.95.

31. [Davidson], "Reminiscences of the Old Brigade," March 29, 1888. The chronology presented here is Davidson's. He clearly writes that the most significant action before Albuquerque occurred on the 2nd day of the battle. Canby on the other hand seems to imply in his after-action report that it all occurred on the 1st day.

33. Ibid. Davidson's second-hand account of Major Duncan's assault, although plausible, probably embellishes the facts. In his diary dated April 11, 1862, Alfred Peticolas, who like Davidson was not present, wrote that the "Abs never came nearer than 800 yards." Colonel Canby noted in his field report that, Duncan was seriously wounded, but did not describe the action. M.H. Hall, in his book "Sibley's New Mexico Campaign," states on page 173 that Duncan seriously injured himself in a fall from his horse, while attempting to dodge a spent cannon ball. Hall does not cite any source. When Davidson asserts that the Federals collected dead and wounded, he directly conflicts with Canby who states clearly that besides Major Duncan, "No other casualties were sustained." See Alberts, Rebels on the Rio Grande, p.99 and OR,I,IX,p.550, E.R.S. Canby to Adjutant General of the Army.

34. Hall, Sibley's New Mexico Campaign, p.173.

35. Mumey, Bloody Trails, p.95. Given the strength of his own command, Canby's demonstrations in front of Albuquerque amounted to little more than posturing and maneuvering. It is doubtful that he ever seriously intended to threaten the town. On the other hand, Alonzo Ickis reported that on the afternoon of the 9th Canby was planning to storm the town around midnight and that Captain Dodd and Captain Plympton had volunteered to lead the attack. Canby is purported to have spoken to his troops, saying that he expected them to do their duty and drawing their "attention to the invincible bayonet in making night attacks." Ickis seems to indicate that this plan was

cut short by an express from Colonel Paul that arrived about 8 P.M.

36. Hall, Sibley's New Mexico Campaign, pp.173-174; Alberts, Rebels on the Rio Grande, p.99; Thompson, Henry Hopkins Sibley, p.294.
37. [Davidson], "Reminiscences of the Old Brigade," March 29, 1888, Davidson.
38. Noel, Campaign from Santa Fe, p.37.
39. Ibid. See also Haas, "The Diary of Julius Giesecke," April 9, 1862.
40. Alberts, Rebels on the Rio Grande, .p97.
41. [Davidson], "Reminiscences of the Old Brigade," March 29, 1888.
42. Thompson, Henry Hopkins Sibley, p.294. See also Hall, Sibley's New Mexico Campaign, p.174; Frazier, Blood and Treasure, p.238.
43. Greely, The American conflict, p.24.
44. Gracy, "New Mexico Campaign Letters of Frank Starr," p.179.
45. Ibid. Sibley was not the only one with transportation problems. On April 11, Alonzo Ickis, who was with Canby's column, wrote that so many mules were giving out that they were forced to burn 2000 blankets and all the clothes except what the men were wearing.
46. OR,I,IX,p.510, H.H. Sibley to General S. Cooper, Adjutant and Inspector General, Richmond, Va.
47. Ibid. See also Hall, The Confederate Army of New Mexico, p.35; Alberts, Rebels on the Rio Grande, p.101.
48. Bloom, "Confederate Reminiscences," p.324. Howland's cavalry entered Santa Fe on April 10th, two days after the Texans pulled out.
49. Ibid.
50. Muster Roll Company H, 7th TMV. The muster roll for Isaac Adair's Company H lists April 20, 1862 as the date of capture for all those left at the Santa Fe Hospital.
51. Bloom, "Confederate Reminiscences," p.324.
52. [Fulcrod], "Reminiscences of the Old Brigade," May 17, 1888. Fulcrod wrote that the eight barrels were buried in Albuquerque, prior to the move to Santa Fe. He also indicates that an unspecified number of cannon were buried at the territorial capital. Twenty years later in 1889, the Albuquerque tubes were located by Major Teel and dug

up. Half of the cannons went to the state of Colorado and the other half to New Mexico. Today one of them can be seen on display in the museum of the Colorado Historical Society. Two are in the collection of the Albuquerque museum and another two are displayed in Albuquerque's Old Town Plaza.

53. [Davidson], "Reminiscences of the Old Brigade," March 29, 1888. M.H. Hall says that Davidson was taken prisoner at Glorieta and "paroled at Fort Union April 5, 1862." If his muster roll states this, then it is at odds with Davidson's personal narrative. See Hall, The Confederate Army of New Mexico, p.146.

54. Ibid.

55. Ibid.

56. Ibid. Three days later on April 15, James A. Darby, again escorting wagons would be captured by the Federals. The thirty-two-year-old lieutenant was paroled on April 16, and sent to Camp Douglas. He was eventually exchanged at Vicksburg on September 22, 1862. See Hall, The Confederate Army of New Mexico, p.200.

57. Alberts, Rebels on the Rio Grande, p.101; [Davidson], "Reminiscences of the Old Brigade," March 29, 1888.

58. Thompson, Westward the Texans, p.99.

59. Hall, The Confederate Army of New Mexico, p.271.

60. [Davidson], "Reminiscences of the Old Brigade," March 29, 1888; Hall, Sibley's New Mexico Campaign, p.168.

61. OR,I,IX,p.511, H.H. Sibley to General S. Cooper, Adjutant and Inspector General, Richmond, Va. Long after the New Mexico campaign was over, General Sibley remained grateful to the territory's Confederate sympathizers. In June 1863, he wrote to CSA president Davis advocating claims of Rafael and Manuel Armijo, Julian Senario, and José Maria Chaves, and praising their unstinting support. See Crist, The Papers of Jefferson Davis, Volume 9, p.205.

62. OR,I,IX,p.659, Henry Connelly to W.H. Seward. The messenger was Canby's adjutant-general, Captain William Nicodemus.

63. Hollister, Boldly They Rode, p.74.

64. Ibid, p.86. Immediate command of the Colorado Volunteers was passed to Lieutenant Colonel Tappan, who declined to take command in favor of Chivington.

65. Mumey, Bloody Trails, p.96; Hollister, Boldly They Rode, p.84. Canby's tired troops marched all day in the rain to reach this position and were then forced to camp in the snow.

66. Hollister, Boldly They Rode, p.89.

67. Ibid.

68. OR,I.IX,pp.550-551, Report of Col. Edward R.S. Canby, Nineteenth U.S. Infantry, commanding Department of New Mexico. Canby's route followed the old road that crossed what is today Kirkland Air Force Base and the Isleta Reservation.

69. Noel, Campaign from Santa Fe, p.39.

70. Alberts, Rebels on the Rio Grande, p.102.

71. Miller, "Hispanos in the Civil War," p.115.

72. Alberts, Rebels on the Rio Grande, p.103.

73. [Davidson], "Reminiscences of the Old Brigade," April 5, 1888. See also Noel, Campaign from Santa Fe, p.39.

74. Ibid.

75. Noel, Campaign from Santa Fe, p.39; [Davidson], "Reminiscences of the Old Brigade," March 29, 1888.

76. Noel, Campaign from Santa Fe, p.39; See also [Davidson], "Reminiscences of the Old Brigade," March 29, 1888.

77. OR,I,IX,p.665, Henry Connelly to W.H. Seward.

78. Hollister, Boldly They Rode, p.91.

79. Bell, "The New Mexico Campaign," p.68. A vidette or vedette is a mounted sentinel posted in advance of outposts of an army.

80. Anderson, "Canby's Campaign in New Mexico," p.386.

81. Hollister, Boldly They Rode, pp.91-92.

82. OR,I,IX,p.665, Henry Connelly to W.H. Seward.

83. Bell, "The New Mexico Campaign," p.68.

84. Ibid.

85. Hollister, Boldly They Rode, p.92.

86. Bell, "The New Mexico Campaign," p.68.

87. Hollister, Boldly They Rode, p.93.

88. Benton Bell Seat Memoirs, p.100.

89. [Davidson], "Reminiscences of the Old Brigade," March 29, 1888.
90. Hollister, Boldly They Rode, p.92.
91. Mallory, "Ferris - Civil War Memoir," p.11.
92. Hollister, Boldly They Rode, p.93.
93. OR,I,IX,p.551, Report of Col. Edward R.S. Canby, Nineteenth U.S. Infantry, commanding Department of New Mexico.
94. Hollister, Boldly They Rode, p.93.
95. Ibid; Mallory, "Ferris - Civil War Memoir," p.12. On the way back to their lines Company F was met by Captain Claflin and his battery moving to another part of the field. The artillery officer took charge of the captured howitzer and according to Hollister "was soon testing its functions against its late owners."
96. Hall, The Confederate Army of New Mexico, pp.138, 160, 167; [Davidson], "Reminiscences of the Old Brigade," March 29, 1888 and April 5, 1888.
97. [Davidson], "Reminiscences of the Old Brigade," March 29, 1888. Davidson's estimate of Union strength was high. Canby's force at Peralta was closer to 2,400.
98. Hall, Sibley's New Mexico Campaign, pp.179, 182.
99. Hollister, Boldly They Rode, p.93.
100. Ibid.
101. [Davidson], "Reminiscences of the Old Brigade," March 29, 1888. See also Ickis, "Diary," April 15, 1862.
102. [Davidson], "Reminiscences of the Old Brigade," March 29, 1888.
103. Whitford, Battle of Glorieta Pass, p.132.
104. [Davidson], "Reminiscences of the Old Brigade," March 29, 1888.
105. [Davidson], "Reminiscences of the Old Brigade," April 5, 1888.
106. Ibid, April 5, 1888. See also Hollister, Boldly They Rode, p.94.
107. [Davidson], "Reminiscences of the Old Brigade," April 5, 1888.
108. Ibid.
109. [Davidson], "Reminiscences of the Old Brigade," March 29, 1888; Noel, Campaign from Santa Fe, p.40; See also Haas, "The Diary of Julius Giesecke," April 15, 1862; OR,I,IX,p.510, H.H. Sibley to General S. Cooper, Adjutant

and Inspector General, Richmond, Va.; Hall, Sibley's New Mexico Campaign, p.184n6; Alberts, Rebels on the Rio Grande, p.103. Theo. Noel places the time of the crossing at 9 A.M., but was not actually present. According to Ovando Hollister, a captured assistant surgeon, named Tolles, claimed that 250 Texans refused to follow Scurry into action, openly threatening his life if he persisted in forcing them. Although this story also appeared in the Santa Fe Gazette of April 26, 1862, no mention of this incident is made in any Confederate accounts, official or private. See Hollister, Boldly They Rode, p.98.

110. Alberts, Rebels on the Rio Grande, p.103. Captain James Walker of Company D from Pyron's battalion was given overall command of the force left at Los Lunas. He was assisted by Lieutenant Ludwig von Roeder, Company C of the 4th, who was made commander of the trains, and Lieutenant Ferdinand A. Fenner, acting adjutant.

111. OR,I,IX,p.510, H.H. Sibley to General S. Cooper, Adjutant and Inspector General, Richmond, Va. Captain Willis L. Robards was one of Sibley's Volunteer Aide-de-Camps and Henry E. Loebnitz was Assistant Quartermaster of the 4th Regiment.

112. Ibid. To have been cut off in the manner described, Sibley must have made his crossing at a point farther north than where Scurry crossed. See also Thompson, Henry Hopkins Sibley, p.296.

113. Gracy, "New Mexico Campaign Letters of Frank Starr," pp.179-180.

114. [Davidson], "Reminiscences of the Old Brigade," April 12, 1888. See also Bell, "The New Mexico Campaign," p.69.

115. Noel, Campaign from Santa Fe, p.39. Noel was not present at Peralta. While his "first shots" report correctly expresses the pride of the Texans in their artillery and gunners it is inaccurate. Physical evidence collected by Dr. Don Alberts reveals that some of the captured Valverde cannon were used at Glorieta Pass.

116. [Davidson], "Reminiscences of the Old Brigade," April 12, 1888. Davidson's figure of 18 Federal cannon may be an exaggeration, but it is probably not too far off. J.M. Bell, one of Canby's artillerymen, mentions two three-gun batteries. Add to these the two four-gun batteries from Fort

Union, under Captain John F. Ritter and Lieutenant Ira W. Claflin, and the Texans at Peralta were outgunned at a minimum 3 to one. The assertion that the Texans had only 4 operational cannon is supported in several accounts. See Bell, "The New Mexico Campaign," p.68.

117. Mumey, Bloody Trails, p.97.

118. [Davidson], "Reminiscences of the Old Brigade," April 15, 1888.

119. Ibid.

120. Mumey, Bloody Trails, p.35.

121. Hollister, Boldly They Rode, p.94. This was the two-column disposition made earlier in the day.

122. [Davidson], "Reminiscences of the Old Brigade," April 15, 1888. Canby's words, as quoted in the Overton Sharpshooter and repeated here, are almost certainly a fabrication. Nonetheless, they correctly summerize the position he adopted in the following days.

123. Noel, Campaign from Santa Fe, p.40.

124. Hollister, Boldly They Rode, p.95. Across the river in Los Lunas, Alfred Peticolas reported the same weather conditions. His diary for the 16th reads; "The wind was blowing clouds of dust through the town and obscuring the view in every direction." Alberts, Rebels on the Rio Grande, p.105.

125. Haas, "The Diary of Julius Giesecke," April 15, 1862. The 4th, 5th, and 7th regiments were commonly refered to as the 1st, 2nd, and 3rd by the men of the brigade. See Noel, Campaign from Santa Fe, p.xiii.

126. Hollister, Boldly They Rode, p.95.

127. Mumey, Bloody Trails, p.98.

128. OR,I,IX,pp.550-551, Report of Col. Edward R.S. Canby, Nineteenth U.S. Infantry, commanding Department of New Mexico.

129. Thompson, Westward the Texans, p.100.

130. [Davidson], "Reminiscences of the Old Brigade," April 12, 1888. Alfred Peticolas states that only one Texan was wounded and "he was accidentally shot by one of our own men." In 1881, J.M. Bell claimed that when the Federals entered the town the found dead men lying as they fell. This was probably a fabrication, but Texan losses may have been higher than reported. Colorado Volunteer Charles Gardiner wrote to his mother; "We found several

graves that looked as if they might contain six or [illegible]...We found sixteen wounded in the town [...]." Gardiner placed Union casualties at "eight killed, wounded." See Alberts, Rebels on the Rio Grande, p.106; ; Bell, "The New Mexico Campaign," p.70; Gaither, "Pet Lambs at Glorieta Pass," p.37.

    131. OR,I,IX,pp.550-551, Report of Col. Edward R.S. Canby, Nineteenth U.S. Infantry, commanding Department of New Mexico.

    132. Hollister, Boldly They Rode, p.95. The generally accepted figure for Union losses is four killed and three wounded. See also Whitford, Battle of Glorieta Pass, p.150.

    133. Benton Bell Seat Memoirs, p.101.

    134. OR,I,IX,p.510, H.H. Sibley to General S. Cooper, Adjutant and Inspector General, Richmond, Va.

    135. [Davidson], "Reminiscences of the Old Brigade," April 12, 1888.

    136. Benton Bell Seat Memoirs, p.101.

    137. [Davidson], "Reminiscences of the Old Brigade," April 12, 1888.

    138. Ibid, April 26, 1888.

    139. Noel, Campaign from Santa Fe, p.40.

    140. Thompson, Westward the Texans, p.100. The reported time of the withdrawal varies between accounts, but fell roughly between 3 and 5 A.M.

    141. [Davidson], "Reminiscences of the Old Brigade," April 12, 1888. Governor Henry Connelly writing to William Seward four days after the Texan crossing, stated that their "whole train, consisting of sixty wagons, was left in the river and on the banks." Connelly is undoubtedly including wagons abandoned on the 18th, nevertheless, his assertion would seem to indicate that at least part of the Confederate train may have failed to make the crossing from Peralta. See OR,I,IX,p.665, Henry Connelly to William Seward.

    142. Hollister, Boldly They Rode, p.95.

CHAPTER 12 - THE LONG WALK HOME

1. [Davidson], "Reminiscences of the Old Brigade," April 12, 1888; Alberts, Rebels on the Rio Grande, p.107.
2. [Davidson], "Reminiscences of the Old Brigade," April 12, 1888; Alberts, Rebels on the Rio Grande, p.107; Haas, "The Diary of Julius Giesecke," April 16, 1862.
3. Alberts, Rebels on the Rio Grande, p.107.
4. [Davidson], "Reminiscences of the Old Brigade," April 12, 1888.
5. OR,I,IX,p.664, General Orders. Canby placed Morris in direct command of all the Union cavalry with the exception of Graydon's company.
6. Noel, Campaign from Santa Fe, p.40.
7. Hollister, Boldly They Rode, p.97.
8. Bell, "The New Mexico Campaign," p.70.
9. OR,I,IX,p.665, Henry Connelly to W.H. Seward. See also OR,I,IX,p.550, Report of Col. Edward R.S. Canby, Nineteenth U.S. Infantry, commanding Department of New Mexico.
10. Hollister, Boldly They Rode, p.97.
11. OR,I,IX,p.550, Report of Col. Edward R.S. Canby, Nineteenth U.S. Infantry, commanding Department of New Mexico; See also OR,I,IX,p.664, General Orders; OR,I,IX,p.552-553, General Orders.
12. Hollister, Boldly They Rode, p.102; OR,I,IX,p551, Report of Col. Edward R.S. Canby, Nineteenth U.S. Infantry, commanding Department of New Mexico.
13. Hollister, Boldly They Rode, p.98.
14. Ibid.
15. OR,I,IX,pp.550-551, Report of Col. Edward R.S. Canby, Nineteenth U.S. Infantry, commanding Department of New Mexico.
16. Mumey, Bloody Trails, pp.100-101.
17. Noel, Campaign from Santa Fe, pp.40-41.
18. OR,I,IX,pp.550-551, Report of Col. Edward R.S. Canby, Nineteenth U.S. Infantry, commanding Department of New Mexico.
19. Noel, Campaign from Santa Fe, p.41.
20. [Davidson], "Reminiscences of the Old Brigade," April 12, 1888.

21. Thompson, Westward the Texans, p.100.

22. [Davidson], "Reminiscences of the Old Brigade," April 12, 1888. The only Joseph Bowers listed on the muster rolls of the Sibley brigade was a member of Thomas Jefferson Helm's Arizona Guards. This company did not take part in the campaign proper, but remained with Colonel Steele's command. If Bill Davidson was not mistaken about Bowers' identity, then the twenty-one-year-old private probably entered New Mexico as part of Captain Coopwood's escort.

23. Noel, Campaign from Santa Fe, p.41.

24. Alberts, Rebels on the Rio Grande, p.107.

25. Ibid, p.108.

26. [Davidson], "Reminiscences of the Old Brigade," April 12, 1888.

27. Haas, "The Diary of Julius Giesecke," April 17, 1862; Alberts, Rebels on the Rio Grande, p.108; Noel, Campaign from Santa Fe, pp.41; OR,I,IX,p.510, H.H. Sibley to General S. Cooper, Adjutant and Inspector General, Richmond, Va.; [Davidson], "Reminiscences of the Old Brigade," April 12, 1888.

28. Crouch, Jornada del Muerto, p.123.

29. OR,I,IX,p.510, H.H. Sibley to General S. Cooper, Adjutant and Inspector General, Richmond, Va.

30. [Davidson], "Reminiscences of the Old Brigade," April 12, 1888.

31. Ibid.

32. Alberts, Rebels on the Rio Grande, p.142.

33. Ibid.

34. OR,I,IX,p.510, H.H. Sibley to General S. Cooper, Adjutant and Inspector General, Richmond, Va. Writing twenty years after the events, William Davidson claimed that Sibley's Volunteer Aide-de-Camp, Willis L. Robards, suggested to the General that he ought not to hesitate to accept the mountain route because "if it failed it would go down in history as Coopwood's failure; while on the other hand, if it was successful Gen. Sibley would receive the credit of having brought his brigade out of the most perilous position in which an army was ever placed." [Davidson], "Reminiscences of the Old Brigade," April 12, 1888. See also Thompson, Henry Hopkins Sibley, p.309.

35. Noel, Campaign from Santa Fe, p.41. General Sibley reported that the men were ordered to prepare seven-days rations. This is corroborated by a number of other primary sources. In his diary, however, Alfred Peticolas states ten-days rations were packed. This seems to indicate that there was some discretion depending on the resources of each mess.

36. [Davidson], "Reminiscences of the Old Brigade," April 12, 1888.

37. Mumey, Bloody Trails, p.98. Colonel Canby stated in a field report that, the Confederates abandoned "38 wagons and the supplies they contained." How much of this equipment was burnt is uncertain. OR,I,IX,pp.550-551, Report of Col. Edward R.S. Canby, Nineteenth U.S. Infantry, commanding Department of New Mexico. See also Noel, Campaign from Santa Fe, pp.41-42.

38. Alberts, Rebels on the Rio Grande, p.109. Shiflett from Company H was taken prisoner the next day, but instead of a northern prison he was paroled at Fort Craig ten days later on April 27, 1862. Muster Roll Company H, 7th TMV.

39. [Davidson], "Reminiscences of the Old Brigade," April 26, 1888, Whitley.

40. Alberts, Rebels on the Rio Grande, p.109.

41. [Davidson], "Reminiscences of the Old Brigade," May 3, 1888.

42. Haas, "The Diary of Julius Giesecke," April 18, 1862.

43. Alberts, Rebels on the Rio Grande, p.110; Noel, Campaign from Santa Fe, p.42; [Davidson], "Reminiscences of the Old Brigade," April 26, 1888.

44. Noel, Campaign from Santa Fe, p.42.

45. Alberts, Rebels on the Rio Grande, p.110. Almost every first-hand account of the camp on Salado Creek complains about the undrinkable coffee. See also Haas, "The Diary of Julius Giesecke," April 18, 1862.

46. [Davidson], "Reminiscences of the Old Brigade," April 26, 1888.

47. Ibid, April 26 and May 3, 1888, Whitley and Peticolas.

48. Hollister, Boldly They Rode, p.100. See also Mumey, Bloody Trails, p.98.

graves that looked as if they might contain six or [illegible]...We found sixteen wounded in the town [...]." Gardiner placed Union casualties at "eight killed, wounded." See Alberts, Rebels on the Rio Grande, p.106; ; Bell, "The New Mexico Campaign," p.70; Gaither, "Pet Lambs at Glorieta Pass," p.37.

131. OR,I,IX,pp.550-551, Report of Col. Edward R.S. Canby, Nineteenth U.S. Infantry, commanding Department of New Mexico.

132. Hollister, Boldly They Rode, p.95. The generally accepted figure for Union losses is four killed and three wounded. See also Whitford, Battle of Glorieta Pass, p.150.

133. Benton Bell Seat Memoirs, p.101.

134. OR,I,IX,p.510, H.H. Sibley to General S. Cooper, Adjutant and Inspector General, Richmond, Va.

135. [Davidson], "Reminiscences of the Old Brigade," April 12, 1888.

136. Benton Bell Seat Memoirs, p.101.

137. [Davidson], "Reminiscences of the Old Brigade," April 12, 1888.

138. Ibid, April 26, 1888.

139. Noel, Campaign from Santa Fe, p.40.

140. Thompson, Westward the Texans, p.100. The reported time of the withdrawal varies between accounts, but fell roughly between 3 and 5 A.M.

141. [Davidson], "Reminiscences of the Old Brigade," April 12, 1888. Governor Henry Connelly writing to William Seward four days after the Texan crossing, stated that their "whole train, consisting of sixty wagons, was left in the river and on the banks." Connelly is undoubtedly including wagons abandoned on the 18th, nevertheless, his assertion would seem to indicate that at least part of the Confederate train may have failed to make the crossing from Peralta. See OR,I,IX,p.665, Henry Connelly to William Seward.

142. Hollister, Boldly They Rode, p.95.

CHAPTER 12 - THE LONG WALK HOME

1. [Davidson], "Reminiscences of the Old Brigade," April 12, 1888; Alberts, Rebels on the Rio Grande, p.107.
2. [Davidson], "Reminiscences of the Old Brigade," April 12, 1888; Alberts, Rebels on the Rio Grande, p.107; Haas, "The Diary of Julius Giesecke," April 16, 1862.
3. Alberts, Rebels on the Rio Grande, p.107.
4. [Davidson], "Reminiscences of the Old Brigade," April 12, 1888.
5. OR,I,IX,p.664, General Orders. Canby placed Morris in direct command of all the Union cavalry with the exception of Graydon's company.
6. Noel, Campaign from Santa Fe, p.40.
7. Hollister, Boldly They Rode, p.97.
8. Bell, "The New Mexico Campaign," p.70.
9. OR,I,IX,p.665, Henry Connelly to W.H. Seward. See also OR,I,IX,p.550, Report of Col. Edward R.S. Canby, Nineteenth U.S. Infantry, commanding Department of New Mexico.
10. Hollister, Boldly They Rode, p.97.
11. OR,I,IX,p.550, Report of Col. Edward R.S. Canby, Nineteenth U.S. Infantry, commanding Department of New Mexico; See also OR,I,IX,p.664, General Orders; OR,I,IX,p.552-553, General Orders.
12. Hollister, Boldly They Rode, p.102; OR,I,IX,p551, Report of Col. Edward R.S. Canby, Nineteenth U.S. Infantry, commanding Department of New Mexico.
13. Hollister, Boldly They Rode, p.98.
14. Ibid.
15. OR,I,IX,pp.550-551, Report of Col. Edward R.S. Canby, Nineteenth U.S. Infantry, commanding Department of New Mexico.
16. Mumey, Bloody Trails, pp.100-101.
17. Noel, Campaign from Santa Fe, pp.40-41.
18. OR,I,IX,pp.550-551, Report of Col. Edward R.S. Canby, Nineteenth U.S. Infantry, commanding Department of New Mexico.
19. Noel, Campaign from Santa Fe, p.41.
20. [Davidson], "Reminiscences of the Old Brigade," April 12, 1888.

21. Thompson, Westward the Texans, p.100.
22. [Davidson], "Reminiscences of the Old Brigade," April 12, 1888. The only Joseph Bowers listed on the muster rolls of the Sibley brigade was a member of Thomas Jefferson Helm's Arizona Guards. This company did not take part in the campaign proper, but remained with Colonel Steele's command. If Bill Davidson was not mistaken about Bowers' identity, then the twenty-one-year-old private probably entered New Mexico as part of Captain Coopwood's escort.
23. Noel, Campaign from Santa Fe, p.41.
24. Alberts, Rebels on the Rio Grande, p.107.
25. Ibid, p.108.
26. [Davidson], "Reminiscences of the Old Brigade," April 12, 1888.
27. Haas, "The Diary of Julius Giesecke," April 17, 1862; Alberts, Rebels on the Rio Grande, p.108; Noel, Campaign from Santa Fe, pp.41; OR,I,IX,p.510, H.H. Sibley to General S. Cooper, Adjutant and Inspector General, Richmond, Va.; [Davidson], "Reminiscences of the Old Brigade," April 12, 1888.
28. Crouch, Jornada del Muerto, p.123.
29. OR,I,IX,p.510, H.H. Sibley to General S. Cooper, Adjutant and Inspector General, Richmond, Va.
30. [Davidson], "Reminiscences of the Old Brigade," April 12, 1888.
31. Ibid.
32. Alberts, Rebels on the Rio Grande, p.142.
33. Ibid.
34. OR,I,IX,p.510, H.H. Sibley to General S. Cooper, Adjutant and Inspector General, Richmond, Va. Writing twenty years after the events, William Davidson claimed that Sibley's Volunteer Aide-de-Camp, Willis L. Robards, suggested to the General that he ought not to hesitate to accept the mountain route because "if it failed it would go down in history as Coopwood's failure; while on the other hand, if it was successful Gen. Sibley would receive the credit of having brought his brigade out of the most perilous position in which an army was ever placed." [Davidson], "Reminiscences of the Old Brigade," April 12, 1888. See also Thompson, Henry Hopkins Sibley, p.309.

35. Noel, Campaign from Santa Fe, p.41. General Sibley reported that the men were ordered to prepare seven-days rations. This is corroborated by a number of other primary sources. In his diary, however, Alfred Peticolas states ten-days rations were packed. This seems to indicate that there was some discretion depending on the resources of each mess.

36. [Davidson], "Reminiscences of the Old Brigade," April 12, 1888.

37. Mumey, Bloody Trails, p.98. Colonel Canby stated in a field report that, the Confederates abandoned "38 wagons and the supplies they contained." How much of this equipment was burnt is uncertain. OR,I,IX,pp.550-551, Report of Col. Edward R.S. Canby, Nineteenth U.S. Infantry, commanding Department of New Mexico. See also Noel, Campaign from Santa Fe, pp.41-42.

38. Alberts, Rebels on the Rio Grande, p.109. Shiflett from Company H was taken prisoner the next day, but instead of a northern prison he was paroled at Fort Craig ten days later on April 27, 1862. Muster Roll Company H, 7th TMV.

39. [Davidson], "Reminiscences of the Old Brigade," April 26, 1888, Whitley.

40. Alberts, Rebels on the Rio Grande, p.109.

41. [Davidson], "Reminiscences of the Old Brigade," May 3, 1888.

42. Haas, "The Diary of Julius Giesecke," April 18, 1862.

43. Alberts, Rebels on the Rio Grande, p.110; Noel, Campaign from Santa Fe, p.42; [Davidson], "Reminiscences of the Old Brigade," April 26, 1888.

44. Noel, Campaign from Santa Fe, p.42.

45. Alberts, Rebels on the Rio Grande, p.110. Almost every first-hand account of the camp on Salado Creek complains about the undrinkable coffee. See also Haas, "The Diary of Julius Giesecke," April 18, 1862.

46. [Davidson], "Reminiscences of the Old Brigade," April 26, 1888.

47. Ibid, April 26 and May 3, 1888, Whitley and Peticolas.

48. Hollister, Boldly They Rode, p.100. See also Mumey, Bloody Trails, p.98.

49. OR,I,IX,pp.550-551, Report of Col. Edward R.S. Canby, Nineteenth U.S. Infantry, commanding Department of New Mexico; See also Hollister, Boldly They Rode, p.100.
50. Thompson, Westward the Texans, p.100; OR,I,IX,p.672, Jas. Graydon, Captain, New Mexico Mounted Volunteers to Colonel Paul; Gracy, "New Mexico Campaign Letters of Frank Starr," pp.172, 181. Captain Graydon later located the buried shells in two caches. He suspected that the three howitzers were left behind and told Colonel Paul, "I believe the Mexicans have the large one buried, and by offering a reward we could find out." There is no evidence that Union troops ever found any of the cannon, but in 1950 one of the mountain howitzer tubes was dug up along La Jerncia Creek. Today it is located at Socorro, New Mexico. Cannon at western posts, before the Civil War, were not inventoried by serial number, so an exact accounting of artillery in use during the campaign is impossible. That said, it appears the Texans started the invasion with fifteen guns: eleven mountain howitzers and four six-pounder field pieces. At Valverde they captured: three six-pounders, two twelve-pounders, and another mountain howitzer. Eight of the mountain howitzers were buried in Albuquerque, one was captured at Peralta, and two were buried along the Salado. The remaining gun was probably the Valverde piece. Of the nine field pieces, one six-pounder was buried. This tally leaves the Confederates with nine cannon on their return to the Mesilla Valley, which corresponds to contemporary accounts.
51. [Davidson], "Reminiscences of the Old Brigade," April 26, 1888. The command structure of the Texan brigade was severely tested by the retreat. Sibley was still its nominal leader, but most decisions were being made at the regimental, and sometimes even company level.
52. Ibid, [Peticolas].
53 Ibid, April 26, 1888 and May 3, 1888; Thompson, Westward the Texans, p.100.
54. [Davidson], "Reminiscences of the Old Brigade," April 26, 1888.
55. Gracy, "New Mexico Campaign Letters of Frank Starr," p.182.
56. [Peticolas], "Reminiscences of the Old Brigade," May 3, 1888.

57. Ibid, [Sharp Whitley].
58. [Peticolas], "Reminiscences of the Old Brigade," May 3, 1888.
59. Thompson, Westward the Texans, p.100.
60. [Peticolas], "Reminiscences of the Old Brigade," May 3, 1888; see also April 26, 1888, Sharp Whitley.
61. Haas, "The Diary of Julius Giesecke," April 19, 1862; Alberts, Rebels on the Rio Grande, p.112n.84. Several contemporary accounts refer to the spring as Bear Springs. This probably stems from the fact that the first Texans to arrive scared away a trio of bears. Howell's diary calls it Steele's Spring.
62. Noel, Campaign from Santa Fe, p.43.
63. [Peticolas], "Reminiscences of the Old Brigade," May 3, 1888.
64. OR,I,IX,p.672, Jas. Graydon, Captain, New Mexico Mounted Volunteers to Colonel Paul.
65. [Peticolas], "Reminiscences of the Old Brigade," May 3, 1888.
66. Thompson, Westward the Texans, p.100.
67. Gracy, "New Mexico Campaign Letters of Frank Starr," p.181.
68. OR,I,IX,p.672, Jas. Graydon, Captain, New Mexico Mounted Volunteers to Colonel Paul.
69. [Davidson], "Reminiscences of the Old Brigade," May 3, 1888.
70. Thompson, Westward the Texans, p.101.
71. [Davidson], "Reminiscences of the Old Brigade," May 3, 1888, Peticolas.
72. Ibid, April 26, 1888; See also Haas, "The Diary of Julius Giesecke," April 20, 1862.
73. Thompson, Westward the Texans, p.101.
74. Noel, Campaign from Santa Fe, p.43. Noel also wrote that many of the men underwent the fatigue and suffering of the march while sick with smallpox.
75. Alberts, Rebels on the Rio Grande, p.114; See also Thompson, Westward the Texans, p.101; Haas, "The Diary of Julius Giesecke," April 21, 1862.
76. Alberts, Rebels on the Rio Grande, p.114.
77. Ibid, p.112.
78. Thompson, Westward the Texans, p.101.

79. Alberts, Rebels on the Rio Grande, p.118. Peticolas also wrote that two other men were abandoned on the 26th.

80. Ibid, p.114; see also Haas, "The Diary of Julius Giesecke," April 21, 1862.

81. [Davidson], "Reminiscences of the Old Brigade," April 26, 1888, Whitley; See also Noel, Campaign from Santa Fe, p.44.

82. Gracy, "New Mexico Campaign Letters of Frank Starr," p.182.

83. Alberts, Rebels on the Rio Grande, p.114.

84. [Davidson], "Reminiscences of the Old Brigade," April 26, 1888; see also Haas, "The Diary of Julius Giesecke," April 22, 1862.

85. Alberts, Rebels on the Rio Grande, p.115. Most of the Texans who kept diaries or journals mistook this stream for the Alamosa. See Haas, "The Diary of Julius Giesecke," April 22, 1862.

86. OR,I,IX,p.672, Jas. Graydon, Captain, New Mexico Mounted Volunteers to Colonel Paul.

87. Thompson, Westward the Texans, p.101.

88. Noel, Campaign from Santa Fe, p.42.

89. [Davidson], "Reminiscences of the Old Brigade," May 3, 1888, Peticolas.

90. OR,I,IX,p.511, H.H. Sibley to General S. Cooper, Adjutant and Inspector General, Richmond, Va.

91. Anderson, "Canby's Campaign in New Mexico," p.386.

92. Thompson, Westward the Texans, p.101. On the 23rd of April 1862, the Texans marched between eighteen and twenty miles. See also [Davidson], "Reminiscences of the Old Brigade," April 26, 1888; Haas, "The Diary of Julius Giesecke," April 23, 1862; Alberts, Rebels on the Rio Grande, p.116.

93. [Davidson], "Reminiscences of the Old Brigade," April 26, 1888.

94. Haas, "The Diary of Julius Giesecke," April 24, 1862; [Davidson], "Reminiscences of the Old Brigade," May 3, 1888; Thompson, Westward the Texans, pp.101-102; Noel, Campaign from Santa Fe, p.44; Alberts, Rebels on the Rio Grande, p.116.

95. Noel, Campaign from Santa Fe, p.46.

96. [Davidson], "Reminiscences of the Old Brigade," May 3, 1888, Peticolas.

97. Noel, Campaign from Santa Fe, p.44.

98. [Davidson], "Reminiscences of the Old Brigade," May 3, 1888, Peticolas.

99. Noel, Campaign from Santa Fe, p.46; See also Alberts, Rebels on the Rio Grande, p.117; Collard, Reminiscences, p.6.

100. Collard, Reminiscences, p.6; OR,I,IX,p.672, Jas. Graydon, Captain, New Mexico Mounted Volunteers to Colonel Paul.

101. Noel, Campaign from Santa Fe, p.47. Noel arrived with Colonel Steele and was consequently in better shape than many of the men who had accompanied Sibley. Burrwell Allen never made it back to Texas. The young private was admitted to the hospital in El Paso with "dysenteria" in June, and later died near Dead Man's Hole on the march home.

102. Ibid, p.145.

103. Crouch, Jornada del Muerto, p.123; [Whitley], "Reminiscences of the Old Brigade," April 26, 1888; Alberts, Rebels on the Rio Grande, p.117. Although the Brigade's march through the mountains was remarkable, it only achieved its goal because Colonel Canby was reluctant to shed further blood and was unwilling face the logistical nightmare of providing for 2,000 prisoners. If Canby had aggressively pursued the Texans the march would have proved an incredible tactcal blunder. Sibley's army was shattered by the trek, and it never managed to get more than a day's march away from the enemy. On the other hand, there is little question that the Texans were better served by the march over another engagement.

104. Collard, Reminiscences p.6; See also Noel, Campaign from Santa Fe, p.47.

105. Hollister, Boldly They Rode, p.116. There is no official record of this movement, but it appears in both the journals of Ovando Hollister and Alfred Peticolas, and fits the personalities involved. See Alberts, Rebels on the Rio Grande, p.119.

106. Alberts, Rebels on the Rio Grande, p.121.

107. Haas, "The Diary of Julius Giesecke," April 25, 1862.

108. Noel, Campaign from Santa Fe, p.45.
109. Alberts, Rebels on the Rio Grande, p.117.
110. Hall, The Confederate Army of New Mexico, pp.269-270.
111. Alberts, Rebels on the Rio Grande, p.117.
112. Ibid, p.117.
113. [Davidson], "Reminiscences of the Old Brigade," May 3, 1888; Haas, "The Diary of Julius Giesecke," April 26, 1862.
114. OR,I,IX,p.669, E.R.S. Canby to Adjutant-General of the Army; See also [Davidson], "Reminiscences of the Old Brigade," May 3, 1888.
115. Houston Tri-Weekly Telegraph, Aug. 27, 1862.
116. Haas, "The Diary of Julius Giesecke," April 27, 1862.
117. Thompson, Westward the Texans, p.102; See also Haas, "The Diary of Julius Giesecke," April 26, 1862; Gracy, "New Mexico Campaign Letters of Frank Starr," p.182.
118. Alberts, Rebels on the Rio Grande, p.118.
119. Noel, Campaign from Santa Fe, p.47.
120. Noel.
121. Ibid, p.48.
122. Noel, Campaign from Santa Fe, pp.47-48; Thompson, Westward the Texans, p.102; Haas, "The Diary of Julius Giesecke," April 27, 1862 April 29, 1862; Alberts, Rebels on the Rio Grande, p.122. The Rio Grande had warmed considerably since the crossings at Peralta, so wading was not same the bone chilling nightmare it was before. Some messes made the crossing even easier by building small rafts to ferry their supplies.

CHAPTER 13 - SHATTERED DREAMS

1. Alberts, Rebels on the Rio Grande, p.123; See also Thompson, Westward the Texans, p.103.
2. Thompson, Westward the Texans, p.103; Noel, Campaign from Santa Fe, p.49; San Antonio Weekly Herald, July 5, 1862.
3. OR,I,IX,p.511, H.H. Sibley to General S. Cooper, Adjutant and Inspector General, Richmond, Va. Musters for the returning companies were begun on and dated May 1, 1862, but because of the amount of work involved, they were still being prepared as late as the 17th.
4. Ibid.
5. Hall, "A Confederate officers letter...," p.332.
6. Hall, The Confederate Army of New Mexico, pp.37, 114, 192, 268; Houston Tri-Weekly Telegraph, Aug. 27, 1862; Muster Roll Company H, 7th TMV. Frank Starr estimated the captured small arms at between 800 and 1000 stand.
7. Gracy, "New Mexico Campaign Letters of Frank Starr," p.182.
8. Ibid.
9. Hall, "A Confederate officers letter...," p.332.
10. Gracy, "New Mexico Campaign Letters of Frank Starr," pp.186-187.
11. Norvel, "New Mexico in the Civil War...," p.10.
12. Hall, "A Confederate officers letter...," p.332.
13. Norvel, "New Mexico in the Civil War...," p.10.
14. Hall, "A Confederate officers letter...," p.332.
15. Teel, "Sibley's New Mexico Campaign," p.700. Although the brunt of the men's anger was reserved for General Sibley, Colonel Green was also clearly implicated in some of the complaints. Teel suggested that "Had Colonel John R. Baylor continued to command, the result might have been different."
16. [Davidson], "Reminiscences of the Old Brigade," May 24, 1888.
17. Hollister, Boldly They Rode, p.170, Purported letter between George M. Brown and his wife, dated April 30, 1862.
18. Alberts, Rebels on the Rio Grande, p.128.

19. Haas, "The Diary of Julius Giesecke," May 25, 1862.
20. OR,I,IX,p.678, Enclosure in report of J.M. Chivington to Brig. Gen. E.R.S. Canby.
21. Alberts, Rebels on the Rio Grande, p.132.
22. Hall, "A Confederate officers letter...," p.331.
23. Gracy, "New Mexico Campaign Letters of Frank Starr," p.182.
24. Thompson, Westward the Texans, p.103.
25. Gracy, "New Mexico Campaign Letters of Frank Starr," p.184.
26. San Antonio Weekly Herald, July 5, 1862.
27. Houston Tri-Weekly Telegraph, Aug. 27, 1862.
28. Ibid.
29. Ibid.
30. Ibid.
31. Ibid.
32. Sibley, Henry Hopkins, "Soldiers of the Army of New Mexico," 1862. Franklin, Texas: Confederate Imprints, 1861-1865; reel 10, no. 653.
33. Alberts, Rebels on the Rio Grande, p.134.
34. Reily, James, "General Orders No.36," May 18, 1862. Franklin (El Paso), Texas: Confederate Imprints, 1861-1865; reel 10, no. 652.
35. OR,I,IV,p.170, H.H. Sibley to General S. Cooper.
36. OR,I,IX,p.682, E.R.S. Canby to Adjutant-General of the Army, Washington, D.C. It is unclear whether Hunter received orders to withdraw, or somehow learned of Sibley's failures and made the decision on his own. See also Mesilla Times, January 8, 1862; OR,I,IX,p.678, J.M. Chivington to Brig. Gen. E.R.S. Canby; Finch, Sherod Hunter and The Confederates in Arizona, pp. 112, 153, 169-191.
37. Thompson, Westward the Texans, p.104.
38. Noel, Campaign from Santa Fe, p.50. Company A of Pyron's command was actually the first unit to head home, having departed sometime in April. See also Hall, The Confederate Army of New Mexico, p.38; Hall, Sibley's New Mexico Campaign, p.209.
39. Hall, The Confederate Army of New Mexico, p.38; Haas, "The Diary of Julius Giesecke," June 7, 1862; Thompson, Westward the Texans, pp.104-105; Alberts, Rebels on the Rio Grande, p.143.
40. Noel, Campaign from Santa Fe, pp.50-51.

41. Ibid, p.52; See also Thompson, Westward the Texans, p.105.
42. Noel, Campaign from Santa Fe, p.52.
43. Ibid.
44. Ibid.
45. Ibid.
46. Ibid.
47. Thompson, Westward the Texans, p.105. Because of the scarcity of water, the brigade was traveling in battalions. These groups were spaced days and some cases weeks apart. Conditions met by one were not necessarily the conditions met by all. See also Haas, "The Diary of Julius Giesecke," June 18-20, 1862.
48. Thompson, Westward the Texans, p.107.
49. Noel, Campaign from Santa Fe, p.53. See also Haas, "The Diary of Julius Giesecke," June 20-23, 1862.
50. San Antonio Weekly Herald, July 5, 1862, Mollie. Major Hampton and his battalion were camped at the Muerto and Colonel Hardeman and his group were in Limpia Canyon.
51. Thompson, Westward the Texans, p.108. See also Haas, "The Diary of Julius Giesecke," June 24, 1862 and July 3, 1862.
52. James Reily, "To the Patriots...," June, 27, 1862.
53. Noel, Campaign from Santa Fe, p.53.
54. Thompson, Westward the Texans, p.108.
55. Noel, Campaign from Santa Fe, p.54; Thompson, Westward the Texans, p.109; Haas, "The Diary of Julius Giesecke," July 15-20, 1862; Hall, Sibley's New Mexico Campaign, pp.213-214. Colonel Green's regiment arrived the 1st week of August and the veteran battalion of the 7th was reported to be about a week behind.
56. Williams, With the Border Ruffians, p.234.
57. Collard, Reminiscences, "My War Horse Pete," p.9. Private Felix R. Collard was part of Colonel Steele's command and did not arrive in San Antonio until mid-August.
58. San Antonio Weekly Herald, June 21, 1862.
59. Finch, Sherod Hunter and The Confederates in Arizona, p.191; Frazier, Blood and Treasure, pp.278-279.
60. OR,I,IX,p.722, WM. Steele to S. Cooper, Adjutant and Inspector General, Richmond.

61. Collard, Reminiscences, "My War Horse Pete," p.6.
62. Ibid.
63. OR,I,IX,p.722, WM. Steele to S. Cooper, Adjutant and Inspector General, Richmond. See also Hall, The Confederate Army of New Mexico, pp.220, 244.
64. OR,I,IX,p.722, WM. Steele to S. Cooper, Adjutant and Inspector General, Richmond.
65. OR,I,IX,p.687, WM. Steele to Commanding Officer United States Forces.
66. OR,I,IX,p.722, WM. Steele to S. Cooper, Adjutant and Inspector General, Richmond; Hall, The Confederate Army of New Mexico, p.47. Dr. Southworth later deserted to the Union and joined the 1st Regiment Texas Cavalry North, "The 1st Texas Traitors."
67. Collard, Reminiscences, "My War Horse "Pete", p.6.
68. Williams, With the Border Ruffians, p.201.
69. OR,I,IX,p.637, Jas. L. Donaldson, to General H.W. Halleck.
70. OR,I,IX,pp.647, 649, 653, G.R. Paul to Adjutant-General U.S. Army, Washington, D.C. March 11, March 17, and March 24, 1862.
71. OR,I,IX,p.506, H.H. Sibley to General S. Cooper, Adjutant and Inspector General, Richmond, Va., Feb 22, 1862.
72. OR,I,IX,p.541, H.H. Sibley to General S. Cooper, Adjutant and Inspector General, Richmond, Va., March 31, 1862.
73. OR,I,IX,pp.669-670, ED. R. S. Canby to Adjutant-General of the Army, Washington, D.C.
74. OR,I,IX,p.714, H.H. Sibley to Brig. Gen. H.P. Bee.
75. Richardson, Messages and Papers of the Confederacy, Volume I, p.231. On June 7, 1862 Jefferson Davis also sent a message to General Sibley offering congratulations "on the distinguished successes of your command," particularly considering the enemy's superior numbers and resources. Crist, The Papers of Jefferson Davis, Volume 8, p.229.
76. OR,I,IX,p.716, R.E. Lee to Brigadier General Hebert, Commanding Department of Texas. Colonel Xavier Debray's 26th Texas Cavalry and the 35th Texas Cavalry were en route to Fort Bliss from the Gulf Coast. An additional regiment was authorized to ride from Arkansas. Both units

were halted 65 miles west of Houston and eventually diverted elsewhere.

77. Anderson, "Canby's Services in the New Mexican Campaign," p.698.

78. Ibid.

79. OR,I,IX,p.511, H.H. Sibley to General S. Cooper, Adjutant and Inspector General, Richmond, Va.

BIBLIOGRAPHY

ARCHIVES AND MANUSCRIPT SOURCES

Adair, Isaac. Will of Isaac Adair. Probate Records of Houston County, Houston County Deeds, Vol. P, pp. 163-4, photocopy courtesy of James B. Evans.

Collard, Felix R. "Reminiscences of a Private Company G, 7th Texas Cavalry Sibley Brigade, C.S.A." Silver City, New Mexico: Robert F. Collard Collection.

Columbus, Texas. Shropshire-Upton Confederate Museum. John Samuel Shropshire Letters, Shropshire to Carrie, December 26, 1861, Fort Quitman.

Evans, James B., ed. Diary of Elizabeth Green Gaines Smith and the John Titus and Elizabeth Gaines Smith Family. Dallas TX: 1988.

Green, Thomas, Letter to Father, May 22, 1861. Typescript courtesy of Dr. Donald S. Frazier.

Haas, Oscar, Trans. "The Diary of Julius Giesecke, 1861-1862." Copied from the collections in The Center for American History, The University of Texas at Austin.

Hall, James Madison. "James Madison Hall family papers, 1813-1865, Houston County, Texas, Diary 1861-1866," Frederick, MD: University Publications of America, 1987

Hanna, Ebeneezer. "The Civil War Diary of Ebeneezer Hanna." 1862, photocopy from the holdings of the Texas State Archives.

Ickis, Alonzo Ferdinand. "The Diary of Alonzo Ickis." Denver Public Library

Mallory, E.H. ed. "Benjamin Franklin Ferris - Civil War Memoir," courtesy of Eugene H. Mallory, Van Nuys, CA

McKenzie, Asa. "Letter to My Dear Wife," November, 1864, photostat courtesy of James Danner, Gresham, OR.

Reily, James, "General Orders No.36," May 18, 1862. Franklin (El Paso), Texas: Confederate Imprints, 1861-1865; reel 10, no. 652, Filmed from the holdings of the Barker

Texas History Center, Library of the University of Texas, Austin, Texas.

Reily, James, "To the patriots of Caldwell, Austin, Gonzales, Victoria, Guadalupe, Milan, Nacogdoches, Angelina, Cherokee, Polk, Houston, and other counties," June 27, 1862. San Antonio, Texas: Confederate Imprints, 1861-1865; reel 10, no. 654, Filmed from the holdings of the Barker Texas History Center, Library of the University of Texas, Austin, Texas.

Robinson, Daniel. "Collection," Fort Laramie National Historical Site, U.S. National Park Service.

Seat, Benton Bell. "Letter to the Hon. G.W. Randolph Secretary of War of the Confederate States of America, Las Cruces New Mexico May 5, 1862." typescript courtesy Paul Harden, Socorro, New Mexico.

Seat, Benton Bell. "Memoirs 1849-1916." courtesy of the Special Collections Division, University of Arkansas Libraries, Fayetteville, AR.

Sibley, Henry Hopkins, Letter to Father of Alexander McRae, May 12, 1862. John McRae Papers #477, selected items, Southern Historical Collection, University of North Carolina, Chapel Hill, NC.

Sibley, Henry Hopkins, "Soldiers of the Army of New Mexico," 1862. Franklin, Texas: Confederate Imprints, 1861-1865; reel 10, no. 653, Filmed from the holdings of the Barker Texas History Center, Library of the University of Texas, Austin, Texas.

Smith-Arrington, Georgiana (Georgia) Viviene. Civil War letters; Dec. 10, 1861 and Feb. 10, 1862. copies and transcripts courtesy of Elisabeth Arrington Montgomery.

Smith-Arrington, Georgiana (Georgia) Viviene. Family Bible. unpublished transcript courtesy of Elisabeth Arrington Montgomery.

GOVERNMENT DOCUMENTS

Abert, J.W. and Peck, W.G., Lieut's U.S.T.E. "Map of the Territory of New Mexico, made by order of Brig. Gen. S.W. Kearney, under instructions from Lieut. W.H. Emory, U.S.T.E.," Washington, D.C.: C.B. Graham's Litho, 1846-7.

Carter, Clarence Edwin, ed. The Territorial Papers of the United States, Vol. XVIII. Washington, D.C.: United States Govt. Printing Office, 1952.

Certification of Houston Co. annual Tax rolls dated May 24, 1855. Houston County, TX: couresty of James B. Evans.

Civil War Muster Roll Abstracts for Isaac Adair, dated Apr. thru Aug. 1861. Austin, TX: Texas State Library and Archives.

Compiled Service Record of B.B. Arrington, 7th Regiment Texas Mounted Volunteers, Civil War. Confederate Adjutant General's Office, Record Group 109, National Archives, Washington, D.C.

Compiled Service Record of Isaac Adair, 1st Regiment Texas Mounted Volunteers, War with Mexico. National Archives, Washington D.C.

Compiled Service Record of Isaac Adair, 7th Regiment Texas Mounted Volunteers, Civil War. Confederate Adjutant General's Office, Record Group 109, National Archives, Washington, D.C.

Compiled Service Record of J.M. Porter, 7th Regiment Texas Mounted Volunteers, Civil War. Confederate Adjutant General's Office, Record Group 109, National Archives, Washington, D.C.

Geological Survey (U.S.) Albuquerque and vicinity, New Mexico-Bernalillo Co. [map]. The Survey, Washington, D.C., 1961.

"H.H.Sibley to D.H.Maury", 28 April 1861, A.G.O., Dept. of New Mexico., Letters Received, Record Group 393, National Archives, Washington, D.C.

Houston County Deeds, Volume Q. Houston County, Texas: courtesy of James B. Evans.

Houston County Probate Records Volume F. Houston County, Texas: courtesy of James B. Evans.

Muster Roll of Company H, 7th Regiment Texas Mounted Volunteers, Civil War. Confederate Adjutant General's Office, Record Group 109, National Archives, Washington, D.C.

National Archives of the United States, Record Group 393: Records of U.S. Continental Commands, 1821-1921, pt1.

United States War Dept. "The Official Atlas of the Civil War. Introd. Henry Steele Commager," reproduction, New York, NY: T. Yoseloff, 1958.

Oregon Governor (1870-1877: Grover). Report of Governor Grover to General Schofield on the Modoc War. Salem, Oregon: Mart. V. Brown, State Printer, 1874.

Original Land Grants in the Name of Isaac Adair and related legal documents. Austin, TX: Texas General Land Office Archives, Records Division.

"Plympton to Capt. Henry R. Selden," Feb. 24, 1862, Record Group 393, "Records of the U.S. Continental Commands, 1821-1920," pt. 1, entry 3183, National Archives, Washington, D.C.

"Santa Fe Trail: Official Map and Guide: Santa Fe National Historic Trail," Colorado, Kansas, Missouri, New Mexico, Oklahoma. Washington, D.C.: National Park Service, Dept. of the Interior, 1995.

Stewart, Charles W., Superintendent Library and Naval Records, Official Records of the Union and Confederate Navies in the War of the Rebellion. Washington, D.C., 1914

United States Census Office. Federal Census 1850: Houston County Texas. Population, Slave, and Agricultural schedules.

United States Census Office. Federal Census 1860: Houston County Texas. Population, Slave, and Agricultural schedules.

"The War of the Rebellion: A Compilation of the Official Records of the Union and Confederate Armies." Four Series, 128 vols. Washington, D.C.: Government Printing Office, 1880-1901.

NEWSPAPERS

Austin State Gazette.
Belville Countryman.
Crocket Courier.
El Paso Herald.
Houston Tri-Weekly Telegraph.
Mesilla Times, "War Size."
New Braunfels Herald.
New Orleans Daily Picayune.

Overton Sharpshooter.
San Antonio Weekly Herald.
Santa Fe Gazette.

DISSERTATIONS AND THESES

Rogan, Francis Edward. Military History of New Mexico Territory During the Civil War. Ph.D. Diss., University of Utah, 1961.

Spurlin, Charles D. Texas Veterans in the Mexican War: Muster Rolls of Texas Military Units. Victoria College, reproduced from the holdings of the Texas State Archives.

BOOKS

Abert, James William. Western America in 1846-1847: the original travel diary of Lieutenant J.W. Abert. San Francisco, CA: J. Howell, 1966.

Alberts, Don E. The Battle of Glorieta; Union Victory in the West. College Station, TX: Texas A&M University Press, 1998.

Alberts, Don E., ed. Rebels on the Rio Grande, the Civil War Journal of A.B. Peticolas. Albuquerque, NM: Merit Press, 1993.

Adair, James Barnett, ed. Adair History and Genealogy. Los Angeles, CA: self-published, 1924.

Aldrich, Armistead Albert. The History of Houston County Texas. San Antonio, Texas: The Naylor Company, 1943.

Bancroft, Hubert Howe. History of Arizona and New Mexico, 1530-1888. San Francisco: The History Company, 1888.

Barr, Alwyn, ed. Charles Porter's Account of the Confederate Attempt to Seize Arizona and New Mexico. Austin, Texas: Pemberton Press, 1964.

Bearss, Edwin C. Steele's Retreat From Camden and The Battle of Jenkin's Ferry. Little Rock, Arkansas: Pioneer Press, 1961.

Beck, Warren A. New Mexico: A History of Four Centuries. Norman, Oklahoma: University of Oklahoma Press, 1962.

Bishop, Eliza H. and The History Book Committee of the Houston County Historical Commission, eds. History of Houston County, Texas 1687 - 1979. Tulsa, Oklahoma: Heritage Publishing Company, 1979.

Blessington, J.P. The Campaigns of Walker's Texas Division. New York: Lange, Little, & Co., 1875.

Boyle, William Henry, Dillon Richard H., ed. Personal Observations on the Conduct of the Modoc War. Los Angeles, CA: Dawson's Book Shop, 1959.

Carroll, John M. The Sand Creek Massacre: A Documentary History. New York, New York: Sol Lewis, 1973.

Colton, Ray Charles. The Civil War in the Western Territories: Arizona, Colorado, New Mexico, and Utah. Norman, OK: University of Oklahoma Press, 1959.

Conner, Daniel Ellis. A Confederate in the Colorado gold fields. Oklahoma: University of Oklahoma Press, 1970.

Craig, Reginald S. The Fighting Parson: A Biography of Col. John M.Chivington. Tucson, AZ: Westernlore Press, 1959.

Crist, Lynda Lasswell; Mary Seaton Dix; and Kenneth H. Williams , eds. The Papers of Jefferson Davis, Volume 9 January-September 1863. Baton Rouge, LA: Louisianna State University Press, 1997.

Crouch, Brodie. Jornada del Muerto: A Pagent of the Desert. Spokane, Washington: The Arthur H. Clark Company, 1989.

D'Hamel, E. B. The adventures of a Tenderfoot: History of 2nd Regt. Mounted Rifles and Co. G, 33 Regt. and Capt Coopwood's Spy Co. and 2nd Texas in Texas and New Mexico. Waco, TX: W.M. Morrison Books, n.d.

Edrington, Thomas S. and John Taylor. The Battle of Glorieta Pass: A Gettysburg in the West, March 26-28, 1862. Albuquerque, NM: University of New Mexico Press, 1998.

Emmett, Chris. Fort Union and the Winning of the Southwest. Oklahoma: University of Oklahoma Press, 1965.

Finch, Boyd L. Confederate Pathway to the Pacific: Major Sherod Hunter and Arizona Territory, C.S.A. Tucson, Arizona: The Arizona Historical Society, 1996.

Frazier, Donald S. Blood and Treasure, Confederate Empire in the Southwest. Texas A&M University Press, 1995.

Gallaway, B.P., ed. Texas, the Dark Corner of the Confederacy: Contemporary Accounts of the Lone Star State in the Civil War. Lincoln, NB: University of Nebraska Press, 1994.

Grant, Ulysses Simpson. Personal Memoirs of U.S. Grant. New York, New York: Da Capo Press, 1982 edition.

Greeley, Horace. The American Conflict: a History of the Great Rebellion in the United States of America, 1860-65. Hartford: O.D. Case & Company, 1866.

Grinstead, Marion Cox. Destiny at Valverde: The Life and Death of Alexander McRae. Socorro, NM: Socorro County Historical Society, 1992.

Hall, Martin Hardwick. The Confederate Army of New Mexico. Austin, Texas: Presidial Press, 1978.

Sibley's New Mexico Campaign. Austin, Texas: University of Texas Press, 1960.

Harris, Gertrude. A Tale of Men Who Knew Not Fear. San Antonio, Texas: Alamo Printing Co., 1935.

Hayes, Augusts Allen. New Colorado and the Santa Fe Trail. New York: Harper and Brothers, 1880.

Hazlett, James C. Field Artillery Weapons of the Civil War. Newark: University of Delaware Press, 1983.

Heartsill, William W. Fourteen Hundred And 91 Days in the Confederate Army. Jackson, TN: McCowat-Mercer Press, 1953.

Heyman, Max L. Prudent Soldier; a Biography of Major General E.R.S. Canby. Glendale, Calif.: A.H. Clark Co., 1959.

Hollister, Ovando J. Boldly They Rode. Lakewood, CO: The Golden Press, 1949.

Colorado Volunteers in New Mexico, 1862. Chicago, IL: R.R. Donnelley & Sons, 1962.

Holmes, William F. and Harold M. Hollingsworth, eds. Essays on the American Civil War. Austin, Texas: The University of Texas Press, 1968.

Irby, James A. Backdoor at Baghdad: the Civil War on the Rio Grande. El Paso, TX: Texas Western Press, University of Texas at El Paso, 1977.

Johnson, Ludwell H. Red River Campaign; Politics and Cotton in the Civil War. Baltimore, Md.: The Johns Hopkins Press, 1958.

Jones, John Beauchamp. A Rebel War Clerk's Diary at the Confederate States Capital. New York: Old Hickory Bookshop, 1935.

Josephy, Alvin M. Jr. The Civil War in the American West. New York, NY: Alfred A. Knopf, 1991.

War on the Frontier: the Trans-Mississippi West. Alexandria, VA: Time-Life Books, 1986.

Karnes, Thomas L. William Gilpin: Western Nationalist. Austin, Texas: University of Texas Press, 1970.

Keleher, William A. Turmoil in New Mexico 1846-1868. Santa Fe, New Mexico: The Rydal Press, 1952.

Kerby, Robert Lee. The Confederate Invasion of New Mexico and Arizona, 1861-1862. Los Angeles, CA: Westernlore Press, 1958.

Kirkpatrick, Charles Edward. The Prudent Soldier, the Rash Old Fighter, and the Walking Whiskey Keg. s.l.: s.n.; Supt. of Docs., U.S. G.P.O., 1987.

Lossing, Benson John. Pictorial History of the Civil War in the United States of America. Philadelphia, D. McKay, 1866.

Mainer, Thomas N. Houston County in the Civil War. Crockett, Texas: Publications Development Company of Texas, 1981.

McPherson, James M. What They Fought For 1861 - 1865. Baton Rouge, LA: Louisiana State University Press, 1994.

Meketa, Jacqueline D. Legacy of Honor, The life of Rafael Chacón, A Nineteenth-Century New Mexican. Albuquerque, NM: University of New Mexico Press, 1986.

Mills, W.W. Forty Years at El Paso 1858-1898. El Paso, Texas: Carl Hertzog, 1962.

Mumey, Nolie. Bloody Trails along the Rio Grande - A Day-by-Day Diary of Alonzo Ferdinand Ickis. Denver: The Old West Publishing Company, 1958.

Noel, Theophilus. A Campaign from Santa Fe to the Mississippi - Being a History of the Old Sibley Brigade. 1865., repr. Houston, TX: Stagecoach Press, 1961.

Autobiography and Reminiscences of Theophilus Noel. Chicago, Il: Theo. Noel Company, 1904.

Nunn, W.C. Ten Texans in Gray. Hillsboro, Texas: Hill Junior College, 1968.

Oppenheimer, Alan J. The Historical Background of Albuquerque, New Mexico. Albuquerque, New Mexico: Albuquerque City Planning Dept., 1962.

Oltorf, Frank Calvert, The Marlin Compound. Austin: University of Texas Press, 1968.

Peterson, Harold L. Round Shot and Rammers. Harrisburg, Pa.: Stackpole Books, 1969.

Petty, Joseph W. Sibley's Campaign into New Mexico. N.p.: N.p., 1955.

Pompey, Sherman Lee. Organization of Brigadier General Henry Hopkins Sibley's Texas Brigade, C.S.A., in the Arizona Territory 1861-1862. Kingsburg, CA: Pacific Specialties, 1971.

Richardson, James D. (comp.) Messages and Papers of the Confederacy Including the Diplomatic Correspondence, 1861-1865. Nashville, Tenn: United States Publishing Company, 1905, 2 volumes.

Rittenhouse, Jack D. New Mexico Civil War bibliography. Houston, Texas: Stagecoach Press, 1960.

Ryan, Andrew. News from Fort Craig, New Mexico, 1863; Civil War letters of Andrew Ryan, with the First California Volunteers. Santa Fe, New Mexico: Stagecoach Press, 1966.

Sanford, Mollie Dorsey. The Journal of Mollie Dorsey Sanford in Nebraska and Colorado Territories 1857-1866. University of Nebraska Press, 1959.

Scott, Robert. Glory Glory Glorieta: the Gettysburg of the West. Boulder, CO: Johnson Printing Company, 1992.

Simpson, Harold B. Hood's Texas Brigade in Reunion and Memory. Hillsboro, Texas: Hill Junior College Press, 1974.

Smith, Duane A. The Birth of Colorado : a Civil War Perspective. University of Oklahoma Press, 1989.

Stanley, Francis Louis. Fort Union. Texas: World Press, 1953.

Stanley, Francis Louis. The Civil War in New Mexico. Denver: World Press, 1960.

State Historical Society of Colorado. History of Colorado, Denver, CO: Linderman co., 1927.

Straw, Mary J. Loretto: The Sisters and Their Santa Fe Chapel. Santa Fe, NM: Loretto Chapel, 1983.

Strickland, Rex W. Six Who Came To El Paso, Pioneers of the 1840's. El Paso, Texas: Texas Western College Press, 1963.

Taylor, John M. Bloody Valverde: A Civil War Battle on the Rio Grande, February 21, 1862. Albuquerque, NM: University of New Mexico Press, 1995.

Taylor, Richard. Destruction and Reconstruction: Personal Experiences of the Late War. New York: D. Appleton and Company, 1879.

Thomas, Betty Wood, ed. Perry County, Alabama marriages, 1820-1832. Willo Institute of Genealogy, 1966.

Thompson, Jerry D., ed. Westward the Texans, The Civil War Journal of Private William Randolph Howell. El Paso, Texas: Texas Western Press, 1990.

Thompson, Jerry D. Henry Hopkins Sibley, Confederate General of the West. Natchitoches, LA: Northwestern State University Press, 1987.

Twitchell, Ralph Emerson. Old Santa Fe, the Story of New Mexico's Ancient Capital. Chicago, Rio Grande Press, 1963.

The Leading Facts of New Mexico History. 2 vols, Cedar Rapids, Iowa: The torch Press, 1911-1912.

Ulrich, Bebe Beasley, ed. Crockett Newspapers 1853-1896. Texas: Publications Development Company of Texas, 1984.

Warner, Ezra J. Generals in Gray; Lives of the Confederate Commanders. Louisiana State University Press,1959.

Webb, Walter Prescott, ed. The Handbook of Texas. 2 vols, Austin, Texas: The Texas State Historical Association, 1952.

White, Gifford E. The First Settlers of Houston County, Texas: from the originals in the General Land Office and the Texas State Archives, Austin, Texas. Austin, Texas: G. White, 1983.

Whitford, William Clarke. The Battle of Glorieta Pass: The Colorado Volunteers in the Civil War, March 26, 27, 28, 1862. 1906. repr. Glorieta, NM: The Rio Grande Press, Inc., 1991.

Williams, Ellen. Three years and a half in the Army, or, History of the Second Coloradans. New YorK: Fowler & Wells, 1885.

Williams, R.H. With the Border Ruffians, Memories of the Far West 1852-1868. Nebraska: University of Nebraska Press, 1982 first published 1907.

Wood, W.D. Leon County CSA Sketches, A partial roster of the officers and men raised in Leon County, Texas for the service of the Confederate States in the War between the States. 1899. repr. W.M. Morrison, 1963.

Wooster, Ralph A., ed. Lone Star Blue and Gary, Essays on Texas in the Civil War. Austin, Texas: Texas State Historical Association, 1995.

Wright, Marcus J., Simpson, Harold B., ed. Texas in the War. Hillsboro, Texas: The Hill Junior College Press, 1965.

PAMPLETS ARTICLES AND ESSAYS

Alberts, Dr. Don E. "The Battle of Peralta" New Mexico Historical Review 58 1983, 369-379.

Anderson, Latham. "Canby's Campaign in New Mexico." in Sketches of War History 1861-1865, Papers Read Before the Ohio Commandry of the Military Order of the Loyal Legion of the United States 1886-1888, 371-391. Cincinnati, OH: Robert Clarke & Co., 1888.

Anderson, Latham. "Canby's Services in the New Mexican Campaign." Battles and Leaders of the Civil War, Volume II, 697-699: New York, The Century Company, 1884.

Bell, J.M. "The Campaign of New Mexico, 1862." In War Papers Read before the Commandry of the State of Wisconsin Military Order of the Loyal Legion of the United States, 47-71. Milwaukee, WI: Burdick, Armitage, and Allen, 1891.

Bishop, Eliza H. "Augusta Louise Smith and Her Husbands Isaac Adair and James Mack Porter." Crockett, TX: courtesy of the Houston County Historical Commission.

Bloom, Lansing (ed.) "Confederate Reminscences," New Mexico Historical Review V (July, 1930), 318.

Boyd, Le Roy. "Thunder on the Rio Grande, the Great Adventure of Sibley's Confederates for the Conquest of New Mexico and Colorado." Colorado Magazine July 1947: 24.

Collins, Thomas Benton. "A Texan's Account of the Battle of Valverde." Panhandle Plains Historical Review, Vol. 37 1964, 33-35.

"Confederate Memorial Day Ceremony Program, Remembering the Battle of Glorietta Pass." Santa Fe, NM: Santa Fe National Cemetery, April 26, 1993, courtesy of James H. Berry, Jr.

Evans, A. W. "Canby at Valverde." Battles and Leaders of the Civil War, Volume II, 699-700: New York, The Century Company, 1884.

Faulkner, Walter A. "With Sibley in New Mexico; The Journal of William Henry Smith." The West Texas Historical Association year book. Abilene, Texas, Vol. 27 Oct. 1951, 111-142.

Finch, Boyd "Sherod Hunter and the Confederates in Arizona." The Journal of Arizona History 10 (Autumn 1969): 137-206.

Gaither, Donald, ed. "The 'Pet Lambs' at Glorieta Pass." Civil War Times Illustrated 15 (November, 1976): 30-38.

Giese, Dale "Echoes of the Bugle", Phelps-Dodge Corporation Bicentennial Booklet, 1976.

Gracy, David B., ed. "New Mexico Campaign Letters of Frank Starr, 1861-1862." Texas Military History. 4 (Fall, 1964): 169-188.

Greer, Thomas L. "Historical Facts about the Battlegrounds and Indian/Spanish Trading Post at Glorietta [sic] Pass." Denver Public Library.

Hall, Martin H. "Planter vs. Frontiersman: Conflict in Confederate Indian Policy" The Walter Prescott Webb Memorial Lectures: Essays on the American Civil War. Austin, Texas: University of Texas Press, 1968.

"An appraisal of the 1862 New Mexico Campaign: A Confederate Officer's Letter to Nacogdoches." New Mexico Historical Review 51 1976, 329-335.

Hayes, Augusts Allen. "An Unwritten Chapter of the Late War." The International Review VIII 1880, 134-149: New York, A.S. Barnes & Co.

Hayes, Augusts Allen. "The New Mexican Campaign of 1862." Magazine of American History XV (February, 1886), 180.

Kajencki, Francis C. "The Battle of Glorieta Pass: Was the Guide Ortiz or Grzelachowski" New Mexico Historical Review 62 no.1 1987, 47-54.

Miller, Darlis A. "Hispanos and the Civil War in New Mexico: A Reconsideration" New Mexico Historical Review 54 1979.

Mitchell, Cheryle. "The 2nd Battle of Glorieta." El Palacio, Magazine of the Museum of New Mexico, March 1991, 24-30.

Norvell, Stevens Thompson. "New Mexico in the Civil War." Military Order of the Loyal Legion of the United States, War papers #45, read January 7, 1903.

Pettis, George H. "The Confederate Invasion of New Mexico and Arizona." Battles and Leaders of the Civil War, Volume II, 103-111: New York, The Century Company, 1884.

Teel, Trevanion T. "Sibley's New Mexican Campaign. - Its objects and the causes of its failure." Battles and Leaders of the Civil War, Volume II, 700: New York, The Century Company, 1884.

Texas Historical Foundation. "Red River Campaign: Centennial Commemoration, Center, Texas - Mansfield, Louisiana April 4, 1964."

Venarde, David. "New Mexico Civil War Site Proposed as Historic Park." National Parks 1988, v62, n1-2, Jan.-Feb., p.13.

ELECTRONIC AND OTHER MISC SOURCES

"International Genealogical Index", Church of Jesus Christ of Latter Day Saints.

Personal communication, Lannie Walker, Sr. 11/26/94.

Sanders, Justin M. "FAQ," alt.war.civil.usa, v2.06, Oct. 19, 1994.

INDEX

A

Adair, Ben, 14
Adair, Emma Ada, 14
Adair, Isaac, 1, 3, 5, 6, 10, 11, 13, 15, 16, 17, 19, 24, 25, 26, 27, 28, 29, 30, 31, 37, 40, 41, 42, 43, 44, 45, 49, 50, 52, 58, 61, 66, 68, 70, 71, 77, 79, 81, 85, 96, 113, 114, 120, 124, 127, 130, 132, 136, 143, 148, 153, 157, 160, 162, 165, 188, 209, 210, 217, 220, 225, 231, 235, 236, 238, 242, 261, 265, 268, 277, 284, 285, 295, 328, 348, 355
Adair, John, 14
Adair, Joseph, 6
Adair, Matilda, 11
Adair, Priscilla, 5
Adair, Thomas, 6
Adair, Zadock, 6, 7, 11, 14
Alabama, 6, 7, 11, 15, 16
Albright, May, 5
Albuquerque, MN, 134, 137, 138, 139, 140, 142, 143, 147, 148, 150, 151, 153, 155, 156, 157, 160, 161, 167, 193, 212, 270, 272, 273, 274, 280, 281, 282, 283, 284, 285, 286, 287, 288, 289, 290, 291, 293, 294, 295, 296, 298, 305, 316, 325, 328, 340, 347, 354, 356, 361
Alexander, William Lee, 64, 108, 114, 133, 354, 356, 358
Allen, Burwell Collier, 346, 366
Alley, Charles H., 180
Anderson, Latham, 322, 343
Apache Canyon, NM, 164, 193, 196, 197, 203, 209, 210, 212, 215, 218, 219, 221, 250, 251, 252, 254, 266, 268, 276, 282, 323
Appalachacola River, 11
Aragon, Francisco, 141
Arizona Rangers, Frazer's, 69, 193, 217, 362
Arizona Territory, 1, 2, 22, 40, 52, 53, 56, 69, 123, 125, 217, 324, 362, 370, 372, 374, 376
Confederate, 35
Armijo, Manuel, 150, 151, 296, 339
Armijo, Rafael, 150, 151, 296, 339
Army of New Mexico, Confederate, 52, 54,

56, 61, 66, 69, 70, 71, 75, 125, 128, 139, 146, 162, 186, 193, 217, 220, 248, 258, 261, 265, 270, 271, 273, 285, 291, 312, 318, 324, 338, 339, 340, 345, 347, 354, 355, 361, 370, 373
Arrington, Bennett Bunn, 30, 45, 285, 349

B

Baca, Pedro, 129
Baird, Spruce M., 137, 148, 149, 296, 299, 351
Baker, John, 226, 260
Bartlett, Love, 224
Bass, Demetrius M., 93
Baum, Benjamin, 73
Baylor, John Robert, 32, 33, 34, 35, 44, 53, 56, 57, 59, 61, 67, 69, 82, 337, 364, 370
Beauregard, P.G.T., 10
Beck, Joseph H., 359
Bee, Hamilton, 375
Belen, NM, 138
Belén, NM, 144, 146, 320
Bell, Joseph M., 303
Bennett, Jordan W., 198
Bernal Springs, NM, 209, 218, 296
Blair, John, 18
Booker, William, 50, 242
Bowers, Joe, 324
Bradford, James, 217, 220, 221, 222, 223, 226, 228, 261

Bradford's Battery, 220, 221, 222, 223, 226, 228
Brigands Phillips', 69, 155, 193, 195, 217, 220, 229, 233, 279, 300
Bronaugh, John M., 360
Brownrigg, Richard T., 339
Buckholts, Charles, 227, 235, 236, 240, 261
Buena Vista, battle of, 9

C

Camp Pickett, 42, 45
Camp Weld, 179, 180, 181, 185
Canby, Edward Richard Sprigg, 50, 62, 63, 64, 65, 67, 77, 78, 83, 97, 98, 102, 107, 109, 110, 111, 112, 113, 115, 120, 122, 123, 127, 128, 139, 168, 171, 176, 177, 182, 186, 191, 195, 265, 281, 282, 286, 292, 296, 299, 308, 315, 316, 318, 320, 323, 324, 331, 349, 373, 374
Canby, Louisa Hawkins, 275, 276, 277, 279
Canõncito, NM, 208, 212, 225
Carey, Asa B., 252
Carleton, James H., 363, 371, 374
Carlton, William A., 349
Carnuel Pass, NM, 298
Carson, Christopher, 64, 65

Carson, James M., 226, 235, 238, 276
Casey Levi, 6
Castron, C.C., 70
Cebeno, Domingo, 372
Central City, CO, 175
Cerro Gordo, battle of, 9
Chacón, Rafael, 73, 83, 90, 102, 112, 120
Chambers, Clark, 260
Chapin, Gurden, 219, 234, 240
Chaves, Jose Francisco, 64
Chaves, Manuel A., 249, 250, 251, 258
Chivington, John M., 175, 181, 183, 185, 190, 194, 196, 197, 199, 200, 201, 202, 207, 209, 212, 215, 218, 219, 221, 222, 249, 252, 253, 255, 256, 257, 258, 259, 261, 262, 265, 268, 282, 297, 302, 304, 308, 309, 314, 321, 347
Cimarron River, 190
Claflin, Ira, 83, 221, 234, 309
Claflin's Battery, 230, 235, 246
Clark, Isaac W., 52
Cleaver, William H., 371
Clough, J. Phil, 91, 113, 237, 301
Cobb, Alfred S, 258
Cobb, Henry P., 242
Collard, Felix R., 3, 51, 58, 347, 370, 373
Collins, James L., 276

Colorado Territory, 24, 64, 167, 171, 175, 177, 179
Colorado Volunteers, 64, 104, 188, 191, 193, 198, 205, 207, 222, 243, 245, 260, 270, 297, 304, 347
  1st Regiment, 167, 175, 196, 197, 202, 220, 236, 241
    Company A, 174, 193, 256
    Company B, 175
    Company D, 223
    Company F, 184, 195, 196, 199, 201, 202, 236, 304, 305
    Company G, 173
    Company I, 222, 226
  Dodd's Independent Company, 64, 73, 90, 93, 104, 115, 177
  Ford's Independent Company, 177, 182
Connelly, Henry, 64, 107, 128, 275, 300, 301, 302, 303, 321
Cook, Samuel, 196, 202, 203
Cooke, Philip St. George, 20
Cooper, Samuel, 353
Coopwood, Bethel, 69, 273, 287, 327, 334, 343
Covey, Edward N., 71, 131
Crocket, TX, 3, 8, 9, 10, 13, 17, 18, 24, 25, 26,

28, 29, 30, 31, 81, 85,
    99, 132, 209, 235, 242,
    284, 296, 328
Crosson, James Murray,
    104, 237, 242
Cubero, NM, 140, 141,
    142, 150
Currie, Edward, 17

D

Daily, T.W., 28
Daniel, James M., 285
Darby, James A., 295,
    301, 305, 306
Davidson, William Lott,
    95, 103, 107, 117, 125,
    134, 135, 143, 144,
    157, 193, 204, 211,
    212, 220, 224, 226,
    229, 241, 249, 254,
    264, 265, 267, 274,
    279, 283, 294, 300,
    301, 305, 307, 308,
    313, 317, 327, 330,
    332, 357
Davis, Jefferson, 9, 16,
    22, 27, 171, 376
Davis, W.T., 272
Dawson, A.J., 105
Dead Man's Hole, 47, 366,
    367
Delaplain, Sam, 300
Denver, CO, 167, 168,
    169, 170, 171, 172,
    173, 174, 175, 176,
    177, 178, 180, 181,
    183, 185, 186, 187,
    196, 222, 248, 356
Deus, Charles, 73
Dickey, M.A., 59
Disease, 15, 55, 59, 70,
    131, 134, 154, 157,
    216, 277, 329, 349,
    358, 359
Dodd, Theodore H., 64,
    176, 187
Doña Ana, NM, 60, 353,
    370
Donaldson, James, 126,
    137, 140, 142, 183,
    249, 374
Downing, Jacob, 223,
    224, 243, 246
Duncan, Thomas, 83, 84,
    86, 87, 104, 288
Dwyer, Joseph, 358

E

Edens, B. Frank, 28
Edmundson, Frank, 15
El Paso, TX, 22, 51, 59,
    353, 357, 366, 370
Elkhart, TX, 28
Elliot, Henry, 227
Enos, Herbert M., 137,
    138, 139, 140
Ewing, Jane, 6

F

Falvey, John, 219
Ferris, Benjamin, 184,
    198, 208, 225, 236,
    237, 306
Ferris, John, 306
Field, Alfred, 91
Fields, Tom, 224
Fillmore, John, 170
Fisher, Morton, 170
Ford, Hiram, 155
Ford, James H., 176
Fort Bliss, TX, 38, 44, 45,
    48, 49, 51, 52, 54, 56,
    57, 74, 185, 351, 353,
    372

Fort Craig, 61, 64, 65, 67, 69, 70, 72, 74, 75, 76, 80, 83, 89, 97, 98, 120, 122, 123, 124, 126, 128, 131, 137, 138, 139, 146, 153, 161, 163, 167, 182, 186, 191, 273, 280, 281, 282, 297, 299, 319, 321, 322, 323, 325, 326, 338, 339, 345, 347, 371, 376
Fort Fillmore, 22, 34, 58, 353
Fort Garland, 64, 172, 177, 182
Fort Lancaster, 52, 59, 364, 367
Fort Lyon, 185
Fort Quitman, 52, 365, 373
Fort Stanton, 34, 281
Fort Thorn, 54, 58, 59, 60, 61, 66, 69, 131, 350, 371
Fort Wise, 176, 177, 185, 186, 187
Frazer, George M., 69
Fulcrod, Philip, 78, 91, 125, 139, 140, 274, 293, 296, 308, 309, 313, 314, 332

G

Gaines Elizabeth Greene, 11
Galisteo, NM, 153, 161, 163, 164, 209, 215, 216, 219, 249, 282, 291, 298
Gardenhier, George, 141
Gardiner, Charles, 193, 253, 256
Gibbs, Alfred, 34
Gibson, J.H., 50
Giesecke, Julius, 48, 143, 156, 158, 161, 163, 263, 315, 350, 357, 366
Gillespie, Richmond, 140, 141
Gilpin, William, 167, 168, 169, 170, 171, 172, 173, 174, 175, 176, 177, 178, 179, 180, 181, 182, 183, 185, 186
Glorieta Pass, NM, 3, 193, 194, 195, 196, 219, 259, 261, 266, 274, 283, 298, 328, 374
Gossett, Zebedde, 90
Graydon, James, 64, 73, 79, 80, 83, 99, 304, 320, 331, 335
Green, Thomas, 40, 61, 65, 67, 68, 69, 71, 73, 77, 78, 89, 92, 96, 100, 101, 103, 105, 111, 113, 114, 122, 124, 161, 212, 213, 218, 257, 264, 267, 272, 273, 284, 290, 293, 295, 296, 299, 300, 301, 305, 307, 308, 310, 311, 313, 316, 317, 319, 325, 326, 327, 329, 330, 331, 332, 336, 351, 353, 358, 360, 364
Grzelachowski, Alexander, 258, 262

H

Hail, Peter, 242
Haley, Charles Q., 285, 348
Hall, Henry, 196
Hall, James Madison, 13, 16, 17
Hall, Robert H., 64, 122
Hall's Battery, 10th U.S. Infantry Company F, 86, 88, 99
Hampton, George J. Hampton, 364
Hanna, Ebenezer, 3, 105, 118, 131, 135, 143, 148, 151, 153, 155, 159, 163, 207, 224
Hardeman, William P., 104, 111, 133, 212, 273, 281, 283, 286, 287, 288, 289, 290, 291, 295, 317, 344, 364
Hartgraves, B.G., 132
Hartgraves, John D., 132
Harwell, John, 16
Hawley, J.H., 306
Hayden, Madgalen, 269, 272
Hays, John C., 9
Hendron, C.D, 176
Hennis, George, 349
Henson, Jake, 224
Higgins, M.C., 59
Hoffman, Gustav, 217, 220, 225, 228
Holcomb, Harvey, 216, 224, 247, 259, 263, 277
Hollister, Ovando, 184, 196, 202, 218, 223, 225, 236, 260, 266, 297, 304, 305, 316, 318, 320, 323
Horn Valley, 118
Houston County, TX, 5, 8, 11, 13, 14, 15, 16, 17, 25, 26, 29, 71, 132, 148, 284, 355
Howard Spring, 47, 48
Howell, William Randolph, 49, 68, 97, 114, 131, 150, 295, 335, 337, 339, 343
Howland, G.W., 196, 219, 220, 292
Hubbard, David, 125
Hubbell, James, 104, 106
Hume, Peyton, 198, 201, 313
Hunter, David, 186
Hunter, Jacob, 283
Hunter, Sherod, 362, 370

I

Ickis, Alonzo Ferdinand, 64, 73, 93, 94, 111, 115, 274, 287, 313, 328
Indian Territory, 19
Indians, 8, 20, 46, 58, 143, 167, 171, 175, 203, 253, 264, 365, 367, 370, 373
  Apache, 58, 118, 164, 193, 196, 197, 200, 203, 209, 210, 212, 215, 218, 219, 221, 250, 251, 252, 254, 266, 268, 276, 282, 323
  Navajo, 21, 142
  Seminole, 19

Wyandotte, 175
Ingraham, Charles, 102
J
Jackson, Alexander M., 270
Johnson's Ranch, 193, 208, 211, 213, 215, 216, 219, 225, 250, 258, 259, 264, 266, 268, 272, 286
Johnston, Joseph E., 10
Jones, B.A., 147, 212
Jones, Lucius H., 255, 257
Jordan, Powhatan, 115, 160, 277, 284
Jornada del Muerto, 326
Juarez, Mexico, 51, 59
K
Kavenaugh, F.E., 141, 142
Kearny, Stephen W., 215
Kelley, Peter, 6
Kelley, Sarah, 6
Kelly, Pvt., 233
Kennedy, S.E., 29
Kerber, Charles, 226, 227
King, Hattie, 30
Kirk, William D., 220, 229, 231, 233
Kozlowski, Martin, 194
Kozlowski's Ranch, 194, 215, 218, 219, 244, 246, 248, 259, 261, 262, 266, 298
L
La Joya, NM, 135, 322
Lancers, 39, 89, 91, 92, 93, 182
Lang, Willis, 91, 94, 124, 159, 182

Las Cruces, NM, 353, 358
Laughter, William, 84
Laurens County, SC, 6
Leddy, Private, 239
Lee, Robert E., 10, 375
Lesuer, Charles M., 104
Lincoln, Abraham, 16, 61, 167, 179, 181, 376
Lockridge, Samuel, 40, 72, 89, 99, 104, 108, 124, 161, 307
Loebnitz, Henry E., 312
Logan, Samuel M., 169, 172, 206
Long, John, 9
Lord, Richard, 104, 109
Loretto, convent of, 269
Los Lunas, NM, 138, 299, 307, 311, 312, 316, 317, 319, 320, 323
Los Padillas, NM, 300
Los Pinos, NM, 299, 300, 307, 308, 316
Lynde, Issac, 32, 33, 34, 35
M
Madison County, TX, 26
Magoffin, James, 353
Magoffin, Samuel, 358
Maney, Samuel B., 131
Manzano, NM, 280
Maxwell, Lucien, 190
Maxwell, Sam, 37, 39
McClellan, George B., 10
McCormick, David, 130
McCormick, David R., 125
McCown, Jerome, 91
McFerran, John C., 321, 324
McGinnis, Joseph H., 198, 309, 313, 314

McGrath, Peter, 260
McIntyre, John, 195
McKee, Joel, 170
McNeill, Henry C., 40, 127, 128, 129, 307, 327
McPhaill, Hugh A., 307, 359
McRae, Alexander, 107, 108, 109
McRae's Battery, 2nd U.S. Cavalry Company G and 3rd U.S. Cavalry Company I, 86, 88, 99, 105, 106, 107, 109
Meinhold, Charles, 87
Mesa Del Contadero, 72, 82, 338
Mesilla, Arizona Territory, 32, 35, 44, 53, 54, 56, 61, 74, 123, 186, 273, 281, 292, 326, 353, 354, 357, 359, 363, 364, 371, 372
Mexico
   Sibley's overture to, 49
   War with, 9, 19, 167
Miller, John D., 191, 199, 262
Mills, Charles H., 261
Mishler, Lyman, 108
Moer, Samuel, 170
Mormon Expedition, 21, 63
Morris, Robert M., 320, 322, 324, 347
Mortimore, William, 105, 107
Mountain Howitzers, 69, 77, 84, 88, 89, 221, 234, 273, 293, 331

Murchison, John W., 30, 295

N

Naile, John C., 135, 157
Natchitoches, LA, 19
Nelson, George, 195, 202
Nettles, Timothy, 198, 199, 201, 216, 251, 254, 313
New Mexico Militia, 64, 97, 126, 128, 145
New Mexico Territory, 1, 2, 21, 22, 23, 24, 30, 38, 41, 44, 45, 51, 52, 53, 55, 57, 61, 62, 64, 65, 72, 83, 84, 86, 89, 91, 99, 104, 106, 107, 115, 119, 121, 123, 126, 128, 129, 130, 136, 143, 150, 152, 157, 161, 168, 171, 176, 177, 182, 185, 186, 187, 188, 192, 193, 203, 215, 230, 238, 249, 251, 259, 269, 271, 275, 280, 282, 288, 296, 299, 303, 304, 322, 331, 335, 347, 348, 350, 351, 354, 358, 360, 361, 362, 365, 373, 374, 375, 376
New Mexico Volunteers, 64, 65, 72, 83, 84, 89, 91, 97, 99, 104, 106, 107, 119, 192, 249, 251, 259, 282, 299, 304
   1st Regiment, 97, 102, 326
   2nd Regiment, 99, 112

3rd Regiment
  Company A, 104, 105, 107, 115
5th Regiment
  Company A, 104, 105
New York, 7, 11, 15, 19, 21, 175
Noel, Theophilus, 37, 38, 42, 56, 61, 69, 75, 117, 134, 290, 313, 338, 346, 350, 365, 366, 367
Norman, Adolphus, 198, 199, 201
Nunn, David Alexander, 25, 26, 27, 71, 81, 85, 90, 91, 95, 100, 105, 132, 355

O

Ochiltree, Thomas P., 100
Odell, James Mitchell, 132, 235, 236, 284, 355
Onderdonk, William H., 91
Otis, Elmer, 177

P

Padre Polaco. See Grzelachowski, Alexander, 258
Patrick, John William, 229, 231, 233
Paul, Gabriel René, 190, 191, 192, 282, 297, 314, 321, 374
Pelham, William, 296
Peralta, NM, 147, 299, 300, 301, 308, 309, 311, 312, 315, 319, 320, 321, 323, 332, 363
Peticolas, Alfred B., 3, 97, 109, 111, 118, 124, 133, 134, 135, 136, 146, 149, 150, 153, 154, 156, 158, 159, 162, 163, 208, 209, 211, 216, 220, 222, 228, 235, 240, 242, 262, 267, 272, 290, 299, 325, 328, 329, 332, 334, 335, 338, 339, 341, 348, 349, 350, 358, 362
Phillips, John, 69, 195, 217, 279
Picacho Pass, AZ, 363
Pierce, George W., 236, 238
Pigeon's Ranch, 195, 196, 207, 215, 216, 218, 219, 221, 226, 230, 231, 240, 242, 256, 263, 274
Pike's Peakers, 197, 202, 220, 237, 241
Pino, Miguel, 99, 112
Pino, Nicolás, 64
Platner, Seth, 59
Platte river, 173, 179
Plympton, Peter, 93, 104, 105, 107
Polvadera, NM, 128, 322, 326, 327, 331
Porter, James Macintosh, 284, 285
Pridgen, Reddin Smith, 25, 26, 28, 29, 100, 355
Purcell, Rube, 224

Pyron, Charles, 67, 69, 81, 82, 83, 84, 89, 104, 134, 137, 138, 139, 140, 142, 151, 155, 156, 161, 164, 167, 193, 194, 195, 197, 198, 200, 201, 202, 203, 207, 209, 211, 212, 215, 217, 219, 221, 223, 224, 231, 239, 242, 244, 245, 247, 261, 273, 276, 296, 299, 307, 308, 309, 312, 319, 327, 364

R

Ragsdale, Dan, 59, 307
Raguet, Charles, 111
Raguet, Henry, 38, 84, 85, 100, 101, 102, 104, 105, 111, 112, 113, 124, 159, 223, 231, 233, 235, 239, 242, 243, 244, 261
Raleigh, Private, 239
Randolph, George W., 360
Raton Mountains, 188
Real de Dolores, NM, 163
Red River, 188
Reily, James, 37, 39, 49, 59, 133, 344, 348, 351, 362, 368
Reily, John, 88
Reily's Battery, 77, 88, 111, 272
Richardson, J.H., 237, 238
Rio Grande, 40, 42, 46, 52, 55, 57, 62, 66, 67, 74, 75, 80, 82, 83, 111, 119, 122, 135, 136, 144, 146, 163, 273, 282, 290, 295, 296, 298, 299, 311, 321, 326, 330, 332, 338, 345, 346, 347, 350, 351, 365
Ritter, John F., 221, 228, 230, 233, 234, 240, 244, 246, 256, 260
Ritter, Simon, 256
Ritter's Battery, 221, 230, 233, 234, 246, 260
Robards, W.L., 25, 312
Roberts, Benjamin S., 85, 87, 89, 97, 314, 315
Robinson, Daniel, 111
Rogers, John M., 163
Romero, Toribio, 299

S

Sabinal, NM, 136, 143, 144
Sabino, NM, 322
Salado Creek, 32, 37, 329, 331
San Antonio, TX, 1, 8, 9, 10, 24, 25, 26, 30, 31, 32, 37, 38, 39, 40, 41, 42, 44, 45, 46, 48, 51, 52, 54, 55, 56, 61, 70, 71, 153, 159, 160, 162, 282, 291, 362, 363, 364, 367, 368, 369, 371, 373
San Augustine Springs, 34
San Cristobal Canyon, NM, 249
San Elizario Spy Company, Coopwood's, 69, 193, 217, 273, 307

San Felipe Springs, 40, 52, 369
San Mateo Mountains, NM, 273, 333, 338
Sandia Mountains, NM, 153, 156, 161, 163, 167, 188, 298
Sanford, B.N., 254
Sangre de Cristo Mountains, 183
Santa Fe Trail, 188, 191, 193, 195, 197, 215, 217, 231, 249, 261
Santa Fe, NM, 51, 69, 137, 138, 139, 140, 148, 153, 155, 156, 161, 163, 167, 182, 186, 188, 191, 193, 194, 195, 197, 198, 212, 215, 217, 220, 231, 249, 251, 253, 261, 265, 266, 268, 269, 270, 271, 272, 273, 275, 276, 277, 279, 280, 282, 283, 284, 285, 291, 292, 296, 297, 347, 354, 356
Schmidt, S., 91
Scott, Winfield, 9, 20
Scurry, William Read, 39, 66, 69, 81, 82, 83, 84, 86, 88, 89, 90, 91, 95, 99, 103, 104, 111, 112, 113, 122, 123, 133, 143, 161, 162, 163, 164, 209, 210, 211, 213, 214, 215, 216, 217, 218, 220, 222, 223, 224, 225, 226, 229, 231, 232, 233, 234, 239, 242, 244, 245, 246, 247, 255, 256, 257, 259, 260, 261, 262, 263, 264, 265, 266, 267, 268, 270, 271, 272, 273, 274, 275, 276, 280, 283, 284, 285, 290, 291, 295, 296, 297, 298, 299, 300, 311, 312, 319, 326, 327, 329, 330, 333, 336, 337, 338, 339, 342, 344, 346, 347, 348, 349
Seat, Benton Bell, 39, 304, 316
Secession, 16, 213
Seldon, Henry, 90, 95
Shannon, Denman W., 122, 205, 237, 246, 261, 307
Shiflett, John Wesley, 328
Shropshire, John S., 50, 193, 204, 224, 228, 231, 232, 235, 236, 238, 239, 240, 246, 261, 307
Sibley Brigade, 26, 30, 31, 56, 117, 130, 137, 141, 142, 217, 280, 282, 283, 296, 298, 321, 325, 326, 340, 351, 355, 363, 376
Sibley Tent, 20
Sibley, Henry Hopkins, 1, 3, 19, 20, 23, 24, 32, 35, 38, 39, 40, 41, 42, 44, 45, 49, 51, 53, 54, 55, 56, 57, 59, 60, 61, 62, 64, 65, 69, 70, 81, 82, 89, 96, 114, 122, 123, 132, 133, 150,

151, 153, 155, 160,
161, 167, 210, 213,
217, 258, 265, 270,
272, 273, 280, 281,
284, 286, 292, 296,
307, 311, 312, 316,
319, 327, 330, 332,
339, 342, 348, 351,
353, 354, 355, 356,
357, 360, 361, 362,
363, 364, 367, 369,
370, 374, 375
Sibley, John, 19
Simpson, G., 93
Slater, Benjamin, 314
Slaves and Slavery, 11,
13, 15, 159
Slough, John P., 174,
183, 185, 186, 187,
188, 189, 191, 192,
194, 209, 215, 218,
219, 220, 221, 223,
227, 229, 230, 231,
234, 243, 245, 246,
248, 249, 256, 258,
259, 260, 265, 266,
267, 272, 281, 282,
289, 296, 297
Smith,, 243
Smith, Augusta Louise, 5,
11, 14, 15, 41
Smith, G.H., 239
Smith, Georgia, 30
Smith, John Titus, 14
Smith, John Titus., 11, 13
Smith, William Henry, 67,
156, 270
Socorro, NM, 127, 128,
129, 130, 131, 144,
149, 159, 283, 284,
286, 354

Southworth, Malek A.,
372
Stapleton, Robert H., 127
Starr, James Franklin, 2,
77, 281, 312, 333, 336,
353, 355, 356, 358
Steele, William, 44, 292,
344, 345, 346, 349,
350, 370, 372
Stephenson J.P., 85
Stokes, Charles, 30
Stracham,, 283
Sturdevant, J., 357
Sumner, Edward V., 20
Sutton, Janette B., 213
Sutton, John Schuyler,
45, 54, 66, 69, 77, 81,
89, 96, 97, 103, 120,
124, 160

T

Taos, NM, 21
Tappan, Samuel F., 175,
185, 186, 187, 222,
233, 234, 236, 239,
240, 241, 242, 246
Taylor, G.N., 242
Taylor, John W., 209, 216
Teel, Trevanion T., 55,
272, 293, 295, 311,
312, 370
Teel's Battery Company B,
1st Texas Artillery, 65,
69, 77, 81, 88, 91, 95,
193, 198, 229, 272,
273
Texas
Land Grants, 8, 12
Texas Militia, 16, 18, 24
Beat No. 1, Houston
County, 18

Crockett Southerners, 17, 18
Texas Mounted Rifles
  2nd Regiment, 32, 57, 59, 67, 69, 82, 83, 89, 134, 217, 364
    Company D, 104, 273
Texas Mounted Volunteers
  4th Regiment, 26, 37, 66, 81, 85, 87, 88, 89, 90, 91, 104, 132, 134, 153, 156, 165, 210, 211, 212, 215, 224, 255, 260, 272, 284, 311, 317, 319, 328, 333, 342, 364
    Company A, 131, 273, 368
    Company C, 91, 224, 226, 228
    Company E, 226, 235
    Company F, 39, 216, 235
    Company G, 48
    Company H, 114, 356
    Company I, 243
  5th Regiment, 39, 40, 61, 67, 91, 94, 105, 107, 125, 127, 202, 206, 217, 237, 257, 260, 284, 301, 309, 321, 325, 337, 350, 358
    Company A, 95, 203, 228, 235, 314
    Company C, 96, 113, 237
    Company E, 307
    Company F, 59, 272, 304
    Company G, 272
    Company H, 272
    Company I, 272, 294, 295
    Company K, 272
  7th Regiment, 156, 165, 209, 211, 212, 215, 217, 260, 284, 292, 311, 317, 319, 328, 342, 344
    Battalion of, 45, 51, 54, 61, 66, 68, 71, 81, 89, 153, 160, 161, 210, 224, 364
    Company A, 96, 113
    Company B, 217, 225, 228
    Company D, 371
    Company F, 115, 163, 235
    Company G, 3
    Company H, 10, 29, 37, 40, 44, 50, 58, 61, 66, 70, 71, 96, 115, 124, 136, 225, 235, 242, 284, 285, 348
      at Valverde, 85
    Company I, 209
Thompson, R.T., 141
Thurmond, Alfred S., 140, 141, 142, 212, 327
Tijeras, NM, 153, 156, 157, 160, 291, 298, 301
Tooke, Lovard, 206
Tremble, Fred W., 263, 307, 309, 327
Trinity River, 11, 12

Tucson, AZ, 362
U
United States Cavalry, 196
  1st Regiment, 104
    Company G, 83
  2nd Regiment
    Company I, 239
  3rd Regiment, 34, 219
    Company E, 218, 219, 221
United States Dragoons., 19
United States Infantry
  5th Regiment, 67, 104
    Company E, 239
  7th Regiment, 102, 104, 111
    Company F, 115
    Company H, 102
V
Vallé, Alexander, 195, 221, 242, 245, 252, 266
Valverde, NM, 2, 74, 83, 103, 113, 114, 115, 127, 137, 139, 140, 141, 143, 152, 155, 160, 162, 183, 187, 195, 212, 213, 241, 245, 249, 259, 263, 264, 273, 283, 307, 309, 312, 313, 325, 336, 347, 355, 356, 361, 374
Van Der Heuvel, Marinus, 124
W
Walker, Charles J., 207, 218
Walker, D.L., 206
Walker, James, 104, 288
Walker, R.P., 242
Weather, 12, 13, 15, 17, 46, 47, 50, 60, 66, 74, 131, 136, 143, 153, 154, 156, 157, 158, 160, 162, 190, 193, 210, 299, 310, 317, 323, 350, 358, 365
  Dust, 46, 48, 50, 74, 104, 153, 164, 203, 294, 295, 315, 319
  Rain, 12, 290
  Snow, 66, 68, 74, 84, 90, 98, 135, 148, 154, 156, 157, 158, 160, 183, 187, 190, 194, 210, 264, 290
  Wind, 68, 75, 135, 136, 148, 152, 154, 160, 180, 190, 282, 310, 315, 319, 323, 374
Weld, Lewis, 182, 185, 186
Wesche, Charles, 126, 128, 129
Wheeler, Otis M., 213
White, Benjamin, 227
Whitley, Sharp, 163, 222, 223, 227, 228, 332, 334, 337, 341
Whitsett, Richard, 170
Wilbar, Alexander P., 296
Wilkenson, C.A., 15
Wilkenson, C.R., 15
Willamette Valley, OR, 168
Williams, R.H., 369
Williams, Wady T., 145
Wingate, Benjamin, 67, 102, 104, 110
Woolsey, Private, 239

Wright, Henry C., 264,
  275, 278, 292
Wright, Thomas G., 359

Wynkoop, Edward W.,
  252, 254
Y
Ysleta, TX, 370, 371

ABOUT THE AUTHOR

DONALD HEALEY is an amateur historian with a lifelong interest in the American West. He attended the University of California at Riverside and Humboldt State University, minoring in history. For the past seventeen years he has worked in information technology management, sharpening his research and technical writing skills. He has taught and trained extensively on computer related topics. He has also written a prolific quantity of user documentation, much of it used by a Fortune 500 magazine publisher. Mr. Healey has lived in California and Mexico, and has traveled broadly. Currently he resides in Eugene, Oregon and is Director of Information Systems for the University of Oregon Foundation.

www.ingramcontent.com/pod-product-compliance
Lightning Source LLC
Chambersburg PA
CBHW052136300426
44115CB00011B/1404